DIASPORA'S HOMELAND

DIASPORA'S HOMELAND

Modern China in the Age of Global Migration

SHELLY CHAN

DUKE UNIVERSITY PRESS
Durham and London
2018

© 2018 Duke University Press
All rights reserved

Typeset in Minion Pro by Westchester Publishing Services

Library of Congress Cataloging-in-Publication Data

Names: Chan, Shelly, author.
Title: Diaspora's homeland : modern China in the age of global migration / Shelly Chan.
Description: Durham : Duke University Press, 2018. | Includes bibliographical references and index.
Identifiers: LCCN 2017036969 (print) |
LCCN 2018000173 (ebook)
ISBN 9780822372035 (ebook)
ISBN 9780822370420 (hardcover : alk. paper)
ISBN 9780822370543 (pbk. : alk. paper)
Subjects: LCSH: Chinese diaspora. | China—Emigration and immigration—History—19th century. | China—Emigration and immigration—History—20th century. | China—Emigration and immigration—Political aspects. | China—Emigration and immigration—Economic aspects. Classification: LCC DS732 (ebook) | LCC DS732 .C43 2018 (print) | DDC 909/.0495108—dc23
LC record available at https://lccn.loc.gov/2017036969

Cover art: Beili Liu, *Yun Yan 1* (detail), incense drawing on rice paper, 2008. Courtesy Chinese Culture Foundation, San Francisco. *Yunyan*, meaning "cloud and smoke" in Chinese, describes the temporal nature of all encounters in life. The drawing is created by brushing a stick of burning incense against the rice paper, one mark at a time.

Support for this research was provided by the University of Wisconsin–Madison, Office of the Vice Chancellor for Research and Graduate Education, with funding from the Wisconsin Alumni Research Foundation.

FOR PHILIP KA FAI POON

CONTENTS

A NOTE ON ROMANIZATION ix

ACKNOWLEDGMENTS xi

Introduction 1

1 A Great Convergence 17

2 Colonists of the South Seas 48

3 Confucius from Afar 75

4 The Women Who Stayed Behind 107

5 Homecomings 146

Conclusion and Epilogue 185

NOTES 197

BIBLIOGRAPHY 233

INDEX 261

A NOTE ON ROMANIZATION

I have used the standard system of romanization, *pinyin*, used in today's People's Republic of China for most of the Chinese names and terms in this book. However, I have also kept the commonly known names used by people to refer to themselves and their communities and places, either at an earlier time or at present. These names and terms are rendered in the original regional language or dialect instead of Mandarin, followed by the pinyin form in parentheses at first mention.

ACKNOWLEDGMENTS

This book proposes a new interpretation of Chinese history through diaspora moments. Looking back, I am still startled by how much time and care it takes before new ideas can see the light of day. From inception to print, it requires not only the will of one person, but also the labor, support, and protection of numerous others along the way. I feel fortunate to have reached this point and to have so many people and institutions to thank for it.

Starting from a Ph.D. dissertation at the University of California–Santa Cruz, this book project evolved and expanded at the University of Wisconsin–Madison. A privileged opportunity to work closely with Gail Hershatter throughout my graduate training, as well as with Emily Honig at the dissertation stage, provided an important basis for this book that I hope both of them would recognize. During the fall of 2015, a manuscript workshop attended by Anne Hansen, Kenneth Pomeranz, Francisco Scarano, Steve Stern, and Louise Young helped push along a major reconceptualization of the work. This experience added to my already great fortune of working among some of the kindest and finest people in the profession. From the time of my arrival in Madison, James Sweet has generously supported my research and shared advice on many occasions, even through his busy years as department chair. Francisco Scarano kept me for years under his wise mentorship, patiently commenting on many pieces of work that have gone into this study. During some of the most difficult moments of writing, I benefited from Louise Young's broad intellect and extraordinary kindness, without which I fear I would not have finished this book. Steve Stern took me in at a critical time. During the long conversations we had at cafés on Monroe Street, he helped me improve the architecture of the manuscript and the sound of my voice; both he and Florencia Mallon were a constant source of warmth and encouragement. Ever so generous with her attention, Gail Hershatter read the revised manuscript in its entirety and offered detailed and pertinent feedback. As I have come to enjoy my current academic home, Gail remains one of the greatest inspirations in my intellectual life. To her and to the scholars mentioned above, I owe so much more than they can possibly imagine.

Many other individuals and organizations contributed financial and cultural resources vital to the completion of this book. A yearlong leave in 2014–15, funded by the Institute of Research in the Humanities at UW-Madison and the Chiang Ching-kuo Foundation for Scholarly Exchange, allowed me to focus on writing. I am grateful to Susan Stanford Friedman for my productive residence at the IRH. At Duke University Press, Kenneth Wissoker believed in the project early on. With the expert assistance of Elizabeth Ault, he arranged for review by three attentive anonymous readers. Susan Albury oversaw the production of this book. I should also acknowledge the help of Takashi Fujitani and Reed Malcolm at the University of California Press. For years, the UW-Madison Graduate School provided summer salaries, travel grants, and fellowship top-ups to help me meet the demands of this project. In addition, support for this research was provided by the University of Wisconsin–Madison Office of the Vice Chancellor for Research and Graduate Education with funding from the Wisconsin Alumni Research Foundation. My current position, historian of Asian diasporas, was created with a major grant from the Andrew W. Mellon Foundation. Before moving to Madison, two internal faculty research grants from the University of Victoria enabled me to conduct additional research for the book. At UC-Santa Cruz, my dissertation project was supported by the University of California Pacific Rim Research Program, the History Department, the Institute for Humanities Research, and the Social Sciences and Humanities Research Council of Canada. In these economic and political times, I realize these significant opportunities came from the persistence of many people and organizations to promote young scholars and emerging work.

Apart from the aforementioned, a great many colleagues shared thoughts at various stages of my project and lifted me up with their good will and engagement. My sincere thanks go to Sana Aiyar, Lawrence Ashmun, Cindy I-fen Cheng, Kathryn Ciancia, Michael Cullinane, Joseph Dennis, Nan Enstad, Edward Friedman, Nicole Huang, Stephen Kantrowitz, Charles Kim, Judd Kinzley, David McDonald, Alfred McCoy, Viren Murthy, Leonora Neville, Se-Mi Oh, Steve Ridgely, Mary Louise Roberts, Claire Taylor, Sarah

Thal, Daniel Ussishkin, Thongchai Winichakul, André Wink, and Dianna Xu. I am also indebted to the gracious support of Laird Boswell, Ana Maria Candela, Angelina Chin, Madeline Hsu, Evelyn Hu-Dehart, Huang Jianli, Glen Peterson, Lisa Rofel, and Jeffrey Wasserstrom. At conferences and talks, the sharp intellectualism of these scholars inspired me to keep moving forward: Sunil Amrith, Tani Barlow, Leslie Bow, Tina Mai Chen, Prasenjit Duara, Donna Gabaccia, Michael Godley, Phillip Guingona, Rebecca Karl, Beth Lew-Williams, Tomislav Longinović, Laura Madokoro, Ronald Radano, Leander Seah, Guo-Quan Seng, Shu-mei Shih, Wang Gungwu, Dominic Meng-Hsuan Yang, and Tara Zahra. In Hong Kong and Xiamen, Hon Ming Yip and Shen Huifeng helped me gain access to important research materials and were wonderful interlocutors. On many days, the intelligent, hardworking undergraduate and graduate students in Madison gave me faith in teaching and helped ease the solitude of writing. Jeanne Essame, Anthony Medrano, Billy Noseworthy, and Galen Poor stimulated me with good conversations about their projects. For quite a while, David Krakauer and Jessica Flack at the Wisconsin Institute for Discovery let me eavesdrop on bewildering discussions about science while I was wrestling with my own problems with time and history. Tim and Laura Taylor were kind enough to read my book prospectus at the last minute. During one winter break, Yajun Mo, knowing fully that the Caribbean is the other way, came to Wisconsin from Boston to help make sure I finish the last revisions.

At an earlier phase of my work, I received many excellent opportunities that I had not dreamt would lead me here. Provocative talks at the Center for Cultural Studies at UC-Santa Cruz cracked open a world of interdisciplinary and politically engaged scholarship. My involvement with the graduate student research cluster, APARC, profoundly shaped my interests and thinking. I learned a lot from my friend Andy Chih-ming Wang. For my brief time at UVic, where I was employed to replace the great Yuenfong Woon, I thank members of the faculty and staff for making pleasant my transition from student to professor, particularly Cody Poulton, Michael Bodden, Gregory Blue, Tim Iles, and Hiroko Noro. At the University of British Columbia, where I completed my undergraduate and master's education, Diana Lary, Henry Yu, and the late Edgar Wickberg let me learn, miss, and keep trying.

Over the years, a now diaspora of cherished friends and teachers have influenced and sustained me intellectually and personally: Noriko Aso,

Edmund Burke III, Cathryn Clayton, Elena Casado Aparicio, Stephanie Chan, Catherine Chang, Alan Christy, Nellie Chu, James Clifford, Christopher Connery, Alexander Day, Dana Frank, Conal Ho, Fang Yu Hu, Minghui Hu, Michael Jin, Wenqing Kang, David Palter, Cynthia Polecritti, Xiaoping Sun, Jeremy Tai, Yenling Tsai, Marilyn Westerkamp, Rob Wilson, Dustin Wright, and Alice Yang. Others in Hong Kong and Vancouver have long indulged me with their love and affection: Corina Chen, Euphemia Chow, Elson Kung, Irene Kwok, Antonia Lam, Jenny Lau, Hoying Lee, Patricia Leung, Vivian Liu, Iona Sham, Melanie Sing, Karen Tan, Carman Wong, and Fiona Wong. Regrettably, there are many more names I am leaving out.

To family members who have borne the burdens of this journey, words fail. To my father, mother, brothers, in-laws, and relatives, I feel your patience. To dear Philip, I can only dedicate this book to you.

Parts of this book previously appeared in the following publications and in a different form: "Rethinking the 'Left-Behind' in Chinese Migrations: A Case of Liberating Wives in Emigrant South China in the 1950s," in Dirk Hoerder and Amarjit Kaur, eds., *Proletarian and Gendered Mass Migrations: A Global Perspective on Continuities and Discontinuities from the Nineteenth to the Twenty-First Centuries* (Leiden: Brill, 2013), 451–66; "The Disobedient Diaspora: Overseas Chinese Students in Mao's China, 1958–66," *Journal of Chinese Overseas* 10, no. 2 (2014): 220–38; and "The Case for Diaspora: A Temporal Approach to the Chinese Experience," *Journal of Asian Studies* 74, no. 1 (February 2015): 107–28.

May the ideas in this book be worthy of all the help I received; I shall remain responsible for the shortcomings.

Introduction

Between the years 1840 and 1940, more than twenty million Chinese left China, crossed oceans, and lived in other lands. Part of the first wave of global migration, this massive outflow was not only unprecedented in Chinese history; it was also the third largest after the exodus of fifty-six million Europeans and thirty million Indians during modern times.[1] Chinese emigrants were an indentured workforce for the sugar plantations in the Caribbean, guano islands in Peru, sheep ranches in New South Wales, gold mines in Transvaal, and war trenches in France. They were also present at the historic gold rushes in California and British Columbia and helped build the first transcontinental railroads bringing the United States and Canada westward to the Pacific. All across Southeast Asia, they worked as opium farmers, rubber tappers, rice millers, and tin miners. Some became major players in commerce, industry, government, education, and culture; others were the ubiquitous street peddlers, shopkeepers, vegetable gardeners, laundrymen, cooks, fishermen, and factory workers. Given this broad scope of Chinese mass emigration, numerous studies have detailed its impact around the globe. Yet one question is not often asked: How did it change China?

Such a question invites us to see Chinese history as fragmented and networked, not unlike migration itself, carrying and carried by forces traversing the world. Already significant in the sixteenth century, emigration was a common aspect of life on China's southeastern coast.[2] Families and entire economies in Guangdong and Fujian provinces subsisted and thrived on the ancient Indian Ocean trading economy. The eighteenth century saw an upsurge of Chinese agricultural and mining activities on both the mainland and the islands of Southeast Asia under local and European patronage, leading to a further integration of commerce and production in the region.[3] After Qing China's loss to Britain in the First Opium War and the forced opening to the West in 1842, emigration reached a global scale, as Chinese labor was pulled into a new geography linked by plantations, mines, railroads, and steamships from the Pacific to the Atlantic worlds. After the 1880s, the rise of anti-Chinese racism and exclusion laws dramatically slowed Chinese emigration to the Americas and Australia, but it continued to flow toward Southeast Asia, which absorbed over 90 percent of China's transoceanic total.[4]

Like millions of other people on the move, many Chinese emigrants did not become strangers to the old country because of their departures. Rather, they enmeshed it ever more deeply into the vast circulations of money, goods, ideas, and people. Leaving behind parents, wives, and children and sending money home, they not only transfigured their native clans, villages, and towns, but also drew China into the orbits of empires, nations, and markets far beyond its shores. Given the relatively high return rate of Chinese emigrants, many also wound up transforming the homeland directly by building new ventures and extending old networks after their return.[5] Driven by the same forces that hastened China's transition from empire to nation, the history of Chinese mass emigration was inseparable from the making of modern China.

The mutual constitution of China and Chinese emigrants in the world could be seen through the rise of a new dynamism in the nineteenth and twentieth centuries: a modern relationship between the homeland and the diaspora that changed China. Not just a matter of Chinese nationalist claims, this relationship was powerful and multivalent, because there was as much effort from emigrants to make China an "ancestral homeland" (*zuguo*) as there was from China to turn emigrants into a "Chinese diaspora" (*huaqiao*). More importantly, the new dynamic was far from insular—it was embedded in a wide array of colonial, national, and capitalist forces, often making the results contingent and the causes opaque to the homeland. As China after the mid-nineteenth century became incorporated into the Western-led industrial economy and interstate system, Chinese elites repeatedly encountered the significance of Chinese emigration in a broader milieu where China was hardly the only player. Through recognizing, protecting, and mobilizing the emigrants, Chinese leaders and thinkers entered complex dialogues over slavery and free labor, overseas migration and colonization, Confucianism and Christianity, family and gender roles, and socialism and capitalism. From the 1840s to the 1960s, the weight of this global engagement pulled China's center of gravity outward and created fields of intense activity. It is in this larger frame that Chinese mass emigration helped create modern China.

Modern China, the Overseas Chinese, and Chinese in the Americas

There is now a massive literature on China and the Chinese elsewhere, but more has been written about China's impact on the emigrants than the reverse, suggesting a missed opportunity despite the enormous extent of the scholarship. Making up a collective body of knowledge that might be called "a global Chinese history," the fields of overseas Chinese, Chinese American, and modern Chinese history have traditionally developed separately from each other. Not always in dialogue, scholars of the three fields share a broad concern over Chinese global engagement, though with a focus on different geographical areas.

Focusing on the Asian maritime world, scholars of the overseas Chinese have long recognized Chinese migrants as important subjects linking South China with Southeast Asia, a point to which most historians of modern China have paid scant attention. Plying the open seas as pilgrims, emissaries, traders, and laborers since the tenth century, the Chinese had been active in the Indian Ocean system many centuries prior to the modern migrations.[6] Crucial to their long-distance activities was the role of affinities based on family, native place, dialect, and brotherhood, not the imperial polity. It is well known that even though Zheng He's seven voyages (1405–33) marked Ming China (1368–1644) as the unrivaled naval power in Asia, the state soon turned its back on the seas. Unlike European powers that successively sought to expand their seaborne empires from the 1500s onward, both the Ming and later the Qing (1644–1911) tried to revitalize the tribute system, outflank private traders, and ban maritime travel periodically, leading to Wang Gungwu's apt phrase for those in defiance: "merchants without empire."[7] Therefore, it is precisely Chinese engagement without Chinese state support that makes overseas Chinese history a distinct, vital field of study. China as a political unit was rightly peripheral to this early picture centered on maritime Southeast Asia.

While Chinese emigrants have long been central subjects of overseas Chinese history, they have until recently been relegated to the margins of modern China studies. In numerous narratives depicting China's evolution into a modern nation, the Qing state makes a "belated" acknowledgment of Chinese emigration, after which Chinese emigrants turn up briefly at major junctures of the national story: buying official titles and honors, extending protection to exiled reformers and revolutionaries, playing a supporting role in Sun Yat-sen's 1911 Revolution, and pouring funds into Nationalist China's anti-Japanese war effort.[8] On the whole, Chinese emigrants seem no more than objects and resources commanded by China, whereas the impact of their own actions and agendas remains localized and derivative. Portrayed as an accessory to China's grand transformations, the emigrants could not have been a historical force. Sadly, what historians have long rejected as an overdetermined "impact-response" model in the study of the relations between China and the West persists in conceptions of China and the overseas Chinese: China called, the overseas Chinese responded—or at least some of them did.

As for Chinese American history, racism, exclusion, and assimilation are the earliest themes related to Chinese migration to the United States. Firmly based in the continental United States, this early scholarship has developed separately from overseas Chinese history, which has a heavy focus on Southeast Asia. As participants and leaders of the civil rights and ethnic studies movements in the 1960s and 1970s, Asian American historians sought to write Chinese immigrants and descendants, together with other Asian ethnic groups, back into U.S. national history. They have stressed how Chinese migrants contributed greatly to the development of the American West and the nation at large, but faced the first exclusion laws from 1882 to 1943, as well as continuous marginalization for seeming "foreign."[9] Hence, early scholars have tended to downplay Chinese Americans as sojourners implicated in Chinese history, emphasizing instead their place as immigrants conforming to U.S. assimilation theory and themes of national progress.[10] From the narratives of the "melting pot" to multiculturalism, China appears as a distant, bounded place that Chinese Americans came from but left behind.

Recently, a "transnational turn" in the broader historical discipline has pushed the boundaries of all three fields. During the Cold War, an extended, politically charged inquiry into whether Chinese abroad were sojourners or settlers dominated overseas Chinese history. Given the waves of anti-Chinese, anti-Communist violence sweeping across Southeast Asia, scholarly investments in what became known as "the overseas Chinese question" not only shared a focus on citizenship and assimilation as in early Chinese American history, but also carried a distinct urgency. To repudiate China as the constant frame of reference for Chinese elsewhere, historians declared that their field, "the overseas Chinese," should be renamed "Chinese overseas." Still a standard practice today, the inversion rejects that the "Chinese" are a uniform entity defined by China. Instead, Chinese people are "Chinese" differently in the world, as in Wang Gungwu's tripartite differentiations: *huaqiao*, who are Chinese nationals residing abroad; *huaren*, who locate their cultural origins in China but are politically oriented to their adopted countries; and finally *huayi*, who are well integrated into local society and could only be seen as ethnically—meaning remotely—connected to China.[11] Yet such purposeful efforts to harden the boundaries between politics, culture, and descent met an unexpected softening after the 1970s.[12] The easing of Cold War politics and the expansion of global capitalism, most notably China's reopening since Deng Xiaoping and the subsequent attempts led by international interests to engage a "rising" China, have provoked a reimagining of Chinese identity and power in the world. This shift is evident in an explosion of Chinese transnational studies that challenge nation-based models of self and community.[13]

Meanwhile, the "transnational turn" in Chinese American history is less concerned with the prospects of reconnection with China, as in some recent works on Chinese overseas, but shows new ways to critique a bounded U.S. history. Aiming at claims of American exceptionalism, the Euro- and Western-centric history of migration and empire, and a neglect of the Pacific world, Asian American scholars have adopted wider frames and shown greater sensitivity to U.S. global engagement in Asia and the flows of Asian migrants, capital, and labor into the Americas.[14] Now joined by scholars in Asian Canadian and Latin American studies, they have proposed hemispheric approaches, borderland studies, and trans-Pacific and global frameworks.[15] Influenced by the "transnational turn," today's Chinese and Asian American history may engage the Pacific Northwest, including British Columbia, and a number of sites in Asia and the Americas that were joined by war, racism, capitalism, and colonialism.[16] These far-flung connections suggest how excitingly scholarly efforts have broadened the themes of early Chinese American history and Asian American studies, as well as challenged the scope of traditional U.S. and Canadian history that rarely goes beyond Europe and the Atlantic world. Importantly, some have also begun to consider China seriously as a historical force.

Similarly, the transnational turn in China studies has spurred a search for new horizons. It has laid to rest the already much-critiqued paradigm of "Western impact, Chinese response" and freed the writing of a "China-centered history" from rigid frames vis-à-vis the West.[17] While it is true that scholars have long been at work writing the regional and global back into national history—from political economy to trade and marketing networks to the environment to circuits of knowledge and culture—they have remained slow in recognizing the wider significance of emigration to the task.[18] Yet the history of Chinese mass emigration offers a unique vantage point on the dialectics familiar to many China historians: those between centripetal and centrifugal forces, nation-building and region-making, and borderlands and empires. At present, a more globally engaged China makes it particularly salient to consider it as the cause and effect of economic and cultural flows. The time is right for bringing together the three fields of scholarship—Chinese overseas, Chinese Americas, and modern China—to shine new light on China in global history through migration.

Locating China and Chinese in the World

Given the promise of new insights into shared themes, how does one study the history of Chinese emigrants and China in a single frame? Apart from the risk of sounding essentialist—assuming that Chineseness is given and immutable—there is still the vexing problem of how to organize a massive history and geography into a coherent form. Two dominant approaches exist in the scholarship. The first approach could be called "the sum of parts" through a total mapping of countries and regions. One instructive example is *The Encyclopedia of the Chinese Overseas*, edited by Lynn Pan.[19] Without discounting the excellent contributions of this monumental resource, the encyclopedic approach to global history rests on a flawed conceptual foundation.[20] It presumes nations and regions as fixed, bounded, equal to one another, and existing prior to migration. A concentric-circle diagram in the volume, which sets up China as the center of an outwardly diffusing identity, provokes thought. Reminiscent of the Sinocentric tribute system positing a civilized self and barbaric others, the visualization of "varieties of Chinese" is not so much "symbolic" as mistaken. There is little reason to

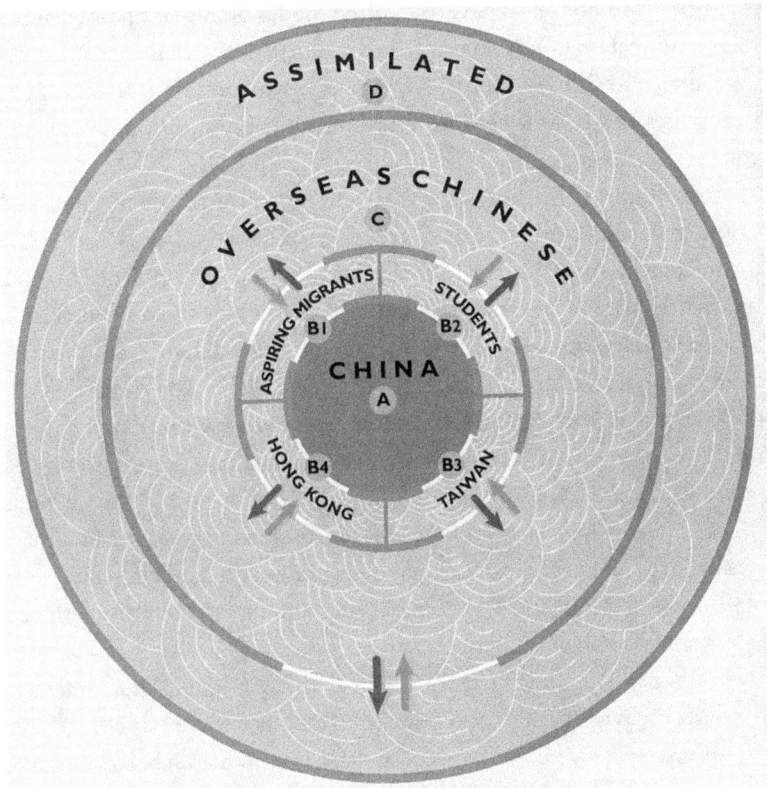

Figure I.1 "Symbolic representation of varieties of Chinese."
Source: Lynn Pan, ed., *The Encyclopedia of the Chinese Overseas.*

believe that Chinese in China naturally possess a unified Chinese culture and that its meaning is stable and never in question.[21] More importantly, even as the diagram recognizes movement between the inner and outer circles, it stops at the circumference of "China." As change passes around but never through it, China appears as a fixed, impervious core.

Another example of the "sum of parts" approach involves the tabulation of ethnic Chinese populations worldwide to highlight numerical range and distribution.[22] Varying between thirty and fifty million people in different estimates today, this sum of Chinese in the world may inform as much as obscure, since it conceals varying methods of counting, categories of identification, and degrees of interaction with China. It also makes invisible the power of bureaucratic institutions, the inherent instability of the label

"Chinese," and nonlinear, less recognized modes of migrant passage other than unidirectional movements.[23] Taken together, the challenge of studying China and Chinese globally demands a greater awareness not only of similarities and differences between the two, but also of the fluidity and complexity of both.

Apart from the "sum of parts," a second general approach to China and Chinese globally could be called "interactions between parts." Eschewing the focus on a fixed totality, historians influencing and influenced by the transnational turn—such as Madeline Hsu, Adam McKeown, Philip Kuhn, and Glen Peterson—have provided useful models linking the disparate fields of modern China, overseas Chinese, and Asian Americas. They include exploring how change occurs in one transnational community, across multiple communities along similar patterns, among others in the world in a *longue durée*, and in the relations between China and the overseas Chinese during a given period.[24] Offering fascinating glimpses of a massive history and geography of Chinese emigration on different scales, each of these models suggests that Chinese emigration was a connecting thread in national, regional, and global change.

Still it is worth going further: How may these insights about "interacting parts" help revise our conceptions of China as a whole?

Toward such a goal, the concept of diaspora can help scholars navigate a fragmented historical geography against which China asserted itself as a unified sovereign nation. A Greek word meaning "to sow or scatter," *diaspora* is traditionally associated with the forced dispersal of Jews, Africans, and Armenians. As a result of decades of innovative work in postcolonial and cultural studies, diaspora now commonly describes a displaced identity or community in cross-cultural contexts that defy fixed and bounded ideas about the nation, race, and modernity.[25] In the Chinese context, diaspora cannot simply be an umbrella term for all Chinese under the sun.[26] Instead, shifting the focus to interactions, scholars may retrace how China and Chinese emigrants were coproduced by the discursive and material history of departures, exchanges, and returns. At no point did China command a single Chinese diaspora. But the relationship between the two brings into focus a process to create a sum out of interacting parts—efforts to designate China as the homeland and to incorporate a variety of actors in the diaspora at a given time. Constructed on both sides, the claims of fixed, unbroken ties, in fact, reflect the palpable effects of living in a world that does not stand still. Seen this way, diaspora can generate the kind of moving edifice that the global historian of China might need.

Several leading scholars in history, cultural studies, and literary criticism—most notably Wang Gungwu, Ien Ang, and Shu-mei Shih—have rejected the use of diaspora, but their criticisms could serve to start rather than end the discussion. In no uncertain terms, they have warned how diaspora misconstrues a homogenous Chinese population perpetually loyal to China, feeds racist and nationalist discourses, and denies immigrants an opportunity to become locals. Politically fraught, diaspora has "an expiry date," occludes how politics and culture are "place-based," and should be abandoned.[27] Undoubtedly, the continuous injustice of racism and discrimination deserves serious attention, but it should not be given at the expense of the historical imagination, an openness to the plurality and contradictions of the human past.[28] Often degraded by progressive narratives of assimilation and integration, diaspora histories remain poorly understood, sometimes appearing as no more than a developmental stage to be overcome. With millions of people moving around the world each day, it seems riskier to avoid rather than learn about the complexity of their lives. Moreover, after decades of groundbreaking interdisciplinary work, historians striving to describe a mobile world can reap the critical insights accumulated in postcolonial, literary, and cultural studies: diaspora is shifting in meaning, intersectional with other social categories, challenges but is not always in opposition to the nation-state.[29] Not a fixed group, diaspora serves as a tactic for political solidarity, a lens onto cultural hybridity, and a reminder that identity is a process.[30] Work remains to uncover how diaspora in the Chinese experience may advance these enlightening conversations, and how global history is yet another dimension of diaspora.

Diaspora in Chinese History

Returning to the central question driving this book—how did Chinese mass emigration change China?—I argue that a new homeland–diaspora dynamic developed, which over the next century inextricably enmeshed China with the world. During the wave of global migrations in the nineteenth and twentieth centuries, huaqiao was the Chinese concept of diaspora that arose in relation to China as the homeland, zuguo. Often translated as "the overseas Chinese," the term *huaqiao* literally means "Chinese who are *temporarily* located," emphasizing at once the spaces beyond China and one's temporary absence from it. This compound had not appeared prior to the late nineteenth century but was a product of old and new forces—*hua* denotes a Chineseness refashioned in racial-national terms vis-à-vis a Western-dominated world, whereas *qiao* evokes familiar meanings of "visiting and lodging temporarily" (*lüyu*) in imperial history, as in the expression *qiaoju*. During the Northern and Southern Dynasties (A.D. 222–589), a period of disunity and war, *qiaomin* and *qiaozhi* referred to the relocation of Han Chinese people and prefectures because of invasions by non-Han nomads. Hence, *qiao* conjures up the ancient tropes of exile, subjugation, and displacement in elite Chinese culture, though the word had only been applied to officials and literati, not traders or laborers, and it certainly had not been about going overseas. A broader label referring to emigration in the nineteenth and twentieth centuries, huaqiao combined old and new meanings to suggest mass, temporary relocations outside China but also bound to it.

Referring to a "temporary" diaspora spread across the globe, huaqiao served as a device to create a "permanent" homeland-nation at home, part of the underpinnings of modern China. In a foundational essay written in 1976 that remains the most cited account on the topic, Wang Gungwu finds that the assumed temporariness in the term *huaqiao* was a sign of official understanding that migration was forced and unwilling.[31] Traditionally, those who wandered were "regarded by the society as unfilial sons and vagrants and by the imperial government as potential if not actual criminals, traitors and spies."[32] What changed in the nineteenth century was official acceptance that migration could lead to settlement, following a series of international treaties, diplomatic reports, revolutionary activities, and nationality laws. These efforts culminated in the widespread use of the term *huaqiao* by the time of the 1911 Revolution and an end to the negative connotation of "enforced and illegal wandering." However, a look across China's century of mass emigration suggests that the idea of a "temporary" diaspora had a greater effect—it undergirded China's national development.[33] Not just a matter of sojourn or settlement ending in official approval, the idea of huaqiao has worked in tandem with that of zuguo, suggesting a productive contrast and a mutual constitution between nation and emigration. In this formulation, the temporariness of the diaspora lends the homeland a semblance of permanence. Dissonances between the diaspora and the homeland are understood as a reality produced by a backward and imperfect nation; until the nation is fully brought into modernity, the future has to be deferred. Thus, despite the rapid transformations of both China and the Chinese in the world, diaspora has served to unify a fragmented time and space, a means through which the homeland-nation can be constituted and reconstituted.

Rooted in the material history of China and Chinese emigration, the coproduction of time and space through huaqiao beckons a reassertion of temporality, thus offering a wider theoretical implication for transnational and diaspora studies that have tended to privilege spatiality. Generally speaking, scholars have more often associated migration with movement in space than with movement in time, even though one cannot be fully understood without the other.[34] It is common to understand diaspora as dispersed communities, while the comparable idea of fragmented temporalities has not attracted much discussion.[35] Furthermore, devoted to the critique of the nation as the basic unit of analysis, the transnational turn in history is a job only half done, as it has more readily challenged the boundedness of a national territory than that of a national chronology. Inspired by the "spatial turn" in critical social theory, the insights on the production of space can be integrated with the parallel work on time that has raised the question of multiple temporalities.[36] Socially and culturally produced, multiple temporalities refer to time not only as a linear succession or an autonomous force, as in the "arrow of time," but also as a diverse product of human and institutional efforts to separate, recombine, and remember it.

In the broader historical discipline, scholars have written about a multitude of times but have yet to consider diaspora time. Some of the most significant works on historical chronologies have focused on non-European contexts and the enduring impact of colonialism and nationalism on notions of the past, present, and future, as in the provocative writings by Prasenjit Duara, Dipesh Chakrabarty, and Harry Harrotunian on Asia.[37] Writing about Latin America, Steve J. Stern also argues that colonial legacies there have created a wealth of "sensibilities about time," calling attention to "cycle and recurrence, continuity, and multiple motion (forward, backward, inertial) in human wanderings through history."[38] More recently, in East Asian history, Stefan Tanaka finds that new reckonings of time during the Meiji period enabled the creation of a temporally and spatially unified society known as "Japan."[39] Louise Young has observed how Japanese urbanites in the interwar period imagined their cities as a "chronotope," a particular time-space in modern society where the future had already arrived.⁴⁰ Pondering rural women's memories of the Mao period, Gail Hershatter has used "campaign time" to describe how agricultural collectivization in the 1950s produced gendered experiences and memories; but these gendered memories do not simply reflect a sequence of state-led campaigns.⁴¹ Overlooked thus far, diaspora is part of this social and cultural assemblage, representing multiple times no less than multiple spaces.

Seen this way, diaspora in the mode of huaqiao was not simply a set of transnational communities, but also a series of transnational moments. During the nineteenth and twentieth centuries, Chinese mass emigration stemmed from an uneven process of globalization that created a coexistence not only of spaces but also of times. As the spread of industrial capitalism, colonial empires, and nation-states spurred a worldwide search for labor, resources, and markets, Chinese time and space proliferated dramatically. This is because Chinese emigrants spun off and became part of other histories from Cuba and Peru to the United States, Canada, and Australia to the Dutch East Indies and the British empire, while China at the same time underwent struggles for modernity of many kinds. These divergent developments sometimes intersected, as industrial, colonial, and national forces did not exist in separate worlds but moved in a constellation of interdependent relations. Thus, what made China and Chinese elsewhere connected and separate was not only a matter of origins or localization, but also a history of globalization that caused Chinese engagement with the world to split, expand, and intertwine in moments of exchange and return. After a century of rupture, transformation, and reintegration, China became ever more fragmented and networked; its modern evolution was at once disrupted and enriched by its condition as a diaspora's homeland.

Diaspora Time and Moments

Using the age of global migration as bookends, this study is an exploration of Chinese history through the temporalities of diaspora. To maintain a clear vision of the different timescales of impact, I will use two concepts: "diaspora time" and "diaspora moments." "Diaspora time" describes the diverse, ongoing ways in which migration affects the lifeworlds of individuals, families, and communities. Though not static, it is a slow-moving and silent condition, continuously combined and combining with other everyday realities. In Chinese history, diaspora time represented the ongoing process in which a family-based strategy of survival and accumulation unfolded in South China and negotiated with the larger forces of globalization. A "diaspora moment" erupts and recurs when diaspora time interacts with other temporalities and produces unexpectedly wide reverberations.[42] At these junctures, diaspora rises to the level of major discussions, demanding a coherent response from leaders and institutions and causing long-term consequences. In Chinese history, diaspora moments were manifest in the development of sovereignty and diplomacy, knowledge about world history and geography, debates over tradition and modernity, reform of marriage and family, and struggles between socialism and capitalism. Momentous encounters took place as Chinese emigrants helped pull Qing China into a Western-led system of nation-states through indentured "coolie" migration to the Americas, inspired an ocean-based national identity in Republican China through the power of Chinese merchants in Southeast Asia, revived Confucianism through the experience of being colonial subjects in the British empire, clashed with the socialist mode of production through maintaining split households, and returned with the effect of embodying a capitalist threat to high socialism through successive waves of refugees. In these political, cultural, and social debates, the Chinese nation took shape not before but during mass emigration, as huaqiao periodically introduced forces that shook the homeland.

Taken together, the changing time and moments of diaspora suggest both a fractured and interconnected Chinese engagement with the world. To assess the effects of Chinese mass emigration on China in a moving historical geography, this study crosses three traditional state periods—the late Qing, Republican, and Communist-Maoist—and connects the territorial units of East Asia, Southeast Asia, and the Americas. This periodization accommodates a global century of mass migration (1840–1940) and extends into the 1960s to highlight the dramatic effects of the Cold War on Chinese migrant flows. Given the breadth of history and geography involved, I draw on a wide range of sources collected in China, Hong Kong, Taiwan, Singapore, and through British government databases, including diplomatic papers, history and geography collections, biographies, newspapers, magazines, and Communist-period archives. The range of my source material suggests a multiplicity of historical agents engaged in the Chinese diaspora–homeland dynamic: indentured laborers, Chinese and foreign diplomats, treaty-port university scholars, colonial and creolized intellectuals, women living in rural South China, well-off and dispossessed refugees, and Party-state officials. Arising from the encounters is a broad array of questions and evidence requiring a cross-field, cross-disciplinary interpretation. Therefore, I also rely on Chinese, Asian American, and overseas Chinese historiographies, diaspora and cultural studies, gender and class analyses, and secondary scholarship about the Americas and Southeast Asia in Chinese and English languages, original or translated. Taken together, this book suggests a moving, interconnected archive of Chinese global engagement, a deep reservoir of challenges and resources for national construction.

Structurally, I have organized this book into five diaspora moments that can be read together like fragments turning in a kaleidoscope during the long nineteenth and twentieth centuries. Far from an exhaustive collection, the moments represent significant shifts in modern Chinese history that have often been narrated without attention to the diaspora, or with too narrow a view about it. While significant segments are new and based on unpublished sources, I also reopen old debates to facilitate a broader analysis and advance a different understanding of the issues at hand. Dynamic and recurrent, diaspora moments reveal a connective tension between migrant histories and national history in the age of global migration.

Chapter 1, "A Great Convergence," revisits the Qing lifting of the emigration ban in 1893, which historians have widely deemed "belated" and inconsequential to China's grand transformations. Revealing that the actual initiative was to invite returns and not simply to endorse exits, the chapter argues that the emergence of China as a "homeland" was not only part of the 1890–1911 sweep that brought down the imperial system, but was also grounded in a mid-nineteenth-century engagement with the indentured "coolie" migration. Contributing to the global spread of diplomacy and sovereignty, this prehistory involves a convergence of Western attempts to recruit "free" labor at the end of the African slave trade, a global crisis provoked by the abuses of Chinese "coolies" bound for the Americas, and Qing assertions of the right to protect the emigrants. By creating new institutions, conventions, and actors, these earlier efforts paved the way for China's transition into a modern nation-state, often marginalized in historical narratives focusing on events at the turn of the twentieth century.

Chapter 2, "Colonists of the South Seas," offers an account of Chinese scholars at Shanghai's Jinan University during the 1920s and 1930s who churned out massive collections of historical and geographical studies about the Chinese in Southeast Asia. Drawing on Western and Japanese discourses that understood migration as colonization, the Jinan scholars, who had been moving across maritime Asia, actively participated in the circulation of colonial power by debating whether Chinese emigration constituted a type of settler colonialism. In so doing, they reinvented received categories of knowledge and portrayed Chinese in the South Seas as critical conduits in China's drive for modernity. As a result of their efforts, which have largely been forgotten, the maritime geography of Chinese settlement became an institutionalized and enduring field of Chinese knowledge about the world.

Chapter 3, "Confucius from Afar," reinterprets the familiar, well-worked story of Lim Boon Keng, a Singapore-born, Edinburgh-trained creole intellectual who famously clashed with the May Fourth writer Lu Xun, but whose colonial experience needs to be taken more seriously. Despite their apparent differences over Lim's belief that Confucian traditions could provide a modern Chinese identity, this chapter argues that both Lu and Lim shared a deep interest in Western colonial and missionary discourses as well as Chinese national projects, hence suggesting their simultaneity rather than Lim's anachronism. Moreover, Lim's commitments to a Confucian revival had originated from his life experiences of moving through the British empire as a colonized subject. Given the great variety of neo-Confucianisms throughout Chinese history, Lim's story highlights the impact of the diaspora experience on Chinese national culture and identity. Even though China was never fully colonized and nationalist discourses typically rejected lasting effects of colonial power, the colonial inflections in Lim's brand of Confucianism have traveled far and wide as a source for Chinese identity and power down to the present.

Chapter 4, "The Women Who Stayed Behind," examines how the Communist Party's land and marriage reforms in the early 1950s backfired in emigrant South China. Aimed to free rural Chinese of feudal oppression and incorporate them into a broader strategy of socialist production, the campaigns of redistributing land and granting women the right to divorce provoked a serious conflict in the transnationally connected south. Revealing a discrepant huaqiao mode of production split between home and abroad, the conflict convinced the Communists to reconceptualize domestic women married to overseas men as new intermediaries between huaqiao men and the state. Widespread confusion ensued. The surprising results suggest that socialism in the 1950s was far from a closed system, but rather continued to be influenced by global circulations through the legacies of mass emigration.

Chapter 5, "Homecomings," looks at the sudden "return" of Chinese from Southeast Asia during decolonization and anti-Chinese movements in the 1950s, and their difficult reintegration at "home" from the time of the Great Leap Forward to the beginning of the Cultural Revolution. An official label of *guiqiao*, meaning "returned overseas Chinese," emerged to cope with a vastly heterogeneous group of arrivals divided by social and geographical origins, but the Communist Party-state increasingly fixated on their collective appearance of disobedience and immutability during an acceleration of socialist building. Although party leaders had recognized and tolerated the transitional nature of guiqiao before the late 1950s, criticisms of the unknown "foreign past" of the returnees became a code for an insidious "capitalism" in the body politic, suggesting a collapse in the efforts to balance different times and spaces in high socialism.

In sum, this book provides a portal to the "diaspora time" operating in Chinese history and the repeated attempts to incorporate it into narratives of the nation. Its point of departure lies in a deceptively simple and understudied question: how Chinese mass emigration changed China. Its conceptual foundation is the "diaspora moments" that emerge in tension with other coexisting temporalities. Not to be reduced to "snapshots in time," diaspora moments conceptualize the opening, closure, and renewal of transnational crossings that resist linear national time. An ever-changing synthesis of the past and future, each moment is a reminder of the plurality and connectedness of the Chinese global experience, as well as a method to study the movements between spaces and times.

CHAPTER 1
———————

A Great Convergence

In 1893, the Qing empire abolished a ban on emigration that had been in place for more than two centuries. Yet most scholars have thought it inconsequential to Chinese history. The historian Wang Gungwu wrote, "Everyone knew how ineffective the prohibitions had been since the eighteenth century, how often they had been modified and reinterpreted, what hypocrisies were practiced after the two Anglo-Chinese wars in the nineteenth century to pretend that the prohibitions were still law, and how impossible it was to implement such laws among the southern coastal Chinese."[1] Others have described the ban as "long overtaken by events,"[2] and its final abolition as "a last-minute move" by a fading empire to recognize emigration.[3] Indeed, the end of the ban had little effect on the already free flow of emigrants, not only because the law was difficult to enforce, but also because a series of treaties permitting labor emigration after 1860 had effectively nullified it. If the 1893 edict meant nothing but the removal of a "defunct symbol," what made the Qing do it?

A look at the memorial that led directly to the imperial edict reveals a misunderstanding: the removal of the ban was not meant to endorse free emigration, but to encourage free returns. Submitted by the diplomat Xue Fucheng (1838–1894), the memorial portrayed a large, long-settled, yet still distinct Chinese population in Southeast Asia that, in spite of being divided into Cantonese, Hokkien, and Teochiu groups, was "deeply devoted to the former homeland." However, fearing that Qing officials and local gentry would use the formal ban on emigration to "accuse them of being fugitives, spies, smugglers, or kidnappers," almost none of these people wanted to return. Warning of changing "times" (*shishi*), Xue wrote that the current uncertainty around return could deprive China of a modern source of wealth and power—the overseas Chinese who were growing in numbers and influence—leaving it permanently at the disposal of the British and the Dutch empires. Instead of "driving fish into other people's nets and birds into other people's snares," implored Xue, the Qing state should sweep away all doubt by giving the overseas Chinese passports and welcoming them home.[4]

Misunderstood and forgotten, Xue's memorial should be restored for the better understanding of China's rapid transformations through trade, diplomacy, and migration during the nineteenth century. Calling for the easing of "barriers" by permitting returns, Xue recounted how a great convergence of events had thrown together the Qing state, the emigrants, and other nations of the world: the opening to Western trade in 1842, the 1860 treaties with Britain and France, the 1868 Burlingame Treaty with the United States, agreements to regulate emigration to Peru and Cuba after 1875, and the establishment of consulates to protect emigrants since 1877. Central to Xue's message was that there was an ever-increasing contact and competition between China and Western powers in an emergent world, but the Qing state could also shape its fortunes by reconnecting with the emigrants and welcoming them home. Almost immediately, Xue's proposal was adopted. Emigration and return without legal impediment became state policy.

More importantly, this new understanding of Xue's memorial brings into focus one particular flow of Chinese emigrants that underpinned his account of trade and diplomatic expansion—the Chinese indentured migration to the Americas (1847–74). Spanning the arc of development underscored by Xue, the flow of indentured laborers to the British West Indies, Cuba, and Peru helped lay the basis of Chinese sovereignty in the global system but has been routinely overlooked in the history of China's modern transformation. Known as "coolies" or the "yellow trade" (*la trata amarilla*) in the West and the "buying of men" or "the selling of piglets" in China, Chinese indentured labor was widely recognized as both a trade and a migration.[5] It arose during the 1840s and 1850s when British and French victories in the Opium Wars forced the opening of Chinese treaty ports, facilitating the amalgamation of the Caribbean, Atlantic, and Pacific worlds into a single marketplace, not only for manufactured goods but also for the extraction and transfer of labor resources. Enabled by Western imperialism, contract-based Chinese labor became a highly demanded, lucrative solution in sustaining the growth of plantation economies after the decline of the African slave trade. Nonetheless, violent kidnapping, mistreatment, and resistance of Chinese laborers soon drew worldwide attention, while Qing efforts to end the global crisis also initiated China into conversations of diplomacy and sovereignty and produced a new mandate to protect the emigrants. Consequently, this encounter with the coolie trade hastened China's modern transformations and was part of the historic integration between China and the world, as noted by Xue.

Readers familiar with the coolie scholarship will know that many scholars have already combed through the vast diplomatic and newspaper sources in various languages and produced outstanding works from them.[6] Deeply indebted to their trailblazing efforts, my intention is not to provide new empirical facts about the trade but to draw out a broader connectivity between indentured migration and China's national development. In recent years, historians and theorists have argued for a larger significance of Chinese coolie migration in the nineteenth-century world and suggested new ways of reading the documents. Pushing beyond the entrenched debate over whether Chinese coolies were actually enslaved or free, Moon-ho Jung and Lisa Lowe have insightfully recast the phenomenon in hemispheric and transcontinental frameworks, suggesting its crucial function in the constructions of capitalism, colonialism, race, and liberal thought.[7] Adam McKeown and Elliott Young have also shown that the Chinese migrant subject helped advance bureaucratic means of control in the Americas, as in the case of the passport during the Chinese exclusion era (1882–1943) and in the case of the labor contract during the coolie trade era (1847–74).[8] Taken together, these new directions have brought fresh insights to the well-studied topic of Chinese indenture, not simply by discovering new sources but by asking questions that have not been asked before.

Joining this growing community of scholars, I ask in this chapter: How did the Qing encounter with the coolie migration transform China? As John King Fairbank has noted, "no foreign activity on the coast of China was more spectacular than the coolie trade."[9] Yet not many scholars have examined its larger impact on China's evolution.[10] This is partly because most historians have stopped seeing China's "opening" to the West in 1842 or the beginning of Western imperialist intrusions as the most decisive watershed in Chinese history, a view now associated with the old, much-criticized model of "Western impact, Chinese response." As for the small number of monographs on the subject, scholars have tended to stress Qing efforts to protect the coolie migrants and abolish the trade, as opposed to a dominant assumption of connivance, which, in the words of Robert Irick, have allowed Western observers to mitigate their "responsibility and guilt" and Chinese scholars to reinforce their preconception of "a corrupt dynasty in decline."[11] Meanwhile, the coolie migration has also largely escaped the notice of historians of the overseas Chinese, who have tended to focus on Southeast Asia and Chinese merchant communities there. This led them to view Qing interest in the overseas Chinese as a late development that did not begin in earnest until the late nineteenth century, culminating in a series of political mobilizations after 1900, the Qing Nationality Law in 1909, and a widened use of the term *huaqiao* for Chinese abroad by the 1911 Revolution. Yet Xue's 1893 memorial serves as a reminder that things did not begin there. Rather, it is necessary to return our attention to a longer arc of developments that began with the indentured migration to Latin America and the Caribbean and largely consisting of poor Chinese laborers after China's forced opening to Western powers in the mid-nineteenth century.

Drawing on the multivolume Chinese collection *Historical Materials on Chinese Laborers Going Abroad* (*Huagong chuguo shiliao*), the British House of Commons Parliamentary Papers, and the extant secondary scholarship, I argue that the crisis over Chinese indentured migration was the first "diaspora moment" that helped create China as a sovereign nation in a global system. Coolies, not merchants, were the first group of emigrants to draw the Qing state into an expansive political economy based on Western industrial capitalism and free trade during the nineteenth century. Lasting fewer than thirty years and involving only a quarter million Chinese, the outflow to the Americas was not the largest in Chinese history, but it remained a major departure from a long-standing, locally regulated pattern of emigration in South China. More importantly, it signaled an emergent space where Qing leaders worked out their relationship with Chinese emigrants in the context of Western attempts to recruit and trade free labor. These intense exchanges on a global scale caused the modern Chinese diplomatic establishment to expand and new ideas about sovereignty and emigration to take root, a direct result of the encounter with the coolie trade. Writing about the rise of extraterritoriality in nineteenth-century East Asia, Pär Kristoffer Cassel has argued that sovereignty could be better understood as a "practice" on multiple grounds.[12] Similarly, I argue that the question of coolies also belongs to a complex environment of different times, spaces, and actors—residents on the China coast, colonial administrators in Europe, planters in Peru, Cuba, and the British West Indies, shippers from around the world—who became intertwined in the wake of the abolition of slavery and in the search for the free Chinese emigrant. The Qing engagement led to some of China's earliest negotiations over sovereignty. Indeed, the official Xue Fucheng was a product of such practice. At the time of the 1893 edict inviting returns, he was Qing China's first consul-general to Britain, France, Italy, and Belgium (1890–94), a modern appointment that came with the mandate of protection of emigrants at the end of their indenture.[13]

Creating the Free Chinese Emigrant

In 1851, the governor of British Guiana, Henry Barkly, called on the home government to provide a loan for the immigration of "hardworking and intelligent" Chinese to the West Indies. Citing a favorable report by John Bowring, the superintendent of British trade in China, who found a "disposition to emigrate" and a supply of labor to "an almost unlimited extent" in China, Barkly wrote that planters in the colony were anxious to "share in the advantages of Chinese emigration," with the hope that Chinese contract laborers would "form a middle class, better capable of standing the climate than the natives of Madeira, more energetic than the East Indian, and less fierce and barbarous than the emigrants from the Kroo coast of Africa."[14] Imagined to be voluntary, unlimited, and racially superior to Africans, the Chinese emigrant seemed like a perfect solution to a nineteenth-century world wrought by Western liberalism, capitalism, and colonialism.

What the British did not expect was that the imagined reservoir of Chinese emigrants was nowhere to be found, a point rarely acknowledged in the vast scholarship on the coolie trade. The importance of the Chinese indenture trade to the plantation regime after the abolition of the African slave trade has been well documented, but what remains neglected is how hard British officials and merchants had to drive into a dynamic, long-established emigrant economy set in local patterns and traditions, much like what sixteenth-century Europeans faced in their first forays into the Asian-dominated Indian Ocean trade. By 1852, the trade had been violently driven out of Amoy and Shanghai by local riots, after which it was forced to relocate to nontreaty ports, opium stations, and Portuguese-held Macao. Even during the British and French occupation of Guangzhou (1858–60), a contract emigration under joint Western–Chinese regulation failed to take off, but kidnapping became the order of the day. Violence enabled by unequal power relations between China and the West, not the safety of the labor contract, succeeded in altering a self-regulating Chinese emigration. A fractured ideal, the free Chinese emigrant was not found but had to be made.

Stressing that the free Chinese emigrant was a construct can help complicate traditional narratives of globalization and explanations of Chinese migration. In a new study of the global historical origins of Western liberalism, Lisa Lowe argues that the Chinese emigrant labor was "instrumentally used as a *figure*, a fantasy of 'free' yet racialized and coerced labor."[15] Criticizing a broad tendency to link the causes of Chinese emigration to a stream of chaos in nineteenth-century China—poverty, overpopulation, land shortages, rebellions, a weak government, and Western imperialism—Adam McKeown writes that "emigration as a family strategy depended more on stability, precedent, and opportunity than on disorder and poverty."[16] Since the coolies made up less than 4 percent of China's mass emigration in the modern period, "the issue was not that Chinese were impoverished and ignorant of migration, but that they already had access to well-developed migration networks and strong commercial acumen." As this chapter will show, historians can no longer reduce the history of Chinese coolie emigration to push and pull, a close cousin of the impact–response model. Far from inevitable, indenture had to rely on a great deal of force and deceit, which provoked great amounts of resistance in Chinese towns and on the high seas.

As we abandon the push–pull model and enter the complex milieu in which Chinese indentured migration took place, a different set of dynamics comes into view. Created to serve planter interests, the free Chinese emigrant ideal ran up against Chinese emigration in reality: well established, male centered, commercially based, and prohibited by the imperial Chinese state. Traditionally, Chinese emigration had been a strategy of flexible accumulation. A calculated family decision, it was not so much based on individual free will as it was embedded in local custom and preexisting networks of maritime commerce. With a lengthy history stemming from the intra-Asian trade across the Indian Ocean, Chinese emigration was nothing new. It was a way of life on the coast of Fujian and Guangdong provinces, controlled by clan and merchant networks, and financed by family groups or a credit-ticket system.[17] Men going overseas intended to settle temporarily, send money home, and eventually return to their families. While away, many strove to work their way up from wage laborers to self-employed merchants and follow a pattern of circular migration involving visits and returns to home villages in China. Never sponsored by the imperial state and occasionally prohibited by law, Chinese emigration had been private and commercialized.

Cutting across maritime trading networks, these migrant patterns gave rise to a geographically flexible yet socially embedded economic practice, one that was at odds with the free emigrant ideal championed by the West. Imagining a new geography in the wake of China's opening, officials on opposite ends of the British empire spoke of a boundless and willing supply of Chinese settler labor that would satisfy the needs of West Indies planters. But British officials in China soon learned that most Chinese emigrated via the Chinese-controlled networks in Southeast Asia, borrowed passage money in exchange for a year's labor, or went independently to the goldfields of California and Australia in search of greater gain. To be effective, Western merchants had to rely on Chinese brokers pejoratively known as "crimps." Given the stiff competition for Chinese labor, it was difficult to recruit enough and quickly without the use of deception and coercion. At the same time, it was almost impossible to find Chinese women to emigrate. Furthermore, local Chinese officials refused to cooperate with British diplomats to regulate emigration, since such efforts to prevent abuses would have implied recognition. Entrenched in the commercial, patrilineal economies connecting maritime Asia but out of the purview of the central state, traditional Chinese emigration had to be radically remade to serve frontier expansion in another world that China was joining. Thus began the creation of the free Chinese emigrant.

Chinese indenture to the Western world began at the intersection of British free-trade capitalism and imperialism in China. In 1833, the British Emancipation Act coincided with another landmark event, the end of the British East India Company's trade monopoly in China, which had lasted more than two centuries. The ascendency of free trade brought the Opium War (1839–41) and the 1842 Treaty of Nanjing, which forced China's incorporation into the Western global economy. This important turning point opened China up not only to the free entry of Western industrial goods but also to the massive transfer of Chinese productive labor to burgeoning colonial and settler frontiers across the globe. By the time Governor Barkly called for Chinese contract immigration to the British West Indies in the early 1850s, mass Chinese emigration had already begun via the new treaty ports of Amoy, Shanghai, and Canton, and the British colony of Hong Kong. It reached as far as Australia, Hawaii, and California. Also growing rapidly was an indentured emigration controlled by Europeans following brief experiments in the colonies of Brazil, Mauritius, and Bourbon. Chinese coolies arrived in Spanish Cuba in 1847, independent Peru in 1849, and the British Caribbean in 1853. British and American merchants among others dominated the lucrative trade, linking coastal China to the global labor market supplying sugar plantations and guano mines. Indenture brought around 125,000 Chinese to Cuba and 92,000 to Peru by its end in 1874, and another 14,000 to British Guiana by its end in 1866. Relatively small and short-lived, this emigration nonetheless incorporated China into an emergent global system based on Western imperialism and industrialization.

Manufactured to satisfy the need for plantation labor, Chinese emigrants in British colonial discourses were a proven, inexhaustible, and superior model of settlers. This image in the British archives contrasted with U.S. discourses during the Civil War and Exclusion eras, which portrayed Chinese emigrants as unfree and unfit.[18] In a series of investigative reports sent to the British West Indies, James T. White, Britain's emigration agent in China, stated in 1851 that the Chinese were a population "prone to emigration" and "in excess of the means of subsistence," so there was no doubt that "any number of laborers may be obtained." Writing that Chinese emigrant labor had been widely used for sugar and spice cultivation in the British settlements of Penang and Singapore, White described the Chinese as "tractable, easily managed, possessing indomitable industry and perseverance." A "strong muscular race, broad shouldered and bony," they were "capable of enduring great and continuous fatigue," making "one Chinese equal to two of the inhabitants of Bengal." "Quiet and inoffensive," unless provoked by harsh treatment, the Chinese were distinctive for being "fond of money" and "extremely shrewd and intelligent," and would quickly become a middle class in the West Indies. Despite government prohibition of emigration, White found that the Chinese were "anxious to emigrate and [would] go anywhere where they have the chance of earning a subsistence," noting their presence in Singapore, Java, Borneo, Manila, and California.[19]

Vast in supply, robust, and disciplined, the Chinese were presented not only as an alternative to East Indians and Africans, but as an ultimate ideal.

Even so, Chinese emigration seemed so bound up with cultural practices and traits that it also confounded the British ideal. Having just acknowledged that the Chinese were so poor and eager to emigrate that they would "go anywhere on any conditions that may be offered," White then criticized how they would not necessarily do so.[20] He pointed out their "habit of combining together for all purposes": "no Chinaman ever acts from individual impulse, but always in concert with others." Clannish yet unwilling to take their families abroad with them, Chinese emigrants preferred sending remittances home and paying occasional visits to the native land.[21] When asked why so few women were willing to emigrate, they said "sea-sickness would kill them," and the men "always sent home money to enable them to live in China." The only way for families to emigrate together was to "take all the collateral branches" of a clan.[22] When interviewing some Chinese about their possible interest in the West Indies, White learned that they expected cash advances to support families during their immediate absence, obtain clothing and other necessities, and cover initial expenses after arrival. Without asking a single question about the colony, nature of work, climate, and the people, White's interviewees seemed only concerned with the cost of living. Furthermore, having recognized that the Chinese were "entirely agriculturalists" and well suited for plantation work, White provided examples that suggested otherwise. In Manila, the Chinese quickly became hawkers or moved into business as soon as they had gotten a little money from agriculture. In Java, they did not work in the field, but were "employed principally as superintendents to regulate and direct the cultivation and the manufacture." Both examples led White to remark that the Chinese were "essentially a commercial people, fond of traffic and barter, of shopkeeping and petty manufactures."[23]

Perhaps to argue for a firm paternalistic control, White also depicted a contradictory Chinese character: "perfectly impassive, cold, and hard as a rock" yet "fond of music"; having "an inexhaustible fund of obstinacy," yet always willing to do anything that [was] required of them; "must be kept cheerful and managed with kindness" and a "consideration for their feelings and habits," yet indulgence would spoil them for they were "extremely cunning."[24] Taken together, these practices and characteristics were deeply incoherent. At once willing and refusing to go anywhere, docile and unyielding, inclined agriculturally and commercially, Chinese emigrants seemed like both a clear choice and an uncertain prospect in the long run.

The conflicting images of the Chinese emigrant were resonant in British Guiana. Looking through the prism of race and empire, officials could not always decide whether Chinese laborers were robust or sickly, hardworking or idle, docile or violent, commercially or agriculturally suited, sometimes acknowledging all the above. In an 1853 report, Governor Barkly, having visited the newly settled Chinese on the plantations, confirmed the "probable value and importance" of the Chinese immigration because of the "docility of their dispositions" and "habits of industry."[25] Despite sickness during the long voyage from China, Barkly noted that the Chinese "vital organism" was confirmed by medical doctors to be "exceedingly strong," whereas Africans and East Indians exposed to the same hardship would have suffered a mortality rate twice as high as the Chinese. Finding the Chinese well-adjusted to the climate and geology and more efficient in labor than any other racial group in the West Indies, Barkly concurred with Bowring, the superintendent of trade in China, who like White thought the Chinese the "most easily managed" of all people, though Barkly's report also briefly mentioned a violent conflict between some Chinese working on the Blankenburg plantation and freed blacks living in a nearby village. When some Chinese immigrants had fallen ill, a series of reports in *The Colonist of British Guiana* in June 1853 implied that Chinese immigrants were "worthless, idle and troublesome," and the experiment was "an expensive failure."[26] The planter of the Blankenburg estate reported that the Chinese were "far more turbulent and refractory than any other immigrants."[27] Another planter commented that the Chinese, even though "more muscular and athletic" than the Indian coolies, were unaccustomed to plantation work and were sometimes prevented by illness from performing regularly.[28] Offering his services in helping import Chinese women into the colony, one merchant wrote from Demerara in 1853 that the Chinese, unlike the Indians, did not bring their women along, making it questionable whether they would ever become "steady or tractable settlers." Despite the contradictions, Barkly found regrettable Bowring's opinion that Chinese emigration to the West Indies would be unlikely to rise as quickly as hoped. Furthermore, it would be almost impossible to expect women and families to accompany the men moving to the colony. In the context of liberal emancipation and colonial capitalism, free Chinese emigration was as elusive as it was necessary.

Another problem facing British officials was China's "connivance," referring to its failure to enforce the official ban on emigration. In response to a British government inquiry about expanding Chinese immigration to the West Indies, Bowring commented that Chinese laws prohibited "self-expatriation" despite a "teeming population." Yet, because emigration was such a "habit" and "the idle, vagrant and profligate population of the coast" was a "source of embarrassment" to the officials, Bowring thought it little surprising that they would tolerate it or even allow convicts to emigrate. The British consul at Amoy, Charles Winchester, made a similar comment. He thought that despite a general prohibition on emigration, there was a "practical limit to the arbitrary authority of the government."[29] Because of "overpopulation," Winchester pointed out, the mandarins knew how emigration could help relieve the pressure on food supply and remove lawless vagabonds from the country. Knowing also that any attempt to stop the annual exodus of "50,000 hungry, abled-bodied men" could lead to an uprising, Winchester thought it unlikely that the Chinese state would interfere with a foreign contracted emigration. Undeniably, these impressions of a corrupt and impotent Chinese government could only raise the appeal of free emigration sponsored by the British empire. But just as unflattering were the descriptions of the uncontrollable prospective emigrants, which contradicted positive accounts about their character elsewhere.

Given the complaints about Chinese state "connivance," it is noteworthy that free Chinese emigration was not meant to be unfettered, but was to be regulated. Soon after the Chinese indenture trade began, alarming mortality rates at sea revealed that the more virtuous Western-sponsored system was, in fact, a cloak full of holes. When the first ship carrying Chinese contract labor, the *Glentanner*, reached British Guiana in early 1853, 43 out of 262 passengers on board had died during a voyage lasting 131 days, and a score of others died while hospitalized. An investigation was immediately launched by the colonial authorities. Apart from recommending the use of larger ships, provision of space for movement, and a supply of fresh meat and vegetables, the report also recommended that the British emigration agent in China, James White, be given power to oversee the selection of proper ships and end "indiscriminate immigration." In particular, it called for an end to all cash advances made by ship captains at the signing of contracts, a practice preferred by the Chinese, because it opened the way to "abuses" on the part of the "collecting sub-agents." In the future, the selection of immigrants should "be left solely to the agent of the colony."[30] However, noting that a sudden increase in the demand for Chinese labor recently had caused Western merchants to transfer contracts to "Chinese speculators" known for "rapacity, recklessness and inhumanity," Bowring added that the resultant "irregularities" greatly increased because of British "isolation from and non-intercourse with Chinese authorities."[31] Paradoxically, free emigration was a state-regulated emigration.[32]

A string of violent incidents in the coastal towns and at sea also made urgent the British push against Chinese prohibition of emigration to make room for joint regulation.[33] One of the first incidents occurred in 1847 when a Straits Chinese from Penang working as a coolie broker for a British firm was seized by angry locals in Amoy (Xiamen), the earliest center of indenture emigration.[34] In 1852, a Chinese mutiny on the U.S. vessel *Robert Bowne* created a great uproar in China. After leaving Amoy in March, passengers on board rose up and killed the captain and part of the crew. After that, the ship was run aground at the Ryukyu Islands, where some passengers were later taken by British officers to Canton and others repatriated to Amoy. While on trial by U.S. officials for piracy and murder, some said that they started the mutiny upon finding out that the ship was not bound for San Francisco as they had been told, but for Latin America. Others described how they had been beguiled on board, kept below deck, and mistreated by the ship captain, who cut off their queues and threw the sick into the sea.[35] Even though the mutiny did not occur on a British vessel, John Bowring noted that those who had returned to Amoy from the *Robert Bowne* incident went around publicizing their cruel treatment at the hands of foreigners. News spread that foreigners were entrapping local residents for shipment overseas. Placards warned the public of "pig stealers."[36] Later that year, local authorities arrested a Chinese broker who had allegedly been kidnapping local residents and confining them in a guarded barracoon. Upon hearing of the arrest, the man's British employer, Francis Darby Syme of Syme, Muir, and Company, went with an aide to the police station and forced a release. Angered by the collusion of Western and Chinese outsiders, Chinese soldiers attacked two Englishmen who happened to be outside the police station. Local residents marched on the foreign quarter in protest. Three days later, unable to turn back the menacing crowd, the British opened fire, killing at least four Chinese and wounding five others.[37] Taken together, the interconnected series of riots and mutinies caused the British to put greater pressure on the Qing government to abandon the emigration ban.

Largely because of the swift popular backlash, the indenture trade in Amoy was displaced. By early 1853, British officials in Amoy reported that shippers found it impossible to recruit willing emigrants to go anywhere except Singapore and Sydney.[38] Instead, the indenture trade had to move to Swatow, Hong Kong, Cumingsoon, Shanghai, and nontreaty ports. In 1858, a British–French invasion of Canton during the Second Opium War allowed the allied forces to dictate a mutually regulated, full-fledged system of contract emigration. Emigration houses were erected, but interest was scant. Instead, foreign occupation inadvertently turned the streets of Canton into an open ground for mass abductions. In Shanghai, a series of riots broke out in 1859 against the Western indenture trade. Angered by the widespread kidnapping, Chinese mobs attacked British sailors, a Catholic church, and Siamese visitors whom they had mistaken for kidnappers.

The incidents of the 1850s brought to light how hard British officials had to work to bring the desired emigrants into being. Following the Amoy riot, the British government ordered its consuls in China not to aid in the shipment of emigrants, but also stressed that they were not bound to prevent cases in which "Chinese subjects of their own free will should prefer to risk the penalty attached to the transgression of the law," because it was "the duty of the Chinese government to enforce its own laws."[39] The logic was elaborated in a rejoinder by the naval commander, E. Gardiner Fishbourne, when a Chinese marine magistrate asked him to stop British merchants from encouraging emigration since it was against Chinese law: "I said that we did not prevent men from emigrating from our country if they were so disposed, and that we could not prevent Chinese from doing so; all we could do would be, to prevent English subjects from sending Chinese subjects out of their country against their will, but that to do this effectually we must be informed by the Chinese authorities of any such circumstance."[40] Asserting a universal right of free emigration for the Chinese equal to the British, Fishbourne did not think that the British should help enforce a Chinese law that impeded it. Instead, the Chinese state had a role to play in the exchange that the British could not fulfill by themselves. Here, nonparticipation was not part of the rationale. In 1854, the governor of Hong Kong, George Bonham, wrote to the British Foreign Office that the need to obtain laborers for the West Indies made it essential to continue emigration in other ports in China. He suggested: "The best mode of dealing with the subject might be to inform the Chinese authorities at the legalized ports that they cannot possibly object to the British authorities assisting in and superintending the fair and honest emigration of Chinese subjects, since it is notorious that the system is carried on under their own eyes, and with their connivance and concurrence, in a manner not free from abuses and risks, while the plan proposed by us would be based upon proper regulations, which would satisfy all parties concerned and entirely do away with past abuses."[41]

"Fair" and "honest," Chinese emigration coming under British assistance and supervision would be free from "abuses and risks." At the center of this statement was how "connivance and concurrence" under the Chinese system jeopardized the well-being of Chinese subjects. A jointly regulated free emigration could only benefit all interests, government and merchant, Chinese and British. What was neglected was that free emigration was mounted by a Western-led system of international relations that brooked no rival others, including China's own tribute system, which remained functional well into the 1870s. During the *Robert Bowne* mutiny in 1852, the Kingdom of Ryukyu Islands, a tribute state of the Qing empire, was the one that first informed Chinese authorities about the incident and assumed care of the stranded Chinese emigrants. During the Shanghai riot in 1859, Qing officials were worried that the attacks on Siamese visitors by a Chinese mob who mistook them for kidnappers would harm relations with the Kingdom of Siam.[42] These two examples suggest that the tribute system continued to operate and generate matters of concern to the Qing state.

Going beyond the push–pull logic, the complex history of Chinese coolie emigration suggests the impact of traditional Chinese emigration and the incorporation of the Pacific into the world economy, signaling a disruption of diaspora time. While British officials expected a ready-made supply of emigrants pouring out of an impoverished and overcrowded China, this was only a fiction to cope with the major transition from slavery to wage work. It denied the reality that Chinese emigration was socially and culturally embedded, meaning that not everyone was willing or available to move to anywhere in the world, despite China's large population. When allowed the options and resources, many preferred to go to California, Australia, and Singapore because of higher wages, greater autonomy, and established practice. Because of emigrant traditions, women and children generally stayed behind; men who emigrated sought to return. Given how baffling British officials found this logic, the free Chinese emigrant was not only a fractured ideal but also one that had to be imposed.

Creating Chinese Sovereignty

Similar to the idea of the free Chinese emigrant, Chinese sovereignty was not found but created during China's encounter with the indentured labor trade. It took the form of a new consciousness that the recognition of Chinese emigrants was essential in a new global age. As discussed earlier, Western diplomats and merchants often criticized the Qing ban on emigration as obstructive to the recruitment of free labor, making it impossible to separate voluntary emigration from involuntary emigration or to prevent the "abuses" and "irregularities" of the trade. In addition, they often couched their disagreements in a language of national wealth and progress, while portraying the inability of the Qing government to actually enforce the ban as a sign of weakness and corruption.[43] One example was a conversation between Captain Dupont, an aide to the first U.S. minister to China, and Tan Tingxiang, the governor-general of Zhili, which took place in 1858. The topic of discussion was whether the Qing should send consuls to the United States:

> VICEROY: It is not our custom to send officials beyond our own borders.
> DUPONT: But your people on the farther shore of the Pacific are very numerous, numbering several tens of thousands.
> VICEROY: When the Emperor rules over so many millions, what does he care for a few waifs that have drifted away to a foreign land?
> DUPONT: Those people are, many of them, rich, having gathered gold in our mines. They might be worth looking after on that account.
> VICEROY: The Emperor's wealth is beyond computation; why should he care for those of his subjects who have left their home, or for the sands they have scraped together?[44]

An example of China's "sublime indifference" toward "her emigrant offspring," this account, recorded by the American missionary W. A. P. Martin, portrayed China as oblivious to a new way to attain wealth and power through the "rich" and "numerous" emigrants. Unimpressed by Dupont's suggestion, Tan implied that China and Chinese abroad were on divergent paths, since the empire was wealthy and secure, while the emigrants had "drifted away to a foreign land" and "left their home." One of the most evocative defenses of the Qing stand on emigration in the mid-nineteenth century, Tan's rebuttal could be contrasted with Xue Fucheng's memorial in 1893. It was also one of the last.

For the next decade and a half, from 1860 to 1874, Qing leaders under the Tongzhi reign confronted a growing crisis of indentured migration that led to new assertions of sovereign rights and eventually the sending of consuls abroad. This dramatic change marked China's transition to nationhood. Traditionally, Chinese emigration resided in the realms of kinship, village, and maritime trade networks. Even though the imperial state had since the Ming dynasty issued periodic bans on maritime travel, it did not do so with the objective of protecting emigrants but in the interest of controlling piracy and subversion. The fact that emigration had not been a mainstay of Qing responsibilities could also be seen in several examples of Dutch and Spanish massacres of Chinese traders and settlers in the Philippines and Java in the seventeenth and eighteenth centuries, with which the early Qing state chose not to interfere. Nonetheless, following the Taiping Rebellion (1850–64), which claimed twenty million lives, and the Second Opium War (1856–60), which brought British and French attacks on Beijing, a new ruling elite made the mandate of emigrant protection a centerpiece of reconstruction during what Mary Wright has called the Tongzhi Restoration.[45] Facing formidable challenges brought on by the Western-dominated treaty system, the Tongzhi leaders sought to improve and enlarge China's place in it, which had the long-term effect of dramatically expanding the borders of the imperial order. If China and Chinese overseas had been on divergent paths, as Tan said to Dupont, a convergence of global forces was unexpectedly rerouting them toward each other.

One of the key examples was the creation of early Chinese sovereignty during the engagement with the indentured migration. The theme of Qing efforts to protect the emigrants is well documented in the literature, but the fact that the emigrants also helped tie the Qing into a system of modern nation-states is not yet well recognized. After China's defeat in the Second Opium War, emigration entered as part of the Qing treaties with the

West for the first time. The 1860 Beijing Convention signed with Britain stated in Article 5: "Chinese choosing to take service in British colonies or other parts beyond the sea are at perfect liberty to enter into engagements with British subjects for that purpose, and to ship themselves and their families on board any British vessel at any of the open ports of China."[46] A concurrent treaty with France contained a similar clause, reflecting a shared desire to expand indentured emigration. As scholars have noted, there followed the establishment of the Zongli Yamen (1861–1901), China's first modern office for foreign relations, which led a full-fledged diplomatic struggle against the indenture trade: translating and poring over every aspect of international law, forming close relations with the Western diplomatic corps, and monitoring world news and affairs. As this chapter will later discuss, the Yamen also dispatched commissions to Peru and Cuba, the first ones sent by the Qing government to investigate migrant conditions overseas. These intense diplomatic efforts suggest that the indenture crisis helped transform China into a proto-nation on the world stage.

A new emphasis on sovereignty illuminates the larger significance of the indentured migration to Chinese national development. The global nature of Chinese labor emigration and the forced incorporation of Qing China into the treaty system meant that the Qing leaders could only exert some control of the matter by engaging in rather than resisting diplomacy with the West. During the process, they learned to define China's rights and interests, negotiate international politics, and expand the practices of the imperial state. This wider interpretation helps extend important studies on the history of China's global integration through emigration, such as the struggles led by Chinese emigrant organizations in the United States to resist racism and develop nationalism.[47] It also suggests that the overseas Chinese contributed to Chinese history not only by supporting disaster relief, reform, and revolutionary causes, a widely accepted point, but also by enmeshing China in an interstate system early on. Though conservative Qing factions would later denounce the Tongzhi leaders as a "foreign affairs clique," and some Chinese communist historians have also accused them of "ceding" Chinese sovereignty to foreign powers, they should in fact be remembered for creating it.[48]

The creation of sovereignty was accomplished in part by combining new and old resources in the struggle against indentured migration. Under the leadership of Prince Gong, the Zongli Yamen was made up of an eclectic group united by an interest in Western affairs and learning. Members rose to the forefront through informal channels of official patronage rather than the civil service examination system.[49] They adhered strictly to treaty terms and forbade labor recruitment by unregulated means or nontreaty nations, turning the treaties with the West into a means to restrain the West. At the same time, they insisted on the continuing utility of Confucian morality. For instance, Prince Gong justified the protection of emigrants by stating that Western labor recruitment was "the same as if China were loaning them to the foreign countries to use."[50] Chinese laborers, being "basically ignorant people" who did not speak a foreign language and lived far away from their native home, deserved state protection. This argument was not based on Western ideologies of liberty and equality; rather, it embodied a Confucian paternalism toward the common people. In this view, emigrant labor was an instrument belonging to the Qing polity that should be respected and returned. In contrast to the Western colonial ideal that the Chinese emigrant was capable of contractual consent, Prince Gong refurbished the Confucian ethic to insist that the government should continue to defend the ignorant and weak in the age of global commerce. In so doing, he also staked out the ground for Chinese autonomy.

To further understand this nascent sovereignty emerging from the indenture trade, the current focus on Qing protection needs to include attention to an emergent global sphere in which it acted. One instructive example is how the officials dealt with a rampant tide of kidnapping and fraud in Guangdong between 1864 and 1867. As Robert Irick has found, joint regulation did not end the excesses of the trade, but instead increased them.[51] Since Britain and France were the only governments that were allowed under the 1860 Beijing Convention to establish emigration houses, others were left unbound by treaty terms. Moreover, as the Zongli Yamen instructed local officials to prevent nontreaty nations from operating in Guangzhou, it inadvertently redirected the unofficial traffic to the Portuguese-held Macao, from which the majority of laborers were shipped to Cuba and Peru. When the Board of Punishments proposed new regulations to stop "crafty" foreign merchants from engaging in the "seizing" and "buying" and "reselling" of people abroad, the Zongli Yamen decided that a bilateral effort would be necessary without seeming to obstruct labor recruitment guaranteed by the 1860 treaties. Therefore, it instructed Robert Hart, the inspector general of maritime customs, to draft new regulations with the help of local officials in Canton.

What the Yamen circulated was a sweeping plan of protection that covered not only the recruitment process domestically but throughout the entire duration of the contract overseas, prompting immediate opposition. In what later became known as the Emigration Convention, the 1866 framework limited the length of contract to no more than five years and forbade the contracted laborer from being taken to unknown destinations, forced to renew a contract, or subjected to harsh conditions. Moreover, it allowed the sending of Chinese officials to investigate work conditions and required that each laborer be given free return passage at the end of the contract. Despite the support of their own diplomats, both the British and French governments refused to accept the new regulations. Britain faced vehement opposition from planters in the West Indies over the provision of free return passage. While France was a major shipper of indentured laborers and did not recruit them for its own colonies, it opposed the five-year limit on the contract because planters in Cuba and Peru demanded a longer period of eight years. On this point, planters in the British West Indies were less concerned because they relied more heavily on the supply of Indian laborers than Chinese laborers. Even the British government was unprepared to increase the bounties that subsidized the hiring of laborers for more than five years.[52] In addition, Spain opposed many of the terms, including those related to hours and wages. Accepting and opposing different aspects of the regulations, the three powers could only agree to omit all provisions protecting Chinese emigrants after leaving China's ports. In an audacious move, the Zongli Yamen rejected the redraft, leveraging the fact that other powers had agreed to the original code and the throne had adopted it into law. Yet an effective solution still depended on the cooperation of Peru and Spain, the largest contractors of Chinese labor, as well as Portugal, under which the indenture trade flourished in Macao. During the course of discussion, it also became clear that the sending of Chinese consuls abroad would be necessary to enforce any regulation.

This incident suggests that the global context in which the Qing acted was just as important as its attempts at protection. The Chinese indenture took place not because the Qing regime was callous or just weak; more importantly, it was not the only player in the field. Instead, the challenges suggest a domain of multiple times and spaces through which indentured Chinese labor traveled. It brought together diverse actors inspired by the promise that Chinese emigration could replace African slavery, simultaneously advancing settler colonialism, liberal humanitarianism, and industrial capitalism. It also created the interdependent interests of home governments, colonial and foreign offices, diplomats, shippers, brokers, and planters, among others, across the Caribbean, the Atlantic, and the Pacific. In other words, it took more than Qing protection to end the indenture trade, not only because many of the activities occurred outside China but also because these activities involved a network of symbiotic interests. Without timely openings for intervention, Qing protection alone would not have gone far enough to bring a lucrative, multinational operation to a halt. What certainly remains critical is that when an opportunity finally came along, Qing leaders seized it.

Such an opportunity arose during an escalation of violence, when a blend of international reporting and Chinese resistance created a new space for action. According to Arnold J. Meagher, there were at least sixty-eight mutinies involving Chinese contract labor between 1847 and 1874, with the overwhelming majority of incidents occurring on vessels bound for Cuba, Peru, and British Guiana.[53] The most serious incidents occurred between the late 1860s and the early 1870s. In 1866, a mutiny on the Italian vessel *Napoleon Canevaro* set off an explosion of fireworks carried on board, killing all of the 662 emigrants two days after leaving Macao, while the crew managed to escape in rescue boats. In 1868, another violent revolt happened on the *Cayalti*, a Peruvian ship flying the U.S. flag. With its deck and cabin covered in blood, the ship ended up in Hakodate, Japan. In 1870, the *Uncovah*, a Salvadoran vessel, erupted in flames during a mutiny near Sumatra, killing more than 100 passengers. Also in the same year, emigrants on the French vessel *La Nouvelle Penelope* killed the captain and forced the ship back to Guangzhou. In 1871, five hundred Chinese emigrants on the *Don Juan* perished in a fire. Other incidents involved large numbers of emigrants breaking free from the ships ashore and leading to local investigations. For instance, the *Delores Ugarte*, a ship flying the Salvadoran flag, was carrying a total of 608 Chinese passengers in 1870, but almost half of them escaped during a stop in Hawaii. It was found that before reaching Honolulu, eighteen people had jumped overboard and twenty-five others had died of illness.⁵⁴ These events became the rallying point for outcries against the Chinese indenture.

It could be argued that Chinese resistance, no matter how serious, played a limited role in ending the indenture, but the volume of the events was certainly turned up by the world press, making it hard to ignore. Emerging across the ports of Hong Kong, Macao, and Shanghai and linked to others in Peru, Britain, and the United States, a cohort of newspaper and periodical writers spoke on behalf of national honor and the greater humanity against what they observed to be a new slave trade. In numerous reports and editorials, they uniformly condemned the indentured migration, portraying Chinese sufferings and mutinies as a series of inhumane tragedies and spontaneous uprisings like those associated with African slaves. Pressing for political and moral action, the international press helped orchestrate public opinion, revitalized antislavery groups and criticisms, and gave structure to government responses. In Hong Kong and Shanghai, the most active English-language newspapers were the *China Mail*, the *Daily Press*, the *Friend of China*, and the *North China Herald*, which frequently carried all aspects of news about the indentured migration. Their global counterparts included the *New York Times*, the *London Times*, and *Harper's New Monthly Magazine*. Taken together, the international press contributed to a sense of a common crisis by publicizing the atrocities and pushing the criticisms to new heights. It is noteworthy that the violent, tragic acts of Chinese resistance arose from complex motives, as there is evidence that some of the mutineers had been pirates and secret society members who enlisted as emigrants intending to plunder and incite others to rebellion.⁵⁵ Regardless of motive, the continual appearance of Chinese mutinies in the news kept up the pressure on different players and helped contribute to an opening that ended the coolie trade.

One such instance came during May 1868, when newspaper headlines in Peru and Britain reported the cruel news of "the branded 48." According to a source from the Society of Friends of the Indians in Peru, a group of forty-eight Chinese who had been brought to Lambayeque from Callao were branded with a hot iron. On the face of each worker was a letter C extending from their chins to their necks.⁵⁶ Sensational reporting escalated criticisms of the coolie trade. Reacting to the news of "branded 48," the Portuguese consul-general in Lima, Narciso Velarde, urged an immediate investigation by the Peruvian government and compared indenture to slavery, saying that "we see the *hacendados*, with honorable exceptions, looking at the *colono* not as a man, but as an instrument and less than a slave." Demanding the release of the Chinese from their contracts and a trial of the criminals involved, he added that the streets of Lima had been filled with an "immense number of Chinese mutilated in the service of their masters and abandoned by them when they are unable to work."[57] Facing international scrutiny, the governor of Macao, Antonio Sergio de Souza, temporarily suspended Chinese emigration to Peru on November 18, 1868, though his government had previously maintained that Chinese "crimps" were the main source of problems. As a result of the efforts of the world press, high-profile scandals such as the "branded 48" kept the Chinese indenture in the news and dealt a blow to the national reputations of those participating in an internationally despised trade that was no longer only China's problem.

A decisive turn happened during the *María Luz* affair in 1872, which set off a chain of responses causing the final closure of the trade in Macao. A Peruvian barque bound for Callao, the *María Luz* made a fateful detour to Yokohama after suffering damage in a storm during the summer of 1872. Alerted by officers on a British warship who found escaped passengers crying for help, Japanese authorities found 230 Chinese on the *María Luz*, many of whom said that they had been kidnapped and forced to sign contracts to work in Peru. Following the arrest of the ship captain, the Japanese court found him guilty of abuse and set all the Chinese men free, a course of action that made Japan an instant hero of humanitarianism and deeply humiliated Peru.[58] A Zongli Yamen report indicates that Chinese community leaders in Yokohama also sprang into action, raising over one thousand dollars to hire a lawyer for the emigrants.[59] As the investigation and court ruling over the *María Luz* case were read around the world, it also had an immediate impact on Portugal. Correspondents between Portugal and Peru quoted an observation by Governor Januario of Macao: "no matter how well organized the emigration might be, it could not continue without involving the colony of Macao and Portugal in very disagreeable conflicts with the English and Chinese governments."[60] Even though Japan was widely credited with the rescue of the Chinese emigrants in the *María Luz* case, the statement indicated that efforts to suppress the trade were also coming from the Chinese. Just as the *María Luz* affair unfolded, Governor-General Rui Lin had begun dispatching river patrols to inspect steamers running between Macao and Canton, searching for crimps and kidnapped victims. Even before Governor Januario announced the closing of Macao to the indenture trade in late 1873, the American minister in China, S. Wells Williams, had reported to the Department of State in June that "the severe measures adopted by the authorities at Canton to prevent coolies of all kinds going to Macao" had left most of its barracoons empty.[61]

Besides leading and joining mutinies that drew the attention of the world press, Chinese emigrants also pulled the Qing state along through other forms of protest. For those who survived the deadly passage and the grueling demands of the contract after arrival, their action sometimes took the form of petitions that have been overlooked in the scholarship focusing on the agency of the Qing state. Two letters were sent to the Qing government in 1869 and 1871, the first overseas Chinese petitions ever to reach China. Interestingly, because Peru was not a treaty nation with China and China did not send consuls abroad until the late 1870s, the petition only came to the Zongli Yamen via the American consul in Lima. Speaking of cruel oppression and discrimination in Peru, the 1869 petition was jointly submitted by three Chinese native place associations in Guangdong province: the Gugang Gongsi, representing the five counties of Xinhui, Kaiping, Enping, Taishan, and E'shan; the Yuedong Huiguan, representing eastern Guangdong; and the Tongsheng Gongsi, consisting of Hakkas from Zhongshan county. It reads: "We the commoners were born and raised in China, a land of moral teachings, but are forced by hunger and cold to live in a foreign land. This is because during the first year in the Xianfeng reign [1850], local bandits rose up, making all lines of work and craft difficult. Meanwhile, there was hiring of labor, so we boarded ships in Macao or Jinxing. At that time, both sides agreed to a contract that no one suspected would change."[62] Alluding to the Taiping Rebellion (1850–1864), this petition provides evidence that at least some Chinese emigrants entered into labor contracts of their own volition, though they stressed that chaos at home had been the reason for their exile. Saying that it had been more than twenty years and that tens of thousands had arrived, the petitioners then portrayed themselves as reasonable, hardworking people forced to endure harsh conditions in a strange land:

> We herd cattle and horses, following every command; we open up farmland and dig wells, submitting to every assignment. Our work goes beyond sunrise and sunset; our laboring continues through winter and summer. To make a living, we accept the difference between master and servant. Yet there are evil foreigners who use their wealth to oppress the poor, completely disregard morality and reason, treat the contract like waste paper, and are indifferent about human life. They are stingy about clothing, food, and pay. They have no mercy for misery and fatigue. They are often cruel and constantly beat us, forcing us to work in chains or labor in the fields through hunger and cold.[63]

Finding the employers inhumane, the petitioners wrote that government officials were also corrupt and the townspeople hostile. Sounding a note of despair, they told of the ignored protests and tragic suicides:

> When we complain to [government officials] about injustice, we get harshly condemned instead. From time to time, we hear how people die unjust deaths. In many places, some have tragically killed themselves. We have not forgotten our debts to the emperor and our fathers, but it is hard to go on suffering in a foreign land. Even though there are sometimes good employers and officials who pity us, they are rare and can do little to remedy the situation. Running shops and businesses, we fear robbers. Walking down the street, we get insulted by children. Everywhere is covered in thorns. All around town are abysses.

Voicing a common plight, the petition reflected the fact that emigrant Chinese in Lima had grown into a stable community, consisting of those who had completed their labor contracts, settled among the locals, opened shops and businesses, and led Chinese organizations. It shows that the community had amassed an ability to mount an organized, eloquent protest to demand protection and respect. Learning that as many as thirty thousand Chinese from Guangdong were living in Peru, a nontreaty nation, the Zongli Yamen asked U.S. officials to extend help to the emigrants. After translating the letter into English, the U.S. legation in China sent a copy to Washington, which was later published in both U.S. and Peruvian newspapers.[64]

Two years later, in 1871, a second petition reached China via American consuls. As reported in the Peruvian paper *El Comercio* on January 17, 1872, a seven-member commission was formed by Chinese living in China, some of whom had returned from Peru. Members came from elite and educated backgrounds, and the leader was the son of a viceroy who had been kidnapped and taken to Peru: "this young man was robbed, drugged with opium, and embarked in Macao ten years ago, and he returns to his country an invalid with one foot less, after being forced to fulfil an illegal contract." The secretary of the commission had been a teacher for the family of an official: "Now 16 years ago he found himself and his two students of 13 and 15 years taking a ride in a two-oared boat in the Bay of Canton, when in a fog he was stopped by an armed launch." After being taken to Peru, the man was "thrice sold to different persons" and "obtained his liberty only after 15 years of hard labor, and when he had become completely deaf"; his two young students had already died.[65] Besides the evidence of the abuses on their bodies, members of commission also brought along three thousand pages of depositions collected from Chinese in Peru.

Taken together, these petitions provided resources for the Qing to rein in the emigration trade. In the aftermath of the *María Luz* affair, the Peruvian government in 1873 sent a mission to China to seek a treaty on trade and migration. Appointed to lead the negotiations, the high official Li Hongzhang (1823–1901) demanded repatriation of the emigrants before a treaty could be discussed. Repeatedly, he stressed the Chinese petitions and international news reports as evidence of abuse. However, the Peruvian representative, Captain Aurelio García y García, rejected the demand. Saying that there were as many as 100,000 Chinese living in Peru, he denied the charge that they had been mistreated. Rather, they were content workers and businessmen who should not be sent back against their will. Questioning the veracity of the petitions, García asserted that they did not contain records of individual identity, could not be verified, and were no proof of exploitation. Here, the inability of the Qing state to document information about individuals, including subjects beyond its territorial jurisdiction, became the point of contention. Thus came Li's idea of arranging investigative missions to Cuba and Peru, the first time that an imperial dynasty in China would send officials overseas to collect information about the conditions of emigrants.

While scholars have closely studied the Cuba Commission led by Chen Lanbin and have translated the extensive report into English, the Peru

Commission is less well known.⁶⁶ Undertaken concurrently but under the radar of Peruvian officials, the Peru Commission was unlike the Cuba Commission, which was formally arranged with Spain. Yet, as discussions for a treaty reached an impasse in 1873, García also rejected Li's proposal to send a commission to Peru to investigate emigrant conditions. In response, Li decided to outmaneuver him by planning a secret mission and choosing Yung Wing for the task. Yung had become the first Chinese graduate of Yale College in 1854. Together with Chen Lanbin, Yung had led the Chinese Educational Mission to the United States.⁶⁷ Both men came from the home region of most of the emigrants to Peru and Cuba, spoke Cantonese, and were further assisted by interpreters. Even though Li remarked that Yung's character was not as reliable as Chen's, perhaps referring to Yung's U.S. education and Westernized outlook, he explained in a memorial to the throne that Yung would be unafraid to engage in debate with his peers and would stand up for Chinese interests, and was thus a decent choice.⁶⁸

Demonstrating a keen awareness of international law and the power of state-produced documentation, both commissions were impeccably designed and executed. Both Chen and Yung were chosen for their Western learning and experience. Western officials were appointed to offer advice, ensure the correctness of procedures, and lend a sense of impartiality to the commissions. Once in Peru and Cuba, the commissions conducted a large number of visits in different locations, from plantations to jails to city streets, over the course of a few months. They collected a wide variety of evidence and generated clear records of depositions that indicated the name and background of each individual, as well as the conditions under which the emigrant was brought there, whether voluntarily or involuntarily. In Cuba, all the interview questions and answers were aligned with contractual terms over wages, hours, and treatment, by which the employers were expected to abide.

Since scholars have studied the Cuba Commission carefully, it is worth a look at the Peru Commission, which also contributed to the end of indentured emigration. Accompanied by two Americans, Reverend J. H. Twichell and E. W. Kellogg, Yung Wing arrived in Lima, Peru, in the summer of 1873. In his report, he wrote that Peru was an independent country but that it largely followed the old Spanish tradition. Finding an "underdeveloped" economy, Yung noted that the native population numbered two million, but that the wealthy did not wish to hire the natives because the wages were too high and the natives, being locals, could not be easily oppressed. Therefore, the wealthy "colluded with the Portuguese to kidnap Chinese laborers in order to satisfy their own needs"; "as many as 120,000 Chinese had been sold and kidnapped" over the previous twenty years, with numerous cases of abuse, sickness, and death. Only three-fifths of the laborers survived the full term of the contract. According to Yung Wing, he also took two dozen photographs of the coolies, "showing how their backs had been lacerated and torn, scarred and disfigured by the lash," and telling "a tale of cruelty and inhumanity perpetrated by the owners of haciendas."[69]

Because the Peru Commission was conducted in secret, Yung did not venture beyond the city of Lima. Instead, he had to rely on the help of American diplomats and merchants, as well as Chinese associations, merchants who had relocated from California, and emigrants who had completed their contracts and resided in Lima.[70] The latter group recounted that they had been sold to cotton and sugar plantations, where food was hardly adequate and clothing was made out of rice sacks. They lived in straw huts that they had to build themselves, and they slept on damp floors. Many suffered beatings or witnessed the beatings of others. Pay was irregular and subject to arbitrary deductions. One person described how a fellow worker "escaped by walking backwards at night and hiding in caves during the day so that his footsteps could not be retraced." Another laborer told of his ordeal on the Chincha Islands. He had to fill two carts with guano every day or he would be tied up and beaten. Every day, at least two or three people committed suicide by drowning themselves in the ocean or burying themselves in a pit under loads of guano. Because of the wave of suicides, soldiers were brought in to keep watch on the workers. After working there for two years, the man persuaded one of the guards to let him work as a carpenter in Lima to fulfill the rest of his contract. After that, he stayed and started a small business.

These testimonies from Peru, together with a similar and larger collection of others gathered in Cuba, were written into detailed reports. To the chagrin of Peruvian and Spanish diplomats, the reports were widely distributed in China and closely studied by Qing officials. Xu Qianshen, a rising diplomat and close aide of Li Hongzhang, reflected on the treatment of emigrant laborers in Spanish Cuba:

> According to those kidnapped to work in Cuba such as the scholar Li Zhaochun and others, after boarding the ship, they were either forced

into a bamboo cage or locked up in an iron cell; a few people were beaten to intimidate the others. What propriety was there? Liu A'shou and others said, many died in humiliation and lost their lives. What dignity was there? After arriving in Havana, as Ye Junfu and others said, they were sold by classification into good, average, and poor, removed of clothing, and inspected and priced while naked. This is shameless and insulting. As Lin A'bang and others testified, buyers removed all clothing of the laborers to check if they were strong or not, treating them like cattle and horses. After beginning work, as Xi Zuobang and others said, Chinese laborers ate scraps that dogs would not eat, did work that cattle and horses would not do. There were prison cells everywhere, constant beatings by whips and clubs. Every day, people with broken arms and legs, open and bleeding wounds could be seen; word of people hanging themselves, slitting their own throats, or swallowing poison could be heard.[71]

Besides speaking in the traditional language of Confucian order, propriety, and humaneness, Xu went on to document violations of the 1866 regulations in a new language of diplomacy and sovereignty. He pointed out that after 1866 as many as 35,000 laborers departed from Macao, where no Chinese officials were present to regulate the process. They had not been recruited from an official emigration house but in Macao, Whampoa, Swatow, and Xiamen. In Macao, emigrants were detained in barracoons, refused exit, and forced to sign contracts. Contracts were eight years long, rather than the lawful limit of five years. Some did not have a contract, did not understand it, or had been told that they were being taken to Vietnam, Singapore, San Francisco, or New York. While on board, emigrants had to buy water and food from the crew and suffered beatings if they dared to ask for more. After arrival in Cuba, employers forced the emigrants to work beyond the stipulated nine and a half hours each day, and sometimes hired under the legal age of twenty years. In the case of sickness, laborers were subject to threats, beatings, and docking of pay. Upon completion of the contract, many could not simply regain their freedom but were forced to renew the contract or were resold to another employer. Apart from the oral testimonies of mistreatment, the most damaging was a horrific tale that was widely believed: when the Chinese died on the plantations, their bones were ground to make sugar. Concluding the report with this ghastly image, Xu remarked, "Spain is a sovereign nation (*zizhu zhi guo*), meaning that it has sovereign rights (*zizhu zhi quan*). Now that the violations are found, would Spain correct them? Or would it pretend that they did not happen?"[72]

This brutal narrative of displacement, exploitation, and expropriation of remains after death constituted a "diaspora moment" through a mutual construction of the suffering emigrant and a new Qing sovereignty. As the Qing state imagined that Chinese emigrants were under complete foreign control, it re-created itself as a nation among others. Xu's report indicated how far the officials had come to grasp their place in a world transformed by mass production, communications, and transportation. Acting in an emergent sphere of diplomats, court judges, the printing press, free traders, protestors, and activists from Britain, the British West Indies, the United States, Spain, Peru, Portugal, and Japan, among others, the Qing state studied international law, enforced its treaties, and policed its borders. Exploiting the attention generated by the world press and Chinese resistance in a global public sphere, it spearheaded a diplomatic struggle through the Zongli Yamen, successfully ending the coolie crisis in 1874. In the wake of this diaspora moment, China came away with the lasting insight that a capacity to recognize, protect, and lead emigrants was integral to its existence in a new global age.

Conclusion

Part of the first modern wave of transoceanic movements, Chinese indentured migration to the Americas marked the first diaspora moment in modern Chinese history. It was a rupture in "diaspora time," representing a departure from the relatively stable, deep history of Chinese emigration based on kinship loyalties and maritime trading networks in Asia going back four centuries. For the participants, Chinese emigration had long been commercialized, male-dominated, and circular. After the 1840s, the triumph of Western imperialism and free trade partly altered this picture by introducing indenture, but diaspora time continued in the resilience of emigrant communities on the coast and the inability of the Western powers to find a ready-made supply of willing emigrants. However, a deepening incorporation of China into the global economy also brought together actors and frontiers eager to experiment with indenture during the transition from slavery to free labor. At this diaspora moment, Qing China was pulled into the dynamic orbit of Chinese indentured emigrants bound for the Americas.

While the impact of Chinese indentured emigration on the Americas might be well known, how did it affect modern China? It changed China by binding the Qing state into a complex sphere of production and labor regimes, print and public debates, and an interstate system of diplomacy and sovereignty. The enormous range of interests made the Chinese indenture trade extremely profitable, coercive, and hard to control, but the extensive draw across multiple geographies also planted the seeds of its demise. Qing protection played a role in ending the global crisis, but it also took the international press and Chinese emigrant resistance to create the opportune timing. Seen more broadly, the encounter forces us to take apart the notions that "China" and "the West" were single, bounded entities and "the world" was the sum of its parts. Instead, each was a plural, contradictory assemblage of interacting times, spaces, and subjects. Pointing out that Chinese indenture ended in 1874 while Indian indenture went on until the early twentieth century, Adam McKeown thinks that it was because "Chinese indenture did not take place within the surveillance of a single empire but across multiple frontiers."[73] David Northup also finds that the imperial networks were shifting in the late nineteenth century, causing some of the indenture trades to shut down and others to open or replace the old ones.[74] Similarly, the end of Chinese indentured emigration resides in a great convergence of fragmented temporal and spatial interactions. One of the most profound effects was that in the process China began to assume its place in a "family of nations."

This impact is evident in the immediate and rapid expansion of Qing diplomatic representation in the aftermath. Though a similar proposal had been made earlier by one of Li Hongzhang's subordinates, Ding Yuchang, in 1867, the imperial court did not begin sending permanent diplomatic missions abroad until 1875, a sign of momentum rather than coincidence. Recognizing their contributions to the end of the indenture trade, the Zongli Yamen promptly appointed Chen Lanbin and Yung Wing as envoys to the United States, Spain, and Peru. By 1880 there were new Chinese legations in England, Germany, France, Russia, Japan, and Singapore. These initiatives were launched on the basis of international law, not because the Qing was forced into them by new treaties.[75] In particular, Chinese diplomats were active in informing and advising the court on matters related to the overseas

Chinese. Xue Fucheng, who penned the 1893 memorial, was part of an itinerant group of reformer-diplomats that included Guo Songtao (1818–1891) and Huang Zunxian (1848–1905) who were instrumental to China's transformation in a global system.

Finally, the prehistory of indentured emigration should be restored for a broader understanding of the 1893 memorial. Emerging from a series of encounters with global commerce and labor, the Qing initiative to invite the return of Chinese emigrants belonged to a long arc of development beginning in the 1840s. Known as huaqiao by the turn of the twentieth century, the emigrant came to be regarded in national narratives not as absent but always revenant, hence the meaning of "Chinese *temporarily* located [overseas]." As Rebecca Karl has pointed out, after the formal removal of bans and stigmas against emigration in 1893, "the juridico-legal as well as the sociopolitical and economic conditions of possibility through which overseas Chinese could be 'captured' as political subjects for China had been established."[76] The call for returns thus sparked broader and more intense attempts not only from China to mobilize the emigrants as a diaspora, but also from the emigrants to recognize China as a homeland, a process contributing to the development of Chinese nationalism. The succeeding series of events would be familiar to many historians of China and Chinese overseas: the exiles of Qing reformers and revolutionaries such as Liang Qichao and Sun Yat-sen among the overseas Chinese after 1898, the first Chinese transnational protest against exclusion in the United States in 1905, the overseas development of Chinese chambers of commerce after 1905, the 1909 Nationality Law on the principle of *jus sanguine*, and the 1911 Revolution that drew on overseas Chinese support and launched a modern republic. Occurring in the mid-nineteenth century, indentured emigration serves to rejoin narratives of Chinese and global development by bringing the Americas and Chinese laborers into the purview of history, complementing the literature's dominant focus on Southeast Asia and the merchant and intellectual elites. In these early interactions, the Qing state and the emigrants had not intended to influence each other, but they ended up doing so in an emergent, interconnected world.

CHAPTER 2

Colonists of the South Seas

During the 1920s, Japan's growing interest in Chinese in the South Seas (*Nanyang*), a maritime region linking the port cities of China, Japan, and Southeast Asia, greatly alarmed Chinese intellectuals who had been traveling and working there. A leading member of the group, Liu Shimu (1889–1952) was a Guangdong native and a veteran of Sun Yat-sen's Revolutionary Alliance. He had taught in a Chinese school in Sumatra, later studied at Tokyo University, and worked as a secretary of overseas affairs for the Guomindang Party in Shanghai.[1] In 1923, Liu translated one of the earliest Japanese statements about Nanyang Chinese by Umetani Mitsusada (1880–1936), head of the police of the Taiwan Office of the Governor-General. In his speech, Umetani declares that *Nanyang huaqiao* (*Nan'yō kakyō*) were "the hegemons of the South Seas" (*Nanyang zhi bazhe*). Given their size, ubiquity, and commercial vitality, despite their lack of political power, he argued that Japan should learn to guide them through Taiwan because Chinese there shared "racial ties" with their Southeast Asian counterparts. Parallel commentary by Liu and other contributors to the publication contained both praise and caution: "Our *huaqiao* [Chinese diaspora] have neither depended on the government nor had an army or a navy. Yet they were able to grow their influence. How did they manage to do that?" "Japanese imperialists have long planned to expand their power in Nanyang," but since they "dare not openly invade Nanyang," they "use stealthy tactics to weaken the power of the five million overseas Chinese."[2]

This mix of praise and caution came to underpin a flurry of publishing activities led by Liu Shimu at Shanghai's Jinan University, which evolved into the most important center for Nanyang studies under Guomindang rule (1927–45) and left a profound impact.[3] With Liu serving as head of the new Department of Nanyang Cultural Affairs (*Nanyang wenhua shiye bu*) in 1927, more than thirty polyglot Chinese intellectuals began producing a massive volume of work on the history and geography of the South Seas through intense research and translation of Japanese and Western titles.[4] Some of their original works on *Nanyang huaqiao*, such as those by Li Changfu (1899–1966) and Chen Da (1892–1975), were translated into Japanese by the South Manchuria Railway Company (Mantetsu) in the late 1930s.[5] Besides compiling more than thirty books, the department published two periodicals, *South Seas Research* (*Nanyang Yanjiu*) and *South Seas Bulletin* (*Nanyang Qingbao*), and a wide array of maps, reference materials, and school textbooks, which found their most important outlet among overseas Chinese newspapers and schools in Southeast Asia.[6] During Japan's invasion of China (1937–45), several core members of the Jinan group including Liu Shimu fled south to Singapore, where they joined local Chinese intellectuals to establish the South Seas Society in 1940 and started the influential publication *Journal of the South Seas Society* (*Nanyang Xuebao*). Others in the group continued to work for the wartime Nationalist government in Chongqing or returned to the mainland after the 1949 Communist Revolution and remained active scholars. Internationally, prominent postwar historians of Southeast Asia such as Victor Purcell and Suyama Taku drew on the work produced by the Jinan intellectuals.[7] The tradition of overseas Chinese studies in China, Taiwan, and Southeast Asia that the Jinan intellectuals pioneered has endured to this day, inspiring reprints of their publications and new studies heavily modeled on them.[8] The impact of the Jinan group was far-reaching.

This chapter focuses on the height of the Jinan activities during the 1920s and 1930s, a valuable case study of how Chinese mass emigration to the South Seas transformed China. Accelerating after the 1870s and reaching a peak in the 1920s, Chinese migration to Southeast Asia created a new cultural frontier for Chinese intellectuals from China. A revolution in transportation and communications, particularly since the opening of the Suez Canal in 1869, had ushered in the era of high European colonialism, later followed by Japan's "southward advance" during and after the First World War.[9] As Chinese laborers and merchants flocked to tin mines, rice fields, and rubber estates, they also swelled ports and cities, stimulating a rapid growth of Chinese newspapers and schools across Penang, Rangoon, Saigon, Singapore, Batavia, Bangkok, and Manila.[10] Attracted to the burgeoning publics, Chinese intellectuals became writers, editors, teachers, and researchers. Situated in this context, Liu Shimu and other itinerant members of the Jinan group were not merely mobilized by the Guomindang state, but had been part of the Nanyang circulations that caught Guomindang attention. In turn, their intellectual energies opened China to European and Japanese views of migration and melded new knowledge about Nanyang into Chinese narratives of the nation.

Largely absent from modern Chinese and overseas Chinese historiographies, the voluminous Jinan writings suggest an intertwined, circulatory history of European, Japanese, and Chinese thought across the South Seas. Though many scholars have recognized the founding significance of Nanyang studies at Jinan University, few have investigated the large corpus of the writings.[11] Vigorously engaged with a colonial world, the Jinan writings suggest that the intellectuals admired European colonial power, rediscovered maritime thinking through imperial Japan, and contemplated a Chinese settler colonialism. These ideas became greatly problematic at the end of World War II, when new territorial states emerged and turned their backs on the seas. By bringing this history out of the shadows, I do not intend to revive or simply critique the colonial logic in the Jinan scholarship. Rather, my goal is to show how the researchers did not simply reproduce colonial ideas about Nanyang, but actively negotiated them and made them Chinese.

Most importantly, the Jinan efforts produced a Chinese national identity inextricably tied to Chinese emigrants, though there is far greater recognition of the reverse. At this "diaspora moment" of Chinese national formation, the intellectuals portrayed Nanyang huaqiao as incomplete colonists without China's protection, China as an incomplete nation lacking overseas colonies, and the two as bound to reunite against a rising Japan. Focusing on how the writing of Enlightenment history helped produce the modern nation-state, Prasenjit Duara has pointed out that "the past is not only transmitted but also dispersed in space and time," therefore history tends to "appropriate dispersed histories according to present needs."[12] The Jinan writings show that Chinese intellectuals also appropriated the dispersed histories of mass emigration to forge a national identity. They insisted that Nanyang huaqiao contained both the fragments of China's past glory and the key to China's future resurgence, suggesting that the nation was as much a creation of the diaspora as the diaspora was a creation of the nation.

Locating this national formation in the South Seas, this chapter examines how Chinese intellectuals contributed to the circulation of colonial ideas about migration and then turns to their writing of a Chinese settler colonialism during the early twentieth century. My loose label "Jinan intellectuals" refers to Chinese researchers, editors, and translators who were associated with Nanyang studies at Jinan University, though some of them also published with other major presses in Shanghai.[13] To deal with the enormous range of published materials, I will focus on the writings of leading scholars Liu Shimu (1889–1952), Li Changfu (1899–1966), Wen Xiongfei (1885–1974), and Zhang Xiangshi (1894–1989) to examine how they redefined Chinese identity and power in the context of maritime Asia.

Colonial Circulations

Spanning littoral Southeast Asia, China, and Japan, Jinan activities during the 1920s and 1930s offer a valuable look into how colonial ideas about migration circulated and became a resource for the Chinese nation. Reading, translating, teaching, and publishing, the intellectuals incorporated Western and Japanese discourses of history and geography marked by geopolitics, imperialism, and social Darwinism: oceanic spaces are free and open, climate determines human attributes and activities, and settlers of the new frontier should civilize the natives for control. These assumptions were embedded into a new understanding of China in the world. At the same time, since Europeans and later Japanese were the protagonists of the colonial story in the late nineteenth and early twentieth centuries, the Jinan researchers had to do much to modify what they lifted from European and Japanese knowledge to insert China into the center. Thus, they brought China into the exchanges of modern knowledge and power and created a national identity tied to the Chinese diaspora. Far from being derivative, the Jinan efforts made it possible for colonial ideas to traverse the South Seas, and more importantly to become Chinese.

A focus on the Jinan contributions to colonial circulations allows historians to consider the South Seas as an integrated region and rejoin historiographies of Asian transformation that have traditionally been separated by colonial and national borders. In modern Chinese history, scholars have highlighted the triangular relations among China, Japan, and the West, but they have not often considered maritime East and Southeast Asia as sites of these important exchanges. Scholars focusing on Chinese and Asian maritime networks generally do not go beyond the eighteenth and nineteenth centuries, given Western expansion. Yet, as Mark Ravinder Frost has perceptively suggested, the traditional networks of intra-Asian trade and migration were reworked but never completely replaced.[14] Asian actors frequently appropriated the new tools of empire for their own agendas, creating and intensifying the multilateral connections in the region, not only those between colony and metropole or between core and periphery of a world capitalist economy. Through travel, print, research, and education, the Jinan scholars also immersed coastal China in a cultural maritime zone that included Shanghai, Tokyo, Guangzhou, Xiamen, Hong Kong, Taiwan, Penang, Singapore, and other Asian port cities, building upon new technologies of communication and transportation provided by steam shipping, the postal service, and submarine telegraph lines. Attention to the Jinan group thus helps advance the new scholarship on capital, labor, and commodity flows in Asia by suggesting that "Chinese circulations" were not only economic but also cultural, including a significant traffic in books, newspapers, periodicals, writers, translators, researchers, and teachers moving across the maritime region.[15]

This fluid, interconnected nature of maritime Asia is evident in the evolving meaning of *Nanyang* and its relatively recent vintage. Surprisingly, despite being a seemingly ancient Sinocentric term, the meaning of *Nanyang* that the Jinan scholars helped propagate did not come straight from the imperial Chinese past, but via modern Japan. As I will show, it referred to a historical geography specific to the early twentieth century—the European colonies of the Dutch East Indies, British Burma and Malaya, French Indochina, the American Philippines, and also independent Siam, where numerous Chinese had gone and settled. Wang Gungwu has suggested that a different term, *Nanhai* rather than *Nanyang*, was used in ancient Chinese records, though the words *hai* and *yang* can be understood to have the close meanings of "sea" and "ocean." Nonetheless, compared to *Nanyang* in the early twentieth-century usage outlined above and the contemporary territorial construct of "Southeast Asia," *Nanhai* was a much smaller region of Chinese trade and conquest. It roughly covered today's South China Sea, extending westward from Fuzhou to Palembang and eastward from Taiwan to the western coast of Borneo, and including only the coastal strips and islands of Indonesia, Borneo, and the Philippines.[16] As

Chinese maritime trade gradually increased after the tenth century, the term *Nanyang* began to appear in the Song and Yuan dynasties, but it did not come into general use and replace *Nanhai* completely until Ming and Qing times.[17]

Another change came in the late Qing period after 1860, when *Nanyang* served to distinguish that area from *Beiyang* (North Seas), a set of coastal administrative regions divided at the Yangzi River for the management of foreign commerce and naval reforms. But this usage ended abruptly when Japan destroyed China's first modern navy in the Sino-Japanese War of 1894–95.[18] In other words, the modern meaning of *Nanyang* as a southern maritime region of European colonies and Chinese settlements did not follow a straight path. It was also different from the way Wang Gungwu has put it: "never a geographical or political concept, only a Chinese commercial one," or "the name for the territories the Chinese had reached by sea."[19] On the contrary, it acquired a new geopolitical meaning in the modern period.

To that point, a study of the Jinan activities suggests that the meaning of *Nanyang* transformed and expanded because of a geopolitical shift in maritime Asia after the mid-nineteenth century. In late Qing China, it appeared as a series of unsettling encounters with maritime imperialism and a slow disintegration of the tribute system. During the First Opium War, Britain was the first Western naval power to challenge and defeat the Qing. Another naval power, France, closely followed this pattern of assault. Not only did it join the British forces in the Second Opium War that captured Beijing, it subdued the Qing again in 1885 and gained control of Vietnam, a major state in the Sinocentric tribute system. At the same time, a rapidly modernizing Meiji Japan further undercut Qing dominance in the Asian maritime world. From the 1870s to the 1890s, the Qing lost to Japan its overlordship in Okinawa, Korea, and Taiwan. In a quick succession of five decades, the most serious foreign attacks facing the Qing came by way of the sea. They chipped away at the Sinocentric tribute order, hastened the downfall of the imperial system, and remapped Asia to a significant degree.[20] This structural change underpinning China's transformation drew the attention of the Jinan group.

Furthermore, the broader geopolitical shift was reflected in a surge of Chinese interest in oceanic history and geography from the mid-nineteenth century onward, even though the Jinan scholars frequently complained about a neglect of the South Seas. Soon after the Opium Wars, prominent scholar-officials and geographers Lin Zexu (1785–1850), Wei Yuan (1794–1856), and Xu Jiyu (1795–1873) led efforts to study Western naval power and pivot Qing attention from inner Asia toward maritime Asia.[21] Stunned by the display of British naval power, Lin Zexu, who had led the suppression of the opium trade in Canton in 1839, organized a translation bureau for Western works of geography and history. Drawing on Western missionary publications written in Chinese, Lin later completed the study, *Geography of the Four Continents* (*Sizhou zhi*).[22] His efforts were joined and expanded by Wei Yuan's *Illustrated Treatise on the Sea Kingdoms* (*Haiguo tuzhi*, 1843) and Xu Jiyu's *Record of the Ocean Circuit* (*Yinghuan zhilue*, 1848), both of which were not only widely read in China but were almost immediately translated into Japanese.[23] By 1852, Wei Yuan's treatise had gone through three editions and grew to a hundred volumes. Warning of an unprecedented threat from the West, Wei urged his contemporaries to "comprehend the appearance of the entire globe because the bases of the English barbarians encircle the world."[24] Nonetheless, by the early twentieth century, these writings on the maritime world were no longer circulated. None of the Jinan historians and geographers discussed or showed awareness of Wei Yuan's multivolume treatise.

The displacement of this earlier generation of writings suggests that radically transformed seascapes created an opening for the Jinan activities. Even as Jinan scholars inherited a long geopolitical shift that helped launch their predecessors' work on maritime Asia, there were salient differences in the premises between the two sets of scholarship. Compared to the Qing scholars, Chinese intellectuals pursuing Western knowledge in the early twentieth century were no longer suspected of traitorous conduct, as was sometimes the case for members of the Opium War generation. On the contrary, they were valued participants in a mainstream enterprise to modernize China. Sponsored by the Guomindang government, the Jinan group spearheaded efforts to institutionalize a modern study of the South Seas along the lines of Western history and geography, as the next section discusses. Rather than continuing to see Europeans as barbarians living on the periphery of the Qing empire, as did Wei Yuan, the Jinan intellectuals were acutely aware that China was in fact on the periphery of Europe. Even more importantly, in contrast to attempts led by Wei Yuan to revive Nanyang as part of the Sinocentric tribute order, the Jinan group firmly recognized that it was a site of well-established European colonies and Chinese settler communities. Moreover, Japan had emerged as an admired model of progress and a vital source of mediated knowledge about the West. Several members of the Jinan group, including Li Shimu, Li Changfu, and Zhang Xiangshi, were natives of Chinese coastal provinces who were educated in Japanese universities in the fields of history, geography, and economics, and became heavily involved in introducing Japanese works in their own research and publishing activities. Embodying a major generational shift, the Jinan works helped integrate China into an emergent maritime world.

Further differentiated from the earlier generation engaging a rising Europe, the Jinan scholars often acknowledged in their work that they were responding to Japanese imperialist expansion in Asia. Historians of the Japanese empire Ken'ichi Goto and Mark Peattie have suggested that World War I marked a high point in Japan's southward advance, which consisted of naval and commercial expansion into the South Seas, known in Japanese as *Nan'yō*, a rendering of the Chinese term Nanyang.[25] During the mid-1910s, the Great War in Europe created a power vacuum in maritime Asia, allowing the Japanese navy to take over the German-occupied Mariana, Caroline, and Marshall Islands in the South Pacific, collectively known as Micronesia. At the same time, Japanese businesses seized the opportunity to secure outlets for manufactures and investment in Singapore, Java, and the Philippines. As a result, Japanese trade with the region increased from 3.8 percent in 1914 to 9.5 percent in 1920.[26] Apart from trade, business intelligence on colonial Southeast Asia was also gathered through "Japan's south gate," Taiwan, through the Office of the Governor-General and the Bank of Taiwan, which produced the earliest study of overseas Chinese remittances in 1914. In China, Japanese incursions during this time also included the 1915 "twenty-one demands" and military actions on the mainland. Its army clashed with Nationalist forces in Jinan, Shandong, and massacred thousands of local residents in 1928, sparking a fundraising drive and anti-Japanese boycotts among Chinese in Nanyang. In 1931, Japan invaded and occupied Manchuria, and in the following year bombed the treaty port of Shanghai. A full-scale invasion began in 1937. From 1940 onward, the Japanese government launched a research program on "the southern sphere," in which one of the key subjects was huaqiao commercial interests. It was estimated that the program generated more than a hundred books and three hundred essays on huaqiao studies within two years.[27] Given Japan's economic and military rise, its growing interest in Nanyang huaqiao further raised the stakes for Chinese intellectuals to compete on behalf of Nationalist China.

As the Jinan intellectuals sought to reorient Chinese attention toward the maritime world, the meanings of the South Seas took on a new colonial dimension during the 1920s and 1930s. Turning away from traditional Chinese knowledge of the maritime world based on the tribute system, Jinan researchers created themselves as the chief interpreters of Nanyang by mobilizing the latest currents in European and Japanese thought. Many members of the Jinan group had studied in Japan or colonial Southeast Asia and were multilingual. Among the most important premises that they reproduced in the work was that colonialism and colonization were civilizing missions. Commenting on the mass migration of huaqiao laborers to the South Seas, leading scholar Wen Xiongfei attributed it to the fact that "the natives had low living standards, therefore their materialist desire was low," unlike the huaqiao. Lacking desire for improvement, the natives "obtained basic necessities from neighboring hills and did not want to labor for others," making it necessary to introduce slavery, indenture, and foreign laborers for economic development. Though neither Chinese migrants nor the natives produced many written records about their lives in the precolonial past, Wen reasoned that huaqiao "did not leave genealogies or travelogues," while blaming the natives for being "too uncultured and illiterate." Crediting huaqiao handsomely for the wealth and prosperity of the South Seas, authors like Wen consistently portrayed Chinese migrants as racially and culturally superior to the native peoples and comparable to the European colonizers. They did so by freely adopting European ideas that colonialism and colonization served to spread progress to undeveloped frontiers.

Apart from assimilating Western colonial thought, the Jinan writings also recombined modern Japanese epistemology and Chinese culturalist discourses to highlight huaqiao success. In Western colonial narratives, the figure of the lazy native dominated centuries of encounters with the Malays, Filipinos, and Javanese.[28] In modern Japanese discourses, the South Seas was "an inferior cultural zone."[29] Anthropologists found the Micronesians "lazy," "sexually loose," and "uncivilized," and the Taiwanese aborigines in need of taming and assimilation.[30] Influenced by European colonial and scientific racism in the nineteenth and twentieth centuries, these modern

Japanese views nonetheless echoed traditional Chinese ideologies of non-Han barbarism and could be seen as a refurbishment of the old Sinocentric order—only Japan had now replaced China as the center of the civilized universe surrounded by others on the margins.[31] Joining a complex conversation of civilization and progress in the South Seas, the Jinan writers rarely questioned the premise that the peoples of the South Seas were uncivilized. Rather, they routinely agreed with colonial views of native backwardness.

Even so, many Jinan authors were not engaged in a simple reproduction of colonial categories but often reworked them to highlight China's geopolitical interests in maritime Asia. Given the impact on the Jinan authors of Japan's increased involvement in the South Seas, a good example was how they dealt with Japanese spatial divisions of the region. As Hajime Shimizu has shown, Japanese intellectuals arguing for a southward advance redefined Nan'yō as a region of predominantly Western colonies, including the Dutch East Indies, French Indochina, British Malaya, the American Philippines, and an independent Siam. This remapping displaced older divisions between continental and insular regions and between Asia and Oceania that had pervaded early Meiji writings. At the same time, Japanese writers reconceived the newly annexed Micronesia as "inner" and "rear" Nan'yō, a potential stepping-stone for a next stage of expansion into the "outer" and "frontal" Nan'yō, a core region controlled by Western colonial powers. These configurations of the South Seas informed the vast body of Jinan studies, but Jinan writers also redefined them to throw light on Chinese interests. Departing from Japanese usage, the scholar Li Changfu, who was educated at Waseda University, used "inner Nanyang" to stress a historically high concentration of Chinese migrant settlements in places that had only become European colonies recently. At the same time, Li used "outer Nanyang" to refer to India, Australia, New Zealand, and the Pacific Islands because Chinese populations and connections with China seemed less dense.[32] These modifications suggest that the Jinan researchers consciously adapted colonial categories.

Another example was the efforts to negotiate ideologies about climate and race in the study of the South Seas. In the late nineteenth and early twentieth centuries, a new practice in global geography of differentiating world regions into temperate and tropical zones reflected what Martin E. Lewis and Kären E. Wigen have called a Eurocentric "environmental determinism," a set of assumptions claiming that "temperate climates alone produced vigorous minds, hardy bodies, and progressive societies, while tropical heat (and its associated botanical abundance) produced races marked by languor and stupefaction."[33] Writing in a similar vein, the Jinan researcher Zhang Xiangshi went on to portray a grand struggle between the people of the temperate zones and those of the tropical zones: "In today's world, the masters of colonies are all white temperate nations. The societies that have been reduced to white colonies are overwhelmingly concentrated in the tropics. The level of culture in the temperate zones is higher, while the level of culture in the tropical zones is low. Even though this is not the only reason, in recent world history, it is [in the temperate zones] where important transformation has taken place. What is the transformation? The development of nationalism and the discovery of oceanic routes between East and West."[34]

Echoing the idea that climatic differences determined racial and cultural progress, scholars like Zhang helped justify European domination of the South Seas. Others such as Li Changfu also reinterpreted the claim to mean that Chinese migrants had long been pioneering settlers in the tropical frontiers where "no whites dared to go," hence their presence displayed an important accomplishment rather than a "low level of culture." Furthermore, unlike Europeans, Chinese settlers thrived without any government backing, said Li. Rather, they acted on their own initiative and confronted many difficulties independently, making them a group potentially superior to Europeans who received state support. Furthermore, many Jinan scholars strongly refuted racial assumptions about the Chinese in Japanese geographical writings. When quoting and reprinting Japanese works on Nanyang huaqiao, Jinan editors and translators took special care to convert all references to China from the disparaging *Shina* to the centralizing *Zhongguo* (the Middle Kingdom), thus purging from the original texts an implied inferiority of China to Japan. Taken together, these efforts suggest that the Jinan scholars not only imported colonial models but reworked them to advance a China-centered geography of the South Seas.

An example could be seen in Li Changfu's critique of Western colonial explanations of Chinese mass emigration by incorporating Marxist analysis. In an argumentative essay, Li rejected the dominant model of geographical materialism—a focus on the relationship between nature and human society—and argued in favor of historical materialism—a focus on the forces of production. Cautioning against an "overemphasis on geographical environment" and a "neglect of historical turning points" (*lishi de qiji*), Li warned of an excessive focus on how nature influenced human activities, reducing Chinese migration to preconditions of physical geography. Pointing out what he believed to be a popular but false assumption that littoral regions should naturally produce vast amounts of emigration, he explained that Hakka emigrants did not live by the sea and Wenzhou natives living on the Zhejiang coast did not emigrate en masse until the twentieth century.

At the same time, Li rejected dominant accounts stressing how overpopulation, natural disasters, political chaos, migrant character, or middleman institutions had caused Chinese emigration. Calling them "errors of simple materialism or subjective idealism," he instead drew upon Marxist theses to posit that a growing agricultural crisis in China during the nineteenth century had caused three concurrent kinds of migration, one toward the cities, one toward undeveloped frontiers, and one toward wealthier destinations overseas. These forces intersected with the expansion of European capitalism, which had led to agricultural disruptions in South China, the creation of colonies elsewhere, and a great demand for labor. To Li, some of the Western claims attributing huaqiao success to their adaptability to tropical climates and resistance to tropical diseases were also common kinds of geographical materialism that perpetuated the exploitation and exclusion of Chinese migrant labor around the world. To prevent the "control of foreign thought," he called for research "grounded in science," by which he meant a more central place for historical materialism rather than geographical materialism in the studies of Chinese emigration.[35] Downplaying both environmental essentialism and traditional emigrant networks, Li thought that the tools of world geography should accommodate China's capacity to generate historical change.

What's more, the Jinan authors not only appropriated colonial ideologies but also the colonial experiences of Chinese emigrants to construct a Chinese national identity. Well immersed in the circulations of maritime Asia, the Jinan group shared the belief in a transoceanic bond between China and huaqiao that could overcome colonial history and geography. The most prolific writer on this problem, Li Changfu was often attracted to expansive statements made by Nanyang Chinese and deliberately included them alongside the more empirically driven studies: "People say that wherever the sun may shine, there is always a British flag. I think that wherever sea water may reach, there is always a sojourning compatriot of my country."[36] The appeal of this claim lay in the imagination of a vast geography that was connected by the seas and was decidedly Chinese. Another statement included by Li took it even further: "When I was in China, I knew nothing of what a nation was. After arriving in France, I saw how Indians and Vietnamese were abused, and how Chinese were derided. It was only then that I realized the role of the nation. On my return to China, none of the ships that came and went was Chinese. It was depressing. After getting to Singapore, we finally saw a ship that flew a five-color flag. We came on to the deck, hollering and jumping up and down. It was great joy!"[37] Evoking a maritime imagery of oceans and ships, the quote expressed a pan-Asian, pan-Chinese cultural pride, at once injured and inflated because of lived experiences as colonized subjects in a European world. But Li thought the sentiment was still a long way from being a national consciousness (*minzu yishi*). For even though Chinese migrants were "as widespread as the British, as wealthy as the Jews, as persistent as the Indians, and as agile as the Japanese," he found them to be politically and culturally fragile, lacking a proper awareness of the ancestral homeland and a Confucian moral education, and too easily assimilated by the British, Dutch, and Malays in the colonies.[38] Reaffirming Liang Qichao's criticism of Chinese in San Francisco in 1903, Li found a prevalent "village mentality" among Nanyang Chinese, meaning that they failed to develop a national consciousness. In other words, he considered a Chinese identity incomplete without a reorientation toward the homeland-nation.

Interestingly, the claim for a fixed national identity was born in the process of unparalleled circulations. The Jinan repurposing of colonial knowledge and power resulted in the belief in a recoverable bond between homeland and diaspora, capable of transcending time and space. As Li elaborated, "being Chinese [*Zhongguo ren*] was neither defined by blood nor by nationality" and "*huaqiao* are Chinese who have migrated to a foreign territory to perform economic activities" and included "their descendants who have not lost Chinese national consciousness."[39] According to this view, blood could be diluted over time by intermarriage, and nationality could be altered by colonial laws, but national consciousness was eternal and could be recuperated. While Li's definition of huaqiao excluded officials and intellectuals who "did not engage in production" and only applied to laborers, workers, farmers, and merchants, it was designed to encompass not only the China-born but also the native-born (*tusheng*) who were vital to the colonial economy. Referring to the Straits Chinese luminaries Lim Boon Keng (discussed in chapter 3), Wu Liande, and Song Ong Siang, who "called themselves *baba* and had British nationality," Li wrote that they could still be huaqiao, implying that national consciousness, once brought back, could trump coloniality.[40] Circulating across the South Seas, the colonial ideologies and experiences of migration provided an unlikely resource for a modern Chinese identity.

What the Jinan intellectuals effectively produced was a national identity tethered to the diaspora, a means through which China could transform into a subject of history and geography on the fringes of empires. Saying that "China has yet to reach the time by which the nation is formed," Li Changfu worried that there had already been an assimilation of huaqiao into the European colonies through nationality laws and education, while anti-Chinese movements led by the native inhabitants also attempted to push huaqiao out of local society, and thus were likely to undercut the prospects of mobilizing huaqiao for Chinese nation-building.[41] In a preface written for a translated Japanese work on Chinese development overseas (1929), Liu Shimu observed that Chinese migration in the last century had gone beyond the South Seas to "the opening of roads and mines in the Americas, the construction of the Panama Canal, and labor on the battlefields of the European War, and among the seamen working on ships going between Asia and Europe."[42] Linking Chinese emigrants to the burgeoning frontiers around the world, Liu also linked China back to Chinese emigrants. As huaqiao contributed to the "making of the civilized world," Liu reminded readers that they also contributed profoundly to the salvation of the homeland: remittances reaching $500 million every year boosted the national economy and "saved it from bankruptcy"; contributions to the 1911 Revolution had led the late Sun Yat-sen to recognize huaqiao as "the mother of the revolution."[43] Furthermore, huaqiao not only donated more than $7 million to China after the 1928 Jinan incident instigated by Japan; they also led fierce boycotts against Japan in Nanyang that would never have happened in the homeland. Just as the British declared that "if it were not for *huaqiao* there would be no Malay peninsula," Liu wrote, he ventured that "if it were not for *huaqiao*, there would be no Republic of China."[44] This portrayal of huaqiao as instrumental to the simultaneous development of China and the world underscored a double point: huaqiao were worthy Chinese national subjects and China was a promising global player. In this formulation, while huaqiao can be loyal to China, China wholly depends on it.

Writing Chinese Settler Colonialism

Tying Nationalist China to Chinese in the South Seas, the Jinan writings also served as a fulcrum of an imagined Chinese colonial empire. In the publications, the figure of the Nanyang huaqiao lacking national consciousness symbolizes not the diverse lived experiences across the South Seas but China's predicament of lacking an overseas empire in a colonial world. Inspired by the dominant notion in Eurocentric history and geography that migration was colonization, the Jinan scholars were nonetheless forced to admit that Nanyang huaqiao were not colonists and that China did not have colonies. But they found a solution by interpolating fragments of emigrant histories and geographies across maritime Asia into a national history extending into the future. The result was a productive narrative of Chinese migrants as incomplete colonists in the South Seas and China as an incomplete nation in the world. By realizing their common destinies, Chinese in the South Seas would finally receive the overdue protection of a nation, while China would also become fully modern by having in its possession a colonial empire.

Structured in the colonial and Enlightenment models of progress, the master narrative produced by the Jinan publications was a synchronized evolution of China and Nanyang huaqiao in the world. Following a European tripartite progression of historical time—ancient, medieval, and modern—the Jinan historians mapped onto this timeline the intersecting paths of Chinese migrant dispersal and national development. According to Li Changfu, Chinese emigration began in Qin and Han times, the dawn of China's first unification and imperial system. It climbed through the Tang and Song dynasties as the early empire morphed into a continental power pushing south. At the apex of Chinese power were the Ming voyages across the Indian Ocean led by Zheng He, which also fostered greater emigration overseas. However, a period of dynastic stasis followed, during which Europeans discovered sea routes to the Indian Ocean and Chinese emigration gained momentum. From the nineteenth century onward, as late Qing and Republican China remained backward, European hegemony consolidated in Asia and colonial governments began to impose unjust laws and treatment on huaqiao, just as the European powers dealt China the heavy blows of wars and unequal treaties. A new threat loomed on the horizon. A rapidly expanding imperialist power, Japan now endangered the interests of both huaqiao and China. To survive into the future, huaqiao and the nation must reunite in the upcoming struggles.[45] Rising and falling in perfect correlation, the intertwined fortunes of China and huaqiao lay at the foundation of almost all Jinan publications.

By assuming synchronicity, the Jinan historians uncovered a splendid national past that continued to be transmitted through Nanyang huaqiao, thus not only reifying the diaspora but also giving it a unique role in unlocking the progress of the homeland-nation. In the historiography of relations between China and the overseas Chinese, scholars have noticed the periodic attempts at "re-Sinicization" among Chinese elites abroad, but historically Chinese intellectuals in China also engaged in the recuperation of "disappearing" traditions and values.[46] This suggests that Chinese identity, even in China, was often in flux. For the Jinan intellectuals, writing about the long history of Chinese dispersal overseas was a means to narrate Chinese hegemony prior to the rise of the West. The pursuit of a unified history and geography also told of a Chinese nation and culture emerging not only within land borders but in the oceanic crossings between Republican China, imperial Japan, and colonial Southeast Asia. Reflecting a traffic of jostling ideas, the narration of huaqiao history was nonetheless highly selective. It focused on the wealthy and powerful, and primarily those located in the South Seas. Such configurations formed the basis of the Jinan efforts to construct Nanyang huaqiao as significant historical subjects who could rejuvenate modern China.

However, this putative role of Nanyang huaqiao was not an insular formation but an active engagement with a global imaginary of national power residing in overseas colonization. As discussed in the last section, the Jinan scholars never once referred to the Qing geographer Wei Yuan and his counterparts in their writings about the maritime world. Instead, they found inspiration in the preeminent intellectual Liang Qichao (1873–1929), whose writings about "colonization" (*zhimin*) helped initiate settler colonialism into national conversations. Writing about Liang's call for a new poetry in 1899, Xiaobing Tang finds that Liang compared the necessity for Chinese poetic innovation to that of European colonial expansion led by Columbus and Magellan, "when [Europe's] land was exhausted and state of overproduction was reached."⁴⁷ Shortly after, as though to expand his own metaphor, Liang's interest in colonization went beyond poetry into history writing. Well recognized and cited by the Jinan scholars, his 1904 essay "Biographies of Eight Great Chinese Colonialists" is the first piece of Chinese writing to link migration with colonization. Arguing that one could tell a nation's spirit from the historical figures that it lionizes, Liang tried to "rescue" the colonial heroes "buried" in Chinese history: natives of Guangdong and Fujian provinces who were fearless rulers of principalities, military leaders, and brotherhood chieftains in Java, Sumatra, Borneo, and Malaya during the Ming and Qing periods. To stress their accomplishments in the contemporary context of a colonial world, he added, "If they could not be compared to Moses, they should at least be mentioned together with Columbus and Livingston."

Intensely focused on overseas migration and settlement, Liang's description created a new global template for Chinese history that deeply impressed the Jinan researchers. As Philip Kuhn has pointed out, Liang chose his eight men for celebration because they had led heroic struggles against European powers or settled in places that later became European colonies.⁴⁸ Moreover, he did so to reimagine Chinese history by adopting a larger frame and putting emigrants at its center:

> To the south of the sea, the population of more than a hundred kingdoms is largely made up of the sons of the Yellow Emperor. Whether it is in terms of geography or history, they should have been the natural colonies of our nation [*tianran wozu zhi zhimin di*]. Yet, [our people] are now living like dependents in the house of others and treated no differently than cattle and horses. Alas! Whose fault is that? Whose fault is that? Since we cannot even protect our land, which has been handed down from the Yellow Emperor, how can we expect to do so south of the sea?⁴⁹

Asserting that migration was colonization, Liang's account points to the South Seas as a historical site for huaqiao settlers and China's "natural colonies" that had sadly fallen into the hands of Western powers. He compares China without colonies to huaqiao without state protection, making them both "dependents in the house of others" and "cattle and horses." Recasting huaqiao as "sons of the Yellow Emperor," Liang further suggests that migration was part of a long, unbroken Chinese expansion not only overland but also overseas, though the latter had been cut short and reversed by European incursions into maritime Asia.

Though Liang Qichao might have been the first to connect migration and colonization in the South Seas, the Jinan intellectuals were the ones who cemented the link. Their geopolitical preoccupations reflected Liang's astute observation of the connections between maritime thinking (*haishi sixiang*) and national vitality (*guomin yuanqi*), colonial enterprise (*zhimin shiye*) and government sponsorship (*zhengfu jiangli*), and political power (*zhengzhi nengli*) and international competition (*guoji jingzheng*). Nonetheless, it is worth remembering that Liang's positive impression of emigrants remained highly tenuous in early 1900s. One may contrast his celebratory piece with a much less flattering account that he published in the same year, in which he declared that the Chinese in San Francisco were chaotic and divided, reflecting a deficient Chinese national character compared to that of Westerners.[50] According to Liang, they behaved like clansmen, rather than citizens; exhibited the mentality of a village, not of a nation; showed an aptness for despotism, not freedom; and lacked lofty objectives. Drawing on social Darwinist notions of racial struggle and survival, Liang's list of criticisms hardly made Chinese emigrants a favorable model, suggesting that the relationship between the nation and the diaspora was still being worked out in the closing decade of the Qing.

By the 1920s and 1930s, the Jinan researchers had helped consolidate the figure of the huaqiao partly by shifting the focus of colonization to the Chinese state as an agent. As Zhang Xiangshi wrote, to have a colony was to "transplant part of a nation's people to another place but they remain subjected to the rule of the nation, while building a civilized society like the nation."[51] Thus, though there were many Chinese settlements in Nanyang, they were not under Chinese rule, did not contribute to Chinese nation-building, and were not Chinese colonies. In a similar fashion, Li Changfu defined colonization as the process of "leaving the motherland for a relatively undeveloped country to permanently settle, participate in economic activities, and maintain political relations with the motherland."[52] According to him, though China during the Yuan and Ming dynasties had sent armies to the South Seas, its aim was to demonstrate power and invite distant kingdoms to send tribute, but not to colonize. The Qing dynasty even banned maritime travel and severed its ties with Chinese emigrants. Hence, the long history of Chinese migration overseas was best known as "development and settlement" (*tuozhi*) or "migration and settlement" (*yizhi*), not "colonization" (*zhimin*), which resulted in Chinese migrants but no Chinese colonies. At the same time, Li did not recognize Chinese migration to Manchuria as colonization but simply as an internal movement, suggesting that his idea of colonization was not only seaborne but required a radically different technology of state power than if it were overland.

Moreover, the Jinan intellectuals tried to redistribute agency from the emigrants to the state by writing a new Chinese history according to the geography of Chinese emigration and the European model of modern chronology. Their efforts created a standard still practiced today. Using China and the West as reference points, Li Changfu (1931) divided the history of Nanyang huaqiao into four periods mirroring China's supposed evolution in the world: early migration, Chinese hegemony, contact between China and the West, and European hegemony. Mapped onto a linear plane, Chinese emigration unfolded during a period of early movements in the Qin–Han dynasties, trade expansion during the Tong–Song periods, and a political exodus after the fall of the Song dynasty and rise of the Yuan dynasty. Then came the early Ming dynasty in the fifteenth century, during which China under the Taizu and Chengzu emperors expanded and "conquered" various islands in the South Seas. The voyages led by Zheng He stimulated greater migration because of the "advantage" provided by Chinese power. From the sixteenth to the nineteenth centuries, as China moved from the late Ming to the late Qing, Europe expanded toward the east, while China became "stagnant." This phase began with the arrival of Portugal and Spain, followed by the Netherlands and Britain. The contact led to "frequent conflict between huaqiao and Europeans," as in the cases of the Chinese pirate Limahong (Lin Feng) attacking Spanish Manila in 1575, the Ming loyalist Zheng Chenggong driving the Dutch out of Taiwan and clashing with Spanish forces in Manila, and a series of massacres of Chinese in Spanish Manila in 1602 and 1639 and in Dutch Java in 1740. Despite these violent conflicts, Chinese migration rapidly increased because "[colonial] development led to demands for labor," and China gradually relaxed the ban on maritime travel.[53] In other words, China and the West were the principal drivers of Chinese mass migration in this narrative.

Entering the modern period, Li's narrative of Chinese emigration continued to reflect the transformation of China in a divided world. From the late nineteenth century onward, huaqiao became "oppressed by European hegemony" and were "on the brink of life and death": Britain took Burma, France took Vietnam, Siam was sandwiched between Britain and France, the Malay Peninsula had fallen completely into British hands, and the United States had replaced Spain as the overlord of the Philippines. The indentured "piglet" trade and Chinese secret societies spread, as the latter came to control the trade in the South Seas. At the same time, colonial governments "passed restrictive laws, increased taxes, even killed, and stirred up native hostilities against the Chinese." Yet, even as huaqiao began to develop active relations with the ancestral homeland, China "had not yet strengthened itself," says Li.[54] This linear narrative of Nanyang huaqiao dovetails with that of China, whereas the South Seas exists merely as a staging ground for the fated rivalries between China and Europe. At the same time, it resets Chinese history in a traditional dynastic cycle to a Eurocentric chronology and geography.

Offering a similar narrative of Chinese development in a wider framework, another Jinan scholar, Wen Xiongfei, situates it slightly differently within the context of geographical knowledge, navigational technology, and transportation and communication.[55] Largely following a European periodization of ancient, medieval, and modern history, his study of Chinese southward movement in the ancient period begins with the opening of sea routes between East and West Asia, religious monks traveling to India, and political refugees following dynastic change. Then it turns to the development of Chinese sea power, starting with the Jin–Tang expansion in maritime navigation and trade, proceeding through the Song–Yuan advances in navigational technology, and followed by Yuan military expeditions to Java and the early Ming voyages of Zheng He. But the Manchu invasions and founding of the Qing dynasty sparked another round of political exodus abroad, suppressed Zheng Chenggong's forces in Taiwan, and brought an end to Chinese maritime influence. Like Li Changfu and many of his counterparts, Wen's portrayal of Chinese history runs along the path of a glorious past, a failed present, and an uncertain future.

Given a rising West and a fallen China, Wen seeks to explain the economic autonomy and status that Nanyang huaqiao managed to achieve through commerce and labor, despite a lack of political power. As he observes, "Last year, I was traveling around the Nanyang islands. Wherever I went, I saw how my nation (*minzu*) was living under the political control of another people, receiving neither help nor protection from the ancestral homeland (*zuguo*). Yet, they united, grew stronger, and survived. The best ones held great economic clout, were rich and powerful, and became part of the elite in the host society." According to Wen, huaqiao and natives lived in "a self-sufficient condition" during the ancient period. After the consolidation of European power, huaqiao obtained a degree of autonomy by laboring on a "vast and undeveloped land." Chinese pirates, secret societies, and indentured laborers became active, and the leaders of all three groups later became rich and powerful. As for the more recent elite, they had gained enormous influence by engaging in tax farming, colonial service, agriculture, mining, and port business.[56] To Wen, these activities gave rise to the economic dominance of huaqiao in the South Seas, despite a lack of Chinese state protection. Here, huaqiao seemed to be self-made successes that were only second to their colonial masters.

A third example of a new history is centered on a world reordered by the spread of Western colonial mercantilism and capitalism, a line of analysis anticipating Wallersteinian world-systems theory. The writer Zhang Xiangshi argues that huaqiao history in the South Seas was a process of "Western power diffusing to the East" (*xili dongjian*) and "white expansion." It began with the exploration of Vasco da Gama around the Cape of Good Hope to reach the Indian Ocean in 1498, resulting in a new sea route to Asia. This development brought many Europeans eastward, establishing colonies and attracting Chinese migrants. As the boost in the spice trade brought an influx of gold and silver, Europe's economy transformed from a natural economy based on primary production to a financial economy based on trade and commerce. This shift set in motion an "internal unification and external expansion," giving birth to colonial mercantilism, manifest in the founding of the British East India Company and the Dutch East India Company. Recently, a major shift had occurred in colonial policy. European powers now sought to occupy territories with rich resources, turn them into markets for manufactured goods, and monopolize shipping. At the same time, they banned direct trade between their colonies and other nations and prevented industrial development in the colonies. However, even though the whites had "more advanced scientific knowledge and capitalist organization," Zhang observes that they still had to rely on huaqiao labor in the tropical zones, thus opening the colonies further to Chinese mass emigration.[57]

Differing significantly from the narratives of Li Changfu and Wen Xiongfei, Zhang introduces a global framework that not only deploys European conceptions of history and geography, but firmly recognizes the formation of a world-capitalist system. Zhang makes no claim of a magnificent Chinese past that might suggest a hidden reservoir of national strength. Nor does he argue for a synchronicity between China and Nanyang huaqiao that turns the Chinese state into a historical force. Instead, a core–periphery structure in a world capitalist economy frames the study. Situated at the margins of an all-powerful system, China seems ahistorical and its survival prospects grim. Even the common portrayal of resourceful huaqiao recedes from this picture. A narrow opening exists in which China could eventually follow the footsteps of Europe to exploit the South Seas. Because "Chinese in Nanyang live in social conditions no different [from those in China]," as commerce and industry in China became better developed, its goods could supply all the needs of Nanyang Chinese. This implies that the settled communities in Nanyang could become the quasi-colonies of a future China, performing the same function as they did in the rise of the West. In other words, the key to China's future, in Zhang's view, is whether it could develop industrial capitalism, turn the South Seas into its own periphery, and replicate the European model of success.

Taken together, the three historical narratives offered by Li Changfu, Wen Xiongfei, and Zhang Xiangshi represent a patchwork of strategies to engage a colonial South Seas. Replete with contradictions, their search for a Chinese settler colonialism challenges scholars to read it not only critically but also broadly into the connectivity of European colonialism, Chinese emigration, and modern China. First, even as the Jinan writers reduced the South Seas to an empty arena in which struggles between China and the West took place, it remains possible to uncover through their efforts a dynamically integrated region that changed China. Adopting a colonial lens, the Jinan intellectuals assimilated Western and Japanese notions of geography and history, reconciled them with Chinese purposes, and created a new field of Nanyang studies. This outcome, as I have argued, emerged from a process of circulation rather than diffusion of already dominant ideologies across the South Seas. A focus on how the Jinan group moved and reorganized colonial knowledge allows us to sift through the complex process of cultural formations in modern maritime Asia. Borrowing from historian Sugata Bose's idea of the Indian Ocean as a "well-integrated interregional arena of economic and cultural interaction and exchange" that persisted well beyond high colonialism, historians of Chinese emigration may also find the South Seas one such arena of increased interaction in the early twentieth century. This sheds light on the mutual connectedness of Chinese, Japanese, and Southeast Asian port cities in modern times, beyond the more general views of the region as comprising discrete colonial and national territories—such as Dutch East Indies, British Straits Settlement, French Indo-China, Nationalist China, and Imperial Japan, or bounded nation-states destined to be born—such as Indonesia, Singapore, Malaysia, Laos, Cambodia, Vietnam, Communist China, Nationalist Taiwan, and postimperial Japan in the postwar period.

Second, while the Jinan narratives siphoned much agency from Nanyang Chinese to orchestrate a hegemonic China prior to a dominant West, the impact of Chinese circulations resounded throughout the region. More than a national fantasy, Chinese merchants, laborers, and intellectuals, like their Indian counterparts, were important economic intermediaries linking port cities and their hinterlands, as well as Europe, the colonies, and other parts of maritime Asia. Revising the thesis of Western impact on Asia, many historians have pointed out that Chinese migrant networks were highly adaptive to the shifting commercial ecology, and not simply overridden by colonial states. As opium monopolies and tax farms in the colonies gave way to export economies and consumer markets, Chinese settlers who had been made rich under the old system reinvented themselves into plantation, mine, and factory financiers and operators, indentured labor brokers, retailers, and distributors. Providing indispensable capital, labor, skills, and services, Chinese in the South Seas, whether the creole *peranakan* or the newcomer *totok*, were commercial middlemen successfully exploiting new niches, intensifying traditional links within the region, and creating new ones through Singapore, Hong Kong, Xiamen, and Shanghai.[58] In the same manner, the Jinan intellectuals could also be understood as cultural intermediaries shaping and shaped by the rise of cities, printing, research, and education. Traveling in a world of rapid urbanization, transportation, and communication, they recombined Chinese, Japanese, and European thought to refashion the Chinese nation and identity in an age of mass migration.

Third, while constructing Nanyang huaqiao as a diaspora and China as a homeland-nation, the Jinan writers downplayed the economic and cultural fragmentation generated by mass emigration. From 1870 to 1940, Chinese movements to the South Seas produced a bewildering variety of social formations along dialect, regional, generational, and class lines, intersecting with a broad assemblage of older colonial orientations, new communist internationalisms, and emergent nationalist movements. Chinese nationalism was only one of the many forces that attracted sectors of the Chinese publics in the South Seas. In addition, the counter-efforts of colonial and native states limited the spread of a political nationalism. In British Malaya, the Dutch East Indies, French Indo-China, and Siam, the authorities closely watched a growing pan-Chinese cultural politics and combated it through press censorship, nationality laws, and regulation of Chinese schools. Furthermore, traditional migrant identities and commercial interests continued to exist alongside Chinese nationalism. Even during the anti-Japanese boycotts in 1928 and 1937, initiated by local leaders to aid national salvation, not all Nanyang Chinese merchants complied. The Cantonese and some of the Hokkien merchants conducting trade with colonial Taiwan adamantly did not. This "disunity" exasperated the Hokkien-Malaysian leader and rubber magnate Tan Kah Kee, who founded a university in his native Xiamen that will be discussed in the next chapter.[59] These examples suggest that the Chinese nationalist movement remained limited in the South Seas, but the Jinan group built a provocative case to transcend the divisions by using the tools of history and geography. By suggesting that China was inextricably bound up with Nanyang huaqiao in the past and how it would remain so in the future, the intellectuals constructed an emergent homeland-nation that would not be complete without unifying with its diaspora.

Seen this way, the Jinan influence on China was profound. Bringing an unprecedented awareness to a world of emigrants, their studies contributed to the reimagination of Chinese modernity and power. One example is how the Jinan studies of Nanyang informed institutional policy and geopolitical interests during Guomindang rule. Partly because of their efforts, education and investment became key areas of outreach. In 1929, Jinan researchers led by Liu Shimu organized the first Nanyang Huaqiao Educational Meeting at Jinan University, well attended by representatives from institutions in the coastal cities of China and Southeast Asia.[60] Japan's invasion in 1937 led to an intensification of directives to drum up return investment in commerce, agriculture, and industry, many of which targeted Nanyang Chinese.[61] To mobilize huaqiao resources and foster a national consciousness, the colonial views propagated by the Jinan researchers resonated in the directives. The following example came from party discussions to attract huaqiao investment in agriculture: "More than a hundred years ago, Nanyang was a wild, thorny land. It was only because of *huaqiao*, who were poor and braved the risk in opening it up, that [Nanyang] became wealthy and prosperous. Therefore *huaqiao* were the strongest at developing lands and the economy."[62]

Since huaqiao "live so far away" and "do not know anything about conditions of soil, transportation, wages, and markets," the government should designate special agricultural zones in Sichuan and Yunnan provinces to encourage investment, said the report. Another example concerns negotiations with the authorities of the Dutch East Indies to raise the legal status of Chinese there in 1941: "In the Dutch East Indies, the number of *huaqiao* has reached more than 1.5 million. Over several hundred years, through mind, body, blood, and sweat, [*huaqiao* have] worked silently, cleared weeds, opened up jungles, developed agriculture and husbandry, built facilities, thus contributing to the prosperity of the Dutch East Indies today."[63] Pointing out the long and vast achievements of huaqiao, Guomindang party officials protested the legal subordination of Chinese residents to Japanese and Europeans in the Dutch colony. They did so by invoking a familiar historical geography stressing Chinese migrant contributions to colonial development.

From 1940 onward, the shifting events of the Second World War brought both hope and despair to the diaspora's homeland. Fighting in China had reached a stalemate, but a fresh outbreak of war in Europe threw Nanyang into turmoil, observed Nationalist Party officials. They saw a new opportunity to attract huaqiao capital seeking refuge. The strategic importance of Nanyang also rose dramatically, becoming a "lifeline of national security" to the Chongqing government threatened by a southward-advancing Japan. Given the large Chinese population in Nanyang, party leaders saw it as a potential base to build alliances across the Pacific. Things took a turn for the worse when much of Southeast Asia fell into Japanese hands in 1942, suspending most remittances to China and causing widespread dislocation in the emigrant-sending towns and villages. At the same time, China rose to the ranks of the Big Four, signaling a turning point in the Allied war effort and an end to the unequal treaties and discriminatory immigration policies imposed on China since the nineteenth century. For a brief moment, a glimmer of hope appeared for Nationalist China to lead huaqiao as a newly recognized power.

Conclusion

A "diaspora moment" in Chinese national formation, the massive Jinan scholarship suggests how diaspora time and national time intersected during the 1920s and 1930s. Spurred by the spread of production, trade, and transportation after the 1870s, Chinese mass emigration to the South Seas contributed to the growing, interconnected port cities in the region and inspired the colonial imagination of a Chinese nation renewed by Guomindang rule. The enormous interest that the Jinan group took in Nanyang and Nanyang huaqiao reflects how ideologies and experiences of migration and settlement were woven into the fabric of Nationalist China. By inventing Nanyang huaqiao as subjects of Chinese history, the intellectuals also integrated China into a modern geography of nations and empires. Heavily influenced by Western and Japanese discourses, their portrayal of Nanyang huaqiao as "hegemons of the South Seas" who remained incomplete colonists was a mirror image of the homeland that had once ruled the seas but failed to build a colonial empire. The constructed teleology of origins and destinies turned the diaspora–homeland dynamic into a means for national progress. But it also suggested China's dependency on the diaspora, whose members held a unique key to its future revival. This surprising mode of self-understanding tends to return whenever a Chinese state seeks global status and rediscovers itself as a diaspora's homeland, as in the official celebration of "new migrants" (*xin yimin*) in present-day China.

A layered product of knowledge and power, the Jinan activities highlight the South Seas as an open yet networked region that helped transform China. They remind historians of how rarely China, Japan, Southeast Asia, and Europe are recognized as intertwined through travel, print, education, and research. They also reveal how the traditional structure of an Indian Ocean emporium continued to operate in a changing matrix of colonial, native, and treaty-port cities. During the early twentieth century, what was traded in bulk no longer included spices, silks, and silver, and was not limited to tin, rubber, and rice, but also consisted of books, periodicals, and newspapers. Serving as powerful intermediaries in this cultural flow, the Jinan intellectuals taught, researched, translated, and published, activities that grew along with urbanization, mass education, the printing press, and steam transportation. These forces were reflected not only in the Jinan adaptations of colonial writings about the South Seas, but also in their life experiences as part of a "cultural diaspora," akin to a "trade diaspora" in the early Indian Ocean economy.[64] Contributing to the links between modern East and Southeast Asia, the Jinan cosmopolitans helped spread colonial ways of seeing by incorporating them into a new historical geography of China in the world.

Furthermore, this diaspora moment powerfully demonstrates the pull of the sea on modern China. It shows that the writing of Chinese history cannot simply mean looking within and across the landed borders of China, but also involves searching seaward for connected transformations. By recognizing China and Chinese emigrants as part of an integrated maritime Asia, it becomes possible to assess how they helped transform it and were transformed by the circulations of capital, labor, goods, ideas, and culture. Awash in the exchanges across the South Seas, the Jinan writings provide a valuable archive of a China unmoored.

CHAPTER 3

Confucius from Afar

In early 1927, Lu Xun abruptly left Amoy University (Xiamen University or Xiada) four months into a two-year term as professor. In letters written to his lover Xu Guangping, he had repeatedly complained about university mismanagement, funding cuts, and old colleagues from Beijing whom he thought were reactionaries.[1] Adding to his frustration was someone he had just met, the university president, Lim Boon Keng (Lin Wenqing, 1869–1957), a little-known English-speaking Chinese from Singapore who spearheaded a Confucian revival at Xiada. Lu Xun called him "a Chinese of British nationality who cannot open or shut his mouth without the word 'Confucius.'"[2] At his first public lecture at the university on October 14, 1926, Lu Xun lampooned the neo-Confucianists for reviving old forms of oppression and being useless in solving new problems, while Lim was listening in the audience:

> Lately, the calls to revere Confucius, venerate Confucianism, read the classics, and revive the ancient past, so as to save China, have gotten louder and louder. In the past, those who advocated reading of the classics often had ulterior motives. They wanted to turn other people into filial sons and subservient subjects, virtuous women and chaste widows, so that they themselves could act superior and ride high above other people's heads. They frequently boasted their knowledge of the classics and old Chinese culture. Yet, did they ever succeed in using *The Analects* to dissuade the foreign soldiers from shooting during the May Thirtieth tragedy? Did they ever use *The Book of Changes* to sink the invading battleships that destroyed the Dagu fort on the eve of the March Eighteenth tragedy?[3]

Instead of poring over "dead" Chinese books with "little application," Lu Xun urged students to read Western newspapers and magazines and to become "busybodies" (*haoshi zhi tu*), agents of change like European explorers Christopher Columbus and Fridtjof Nansen. Speaking after Lu Xun, Lim Boon Keng avoided responding to the attacks on a revived Confucianism but remarked that the university founder Tan Kah Kee (Chen Jiageng, 1874–1961), a successful Hokkien rubber industrialist in Malaya, could well be admired as a "busybody" in Lu Xun's terms.[4] Baffled by Lim's apparent unawareness that the criticisms were meant for himself, Lu Xun wrote to Xu Guangping afterward, "this is how confused things are in this place!"[5]

A well-known controversy, this conflict between Lu Xun and Lim Boon Keng has been told and retold against changing models of political and cultural citizenship in both China and Singapore.[6] After 1949, Chinese Communist historians criticized Lim for failing to come to terms with modernity, as they made Lu Xun synonymous with revolution and the 1919 May Fourth Movement. In post–World War II Singapore, the long history of interactions with China underlying stories like that of Lim was swept up in an upheaval of decolonization, nationalism, and Cold War struggles. Since the 1990s, scholars and politicians in both places have rediscovered Lim as a representative of a "bicultural elite," trying to refurbish Confucianism for the needs of national reform and global capitalism. In Singapore, scholar Lee Guan Kin has portrayed Lim as a hybrid of "East and West" and a Singapore-Malay Chinese (*xinma huaren*) who located his "cultural roots" in China while remaining "locally oriented toward Singapore-Malaya."[7] Singapore statesman Lee Kuan Yew called Lim a historical model that must be "replicated" and urged citizens to become "multicultural players" to engage the growing economies of China and India.[8] Meanwhile, in China since the 1980s, Deng Xiaoping's interest in how Confucianism contributed to the economic success of Singapore and other overseas Chinese societies has evolved into a state-patronized movement at home, support among academics in the West, and most recently a spread of Confucius Institutes abroad.[9] New biographies of Lim in mainland China portray a patriotic overseas Chinese and a modern Confucianist whose differences with Lu Xun have been exaggerated.[10] Taken together, the revisionist portrayals of Lim have not gone beyond the traditional/modern, East/West binaries, but they also suggest that political and cultural assertions in both China and Singapore are not only changing but occasionally intertwine.

Revisiting Lim's story as an example of connected transformations, I seek to highlight a still-neglected context of colonial power across South-

Figure 3.1 Statue of Lim Boon Keng at Amoy University, Xiamen. Photograph by the author.

east Asia that implicated Nationalist China.[11] Born to a third-generation creolized Straits Chinese family in Singapore and educated at the University of Edinburgh as a medical doctor, Lim was groomed to be an elite subject of the British empire. Surprisingly, he discovered traditional Chinese culture while in Scotland, led a Confucian movement after returning to Singapore, remade himself into an anti-Christian, anti-imperialist critic on behalf of China, and went on to serve as the inaugural president of Amoy University (Xiada) for sixteen years. Though the general characterization of Lim as "bicultural" or "multicultural" seems valid, I find that for the most part Lim understood himself to be bringing back an "authentic" Chinese culture. Repeatedly, he argued in his writings that it should be free of European, Malay, and "superstitious" Chinese influences. Subsequently imported to Xiada, his blend of neo-Confucianism not only advocated a return to the "original" teachings of Confucius, but rationalized them as modernizing, secular, and compatible with science—a process unfolding all across Asia that scholars have termed "religion-making."[12] Understanding the source of Lim's inspiration requires taking seriously his negotiations with colonial discourses of race, gender, science, and religion, no less than the influence of Confucian learning on his formulation of an "authentic" Chinese culture.

By situating Lim's revivalism in dialogue with colonial forces in Asia, it becomes possible to discern a series of "diaspora moments" through a shared making, unmaking, and remaking of Confucianism that helped shape China. While Prasenjit Duara has argued that Chinese intellectuals in China, unlike the creolized Peranakan Chinese in the Dutch East Indies, did not "need" Confucianism to sustain a Chinese identity, Lim's revivalist journey, when viewed across the long twentieth century, has contributed to recurring discussions about the place of Confucianism in China and beyond.[13] Distinct but far from unique, his story was part of a "returning" movement of Western-educated Chinese colonial intellectuals seeking to interpret the West for China and to interpret China to the West since the late nineteenth century, a group that included Gu Hongming (1857–1928, b. Penang), Wu Tingfang (1842–1911, b. Singapore), Wu Liande (1879–1960, b. Penang), and Eugene Chen (1878–1944, b. Trinidad). Similarly, the recent rediscovery of Lim in China and Singapore is part of a greater return of Confucianism that partially began overseas. To illustrate the homeland-diaspora dynamic historically, this chapter will reinterpret Lim's writings and life story in Singapore and China as a series of disjunctions and convergences in the meaning of traditional Chinese culture in the world. It will also locate Lim's innovations in an overlay of times and spaces from the colonial Straits Settlement to imperial Britain to late Qing and Republican China, rather than in the terms of closed, bounded opposites between East and West and between tradition and modernity.

Colonialism and Reformism

The Chinese-born British subjects are now in the state of transition, socially and intellectually, between the old ways of our forefathers and the new doctrines of European civilization.
—LIM BOON KENG, 1897

The people in transition portrayed by Lim Boon Keng were the Straits Chinese, the descendants of Chinese migrants and subjects of the British empire in nineteenth-century Singapore. Founded in 1819, Singapore was incorporated into the Straits Settlements in 1826. The 1881 census showed that the Settlements had a total population of nearly 140,000, of which over 60 percent were Chinese. The Straits-born accounted for approximately 11 percent of the Chinese total.[14] In colonial and Chinese travel narratives, these *babas* (males) and *nyonyas* (females), the Malay terms denoting local birth and Chinese or Chinese-Malay ancestry, spoke patois Malay but were still recognizably "Chinese" because they adhered to Chinese dress and customs, with men still wearing the distinctive queue.[15] Under British colonial rule, the introduction of English education through local schools and exclusive scholarships to study in Britain gave rise to a class of English-educated elites who were to serve the needs of trade and colonial administration. Aimed at producing loyal British subjects, the educational apparatus in the colony and metropole, however, also instilled a sense of purpose into men such as Lim Boon Keng, who returned from Britain in 1893 to herald a new era for the Straits Chinese.

When assessing the origins of Lim's Confucian revivalism, scholars have typically emphasized China's influence in an impact–response paradigm and have not always acknowledged that the Straits-born Chinese made significant cultural innovations of their own. Yen Ching-hwang finds it "ironical that the Confucian revival movement [in Singapore] should have been led by a Westernized intellectual like Lim."[16] He argues that the ideology of the movement "sprang directly from [Qing intellectual] Kang Youwei's reformism," seeking to make Confucianism China's state religion, which "partly testified to the impact of Confucianism on overseas Chinese intellectuals, and partly to [Lim's] political intention of mobilizing support of [Kang's] reform movement."[17] Lee Guan Kin argues that Lim's political sympathies with Kang Youwei and his association with other China-born Confucianists in Singapore would suggest their heavy influence on him.[18] But she also notes incidentally that Lim might have been a Confucianist before knowing them, given some of his early writings on Confucianism from the mid-1890s. In other words, discussions of Lim's revivalism have largely assumed China to be the storehouse of traditional Chinese values and Chinese intellectuals from China the key mediators, from whom overseas Chinese intellectuals then learned and chose according to their own needs.

Nonetheless, a greater sensitivity to Lim's formation as a Straits Chinese intellectual suggests that his cultural influences were diverse and interlinked. Born in Singapore on October 18, 1869, Lim Boon Keng could trace his family lineage back to China and locally in Malaya, beginning with his grandfather's arrival from Fujian province in 1839 and marrying a nyonya in Penang. Later, their son, Lim Boon Keng's father, also married a nyonya in Singapore whose family was from Malacca. When Lim Boon Keng was ten years old, his mother died. His father remarried but died of infection from a shaving cut soon after Lim turned sixteen. This tragic turn of events left Lim Boon Keng and his eleven siblings in the care of their grandparents. It also caused him to later become a medical doctor, a common ambition among young men from China such as Lu Xun and Sun Yat-sen. At home, Lim Boon Keng spoke baba Malay, a creole speech of Hokkien and Malay. He received a brief classical Chinese education from the Hokkien clan association in Singapore and a formal education in English from the Raffles Institution. In 1887, Lim, at age eighteen, became the first Chinese to win a Queen's scholarship to study in Britain.[19] In 1892, he earned a degree in medicine and surgery from the University of Edinburgh. Yet, while there, his experience of witnessing white humiliation of the Chinese, being isolated by students from China because he could not speak Chinese well, and feeling ashamed over his inability to translate a Chinese paper for a professor had also prompted him to ardently take up Chinese language and classical studies in his spare time.[20] From emigrant China to colonial Malaya to imperial Britain, this circuitous path of Lim's family and life experiences suggests how these different times and spaces were imbricated.

After returning to Singapore in 1893, Lim began to advance his interest in traditional Chinese culture as the basis of moral reform. Appointed as a Chinese member of the Straits Settlements Legislative Council in 1895, Lim helped found the Chinese Philomathic Society in 1896 to promote the study of English literature, European music, and the Chinese language. He also coedited an English-language quarterly journal, the *Straits Chinese Magazine* (1897–1907), with Song Ong Siang (1871–1941), a fellow Queen's scholar and Cambridge-trained barrister. The magazine targeted a "better-educated" and "permanently residing" generation, the locally born, creolized, and colonially educated who were "unfortunately bound to know increasingly less about the traditions and histories of their ancestors."[21] Though it was originally intended as a forum to discuss matters concerning "Straits-born people of all nationalities," topics related to the Chinese came to fill the pages of the magazine. Not interested in the mere reinstallation of "past knowledge," editors and writers of the magazine sought to filter that knowledge through a reformist agenda. Chosen for the cover of the inaugural issue was a Confucian saying from *The Analects, guo ze wu dan gai*, which Lim Boon Keng translated as "if you have faults, do not fear to abandon them."

One of the most significant creations of the *Straits Chinese Magazine* was the ideal of a progressive reformer who rejected "Malayness" and "Europeanness" and sought to recapture the morality of Confucianism lost in the passage of time. Calling to account "conservatives" who feared change at a moment of transition, Lim Boon Keng wrote in 1897, "we are almost afraid that our sons, when enlightened by the culture of Europe, will turn against their fathers, and discard the heritage of our customs and religions for the usages and beliefs of the Aryan races." Yet, he stressed, what was left unexamined was the truth behind the widespread renunciation of Chinese culture among local youth—the lack of a systematic Chinese classical education, the association of Chinese culture with "barbaric customs" in China such as infanticide and foot binding, and the irrationality of social traditions such as ancestor worship. Reforms to eliminate superstition and ignorance, accompanied by the study of Chinese classical literature to ennoble the mind, would be essential in order to restore faith in Chinese culture and to end the moral decline of the babas.[22]

Calling themselves "reformers" and their opponents "conservatives," the young Straits Chinese developed a broad social critique identifying a hedonistic, ignorant, and superstitious population and delivered it in gendered terms. Highly self-critical, many writings in the *Straits Chinese Magazine* described how the local community had been lost in the mixture of cultures, lacked a coherent code of ethics of its own, and was given to opium addiction, gambling, patronage of prostitutes, and idolatrous worship. Frequently, contributors concretized the siren call of malaise in distinctive problems for men and women. In one of the pieces, Lim Boon Keng observed that the babas grew up guided only by "instincts," and hence were indulgent in physical and sexual pleasures (1900):

> There is no greater eater than the extravagant Chinese. Foods for them are prepared in different ways. You have the Malay sambal, the Indian curry, the European dishes and pâtés and the Chinese pork. All these preparations are served at one meal, accompanied by the choicest and strongest wines and drinks of all nations . . . to further enliven the occasion, singing girls and female dancers are employed. These serve

to fill the gap in their social life, which ought to have been filled by respectable women of their own position—the wives and daughters of the men.[23]

Disorder was also found among the nyonyas, who were illiterate, dependent, and addicted to gambling, wrote Song Ong Siang (1897):

> [They have] become selfish and careless and ignorant, with a propensity for gambling and some even for drinking... rather than to be occupied with the training, moral and mental, of their children, or to study to make their houses and their surroundings real homes for their husbands and grown-up sons, to wean them and draw their attention and desires away from the temptations and vices and evil companions that dog their every step and to woo them to the comforts and the pleasures of an ideal family circle.[24]

To Lim and Song, these gendered transgressions indicated the urgent need for a moral order in the Victorian image, whereby the man would be restored as the public figure of self-restraint and probity and the woman as the buffer against moral contamination in the home.

Generally overlooked in the scholarship, the gendered rhetoric of Lim and Song suggests that their reformism resembled British Victorianism more than Qing reformism, even though the latter is often assumed to be the main inspiration. While their emphasis on women's roles as wives and mothers and the call for female education may sound similar to the late Qing project, much less so was Song's desire to curb nyonyas' visibility and reinvent them as moral guardians in the home. The same could be said of Lim's endorsement of women who were men's respectable social companions rather than prostitutes. This cult of female domesticity was markedly Victorian. Additionally, the immense concern with baba self-restraint against carnal indulgences and the stress on cultivating male interests in athleticism, debate, literature, and music through the Chinese Philomathic Society were hallmarks of the Victorian ideal of masculinity.[25] This heavy borrowing from British imperial culture suggests the impact of living in and across the colony and metropole. It also shows that a critical analysis of the two men's gender ideology, a common blind spot in previous scholarship, can contribute to a fuller picture of their intellectual adaptation.

Furthermore, a closer look at Lim Boon Keng's series of essays indicates that his engagement with colonialism as a Straits Chinese elite made his Confucian movement both independent of and intertwined with the one led by Kang Youwei in some significant ways. From 1899 to 1901, Lim delineated a reform agenda that included the end of queue-wearing, modernization of dress and costume, emphasis on Mandarin Chinese as the "father tongue" (*fuyü*), and standardization of marriage and funeral rites.[26] Wide-ranging and locally specific, the proposal did not fit within Kang's concurrent Confucian reformism. Instead, it sought to redefine the babas as a distinct group who would and should never become fully British, were no longer purely Chinese, and had succumbed to bad influences, but could become subjects in their own right through reviving "lost" traditions. This is not to say that Lim's Confucian movement was particular rather than universal. Rather, it was a case of attributing the moral shortcomings of the babas to a history of emigration and settlement, and reimagining that they could become complete again by reconnecting with Chinese traditions. Yet it could also be said that both Lim and Kang were reacting to a single process of Western expansion that assumed different forms in their respective times and spaces.

Seen this way, the queue-cutting ("anti-towchang") movement offers a remarkable example of how the Straits Chinese reformism was embedded in colonial forces that also implicated China. Though not to be confused with support for the anti-Qing movement led by Chinese revolutionaries, the Straits Chinese effort to end queue-wearing was also meant to abolish "a sign of allegiance to the Manchu sovereign" and a local custom coming under scrutiny for its "absolute uselessness and inconvenience," in Lim Boon Keng's words.[27] As he wrote, since the "conservative instinct" of the Chinese race was deeply rooted, losing the outmoded queue was a necessary first step toward progress.[28] Nonetheless, the queue had also been a distinctive symbol of Chinese ethnicity and patriarchal descent in Malaya. Over a long period of migration and settlement, queue-wearing by Malayan Chinese men functioned to distinguish themselves from Malays and Europeans in local society. In the Straits Settlements, British colonial authorities cut off the queues of Chinese convicts in prison, a severe stigma that would cause some to wear an artificial queue upon release.[29] The importance of the queue as an ethnic and masculine symbol, locally sustained by both the Chinese wearers and the colonial state, can be further gleaned from an account by

Wu Liande (1879–1960), a Penang-born Chinese and Queen's scholar who later trained as a doctor in Britain like Lim Boon Keng. In his 1959 memoir, Wu recalled having his queue cut while en route to Cambridge, England, in 1896:

> Before I reach [sic] Gibraltar, I decided to remove my cumbersome queue, which seemed to have provided considerable amusement to some passengers and children on board. I paid the barber five shillings for his service and preserved the long hair in a paper packet to be posted later from England to my mother. I felt most miserable for days after its removal, as if part of my head had gone. For the queue had almost been part and parcel of myself since infancy when the little tuft of hair had been left in the middle of the scalp, and we had been taught from childhood days that it was the hallmark, so to say, of a true Chinese, forgetting that it was rather the emblem of servitude imposed by the conquering Manchus upon a helpless Chinese nation.[30]

This emotional anecdote, remembered decades later, spoke affectingly of the centrality of the queue to a male identity descended along the family line, a symbol so intimate that when the young Wu had it cut off, he sent it to his mother for preservation. As the queue had become a broad symbol of Chinese backwardness in the Western world by the late nineteenth century, it invited insult and mockery, forcing Wu to abandon a significant part of his identity as "a true Chinese." Instead, he rejected it as a racialized "emblem of servitude" to the Manchus in China, as newly propagated by colonial beliefs.

As colonialism reified traditional Chinese culture but also eviscerated it as a source of modernity, a wave of new arrivals from China further motivated a search for alternatives among the Straits Chinese. Local traditions, such as queue-wearing, ceased to be an exclusive marker of Chineseness to the Straits-born, but became tangled with imperialist images of stasis and barbarism in China. A prominent colonial official, G. T. Hare, made the connection clear in a lecture to the Chinese Philomathic Society in 1897:

> But though you retain the Chinese national customs and dress . . . [you] should as Chinese born British citizens remember that you have great rights and privileges here, institutions that you may well be proud of,

for they have only been won by the British people after many centuries of struggle and sacrifice of many noble lives.... In China, as you know well, Chinese citizens do not exist. The Chinese people are constitutionally slaves. They have no political rights and very few privileges as citizens. Their one duty is to obey.... They will have nothing to do with [the government] for fear of getting into trouble. This feeling has to some degree reacted on you, and explains why it is so difficult to get Straits-born Chinese to come forward in public life. You are too much influenced by the China-born Chinese in this respect.[31]

Rendering shared traditions with China-born Chinese as a political handicap for the Straits-born, this account is an important reminder of how colonial flows reshaped the meaning of a "Chinese" identity simultaneously in China and Singapore by linking them together. The characterization of British citizenship as the source of "great rights and privileges" obscured the fact that non-Europeans were barred from employment in the colonial civil service until the 1930s, an issue of great aggravation among many English-educated Straits Chinese in the early twentieth century.[32] Treating Britain as the source of progress and China as the lack thereof, a colonially defined Chinese identity had limited utility to aspiring social leaders like Lim Boon Keng. Instead, they sought to reclaim traditional Chinese culture as fully compatible with modern life.

A vigorous engagement with colonial power, Straits Chinese reformism at the turn of the twentieth century embodied not only a resistance against colonial assumptions but also a recombination of them to reconstruct Chinese culture as comparable to European culture, traditional and yet also rational. As Lim Boon Keng (1900) wrote:

"Europa" becomes in the half-awakened consciousness of the Chinese youth the Utopia where love reigns, poverty is unknown and all is good. But sad to say the same course of reading often creates a prejudice against things Chinese. The contemptuous tone and often erroneous statements of European writers, when referring to the "Chinaman," cannot but prejudicially influence the young and growing mind ... it is extremely prejudicial, indeed monstrous, to bring up our children into the belief that the Chinaman qua a Chinaman is vile ... they abhor the Chinese customs and they feel they may just act as their convenience dictates.[33]

Crucial to the effort was the call to modernize Chinese "superstitious" and "idolatrous" practices such as ancestor worship, which were frequent objects of Western exoticization and abhorrence. Fearing the erosion of affiliation with Chinese culture among youth because it did not suit the modern mind, Lim attempted to eradicate what he considered scientifically absurd ("offering a material dinner to ghosts"), morally invalid ("it was almost better for the parents to be dead than alive!"), and a radical departure from the original teachings of Confucius, who "lived 2500 years ago" and "would not sanction the present extravagance and waste for no good purpose."[34] Instead, he held, respect paid to the ancestors should conform to the "principles of the ancients" and engage no "Buddhist priest" or "feng-shui professor." Any signs of "grand display for effect," "lamentations calling upon the dead to rise, eat, and sleep," or "gaudy shows and discordant noises" should be discouraged.[35]

Another example was Lim's idea of a universal set of marriage practices designed for all Straits Chinese regardless of native place, religious sect, or social class. Chinese marriage customs, Lim found, were controlled by women, often entailing elaborate consultation with "horoscopers" and a number of feasts that would last for a week. "Superstitious" and "wasteful," they should be replaced by a few simple steps finished in two days: the exchange of betrothal gifts, a preliminary feast for family and close friends, a ceremony witnessed by the family, signing and registration of the marriage contract, and visits paid by the wedded couple to relatives and friends.[36] Traditional yet rational, a modernized Confucian society would not be singular but would stand among others in a comparative cultural scheme.

Distinct but comparable to other traditional cultures, Lim's vision of Confucianism could also be seen in the area of education. Arguing that superstition stemmed from ignorance, Lim Boon Keng advocated that Straits Chinese children be given moral training, which he thought absent in most schools and homes. Just as "the Mohammedans read their Koran, the Christians teach the Gospel," Lim contended that the Chinese should learn the Chinese language and the basic tenets of Confucianism. Mandarin Chinese, the speech of China's capital, not the various southern topolects spoken in the Straits such as Cantonese, Hokkien, Hainanese, Hakka, and Teochew, was chosen as the universal medium of instruction so as to overcome the linguistic divisions in the Chinese community. Furthermore, the education of women and girls would be vital to the moral uplift of the community because Lim felt that to keep "women in a low, ignorant, and servile state and in time [all would] become a low, ignorant and servile people." Besides sewing, cooking, and other household duties, girls should be taught language, music, and physical exercise.[37] In 1899, together with Song Ong Siang, Lim Boon Keng founded the Singapore Chinese Girls' School, the first of its kind. He also led fund-raising efforts responsible for the spread of modern-style Chinese schools during the early 1900s, schools that taught a variety of new subjects including mathematics, history, science, and physical education. Here the expansion of education served as means to innovate a rational Chinese society in a multicultural setting.

Moreover, Lim's complex interaction with colonialism involved a reproduction of racial ideologies, an aspect largely unexamined by scholars who have stressed a clash of already formed "Chinese" and "Western" cultures or "bicultural" tendencies in his thought.[38] In his writings, Lim repeatedly expressed anxiety over interracial contact and formations in social Darwinist terms, rejecting what he considered "Malayanization" and "Europeanization" among baba Chinese. His notion of a "European" influence involved the renunciation of Chinese language in favor of English and the emulation of an extravagant manner of living that was "foreign to their forefathers." His idea of "Malayness" was far more disparaging, even though Malay culture was an integral part of the creole baba culture. Invoking the fact that baba society in Malaya originated from Chinese intermarriages with native women, Lim and other contributors to the *Straits Chinese Magazine* frequently gendered Malay culture as female and associated their "maternal blood" with the "spirit of independence and thriftlessness," "the love of gewgaws," "the hatred of continuous hard work," and the barbaric practices of keeping nyonyas confined and uneducated.[39] "Chinese blood," on the contrary, was credited with the masculine spirit of enterprise, adventure, industry, and frugality.[40] Despite evidence that native wives traditionally ran family trading businesses in the absence of their sojourning Chinese husbands and contributed essential labor, connections, and skills to the household, the degree of "blood dilution" was made a barometer of morality, energy, and success—the more Malay blood there was in the ancestry, the less moral, energetic, and successful would be the person.

This rejection of "Malayness" reproduced a dominant hierarchy of races in terms of their value to the British empire, attesting to the fact that the new Straits Chinese identity was also an assimilation of colonial discourses.

Reporting on the early progress of Singapore in the 1820s, for instance, Governor John Crawfurd (1823–26) estimated "the worth of one Chinaman to the State as equal to two Klings [Tamil Indians] or four Malays." According to one retired colonial official writing in 1879, "not a single Malay can be pointed out as having raised himself by perseverance and diligence, as a merchant or otherwise, to a prominent position in the Colony"; most remained "nearly stationary" as fishermen and paddy planters. The Chinese, on the contrary, were "the most active, industrious, and persevering of all."[41] Nonetheless, subordinated to European power, Chineseness in the colonial context was also a contradictory formation that could easily shift from positive to negative. One Western observer offered the following view of the Chinese: "The Chinese are sober, industrious, domesticated, methodical, ingenious, honest and persevering in business, respectful to their seniors, and dutiful to their parents, polite in their intercourse with each other, law loving, easily governed with firmness; on the other hand they are crafty, proud, conceited, treacherous, unscrupulous, revengeful, cowardly, cruel and untruthful. Superstitious to a degree. Their features are stolid and never indicate the working of their minds."[42] Painted in a broad sweep, this impression implies that Chinese character was unpredictable and could be found anywhere on a continuum of opposites. Even though colonial elevation of the Chinese was ambivalent and limited, it no doubt resonated with Lim's larger project of inventing a modern Chinese identity with hard boundaries.

Perhaps most decisively, the Straits Chinese efforts to create modern Chinese subjects intersected with a modernizing China. Given that a growing class of English-educated Straits Chinese continued to face limited prospects for advancement locally, China increasingly appeared to be an exciting site of transformation. During the 1898 reform movement, the Chinese consul in Singapore encouraged the Straits Chinese to seek employment in China: "With a tolerably good knowledge of English, and with the advantage of having come into contact with Europeans, the Straits-born Chinese now working as clerks on poor and inadequate salaries would find lucrative employment in the railway, mining, and other new enterprises now being opened up in China."[43] Although the reform movement ended in disaster and sent Kang Youwei and other reformers into exile, the drive for modernization resumed in the early 1900s, as the Qing court reached out to overseas Chinese communities for funds and expertise to launch a new program of reforms.⁴⁴ Urging the Straits Chinese to rise to the occasion, Lim Boon Keng declared that China was undergoing "the grandest struggles for wealth or fame that the history of the Far East has ever witnessed," and "all the nations of the world are directing their attention to China." What China needed the most were experts who could act as "middlemen who thoroughly understand the foreigner and who will successfully bring about the reconciliation of the East and the West." To Lim, nobody would be more capable of filling that role than the Straits Chinese.⁴⁵

Calling upon the Straits Chinese to be middlemen for a modernizing China, Lim also exhorted them to seek a higher footing than that of the Chinese in China. Indeed, cultural affinity would give the Straits Chinese a competitive edge over the Japanese and Westerners in "a new and almost limitless field for their exploitation," wrote Lim (1903):

> In this new line there is enough of variety to suit every son of the Straits from the poorest to the richest. And when the Straits-born Chinese with proper qualifications arrives in China he finds that he is the sort of individual destined by nature to reconcile the great Chinese Nation to the ways of the great world beyond China. Naturally the natives of China have more confidence in their kinsmen from abroad, much more than they would have in foreigners however friendly. They look upon the returned of Chinese as practically their own people. They are prepared to trust us and we can read their hearts as no other people can do.⁴⁶

Arguing that the babas had "imbibed certain Malay tendencies" that were not to their advantage, Lim thought it fortunate that they were otherwise cosmopolitan in tastes and habits and could operate in China as the Apostle Paul did in different environments and blend in easily, like "a Greek among the Greeks" and "a Gentile among the Gentiles." Finally, Lim cited a famous Penang-born Chinese, Gu Hongming (1857–1928), who studied in Edinburgh and worked for Viceroy Zhang Zhidong, as a model for the Straits Chinese. As British subjects, Lim noted, the Straits Chinese should be able to enjoy the benefits of the spread of British influence in China and make good use of every opportunity. Here, the colonial status of the Straits Chinese became useful at China's opening to the Western world.

Lim Boon Keng's vision of how the Straits Chinese might play a unique role in China's modernization suggests that Chinese cultural expressions were far from shared across Chinese times and spaces, but they were also intertwined because of moving historical forces. By racializing certain social traits and practices that he deemed undesirable—extravagance as "European," indolence as "Malay," and "superstition" as contradictory to ancient Chinese principles—Lim aimed to restore a timeless and homogenized essence to the descendants of Chinese emigrants, making it possible for them to defy colonial representations and be both Chinese and modern. A reorganization of colonial assumptions, this identification precluded the formation of interracial subjectivities locally but did not simply mean yielding the cultural autonomy of the Straits Chinese to China. Rather, it allowed the Straits Chinese to become exemplars of progress, comparable to the Westerners and Japanese who were agents of modernity, and without being reduced to objects of modernization like the Chinese in China. Emerging at this historical conjuncture, the project of reviving Confucianism gave Lim confidence to "reconcile the great Chinese Nation to the ways of the great world beyond China" at a diaspora moment.

Christianity and Confucianism

In an 1898 essay entitled "The Renovation of China," Lim Boon Keng mounted an impassioned critique of the American missionary Arthur Smith's influential book, *Chinese Characteristics*, published in 1894.[47] The book was featured as a series in Shanghai's English-language paper, the *North-China Daily News*, and later became one of the most widely read Christian accounts of Chinese civilization in both China and the West. Lim quoted a famous prescription for China's presumed backwardness from the book: "What China needs is righteousness, and in order to attain it, it is absolutely necessary that she have a knowledge of God and a new conception of man, as well as of the relation of man to God. She needs a new life in every individual soul, in the family, and in society. The manifold needs of China, we find, then, to be a single imperative need. It will be met permanently, completely, only by Christian civilization."[48] Responding to Smith's call to replace Chinese traditions with "Christian civilization," Lim argued that Chinese institutions, in spite of their shortcomings, had "withstood the crucial test of time." He also criticized Smith for misunderstanding "the nature of Chinese culture" and assuming that Confucianism was obsolete, or as Smith put it, a piece of "rotten wood" that could no longer be carved but "must be wholly cut away."[49] Situating Smith within a larger body of

Western views on China, Lim found that these views contributed to "an unjust view of the character of the Chinese people," evident in the deplorable treatment of Chinese by Westerners in the treaty ports of China and various parts of the world. They also propagated "a more unfair estimate of the value of Chinese institutions" and the false belief that European progress was the result of Christianity. Implying that these views of Chinese traditions did not reflect an objective condition but were a sign of racism and imperialism, this critique of Christianity was integral to Lim's ideas of Confucian revival.

When writing about the conflict between Lim Boon Keng and Lu Xun in 1926, scholars have generally overlooked a convergence despite the men's respective revivalism and iconoclasm: their deep interest in Christian missionary discourses about China. As Lee Guan Kin notes, from 1895 onward, Lim produced a vast body of writings in Singapore comparing Christianity with Confucianism. In China, Smith's *Chinese Characteristics*, considered by Lim to be "unjust" and "unfair," sparked enthusiastic discussions about "national character" among May Fourth intellectuals. As Lydia Liu writes, Lu Xun used the imported missionary theory to advance his critique of the "indigenous tradition, culture and the classical heritage."[50] While he thought that missionary portrayals truly reflected the weakness of Chinese national character and should be heeded, Lim believed that missionaries threatened to undermine the viability of Chinese traditions and therefore must be resisted at all cost. Their divergent reactions to the same body of missionary knowledge suggest cultural reckonings from distinct yet intertwined Chinese times and spaces.

To better understand Lim's revivalism, it is necessary to resituate Lim's ideas in a wider context of what scholars have termed "religion-making."[51] A global phenomenon in the nineteenth and twentieth centuries, "religion-making" refers to the bifurcation of the religious and the secular, a development accompanying the spread of modernity—a discourse of science, reason, and individualism associated with the Enlightenment—and forces of modernization such as urbanization, industrial and capitalist innovations, mass education and politics, and increased state power. During this process, colonial rule and national movements were intertwined with attacks on "superstitions," reification of "religion" as a separate realm of moral ethics, and building a secular society. As long-existing multicultural communities in Southeast Asia became newly transformed by mass migrations and high colonialism, the region became a hotspot of religion-making in the modern era. There, Asian "religions," including Confucianism, Islam, Hinduism, and Buddhism, were invented as comparable to one another, as each underwent a similar process of rationalization—an end to mythology, a return to "authentic" and "original" texts and values, and new assertions of compatibility with modernity. Lim's Confucian revivalism could be understood as part of this structural transformation across Asia.

The same development took a different form in May Fourth China, though the impulse underneath the attacks on religion was remarkably similar. As Mayfair Yang writes, during the late nineteenth century, Confucian reformers such as Kang Youwei, Tan Sitong, Yan Fu, and Liang Qichao tried to incorporate Western evolutionism and rationality into a traditional religious cosmology that had emphasized the power of divine forces. Since Western imperialism increasingly threatened China's survival, these reformist intellectuals also accepted that China's cultural and religious traditions were "backward," especially in the May Fourth period of the 1920s. During this time, violent attacks on the patriarchal family and the worship of ancestors and gods went hand in hand with a revolutionary nationalism seeking to "liberate" the individual and embrace Western science and progress.[52] Therefore, even though China was not fully colonized, unlike most of Southeast Asia in the early twentieth century, it also underwent a similar process of religion-making to destroy "superstitions" and build a modern nation.

Seen in this interconnected context, Lim's revivalism was a project to make Confucianism compatible with Western science and comparable to modern Christianity. Part of his approach was to discredit the claims of a natural divide between traditional China and Christian Europe in missionary knowledge. During a 1904 lecture, he spoke to an audience of Straits Chinese youth whom he assumed were attracted to Christianity because they felt "sorry" that they were Chinese:

> It is our consciousness of the absurdity of our traditional religions and customs that drives many of us without study or thought to embrace the creeds of other races. With a crude notion of Christianity, we vainly imagine that modern Christianity as professed by the missionaries whom we know is the source of life and power to the Europeans. We are assured of this by the average missionary. We believe this, and from this to join-

ing the Christian Church is only a question of time. But surely it is only right that before we forsake the old customs, the old faiths, and the ancestral relics, we shall faithfully enquire whether these are really what outsiders represent them to be.[53]

Acknowledging that Chinese "traditional religions and customs" needed reform, Lim spoke out against what he saw as a mindless acceptance of a foreign religion among the Straits Chinese. Rejecting the idea that Christianity contributed to Europe's success, he recounted the history of Christianity, invoking a past when the Christian Church "burned or destroyed all who dared to declare opinions contrary to her established dogmas." Instead, it was the growth of science and education that finally weakened the power of the Church, making religion "purer, freer from superstition, more tolerant and more ethical." Here, it seems that all Confucianism needed was a similar kind of purification without having to be replaced by Christianity.

Another aspect of Lim's revivalism was to deny Christianity as a universal source of morality by linking it with the racism and imperialism of Christian nations. Even as missionaries routinely blamed Confucianism for Chinese conservatism and xenophobia, Lim contended, this formulation concealed the modern origins of these Chinese attitudes: the "indiscretion" of missionary activities and "the wars waged to force the Chinese to accept opium."[54] While anti-foreign sentiments were also present among China's reformers, Lim argued, "so long as the foreigner, in his eagerness to secure concessions, disregards the interests and feelings of the natives, he will continue to be hated and disliked."[55] In a 1901 collection of articles published in London for an English audience, Lim argued that European powers were not as morally superior as missionaries claimed. Naming the unjust treatment suffered by China from the treaty clauses of "most favored nation," fixed tariffs on foreign goods, the opium trade, and forced acceptance of missionary activities, Lim reversed the disparaging term "The Yellow Peril," which had originated in the West referring to Chinese emigrant labor, to "The White Peril," meaning the menacing behavior of white Christian nations who refused the entry of Chinese immigrants, denied them the rights and privileges guaranteed by recognized treaties, and demanded unprecedented privileges for themselves in China. Regarding the violent opposition to missionaries in China, Lim explained that missionaries were a source of social strife, violating the "communal rights and customs" of the Chinese people and encouraging some Chinese to take political advantage of the missionary influence. Alluding to the popular missionary discourses on Chinese character, Lim insisted that Chinese attitudes of hostility had historical causes, and could not be attributed to "inherent defects in the native character."[56] Released in London in the immediate aftermath of the 1900 Boxer Rebellion, Lim's commentary went boldly against criticisms of Chinese xenophobic violence in the West.

If the great divergence between China and Europe was not the result of a fixed tradition and religion, what caused it? Lim believed that European progress was the result of a sound education in philosophy and science, while Chinese stagnation was caused by a lack thereof. The solution was a return to "the accurate study of nature" laid down by Confucius: "It is the study of science that has placed Europe in her present enviable position. When men obtain a clear and satisfactory knowledge of things they realize the true nature of the processes which account for the phenomena we see. From pure observation they proceed to experiment, and by the combination of these two methods, distinctly foreshadowed in the 'Ta Hsio' [Da Xue, *The Book of Great Learning*], patient students deduce or discover 'the laws of nature' which reveal to us the secrets that give to modern civilization all her power and her grandeur."[57] Claiming that scientific rationality was a fundamental element of Confucian teachings, Lim's teleological reading of Confucianism aimed to show that "Chinese civilization," when stripped of superstitions and returned to its core, should bear the same fruits of success as "European civilization."

By asserting that the Confucian ethic placed "Chinese culture" on par with "European culture," Lim remained committed to progress as set forth by the example of Europe. His only disagreement was with the claim made by missionaries such as Arthur Smith that Christianity was the universal law of progress. In all his objections to the Christian influence on China, Lim's point was never whether or not Europe's scientific progress should entitle it to conquer and subjugate. Instead, he asserted over and over again that those acts of "injustice" against China were powerful evidence that Western missionaries had no absolute claim to moral superiority or any right to insist that they had the final word on Confucianism.

Moreover, Lim's anti-Christian stance reflected a wider investment in a secular world, as he claimed that all religions did more harm than good to the modern mind. If religion was a code regulating human duties and obligations, Lim declared that Confucianism would be "a religion of the highest grade," because "Confucius was not a spirit nor was he an incarnation," but rather a man who clearly saw that it would be futile to "waste human energy in attempting to explain everything which one could not investigate." Instead, he found, Confucius laid down the principle of agnosticism, which Thomas Huxley, "2500 years after [Confucius]," adopted as the foundation of modern science. Lim's secularism led him to reject the value not only of Christianity but also of Islam, Buddhism, and Daoism. Determined to rid Chinese social life of "nonsense and superstition" such as ancestor worship, he applied the same rule to the "refined nonsense and superstition in Western creeds," treating all religiosities as anti-intellectual and incompatible with progress.[58]

Lim's ideal of a modern and secular Confucianism can be further examined through his comparative views of "Confucian women" and "Christian women." Disagreeing with Western missionaries that Confucianism was responsible for the low status of women in China and that Christianity explained their high status in the West, Lim pointed out the portrayal of Eve in the Bible, charging that it made women appear "evil" and "foolish" for causing the fall of humankind. In contrast, he argued, women in ancient China received education to develop their character and "maternal instincts," and women in sericulture typically enjoyed a great degree of independence. Claiming that women were "considered inferior to men insofar they were subordinated to men biologically," Lim went on to argue that women already occupied the position of highest honor and importance in Confucian society, motherhood, and therefore were "compelled by circumstances to play a secondary part in the severe struggles for existence."[59] Concluding that the Confucian treatment of women was "more humane, more reasonable and more in accord with modern European practice," Lim reversed a critique of the status of Chinese women in many missionary writings.

Nonetheless, Lim's determination to rescue Confucianism from Christian "misunderstandings" made him less concerned with the actual complexity of women's experiences than with the appearance of clear opposites. On the topic of Chinese concubinage, Lim argued that it was in fact "more humane and reasonable" than the Western practice of monogamy because Confucian China recognized the "illegitimate births" to mistresses, whereas such children were stigmatized in Christian society. On the topic of Chinese prostitutes and courtesans, he claimed that Confucianists, as "practical men," were prepared to tolerate them in the same way as the ancient Greeks. Asserting that "similar ill-treatment of women by men [was] common enough throughout the whole of Christendom," Lim found that the "Confucian woman," who was less publicly visible, was no less honorable than her "Christian sister": "The Confucianist wife may not have all the ravishing charm of intellect of the Christian women of the West. She may appear to be secluded behind the *purdah* [sic] whilst the Christian wife is entertaining the friends of her husband, but who can say that in unselfish devotion to her husband and in her love of her children, the Confucianist woman is in any degree inferior to her Christian sister. . . . Above all is she in any way less happy than the hysterical or neurotic or neurasthenic women of the West?"[60] Charging that "the Christian wife" tended to suffer from depression, Lim argued that her "Confucianist" counterpart enjoyed "the noble dignity of mother of the family" and "the highest honors which the father may expect from his son." Chinese history was in fact filled with great examples of eminent Confucian men who were deeply devoted to their mothers. Besides, as "the highest type of civilized womanhood," the "Confucian woman" defends the "purity of the home" but is not given "the liberty to ruin the family." Instead, she "overcomes the passions by art" and "governs the man who would be her lord by an unfailing courtesy and an enduring devotion."[61] In other words, Lim's gendered critiques did not intend to attack Chinese patriarchy so much as to attack Christian supremacy.

Interestingly, these writings suggest that Lim's Confucian revivalism intersected with May Fourth iconoclasm over missionary portrayals of the low status of Chinese women. Rather than promoting the liberation of women, Lim was determined to show that Confucianism was far more capable than Christianity of sustaining the moral order of a modern world. Treating women as the "weaker sex" that needed men's protection from evil and violence, and as the "better half" that should be exalted and admired, Lim incorporated Victorian sexual and gender norms into his ideal of a Confucian order. Maintaining that women's social functions were predetermined by their biological "subordination" to men, Lim believed that Confucianism enabled women to assume "complementary" and "secondary" roles in the struggle for survival to be shouldered by men, while reserving the highest honor and respect to motherhood, a position attainable only by women. In other words, he argued, Confucianism was more effective than Christianity in producing a durable masculinity that could defend a fragile femininity, making Confucian society "more humane and reasonable" toward women. Whereas the struggle for national modernity took precedence in May Fourth China, the race between Christianity and Confucianism in a colonial world also severely limited Lim's commitment to women's advancement.

Refuting the universal claims of Christianity, Lim Boon Keng went on to construct a universal appeal of Confucianism by embracing new knowledge of Western evolutionism and individualism. Reacting to missionary notions of East–West difference, he rejected the claim that the East was governed by collective interests and the West by the pursuit of individual freedom. Rather, he argued that Confucian society aimed at the production of "the perfect man," the individual in perfect possession of his physical, intellectual, and moral faculties, whose obligation to the family, often criticized by missionaries for stifling individuality, was in Lim's view a value necessary to ensure the longevity of the race in social Darwinist terms. Exercising the five virtues of benevolence, justice, wisdom, politeness, and good faith, which included the knowledge of science and agnosticism, the individual's final stage of evolution was as an "agent of government," the basic unit of society who would then contribute to international peace. In this case, Lim believed, the ideal of Confucianism was "not very far from that of the great religions of the world," but also differed significantly from them in that it claimed no "supernatural sanctions" and allowed each nation to "preserve its ancient faith as the best antidote to national decay." Therefore, unlike Christianity, Confucianism was "acceptable to every educated man in Europe and throughout the world," transcending divisions of race and nation.[62]

By secularizing Chinese cultural traditions and adapting them to Enlightenment knowledge in a colonial world, Lim's revivalism was part of a larger religion-making that also impacted China. He laid down the struggle between the West and the rest as the chief concern for modern Confucianists, and Christianity as the threat that could obliterate access to the invaluable resources of the Chinese past. Breaking up the experiences of migration and settlement in colonial Singapore into "Europeanization," "Malayanization," or Chinese "ignorance" and "superstition," Lim ended up reassembling the fragments to forge a modern and secular Chinese tradition. Claiming a cultural loss induced by the hegemony of Christianity, Lim believed that descendants of the ancient Chinese civilization must redeem the Confucian past in order to refashion themselves as autonomous agents of progress, a conviction that he would carry to China when he became head of Amoy University in the 1920s. Lu Xun, on the other hand, thought that Chinese confidence in the "old culture" was excessive, enslaving people to a traditional morality, and that it should be shaken up to make way for the new.

Education and Modernity

When considering the journey of Lim Boon Keng's Confucian revivalism to May Fourth China, another development for consideration was a rapid expansion of education across coastal China and Southeast Asia. There Chinese merchants and intellectuals in the diaspora played a key role in producing a connected transformation. As the founding president of Amoy University, Lim oversaw an enterprise single-handedly funded by the successful overseas Chinese rubber industrialist in Singapore, Tan Kah Kee. Since the early 1900s, Tan had founded and financed a dozen schools to modernize education in his native Jimei village near Xiamen. Hoping to set an example for Chinese of Fujian origin in the South Seas, who in his view were not only reluctant to return to China but were also squandering their wealth on an extravagant lifestyle, Tan announced in 1919 an ambitious plan to build a private university in Fujian to help close the gap between his native province and the neighboring Zhejiang, Jiangsu, and Guangdong, where a number of Chinese- and foreign-run universities had been established. With a dual goal of providing young people in Fujian and of Fujian descent in Southeast Asia with a modern education, Tan's vision was to provide an initial amount of four million Straits dollars, to be supplemented by contributions of other overseas Chinese donors to support the operation of Xiada. Assisted by a preparatory committee consisting of well-known educators such as Cai Yuanpei, Tan had first offered the presidency of the university to Wang Jingwei, a political aide to Sun Yat-sen who had traveled widely overseas, and later to Deng Cuiying, a native of Fujian educated in Japan, both of whom later resigned to take up government posts.[63] The search finally ended in 1921 when Lim Boon Keng accepted the appointment. Tan's selections suggest that overseas education and experience weighed heavily in the overall scheme of leadership.

Nonetheless, the reception of Lim Boon Keng did not go as smoothly as planned. In the spring of 1921, Xiada opened its doors to a student enrollment of about one hundred, half of whom were natives of the province. Praised by Tan Kah Kee as "the most outstanding person among millions of the overseas Chinese" and "well versed in Western materialistic sciences and Chinese cultural spirit," Lim was soon attacked by the new students as "unqualified, incompetent, outdated, and depraved,"[64] suggesting that the campus climate mirrored the broader turbulences across many other educational institutions in the Chinese republic. In 1924, after Lim sacked some members of the teaching staff, apparently to break up an academic feud, the incident was criticized in a Shanghai newspaper and caught national attention. A standoff between students and the administration ended in the departure of hundreds of students and staff and their founding of a new university in Shanghai named "Daxia," an inversion of characters to suggest the overturn of "Xiada."[65]

Despite the stormy beginning, the building of Xiada got back on track after 1926, when Lim consolidated the blending of different elements into a single curriculum. The curriculum stressed mastery of the national language, Mandarin Chinese, the study of English as a second language, a liberal education encompassing philosophy, history, and literature, as well as professional and practical training in fields such as engineering, economics, medicine, sciences, commerce, law, and education. The university consisted of forty buildings, providing a total of 3,000 rooms and a wide range of facilities such as student dormitories, a gymnasium, a sports ground, a library, a laboratory, a meteorological observatory, and museums. At the height of its success in 1930, Xiada consisted of five faculties, under which seventeen departments operated, along with a medical and an engineering school. Annual student admission ranged between three hundred and six hundred students.[66] Additionally, several eminent literary and cultural scholars from Beijing, including Lu Xun, Shen Jianshi, and Gu Jiegang, came to establish a new field of "national studies" (*guoxue*). This news drew enthusiastic reporting among Shanghai's major newspapers, leading to one hopeful commentary that "it will not be many years from now that Xiada could emerge as one of the most comprehensive universities in China."[67]

The intersection of Confucian revivalism and Western science with national studies under Lim's direction merits some attention. Dating back to the "national essence" (*guocui*) discussions of the 1890s, the national studies movement in the 1920s followed the footsteps of late-Qing intellectuals such as Kang Youwei and Zhang Taiyan in a desire to revive traditional knowledge through modern methods. As Arif Dirlik writes, earlier reformist thinkers sought to "rescue true learning (and hence the 'national essence') from its distortion under imperial rule" and to prevent new Western learning from undermining Chinese cultural independence. However, the place of Confucianism in the revival of traditional learning was not always secure and unchallenged.[68] In the post–May Fourth period, national studies developed into an intellectual field stressing a "scientific" understanding of the past and the possibility of finding a Chinese national identity in ancient texts. To the iconoclastic intellectuals such as the anti-Confucian historian Gu Jiegang, who also worked briefly at Xiada, Dirlik observes that the study of the ancient past was "not to negate the nation but to establish it on firmer modern grounds." This distinct impulse spoke to a fundamental contradiction in recent Chinese history between the urgency to modernize China based on Western models and the anxiety over the loss of cultural autonomy. Interestingly, the development of national studies paralleled Lim's efforts to reformulate Confucianism in colonial Singapore and bring it to China.

These coexisting elements converged in the educational philosophy that Lim assembled at Xiada. Aimed at producing young men in the model of "the Chuntze" (*junzi*), which Lim considered to be the equivalent of the "educated gentlemen" in Britain or "heroes and knights" in the age of European chivalry, his ideal of the modern Chinese was steeped in Confucian teachings, Western knowledge, and devoted to the "revival of national culture."[69] At a ceremony commemorating the birthday of Confucius on October 3, 1926, that preceded the famous attack by Lu Xun, Lim gave a lecture to the attending students and staff on the subject, "Are the teachings of Confucius applicable today?"[70] Alluding to the May Fourth–inspired attacks, Lim told the audience that "what was meant by the doctrine of 'respect the ruler' [*zunjun*] was completely different from the 'imperialism' that people oppose and reject today." Moreover, recent ideologies in the West, such as the idea that "universal love" must start from the family, echoed the Confucian precepts of filial piety and family as the basis of society, suggesting that Confucianism could also be understood as a universal philosophy. To him, the answer to the question "are the teachings of Confucius applicable today?" was resoundingly affirmative.[71]

Yet Lim's defense of Confucianism had a jarring effect on faculty and students seeking new knowledge. Lim had first imported Confucian values to help the babas in colonial Singapore develop a progressive Chinese identity. Not only did he reimport them to the land of Confucius; he did so at a time when Confucian thought was coming under serious attack. Lim did not see the need to reject Confucian culture, as previously shown, but he had to defend it through an interpreter because he was not confident in addressing the students and faculty in Mandarin. To them, many were unimpressed that their leader was an English-speaking, inferior copy of a Confucian culture in China that had become obsolete, but who still insisted on telling them how to be Chinese.

This conflict was apparent in Lu Xun's public criticism of the Confucian revival at Xiada and his subsequent departure in 1927. Citing "illness" in order to obtain a quick release from employment, Lu's resignation aroused suspicions that a power struggle involving an aide to Lim Boon Keng had pushed him out. Within weeks, a futile student movement to retain Lu grew into large-scale protests demanding university reform and, once again, the removal of Lim from the university presidency. It was accompanied by a student strike that lasted several months, a phenomenon that was said to be previously unseen in South China and that drew heavy condemnation from the Xiada founder Tan Kah Kee. Without trying to clarify the rumors, Lu Xun had left Xiamen to take up the position of dean of the arts at Sun Yat-sen University in Guangzhou. In a letter written to the Beijing literary magazine *Yusi*, Lu called Lim "a Chinese of British nationality who could not open or shut his mouth without the word 'Confucius.'" These events made Lim a target of criticism among Chinese Communist historians after 1949.

At the same time, Lim has been an object of rescue in the overseas Chinese scholarship since the 1980s, particularly around a study and translation of the classical verse *Li Sao* that Lim published in 1929, originally written by the ancient poet Qu Yuan (c. 338–288 B.C.E.). Drawing on a 1955 interview conducted by Lian Shisheng, Bi Guanhua, the writer of a short biography of Lim in 1985, suggests that Lim had begun the work on *Li Siao* earlier than the encounter with Lu Xun, but it was also because of a slight over his lack of Chinese culture:

> I asked Mr. Lim why he translated *Li Sao*. He told me that when he was [about to become] the president of Xiada, someone ridiculed him for

being a baba and said that he could not have known anything about culture. If he was to continue to make a living in Nanyang, he would not have cared about anyone who ridiculed him. However, at that time, he was going to become the president of Xiada. The word "baba" felt like a cast of hot iron, hurting him a great deal.... [Later,] he asked a friend what was supposed to be the most difficult to learn in China's ancient classics. He was told, in all of Chinese literature, the most difficult was poetry, and in all of ancient Chinese poetry, the most difficult was *Li Sao*. Therefore he was determined to study it thoroughly and became more and more interested as his study went on.[72]

In recent Singapore historiography, sympathetic accounts like this one stress that the painful experience of being denigrated as a baba caused Lim to take up the study of *Li Sao*.[73] Another biography of Lim by Khor Eng Hee describes him as tragically caught in the changing times of May Fourth China, "An aging man, Lim Boon Keng had become an obsolete figure.... How could a pure-hearted and honest third-generation overseas person of Chinese descent withstand such a cruel trial?"

Nevertheless, Lim's elaborate study of the *Li Sao* also suggests that he remained steadfastly committed to a Confucian revival. Critically acclaimed by the British sinologist Herbert A. Giles and the Bengali poet Rabindranath Tagore, Lim calls the work "the outcome of a 'labor of love,' undertaken with the understanding that the best scholars have unanimously declared *Li Sao* to be the most elegant and difficult work in Chinese literature." While he painted Qu Yuan, who was remembered in the classics as a loyal minister to the King of the Chu, as "a true Confucian" and a "refreshingly modern" inspiration, Lim spoke defiantly against the attacks on Chinese traditions:

China has need today of a patriot like Ch'ü Yüan [Qu Yuan]. A man of principle is wanted to stop all lies and shams, and to tell the crowd to do honest work and not to think of clamoring for the moon, before they can stand up and walk.... Though circumstances have changed, the spiritual conditions of existence remain fundamentally the same. Organic life is an endless chain of kaleidoscopic essentials. Therefore, while China is today in throes of the birth of democracy, it does not mean that the lessons of her past are devoid of meaning or value. In fact, loyalty is even more important in a democracy, because without fidelity among the people, no leader will be trusted. Without confidence, there can be no union. Without cooperation, no real republic can exist. Therefore, this ancient tract still has great ethical value in these days when ideals are in the melting pot.[74]

Lim's depiction of Qu Yuan could be juxtaposed with Lu Xun's critique of the neo-Confucianists in 1926 discussed at the beginning of this chapter. A model for those "without the least desire for reward or recognition, in spite of popular misunderstanding, criticism, or attack," Qu Yuan in Lim's mind was fiercely loyal to Chinese values and traditions. Despite "an endless chain of kaleidoscopic essentials," the spirit that Lim discovered in Qu Yuan transcended time and space to reunite with the ancient Chinese past. This desire for a cultural reintegration was not only basic to Lim's revivalism and marked his contribution to the recent resurgence of Confucianism in China and overseas.

Given the scholarly focus on the contretemps between Lim Boon Keng and Lu Xun, it is worth contemplating how the quest for modernity through education intimately connected May Fourth China and colonial Southeast Asia. Despite their different backgrounds, Lu and Lim were brought together by the creation of a university in emigrant-sending Fujian by the overseas Chinese industrialist Tan Kah Kee. Just as universities became a hallmark of progress and sites of cultural debate in China, Lu Xun reacted to a revived Confucianism at Xiada similar to the trends he saw in Beijing, to which Lim Boon Keng responded by saying that Tan Kah Kee was a fine example of Lu Xun's "busybodies."[75] Although Xiada was, for most of its early history as a private university, embroiled in student unrest and academic struggles, its greatest challenge was financial. While fund-raising efforts in Southeast Asia to sustain the operation of Xiada had never been as successful as Tan had hoped, the heaviest blow came during the Great Depression, which almost wiped out Tan's business wealth in Singapore.[76] In the following years, the acute financial crisis facing Xiada prompted Lim to voluntarily stop drawing a salary, to make personal donations, and to lead three fund-raising trips to Southeast Asia. From its establishment in 1921 until 1937, partly because of this financial instability, Xiada was only able to produce a total of 571 graduates.[77] In the spring of 1937, on the eve of the Japanese invasion, Tan handed over the stewardship of Xiada to the Guomindang government.[78]

Finally, the outbreak of war disrupted an era of connected transformation between the coastal regions of China and Southeast Asia in the twentieth century, a sharp turn that could be seen in the story of Lim Boon Keng after his return to Singapore in 1937. After Britain declared war on Nazi Germany in 1939, Lim called for Chinese who were British subjects to donate funds and join the voluntary corps, while also reminding them of the duty owed to the ancestral homeland in the resistance against Japan.[79] After Singapore was captured by the Japanese on February 15, 1942, Lim was arrested and became head of the puppet Overseas Chinese Association. Put in charge of 250 members, Lim was appointed to collect a "donation" of fifty million Straits dollars from Chinese across Malaya to demonstrate loyalty to the Japanese occupation. A practical measure to strip Southeast Asian Chinese of their economic power, the order was also an act of punishment because many including Tan Kah Kee had so fiercely led an anti-Japanese movement on China's behalf since the late 1920s.[80] During February and March 1942, the Japanese military in Singapore massacred tens of thousands of Chinese suspected of being "anti-Japanese overseas Chinese elements."[81]

Because of Lim's role as a spokesperson for the Japanese forces, he was accused of being a collaborator in postwar accounts in the People's Republic of China. Yet historian Lee Guan Kin finds that the collaboration did not happen without extreme personal agony. Drawing on oral sources from the 1980s, she writes that Lim, a man in his seventies during the occupation, spent his days acting like a madman, drinking and dancing in Singapore's Chinese clubs, uttering tearful words of guilt to those around him, and repeatedly attempting suicide.[82] At the end of the war, decolonization and independence struggles burst onto the scene after decades of anticolonial nationalist movements developing across China and Southeast Asia. Lim kept a low profile and retired from public affairs. He died in Singapore in 1957.

Conclusion

This reexamination of Lim Boon Keng's Confucian revivalism as a "diaspora moment" stresses how Western colonial expansion provided a common stage for Chinese intellectuals to mount discussions about traditional culture. Suggesting an intense dialogue with colonial power, Lim drew inspiration from social Darwinist racial thought, Victorian gender ideologies, Christian missionary discourses, Enlightenment ideals of progress, and scientific ideas of evolutionism to reinvent Confucianism as modernizing, secular, and rational. His innovations coincided with May Fourth attacks on Confucianism and with an emerging "national studies" movement in search of a modern China in the world. These connected transformations suggest an imbrication of distinct times and places. While Lim's thought was not simply an offshoot of the Confucian movement led by Kang Youwei in China, he likewise made use of globally traversing resources to assemble "authentic" Chinese traditions.

Furthermore, the meeting of Lim Boon Keng and Lu Xun suggests how assertions of Chinese culture and identity proliferated and became intertwined in the early twentieth century. Despite their disagreements over Confucianism, both men were reacting to a common existence at the fringes of empires. Lim Boon Keng was a Straits Chinese intellectual who traveled to the metropole, returned a changed man, and dedicated himself to renewing China's heritage. Lu Xun was a leading May Fourth writer radicalized by China's deepening crisis and was convinced that its people must break away from its palpable traditions to fully engage a new world. Inhabiting globally connected yet differently inflected cultural flows, both men responded to the predicament of being Chinese in an era of Western dominance. Their braided paths suggest that the intimacy between homeland and diaspora was not given, but emerged through the converging histories of modern empires and nations. In turn, these histories heavily shaped notions of traditional culture and identity in Asia.

Furthermore, Lim's revivalism helped lay the basis for a resurgent Confucianism in the late twentieth century and beyond. Since the 1980s, the figure of Lim Boon Keng has received new and significant reframings in Singapore and China. Brought back by academics and politicians, his story had slipped out of notice during an ascent of anticolonial nationalisms in postwar Southeast Asia and China. Yet, since the waning of the Cold War, the rise of neoliberal capitalism, and China's economic reforms in the early 1980s, reconnections appeared in the form of a renewed desire for an authentic yet cosmopolitan Chinese identity. From "baba" to "Chinese of British nationality" to "bicultural" to "multicultural," the figure of Lim suggests the evocativeness of a global Chinese identity rooted in the traditions of an ancestral homeland. Far from being insular and fixed, diaspora is a recurrent dialogue about Chinese connections in the world.

CHAPTER 4

The Women Who Stayed Behind

By the time the Communist Revolution came to South China in 1949, a century of mass emigration had transfigured many of the region's rural towns and villages, causing a series of surprises in the early building of socialism. In Guangdong province, as many as one in five residents belonged to a transnational *huaqiao* family in which men had moved overseas, women stayed behind, and remittances were an important source of household income. Following the late liberation of Guangdong from Nationalist rule, the new Communist Party-state adopted a hard-nosed approach to land and marriage reform that came to penalize emigration heavily. Aimed at modernizing agrarian production and the rural family, the campaigns struck hard at "overseas Chinese landlords" and "overseas Chinese marriages," igniting a far-reaching backlash. By early 1951, violent expropriations against "overseas Chinese landlords" drew a flurry of pleas from men abroad who complained that their families had fallen into "a world of terror." Similarly, the efforts to liberate domestic women from "overseas Chinese marriages" brought a wave of divorce applications and caused widespread conflicts at home and abroad. In the aftermath of rising discontent, falling remittances, and villages being emptied by a mass exodus, the Party-state was forced to roll back socialist transformation in South China. Surprisingly, it allowed huaqiao families to remain outside the socialist transition and installed the women who stayed behind as chief intermediaries between the state and emigrant men until the height of the Great Leap Forward (1958–60).

Focusing on how the early Communist Party-state reckoned with the effects of mass emigration in rural Guangdong, this chapter situates the events at the intersection of socialist construction and emigrant connections during the 1950s. In the historiography of land and marriage reform, scholars have long rejected the traditional assumption of an orderly expansion of state power across society; instead, they have found that it proceeded in fits and starts and evolved uneasily in response to local conditions.[1] Drawing on archival sources and oral history, recent research has further challenged a linear view of early Communist history. Neil Diamant finds a "bumbling" process in the implementation of the 1950 Marriage Law. Gail Hershatter observes that young rural women activists used the party language of feudalism to critique marriage practices long after "campaign time," suggesting that change occurred "not in response to a single state intervention, but over a longer, more gradual and less easily traceable shift in social interactions and mores."[2] In other words, scholars have stressed how the effects of socialist construction shunned the straight line.

Similarly, the situation in 1950s Guangdong did not fit into the picture of a linear time and unified space, but indicated interaction between different temporalities of human action. Even though most of the country had already been under firm control, the Communist liberation of Guangdong—three weeks after the establishment of the People's Republic of China in October 1949—brought particularly acute conflicts during the land and marriage reforms. This is because, with its distinctly intricate links with emigrant families and overseas communities, Guangdong became a high security concern during the final suppression of Guomindang forces and the simultaneous outbreak of the Korean War (1950–53).[3] This confluence of events prompted the Party-state to abandon a moderate approach to class struggle, provoking immediate protests from overseas Chinese men whose family members in China were branded as "landlords." After the war, as the Party-state became increasingly interested in channeling overseas Chinese remittances toward the building of a self-sufficient economy, officials tried to limit the liberation of women from feudal "overseas Chinese marriages" and scrutinized their functions in the emigrant family. In both instances, the central government and local cadres were actively engaging conditions created by mass emigration in rural Guangdong, suggesting that socialist transformation during the 1950s did not develop in isolation but emerged from a continuous negotiation with transnational networks and resources.

Until recently, the gender of migration has been neglected in the historical study of the overseas Chinese and South China. Contrary to a common view that emigration threatened lineage development, scholars have found that the two reinforced each other through the sharing of remittances and kinship networks through chain migration.⁴ This mutual connection helps explain the unique presence of many powerful, tightly knit lineages in Guangdong and Fujian provinces, areas historically well known for emigration. It also calls special attention to the role of gender, given that most emigrants were traditionally men. Women, with few exceptions, and especially during anti-Chinese exclusion in many settler nations after the 1880s, remained in the home villages. Focusing on the Guan lineage in Kaiping, one of Guangdong's emigrant Four Counties (*siyi*), Yuen-fong Woon argues that many resident women supplemented the remittance income with farming and wage labor, adopted male children in the absence of heirs, and handled the earnings of their overseas husbands, making some of them de facto heads of their households.⁵ In Taishan, another of the Four Counties, Madeline Hsu finds that women in split-household families faced many pressures that came with long separations, but the women also enabled many such groups to endure through mutual support and generational transfer of responsibilities.⁶ More recently, Huifen Shen's work on "left-behind wives" demonstrates how women in southern Fujian actively pursued personal and familial welfare in contrast to the stereotype that they were passive and dependent on their husbands abroad.⁷ Taken together, these groundbreaking studies have revised the traditional understanding of lineage, emigration, and society through a gender perspective.

Bringing together the study of the early People's Republic of China and the overseas Chinese, this chapter asks how the link between gender and emigration influenced 1950s China. I argue that the twists and turns over the question of "overseas Chinese landlords" and "overseas Chinese marriages" marked a "diaspora moment" that confounded socialist construction in the homeland. Culminating in the rise of huaqiao as a category with special privileges, the moment told of an evolving dialogue between different temporalities of development, huaqiao and socialist, each with a gender dimension. For huaqiao families, development was the cyclical continuity of the patriline. It operated by relocating male labor overseas and retaining female labor at home to ensure the accumulation and transfer of resources through the generations. By contrast, socialist development in the 1950s was a linear temporality emphasizing rupture from a feudal past and progress toward an idealized future through a division between rural agriculture and urban industrialization. The new unit of rural production was the conjugal family, not the traditional lineage, to be based on joint, not split, residence and labor. These two modes of temporalities collided during the land and marriage reforms in South China, but as central officials later sought to mobilize remittances, they also ran up against the gender of emigration. Often received and handled by the wives and mothers of overseas Chinese men, remittances had helped balance China's international payments in the early twentieth century and could serve the urgent needs of socialist building in the present.[8] As a U.S.-led international embargo on Communist China and Cold War struggles widened across the 1950s, the Party-state became convinced that attacking huaqiao family practices could end up destabilizing socialism.

The result was a tentative creation of huaqiao families as a special group outside of socialist time and women who stayed behind as intermediaries, contributing to an important fracture in early socialism. To remedy the attacks during the land and marriage reforms, the Party-state announced in late 1953 that huaqiao families were now free to receive remittances and make private investments, would be given higher rations of basic necessities and access to scarce goods, and would be licensed to engage in "feudal" consumption. These efforts marked the transformation of huaqiao into "a special category," an unusual development described by Glen Peterson in a recent study.[9] As a centerpiece of this strategy, women were told to refrain from divorce, join agricultural production, but also "strive for remittances" by maintaining harmony with their husbands abroad. These efforts grew from the premise that this special status of huaqiao was temporary and aimed toward reintegration, while the women who stayed behind could bridge the gap between an imperfect present and a unified future. A means to reintegrate the dispersed times and spaces because of mass emigration, these efforts helped establish socialism as a universal and permanent project. But it also implied a deferral of larger goals, demanded substantial accommodations, and was a constant reminder of the incompleteness of socialism. In other words, the ongoing history of mass emigration demanded a flexible approach, but a flexible approach could also threaten the integrity of socialism.

Based on official documents from the Guangdong provincial and Guangzhou city archives that no scholars have discussed at length, the following is a combined analysis of land and marriage reform in rural Guangdong. These archival sources do not allow piecing together a complete picture of the campaigns and the firsthand experiences of huaqiao families, but they do afford a rare glimpse into how party cadres understood and responded to the shifting conflicts on the ground, causing a sequence of speed-ups, slowdowns, and do-overs. This reading strategy permits me to draw out the stress points between the two orders, huaqiao and socialist, which converged over the role of women. As for terminology, two different terms were used in the reports to refer to resident members of huaqiao families. In the discussions on the land reform, they were generally known as *qiaojuan*, a term emphasizing economic dependence on huaqiao men abroad. Consisting not only of wives but also elderly parents, children, and other relatives supported by huaqiao men, qiaojuan came to represent households in rural Guangdong that were most targeted during class struggle and in subsequent efforts to restore production and that were mostly headed by women. Another term, *qiaofu*, was used during the marriage reform to mean the wives of huaqiao men. Their gender was highlighted to reflect membership in another Party-state category, "woman" (*funü*), an object to be liberated from feudal patriarchy.[10] At the same time, their marriage to overseas men, represented by the *qiao* in qiaofu, was underscored to typify emigrant practices first understood as backward but later as essential to the advancement of socialism. Representing the women who stayed behind, qiaojuan and qiaofu were thus gendered facets of an acute conflict between huaqiao and socialist temporalities in 1950s China.

Land Reform

To the party cadres conducting land reform, South China appeared to be a distinctly backward space compared to the rest of rural China, since feudalism there was "not only rampant, but also extreme." Noting the mass emigration of men and the unusual amount of wealth in the rural towns and villages, officials found that "overseas Chinese landlords" owned and rented out large tracts of land, hired labor, lent money, ran businesses, and seldom engaged in farming. Men were typically absent because they had moved overseas or to the city, or came back at an unproductive old age after spending decades working abroad. Though sons sometimes stayed behind, the wives and daughters-in-law were more commonly in residence. Led by these observations, the land reform in South China provoked a serious conflict with transnational dimensions. Letters came pouring from local residents and overseas Chinese men and organizations, complaining of expropriations, extortions, and violence against family members and fellow villagers branded as overseas Chinese landlords. The letters and corresponding investigations offer a glimpse into the explosive conflict between a socialist ideal and a huaqiao practice: the former penalized a household's disproportionate ownership of land relative to size of household and its contribution of agricultural labor; the latter allocated a household's labor power transnationally according to age and gender. The conflict suggests how local and overseas actors negotiated their place in the new order, as the party drove a wedge into the rural economy by separating "huaqiao" and "peasants."

Letters to the Authorities

The following discussion draws on archival records in Taishan county, where land reform began in May 1951. One of the most spectacular examples of rural prosperity in Guangdong, Taishan county was nicknamed "Little Canton" after the famous provincial capital and international port city. By the 1920s, Taishan had boasted a land-owning middle class, more than a hundred schools, and hundreds more businesses including department stores and a movie theater.[11] By the end of 1953, land reform brought more than five hundred petitions from residents and emigrants, a group making up 35 percent of the county's population.[12] While the pleas commonly expressed shock and dismay at the campaign, two broad patterns were discernible in the tactics of negotiation. One set of petitioners stressed the nonpolitical nature of their activities to downplay class antagonisms. They claimed adherence to patriarchal and Confucian virtues and portrayed themselves as hardworking conservatives who had steered clear of trouble. The second set of petitions was boldly political. They pointed out lawless, arbitrary cases in which peasants ignored central regulations protecting overseas Chinese property in the villages and instead confiscated and tortured. Some writers came close to criticizing the failure of the new government to guarantee basic order. Others appealed to the Communist Party's anti-imperialist, anticapitalist stance by stressing their own exploitation in the West. Four examples of "overseas Chinese landlords" in the archives appeared instructive: Liao Xuanguang (United States), Ye Dashen (United States), C. K. Sheen (Burma), and Li Yihua (Cuba).

The first two examples belong to the group adopting traditional moral tactics to modulate class tensions. In the case of Liao Xuanguang, two of his sons living in the United States wrote to county officials about the mistreatment of their father and wives: "Our father Liao Xuanguang has always handled worldly affairs with a peaceful disposition and has a strong belief in justice.... Now suddenly little men [*xiaoren*] dominated the village and wreaked havoc. They denounced our father and extorted a large sum of over 313 million RMB. They also made our wives suffer various abuses, oppressed them bitterly, and held them in confinement. Such a tragedy is appalling."[13] Invoking the classic trope of "little men" scheming against virtuous men in the Confucian tradition, Liao's sons pleaded that officials visit to conduct an investigation, "so as to end the havoc and pacify the hearts of the people." Two other letters submitted by Liao Xuanguang's brother and grandson in the United States stressed that Liao spent decades working abroad before returning home in old age and poor health, thereby appealing to the patriarchal values of respect for the old, protection of the weak, and filial piety.[14] According to the Liaos, class struggle not only upset their household economy spanning three generations and extending from Taishan to the United States, but also signaled a collapse of the moral order. A similar tactic could be seen in the case of Ye Dashen, who had lived in the United States for almost five decades and had recently returned to live in Guangzhou city. His family remaining in Taishan was handed an 11 million yuan fine that had to be paid within two days. Writing in his own defense, Ye stressed that he had tried to live a honorable life and avoid politics: "For the seventy-seven years [of my life], I have devoted myself to farming and have not handled any affairs in the village. I own a house and a piece of land measuring about five *mu*,[15] which I bought with hard-earned money while working in the U.S. For many decades, I was never involved in any conflict.... I have always helped others and did not engage in exploitation."[16] Enclosed with Ye's plea was an autobiographical sketch chronicling the major events and accomplishments in his life. His example reflected a broader pattern of self-portrayals by victims who maintained that they were honest in character and had never been guilty of any political or interpersonal conflicts in the past. The latter implied a common belief that meddling in power politics would leave one open to retribution, which some petitioners thought had motivated the violence of the land reform.

Another set of letters tried to engage the authorities in political terms. Contesting a massive fine imposed by the peasants' association, a man in the lumber business in Burma named C. K. Sheen (Zhu Jishen) complained that specific regulations protecting the properties of "huaqiao landlords" were ignored. Promulgated in November 1950 to complement the Agrarian Reform Law of June 1950 with reference to huaqiao households, the "Regulations for the Handling of *Huaqiao* Land and Properties during Land Reform" stated that the land of huaqiao landlords should be reallocated but protected their houses and other forms of private property from confiscation.[17] On the contrary, Sheen wrote, the peasants' association hectored huaqiao families by "administering bodily harm," "calling women and children bullies," and "demanding a staggering sum of money." Noting widespread lawlessness and a breakdown of central authority, he even speculated that infiltration by Chiang Kai-shek's Guomingdang forces might have been the cause.[18] Sheen's son, Zhu Yanxiong, who had recently returned from Burma, lodged a similar complaint about the peasants' association. He claimed that it was not headed by those who were exploited, but by "bullies" and "thugs" who were turning Taishan into a "world of terror."[19]

Although most pleas from abroad were sent on behalf of family members at home, they were sometimes submitted collectively by overseas Chinese associations on behalf of fellow villagers, suggesting that some organizations saw it as their role to seek political redress. One example was the Taishan Tielukang Village Association in Havana, Cuba, which entered a complaint on behalf of Li Yihua, the son of a fellow huaqiao. According to news sent from the village, association leaders wrote that Li and his wife were subjected to public trials, beaten, forced to kneel on the ground covered with stones, and given a large fine of nearly six million yuan to be paid within forty days. Declaring that they had welcomed the Communist liberation of China, the leaders wrote that the senseless attacks caused them to question the party's promise to "protect the rightful interests of *huaqiao*" and build a new China.[20] Calling the violence an "excess" and urging a fair trial for Li Yihua, the letter writers beseeched the government to act immediately to restore the confidence of the people.

In other cases, individuals tried to engage party officials in a political language about U.S. imperialism and capitalism. Claiming that he had "toiled like cattle and horses as a hired laborer," one emigrant wrote that the pains of living in a "cruel capitalist society governed by American imperialism" could not be adequately told. Saying that he bought a piece of land and built a house in the home village not to exploit others, but to rely upon in retirement, he urged the new government to honor its promise of protecting huaqiao and allow him to keep his property.

Stopping short of attacking Communist policies, the examples above were nonetheless sharp commentary on the land reform in progress and sought to redefine emigration as an arduous and dignified undertaking that should be shielded from class struggle. Provoked by the interpretation of family wealth as a sign of exploitation, the diverse rhetorical strategies in the letters suggest that the petitioners did not comprehend what the socialist agenda for them was, but strongly felt that they, as huaqiao, had a right to voice their opposition to injustices. Downplaying class tensions, many claimed close observance of Confucian and patriarchal virtues and a lack of interest in politics, exhibiting the exact qualities that would make them seem "oppressive" and "feudal" in socialist terms. Others implored the government to remedy the ineptitude of peasant associations and a slippage in the commitment to defend huaqiao interests. Their dissenting voices contrasted with the Communist Party's goals in the land reform—to dismantle traditional structures of power and modernize the agrarian system.

Local Investigations

The cries of injustice prompted local inquiry into the treatment of huaqiao families in Taishan. However, instead of dispatching independent examiners to the villages, provincial and county authorities simply passed the cases to land reform work teams and peasants' associations. Thus, the task of investigation ended up precisely in the hands of those accused of causing the abuses. Since the disputes inevitably called into question the authority of the new power holders who had led the campaign, the reports represent their efforts to stake a claim to the socialist order when that of the huaqiao remained loosely defined. Their counterstrategies consisted of hewing closely to the standard language of class struggle and maintaining that the struggle sessions were lawful, torture nonexistent, and the conclusions correct. As one peasants' association reported on the case of Liao Xuanguang: "[Liao] could be considered a power holder. Because he was rich, he often connived with bureaucrats and lawyers to bring lawsuits against the masses, and he often won the cases. He went abroad for thirty or forty years, and returned to the village at age sixty. In April 1952, during the land reform, he died of illness. We struggled against him several times and against his two daughters-in-law.... We demanded a compensation of 313 million yuan, but only received 22,970,000 yuan in reality."[21] Similar accounts of overseas Chinese landlords stressed that they were feudal, reactionary oppressors perpetrating "cruel exploitation of the peasants" and "monopolizing power." The report on the case of Li Yihua found that Li was a "bureaucratic comprador" who embezzled the remittances of other families by "setting up a fake village organization of food supplies" and using a youth association as "a front for a gambling and smoking den." Just before Liberation, Li was said to have colluded with the county head to assist anti-Communist forces. After Liberation, he was heard saying to the peasants, "Chiang Kai-shek asked us to be patient for another year."[22] In these accounts, overseas Chinese landlords abused public funds, engaged in seedy operations, and connived with Guomindang forces. In rare discussions of physical altercation, investigators portrayed the victims as despicable enemies staging a pathetic resistance or mocking the leadership of the peasants. In other words, class struggle was maintained as a universal policy, under which huaqiao landlords were to be brought in line just like other landlords.

Another line of argument in the reports emphasized that production required agricultural labor be bound to the village, making it impossible to discuss emigrant practices that did not conform to such a model. Given the official principle of "land to the tillers," "*huaqiao* landlords" were penalized for their lack of full participation in local farming but active engagement in commercial activities including the hiring of labor, landowning, and the making of loans and leases. This interpretation had the effect of effacing the productive labor undertaken by men overseas, as in the report on the family of the U.S. huaqiao Ye Dashen: "The family farmed their land for seven years but did not participate in the principal labor. They only participated in auxiliary labor. Half of the land was farmed by hired labor. For the remaining half, the owner was only responsible for supplying seeds and fertilizer. All the rest of the farm work was carried out by hired labor. All fruits of labor were turned over to the owner."[23] Claiming that "rent exploitation" constituted the main source of household income, the report did not mention whether other household members participated in labor overseas. This silence over the role of production overseas and its possible contribution to the household indicated that the primary objective of the land reform was to liberate and equalize local forces of production. As the formula for class status conveniently left out transnational factors, it is ironic that crimes of local exploitation often had to be redeemed with money earned abroad. Complaints submitted by emigrant men frequently mentioned the letters and telegrams sent by frantic wives and daughters-in-law, asking for massive funds to settle fines and obtain release from imprisonment.

The ambiguity of huaqiao production in the class struggle sometimes led to the assignment of blame to the women who stayed behind in the villages. One example can be seen in a lengthy response from the land reform work team and peasants' association in one district in Taishan. Published in the official provincial newspaper, *Nanfang Ribao*, on December 28, 1951, the open letter of reply addressed the plea submitted by Zhu Yanxiong on behalf of his father and Burma huaqiao Zhu Jishen (a.k.a. C. K. Sheen). Stating that Zhu Jishen was one of the largest landlords in the district, who owned and rented out thirteen *shi* of farmland, the report said that he was a huaqiao capitalist who got rich by investing in the lumber industry in Burma more than ten years before, while his wife, Chen Genghao, stayed in the village. Noting a conversation overheard by a committee member of the peasants' association, Zhu Shujian, who used to be one of Chen's hired laborers, Zhu Jishen had asked Chen after buying up a lot of farmland whether she could manage if he did not send any money home. Chen told him not to worry, suggesting to the peasants' association that she was responsible for overseeing matters in the household.[24] Said to have exploited house servants, Chen was also condemned for being a cunning landlord who lied about the land farmed by hired labor and the actual size of her household: "This year, before the arrival of the land reform work team, she tricked [hired laborer] Zhu Shujian and changed the 1.05 *shi* of land that he was hired to farm to [pretend that it was her household's] self-farming land. In fact, Zhu Shujian was still responsible for all the labor. [Chen] also moved her grandchildren and her son Zhu Yanxiong's whole family back to the village, in order to appear like a larger household and trick the government into changing their class status." Aside from her "trickery," Chen was proven guilty because she was illiterate and once had Zhu Shujian help her read a letter. In the letter, her son in Burma consulted her about returning to the home village to start a soy sauce business using the gold stashed away in the ancestral house. This showed that Chen "owned the gold" and "so she was being held by the peasants' association," said the report.[25] This focus on local practices made Chen a convenient target because she was captive to the land reform. As both her husband and son were absent, the campaign held her accountable for her alleged aversion to agricultural labor, oppression of laborers, and power over family assets. Additionally, her illiteracy and use of hired men gave away important information about the household. As resident women were more likely to be in charge of emigrant households, Chen's position in the class struggle was made more vulnerable because of her gender.

Apart from highlighting the gender of emigration, the negative repercussions of the land reform beyond South China reveal a transnational dimension of the problem. Alienating expatriated men whose families were branded as "*huaqiao* landlords" in the home village, the land reform provided instant fodder for anticommunist propaganda during the Cold War. Many sensational and lurid accounts, some directed by the Guomindang, sprang from a common fear that the Communists were running roughshod over the families of the overseas Chinese.[26] A three-part book series published in Hong Kong in 1952, *The History of Blood and Tears of the Overseas Chinese Home Village of Taishan: A Documentation of Chinese Communist Atrocities*, portrayed Taishan's transformation into a living hell under a corrupt and bloodthirsty regime that tortured, looted, raped, and killed—a horrid image recalling Japan's invasion of China (1937–45).[27] A Taishan native who had fled to Hong Kong, the author wrote that he received death threats from the Communists and a permit to enter Taiwan from the GMD government after the publication of the first two parts of the series.

The damaging effects of the land reform on overseas Chinese support were not only ideological but also material. Immediately, a severe drop in remittances was reported across South China. In Taishan, official statistics from the Taishan People's Bank recorded a 2.8-fold increase in remittances from 1950 to 1951, most likely resulting from the large fines imposed during the land reform. In 1952, the amount fell by 32 percent. The usually higher volume of remittances around the Chinese New Year also dropped nearly 36 percent.[28] Facing the setbacks of rising discontent and falling remittances, the central government became concerned with the long-term impact on overseas Chinese support and national stability and began to seek other ways to carry out socialist construction.

Central Initiatives

The backlash to the land reform revealed to the Party-state that rural South China was a nexus of transnational flows, forcing it to recalibrate its agenda. Emerging from the forays of class struggle was a new understanding that the region's rural landscapes had long been entangled in emigrant networks, that women were important conduits, and that overseas Chinese support for socialism could be won or lost. Manifest in the engagement of emigrant men and resident women, the synchronicity of rural South China with the world beyond caused the Party-state to begin delineating ways to accommodate the "distinct character" (*teshu xing*) of huaqiao families. Until full reintegration was possible, it seemed appropriate to "look after" (*zhaogu*) huaqiao and guide them toward socialism. However, it should be recognized that such an accommodation was motivated not only by huaqiao's distinctiveness but also by the appeal of huaqiao support and remittances. The prospects of powering socialist projects through a large and steady inflow of foreign exchange made it expedient for the Party-state to open a temporary space for huaqiao families to be free from intervention. In fact, the following series of do-overs was partly because the permanent system that the Party-state urged huaqiao to transition into had not yet been formed, and it wanted their help to complete the transformation.

In early 1953, the first set of central initiatives was announced to review the treatment of huaqiao households in Guangdong, though top leaders had learned of the conflicts by the fall of 1951. Estimating that as many as one-fifth of the households had been "wrongly struggled against" (*cuodou*) and "wrongly harmed" (*cuoshang*) and one-fourth of the "landlords" wrongly classified, the central government, having waited until the land reform was officially over, announced that it would correct the "errors" and "excesses" of the campaign.[29] In two public speeches in 1953, Liao Chengzhi, one of the most prominent figures of the Central Overseas Chinese Commission, spoke about the review as it unfolded in Guangdong. In January, he admitted that "hasty" implementation had caused the land reform to "stray" off course, but this was largely the same observation that he had made in 1951. By November, he found a situation worse than expected. Of the 6.4 million qiaojuan living in Guangdong, he reported that 5 percent had been classified as "landlords" but that only one-fourth of them had been classified correctly, making up only 1.25 percent of the total dependents. Seeking to contain the situation, Liao attributed such widespread error to "a deep hatred of peasants who had long suffered feudal oppression," "the infiltration of reactionary landlords into peasant associations," "impure work teams," "inadequate mobilization of peasants," and "an incomplete grasp of the real conditions in the villages."³⁰ Execution, rather than intent, was the crux of the problem.

Nonetheless, at least one other issue seemed pertinent: If so many huaqiao households had been wrongly classified before, how might they be correctly classified now? The new directives maintained a complex set of distinctions. The most important one was feudal exploitation versus capitalist exploitation. The central government asserted that the land reform only penalized the former—the exploitation of poor peasants by occupying large tracts of land in the village—keeping off limits "capitalist exploitation," meaning profits obtained from engaging in industry and commerce abroad. This distinction relied on a clear separation of exploitation between home and abroad, feudal and capitalist.

However, this new distinction was immediately contradicted by two other criteria used to determine correct class status. One was whether the huaqiao was "an overseas Chinese laborer" (*qiaogong*) while abroad, and hence considered "exploited" in the home context, even though the exploitation would have been "capitalist" in nature and occurred overseas. In addition, if the huaqiao owned a small business abroad but performed most of the labor himself or with family members, he was not an "overseas Chinese merchant" (*qiaoshang*), but an "overseas Chinese laborer." The latter distinction drew a line between status before and status after emigration. If the huaqiao landowner had been a laborer before emigration, he would not be classified as a "landlord." If the amount of land owned did not exceed the local average among small landlords, the official class status was "overseas Chinese laborer," and if the land exceeded the average only by a small amount, "small land lessor" (*xiao tudi chuzu zhe*).³¹ Only those who had exceeded a higher limit of landholding would be classified as "landlords." Taken together, such attempts to draw out the "social background and labor power abroad" (*guowai chengfen he laodong li*) of huaqiao households was meant to elicit a fuller picture of those that had been lumped together as landlords, but the distinctions between feudal/capitalist, home/abroad, and before emigration/after emigration could be mutually contradictory and nearly impossible to ascertain.

The layers of complexity in determining the class status of an emigrant household illustrated the pitfalls of measuring an enormously flexible family strategy against a rigid understanding of rural China. With some differentiation among landlord, peasant, and laborer, the land reform had projected the view of an insular countryside awaiting liberation. But what officials kept encountering were families that were at once living at home and elsewhere, integrated in production, and highly commercialized. The maintenance of distinctions in the land reform review obscured how huaqiao abroad were socially diverse and changeable over time, and how the split activities came to reinforce each other. Emigrants were farmers and farm owners, street hawkers and shopkeepers, factory workers and factory owners. Their earnings and savings cycled back to support a range of commercial activities in the home village—buying land, hiring labor, and making loans and leases—not only to serve the future of the multigenerational collective but also to provide individuals with the possible benefit of return for retirement. Seen this way, the land reform review was an uncertain exercise to reify emigrant exchanges that had been circulatory and staggered.

Searching for a middle course, the Party-state began to articulate "special consideration" toward huaqiao households, the greatest concern being the loss of overseas Chinese support and remittances. In addition to the measures outlined above, the Party-state announced that confiscated houses that had not yet been reallocated should be returned and collections of outstanding grain surpluses should be discontinued. An assistance fund of fifty million RMB was provided to help families in hardship.[32] In addition, those whose status remained "*huaqiao* landlords" and "*huaqiao* rich peasants" should be reclassified as peasants "ahead of schedule" before their terms of labor reform expired.[33] Most importantly, the government reaffirmed its commitment to protecting remittances as a legitimate source of family income and prohibiting local infringement of any form. Besides banning uses that would constitute outright exploitation, such as speculation, hoarding, and high-interest money lending, the central government declared that huaqiao households should be as free as they had been to spend remittances on private investment and consumption including weddings, funerals, education, and the hiring of labor. On the participation in geomancy and folk religions such as *fengshui* and *gongde*, Liao Chengzhi remarked that "feudal superstition" among huaqiao families would have to be superseded by a "long period of patient education" rather than terminated by force. His point highlighted the function of a temporary concession to phase out contradictions between contemporaneous agendas.

Besides sorting out the land reform, central officials tried to refocus energies on production, in which the women who stayed behind were assigned a new role. Beginning in 1953, rural production meetings and forums targeting qiaojuan were organized across the province. In Taishan county, about four hundred qiaojuan attended one such meeting in January 1954, during which they were urged to join agricultural production and strive for remittances. Assuming that qiaojuan "depended primarily or secondarily on the labor power overseas," officials told the attendees that "labor is glorious" and "eating all day without doing any work is shameful." Recognizing that "qiaojuan have their own special characteristics," officials said that the Party-state had sufficiently demonstrated "care" and "concern" for them during the land reform review. Now that qiaojuan had *fanshen*ed, they should "unite with the peasants," contribute to agricultural production, and "abandon the misguided idea" that "there is no other way to make a living but to go overseas."[34] Here, abandoning emigration in favor of farming would have been straightforward if the women were not also goaded to "strive for remittances." At the meeting, officials asked them to reassure family members abroad that life in the village had gone "back to normal," hence it was time to resume sending money home. Even though remittances were funds "obtained under or through capitalist exploitation abroad," officials restated the central directive that remittances earned overseas "should not be used as a criterion to determine class status" domestically. By drawing a firm boundary between home and abroad, officials avoided discussing the implications of seeking "capitalist" resources for socialist construction.

The potential contradiction was painted over by official accounts of model behavior after the meeting, all of which were rendered in the voices of qiaojuan women. In these celebratory narratives, initial misunderstanding caused by the land reform was dissolved by party benevolence and qiaojuan self-transformation, ending in unity between the two sides. Reclassified as a "poor peasant" during the land reform review, Mei Huan said that her family of eight was allocated more than ten *mu* of land and she was more than relieved that the "rice jar" of her household, which had been "placed in the U.S. for decades," was now "stored right at home" and "as sturdy as Mount Tai." With her new commitments to frugality and production, Mei declared that her family "would not have to fear going hungry" even if remittances were interrupted.[35] Another story narrated by Li Jinlan laid the blame for the errors of the land reform on "reactionary rich peasants" and cadres who "did not have a good grasp of the policies." Wrongly struggled against, Li now understood it was not the peasants' fault. Instead, because of the "care" of Chairman Mao, she "became determined to unite with the peasant brothers" to improve production and urged other qiaojuan to do the same.[36] Exonerating central intentions, these first-person accounts proclaimed that the problems of the land reform had been corrected by "serious," "concerned," and "receptive" cadres sent directly from the party center. With the repatriation of the "rice jar," state officials portrayed a liberation welcomed by qiaojuan women who had lived uncertain lives dependent on overseas support. Calling upon others to work alongside their "peasant brothers," these female voices embraced a socialist vision of self-reliant modernity, rooted in labor, frugality, a unity of peasant men and qiaojuan women under the "care" and "concern" of party leadership.

Contrary to the triumphant accounts, a series of internal reports in Taishan during 1953–55 suggest that the central directives succeeded in lowering the class status of most huaqiao households, but might also have unleashed new forces that marginalized them. Newly dispossessed by the land reform, many had lost their properties, did not have the means or skills to grow food, or were not given the land that a lowered class status should have provided them. Some also lost the support of remittances because their family members overseas were still reacting to the shock of the land reform or faced new restrictions on sending them from the countries where they lived. In one example, one woman's husband was a laundryman in the United States. Downgraded from huaqiao "landlord" to "laborer" and given one portion of land, she and her son did not have any farm tools or supplies and had not received any remittances since the land reform. They were so poor that they had to use a hemp bag as a sleeping blanket and take a door down to use as a table.[37]

Stories of extreme poverty were a common thread in the reports. In some villages, qiaojuan even lost the portions of land that they tilled. In other villages, all huaqiao households, rich or poor, were "allocated one less portion of land" than others.[38] In one example, twenty-four of fifty-six households in one village, nearly half of them, were in this situation. Blaming peasants who had a "strong economic motive to profit" (*youshui jingji guandian zhong*) and "impure" (*buchun*) low-level cadres who failed to have a firm grasp of central policies, officials wrote that they took advantage of qiaojuan by seizing for themselves more than they should have.[39] But it was clear that the land reform had helped create a new bias that huaqiao families had little need for land because they had always depended on remittances, lacked labor power, or despised farming.[40] One elderly couple who had been supported by a grandson in Burma was not given any land. Since it became difficult to send remittances from Burma, they were going through a tough time. The wife expressed her anger: "I have to write my grandson and tell him not to come back to the village. We have no land to produce food. This is like waiting for death."[41] Another woman lived in a household of four that was classified as "overseas Chinese laborer" and received remittances only occasionally. Because she was older, the family was only allocated three portions of land. She felt discriminated against, saying, "All the people in the country have *fanshen*ed but me. Since I did not get any land, none of the [political] meetings is going to be my business. I am not going to participate."[42] These reactions among huaqiao households suggest that local relations remained tense after the land reform review.

The unresolved tensions were aggravated by the central directives to recognize the privileged status of huaqiao families and prepare local society for collectivization, creating a wide-ranging set of problems rendered by county officials as "disunity." They indicated that qiaojuan were ostracized by peasants and even by local cadres, not only in everyday interactions but in the formation of mutual aid teams, a central campaign to pool together the labor power and resources of rural households to raise agricultural productivity. Some of the excluded qiaojuan complained: "Everyone is walking down the path of socialism. Only I have no path of socialism to walk on," referring to the Party-state slogan for the campaign, "taking the path of socialism."[43] Even though many qiaojuan were suffering and no longer received remittances, leaders of a peasants' association told them, "You can take the *huaqiao* path," suggesting that the special status enjoyed by huaqiao made them incompatible with socialist transformation.[44] Some cadres were reluctant to comply with the new orders to "unite with qiaojuan" because they feared being accused of "changing their political stance," "going down the capitalist path," and "currying the favor of *qiaojuan*" because they had remittances. Personally, the cadres had also struggled against qiaojuan in the past and did not want to appear sycophantic for uniting with them now.[45] In other words, the new central directives placed local actors in a socially and politically awkward situation with regard to each other.

Revealing how the new policies provoked new conflicts, the rift between peasant and huaqiao households also shed light on the web of relations that had closely linked them together in the past. In the reports of common infringement of qiaojuan rights to investment income and remittances by peasants and cadres, officials noted that qiaojuan who had been classified as huaqiao "landlord" or "merchant" were not only forced to remain silent about the rents and loan payments that were outstanding; they were also afraid to make new loans.[46] This included "friendly loans" (*youyi jiedai*), small low-interest or interest-free loans, that they had formerly made to peasants who ran into cash flow problems at harvest times.[47] Qiaojuan withdrawal from "friendly" lending pointed to a broader interdependence between emigrant and peasant families. As officials learned, peasants had been hired to work for emigrant households lacking labor power. In return, the work offered wages that many were resistant to giving up when peasants were called upon to form mutual aid teams. Even though the sharing of labor and other resources suited qiaojuan, peasants in their villages did not welcome it because they used to be paid "20,000 to 30,000 *yuan* for plowing a *dou* [sic] of land for a *qiaojuan* household."[48] But the formation of mutual aid teams would lead to the loss of this valued income.

In other words, despite central attempts to institute a separation in the rural economy—qiaojuan households as remittance-based, and peasant households as farming-based—the common practices of lending and hiring suggest a significant degree of interdependence. Because of the mass emigration of men, local groups had adapted to a smaller pool of male labor and the inflow of remittances by forging commercial relations with each other. Qiaojuan or peasant, few had been left untouched by the effects of emigration in these villages.

Marriage Reform

Largely in the same vein as the land reform, the marriage reform in rural South China portrayed emigrant practices as distinctly "feudal" and "oppressive," but its center of attention was the women who stayed behind. According to party officials, the departure of men not only forced their wives, officially known as qiaofu, to live like virtual widows, abandoned and prone to adultery, but also encouraged female dependency. Assuming that the women were supported by overseas remittances and avoided productive labor, they were important targets of liberation under the Marriage Law. A landmark piece of legislation to abolish "the feudal marriage system based on arbitrary and compulsory arrangements and the supremacy of man over woman," the Marriage Law not only extended free-choice marriage and divorce, but also reconfigured husband and wife as "companions living together"—"bound to live in harmony, to engage in productive work, to care for their children, and to strive jointly for the welfare of the family and for the building up of the new society."[49] This redefinition of marriage as a unit of joint residence and labor poorly described emigrant South China, where mass emigration had split and relinked families across lines of nation and gender for generations. At first, officials were surprised by women who did not want to divorce their absent husbands, attributing their reluctance to feudal backwardness and reliance on remittances. But officials were surprised again by others who did and provoked intense opposition at home and overseas. Concerned about the negative impact of the social conflicts, they suspended the campaign and instead vowed to preserve huaqiao families.

Not specific to the south but occurring across the nation, the ironic reversal of the marriage reform remained instructive, presenting a transnational dimension of socialist construction for analysis. Even as the rapid shift mirrored a national effort to impose family stability, it stemmed from a great fear that the liberation of qiaofu would alienate overseas Chinese men and derail a broader agenda to mobilize remittances for the building of socialism.[50] Similar to land reform in the region, the marriage reform backfired, revealing that the kinship networks giving meaning and purpose to remittances hinged upon a gendered division of labor. This discovery led the Party-state to discontinue the attacks on huaqiao marriage as making women passive, adulterous, and dependent. Instead, it corralled the women who stayed behind into an intermediate role to take up farming and strive for remittances. The conflict also provides a useful means to understand the practice of socialism in 1950s South China. In an uneven geography of transnationally connected villages and women-headed households long engaged in commercial flows, the Maoist vision of a self-sufficient agrarian society could not have been farther from home.[51]

The following recounts how party officials encountered huaqiao marriage in South China and sought to promote among qiaofu a "modern marriage" based on free choice. Not a newly invented ideal, free-choice marriage had been a mainstay in China's search for modernity since the New Culture Movement began in 1915, codified as law under the former Guomindang government, and implemented in Communist base areas during the 1930s and 1940s. The 1950 Marriage Law expanded the scope of free choice, formalized the right of divorce, and transformed marriage into a personal relationship between equal partners mediated by the socialist nation.[52] Though it had not been uncommon for a woman in a huaqiao marriage to remarry if her husband abroad failed to provide economic support, a local practice unacknowledged by the officials, the Marriage Law offered a legal means for women to terminate a marriage at will and for reasons other than economic ones. In preparation for the Marriage Law Month campaign in March 1953, the Overseas Chinese Affairs Committee of Guangdong ordered investigations into marriage in the emigrant-sending counties, all of which were at various stages of implementing the Marriage Law. The efforts resulted in the first detailed reports on the marital conditions of women living in the province, particularly in rural townships but also including Guangzhou city. On average, huaqiao households made up 20 to 40 percent of the population, reaching a high of 70 to 90 percent in a few communities. Compiled by local officials in charge of overseas Chinese affairs, the reports criticized huaqiao marriage for causing qiaofu to have three dominant characteristics—passivity, adulterousness, and dependency—that emphasized their victimization and the challenges of integrating them as socialist subjects.

Passive, Adulterous, Dependent

The first common image of qiaofu was passivity because of the prolonged separation between husband and wife. Often lasting for years or decades, spousal separation was the most criticized aspect of huaqiao marriage in the reports. Emphasizing the effects of separation on the women at home, officials were most critical of marriages involving "wives longing for their men" (*wanglangxi* or *denglangxi*), women who became married to men after their departure and never met their husbands. Although their actual numbers were unspecified, officials explained that this type of union was arranged by parents who feared that their sons overseas would marry a foreign woman and stop sending money home, making these "longing wives" powerful evidence that huaqiao marriage was distinctly oppressive. Finding

TABLE 4.1 The length of spousal separation among *huaqiao* families in Guangdong province, 1953.

Duration of Husband's Absence (yrs)	Guangzhou City	Bao'an County, Songlian and Aohu Townships	Zhongshan County, Datong Township	Dinghai County, Liangou Township	Raoping County, Dongao Township
Under 5	16	34	23	15	6
5–10	6	23	25	45	17
11–20	23	40	19	37	10
21–30	15	96*	31	32**	—
31–40	7	—	16	—	1
41 and over	1	—	3	—	—
Total Interviewed	68	193	116	129	34

*Figure indicates a period of 21 years and over.
**Figure indicates a period of 20–32 years.

Sources: Reports on *huaqiao* marriages from Guangzhou city, Bao'an county, Zhongshan county, Dinghai county, and Raoping county, 1953 (Guangdong Provincial Archives: 237-1-3).

women in similar situations weak and docile, officials wrote that some even acquiesced to a life of widowhood. In one example, a woman in her early thirties had a husband who had gone to Thailand fifteen years before, had never returned, and had recently died. The officials wrote, "In her family, there have already been three generations of widows—she herself, her mother-in-law, and her mother-in-law's mother-in-law. It was because all of their husbands went overseas, forcing them to endure living widowhood [when their husbands lived] and dead widowhood [after their husbands died]."[53] This account of three generations of women sharing the same fate evoked images of widows from a premodern era, implying that huaqiao marriage was anachronistic and backward. As officials observed, many others quietly accepted bigamous husbands and difficult mothers-in-law.[54] Depicting these experiences as cruel and wasteful, investigators reported that huaqiao marriage left qiaofu passive.

The second image of qiaofu had to do with extramarital affairs. Officials found that because qiaofu and their overseas husbands did not live and labor together as promoted under the Marriage Law, there were few prospects for them to develop "affection" (*ganqing*) for each other. The result was a common problem of "incorrect love affairs." In one of the cases, a woman aged thirty whose husband worked in Thailand as a laborer had sexual relations with a younger "poor peasant" and became pregnant. She did not want to abandon her three children, but was so terrified of being punished that she wanted to kill herself.[55] In other cases, a wider than usual age gap between husband and wife caught the notice of officials, who posited that the incompatibility was a root cause of female adultery. Citing a common pairing of "old husband, young wife" (*laofu shaoqi*), officials wrote that "many *huaqiao* only married after they had reached quite an advanced age" because of the need to make a living abroad, while women married young and stayed in the village unaccompanied and neglected. Treating affairs as somewhat inevitable in huaqiao marriage, investigators were only mildly critical of the adulterous qiaofu, but remained reproachful of those who killed infants born out of wedlock or continued to take their husbands' remittances. However, these accounts of sexual transgression would seem to contradict the previous image emphasizing qiaofu passivity.

Compared to these two images, officials were far more contemptuous of the third: dependency. Assuming that the men overseas provided most or all of the family labor and income, officials found that their wives were left stranded when remittances fell short. One example involved a woman whose husband lived in Malaya. Recently, her husband had not been sending remittances home. She wrote many times and even went to Hong Kong to send him a telegram, but she did not receive any news. The loss of economic support caused great hardship for her and her young daughter.[56] Women like her suffered, officials claimed, because they had been dependent on remittances and unaccustomed to productive work. Still, some were unwilling to leave their husbands because they desired both a comfortable life and a love life. In one vividly recorded example, a woman, aged thirty-eight, had a husband who worked in Canada. Officials wrote that she "often had sexual relations with other men" and "had abortions six to seven times." After Liberation, she "fell in love with a hired laborer and became pregnant again." As her husband kept sending her money, her neighbors asked her if she had decided "which man to marry." She said, "I agree to marry both. I want money from the one overseas. I want the company of the one here."[57] Other cases included women who had just filed for divorce but wanted it nullified after receiving new funds from their husbands abroad.[58] In some villages, when the women expressed hope to join their husbands abroad, they were immediately criticized for having "reunion thinking" (*tuanyuan sixiang*) and "desiring an easy and comfortable life" (*tantu anyi*).[59] This suggests that seeking a family reunion abroad was politically unacceptable and was simply regarded as avoiding labor.

Modern Marriage

Though women in huaqiao marriage appeared uniformly backward, the criticism was mediated through a broader agenda of remodeling the family and building socialism. Raising the banner of "modern marriage," official investigators preached to qiaofu that local residence and labor would engender companionate and productive partnerships that were absent in their marriage. Noticing that husband and wife in the huaqiao family did not live and labor together, they surmised that it prevented "affection" (*ganqing*) and "happiness" (*xingfu*) from taking root, but instead encouraged illicit affairs, bigamy, and "green terror," meaning cuckoldry. As monogamous and free-choice marriage "saves money and works well," the women were told that they could be part of it in two ways: by divorcing their overseas husbands and remarrying local men, or by helping their overseas husbands come home.[60] The suggestions provoked what officials came to regard as "resistance," but "resistance" also offered a window onto a wide-ranging and discrepant set of considerations that women had about "modern marriage."

One conversation seemed to reveal the problems from the perspective of the women. In Raoping county, after learning that some women were unhappy about their condition, party cadres tried to convince them to get divorced and remarry some men who were charcoal burners living in the hills and had difficulty finding wives. Stressing that these men had "good social backgrounds and laboring perspectives," cadres were amazed that none of the women would even consider it. Seeing that the women "felt quite low," the cadres suggested that they "devote their energies to production. After laying down a good basis of living, [the women] could then write and send money overseas to ask their husbands to come home." One woman cried out in disbelief, "Hey! I'm already 28 years old. In two more years, I'm finished [meaning unmarriageable].... Even if life improves, there has never been such a thing as sending money overseas from the village to ask someone to come back." In the end, the cadres concluded that the women had "an unenthusiastic attitude toward production and were pessimistic about the future."[61] The women thought that marrying the charcoal burners meant poverty, whereas sending money to their husbands abroad to bring them home was a reversal of gender roles, both of which were utterly absurd. In this sense, flexible family accumulation required flexible gender configurations. All this was tricky for the officials because they sought a bounded model of marriage to benefit national construction.

In many similar cases involving women's apparent apathy toward "modern marriage," officials were rarely able to see the complex calculations behind it. Fixated on the appearance of dependence on remittances, the officials failed to recognize contrasting evidence of the women's independence because of their deep engagement with the family and village economy. Often, women performed waged labor inside and outside the home. For example, officials interviewed one woman who had not heard from her husband in Cuba for years, but because her son had already grown up and worked in a textile factory in Hong Kong, while she earned a living by sewing, she did not have any complaint about her marriage. However, officials interpreted this as a sign of resistance rather than independence.[62] The reports also did not discuss how qiaofu contributions to the household budget were especially pertinent when remittances were infrequent, meager, or nonexistent. As data collected from eight overseas Chinese localities indicated, women who reported few or no remittances ranged from 6 to 33 percent, averaging a significant 18 percent.[63] In one township in Dinghai county, cadres reported that the women worked as tile makers and in other sideline activities. As a result, "the standard of living in a *huaqiao* household was usually higher than that of others," because in addition to remittances from abroad, every woman could bring in wages as much as 10,000 yuan per day.[64] Some cases of adultery also showed that women participated in market activities, ran businesses, and hired farm labor for the household, which brought them into contact with other men. One example involved a woman whose husband had moved to Canada. Even though he kept sending remittances, she ran a rice business with a fictive brother. Later, the two started living together.[65] Another woman hired a neighbor to help farm the land that she received in the land reform. After a while, they had sexual relations.[66] In one case where officials tried to explain that a wide age gap between a qiaofu and her older overseas husband caused her to take up with a younger local man, the two met because they both carried pigs on shoulder poles to sell at the market. Scattered throughout the reports, but largely unexamined, these valuable pieces of information suggest that qiaofu played a productive role far more substantial than was acknowledged by the investigators.

In addition, the resistance of older qiaofu toward marriage reform helped reveal the cooperative functions performed by resident members in the family that sometimes outweighed the contributions of those far away. For women whose husbands and sons were both absent, daughters-in-law were a vital source of support and security. Their productive labor was so important that the idea of their divorcing and remarrying distressed many mothers-in-law. Officials reported one case in which Chen Mufeng, aged thirty-one and classified as "poor peasant," was married to a man whom she had never met and who had been abroad for almost twenty years. Every year, her husband sent five remittances and some packages of goods. The previous year, she wanted to get a divorce, but her sixty-year-old mother-in-law burst into tears and complained to a local official. Chen became worried that if she went ahead with the divorce, other people would accuse her of being "heartless." So she abandoned the idea and instead adopted a girl.[67] Although a stable living guaranteed by remittances did not stop Chen from pursuing a divorce, social pressure from other villagers did. Instead of abandoning her mother-in-law, she avoided criticism by becoming a mother herself to an adopted child.

It is noteworthy that mothers-in-law opposed the Marriage Law not only because of traditional values, but also because of pragmatic concerns about their livelihood as a result of the emigration of husbands and sons. In a rare instance, officials acknowledged that because "the material life at present is harsh, the main productive labor is performed by the daughters-in-law." Some mothers-in-law threatened to commit suicide or taunted the divorce-seekers, saying "it is reasonable for young maidens to marry out. It is a good thing. But if those who are daughters-in-law remarry, there will not be a good ending."[68] Although it was unusual, the mother-in-law could sometimes be an ally of the qiaofu. In one case, Fu Guiying, aged thirty and married at eighteen, had a husband who had been overseas for eight years. A year earlier, she had had an "incorrect love affair," became pregnant, and had an abortion. Her husband overseas heard and wrote home to tell her to leave; the man with whom she had an affair also did not want her. But her labor production was very good and her mother-in-law was very fond of her, so she was still living in her husband's house.[69] This unusual arrangement suggested that older qiaofu sometimes wielded a lot of power in the household because of the absence of men. Despite her son's protest of Fu's affair, the mother-in-law let her stay because she liked and needed her.

The pragmatism behind the resistance to "modern marriage" challenged the dominant portrayal that emigrant men provided the sole income and labor while resident wives indulged in leisure and comfort. This point was evident in the various concerns raised directly by the women in the reports. Instead of trying to fix their marriages, some opted to focus their energies on raising young children and earning a living. Given that divorcees were expected to remarry and not remain single, many decided that having been married would narrow their prospects of finding a suitor locally, making divorce unappealing. One woman who was already supporting herself by working with a sewing machine said that she did not want to end up with a farmer.[70] Others worried about losing their rights to land and abode in a divorce, bringing instability into their lives. Interestingly, some older qiaofu saw that the perfect solution to their marriage problems would be for the Party to bring their husbands home, even though this was beyond state power.

Far from being immobilized by feudal oppression, qiaofu were motivated by active considerations about their social standing and personal welfare. To seek autonomy and protection, they pursued a diverse range of strategies, resulting in a set of mutual obligations. While some aggressively pursued sexual satisfaction outside the patriarchal structure, many more were expected to shoulder a greater amount of work to compensate for the absence of men and the shortfall of remittances, the latter situation a more common one than acknowledged. Finally, women were not the only ones who were skeptical about "modern marriage." As the campaign rested on an invented domain of long-suppressed female emotion awaiting release, officials were quick to turn on any expression that they thought was an excess or a throwback to the feudal era. For example, they condemned cases of "first adultery, then marriage" (*xianjian houqu*) in which women who had become pregnant out of wedlock rushed to marry their lovers without bothering first to inform their husbands and formalize the divorce. Others threatened to kill themselves when the court rejected their divorce applications, misconstruing the official language of "happiness" (*xingfu*) as approval for free love or land for illegitimate children.[71] These examples made "modern marriage" a complex negotiation not only between individuals but also between individuals and the state.

Backlash, Backfire, Reversal

Although the investigations found that qiaofu were uniformly backward and resistant to liberation, some of the women responded enthusiastically to marriage reform, causing officials to worry about an "excessive" use of divorce. By 1955, huaqiao couples accounted for over 20 percent of all divorce applications in Guangdong, a figure proportional to population. However, over 90 percent of the applications were brought by resident women against their husbands overseas. This rate was consistent with a national trend that women formed the vast majority of plaintiffs in divorce cases, but it was also one of the highest, compared to a national average of 77 percent and 75 percent in Shanghai. The wave of divorce led by women in huaqiao families led to great confusion in rural South China. A wide array of problems was reported: village cadres "overemphasized *huaqiao* policy" and were inclined to punish qiaofu adulterers harshly as a warning to others; court officials were too lax or too stringent with huaqiao divorces; huaqiao husbands ignored or objected to their wives' applications for divorce; and mothers-in-law obstructed the divorces of their daughters-in-law.

Attracting the most attention was how the divorces seemed to have bred mistrust between huaqiao men and local officials and could cripple the rural economy. In one township of Dinghai county, cadres related that some huaqiao men wrote angry letters from abroad demanding to know if their wives had been "three togethered" (*santong*), charging that the socialist slogan for party cadres and the masses to "eat together, live together, labor together" (*tongchi, tongzhu, tonglaodong*) was a pretext for sleeping together—sexual transgressions causing huaqiao men to be cuckolded. To guard their own interests, some men began to send less money home, which then upset their wives.[72] The detrimental effects of divorce were also linked to the broader question of rural stability. In Wenchang county, where the number of huaqiao households and qiaojuan population size were reportedly 47 percent (47,841) and 33 percent (187,412) of the total, respectively, officials found that the total remittance income received in 1955 was 6,277,100 yuan. This massive sum of money was "enough to buy over 523,900 plows at 12 yuan each" or to "pay for a year's food consumption for 62,771 people," about 11 percent of the county's population.[73] Given that remittances were funds sent by emigrant men to support their families, huaqiao marriage was a lifeline of the community.

To control the negative repercussions, local officials began to persuade the women to drop their petitions for divorce. Moving away from a focus on qiaofu conditions, officials now depicted their husbands as the true victims of a nation that had been warped by landlord exploitation, Guomindang oppression, and Japanese attack. In one township, officials explained to qiaofu that prior to Liberation, a landlord class of about 6 percent of all households used to monopolize 69 percent of all land. People had lived in dire poverty, subject to constant extortions, heavy taxation, and forced conscription. Japanese occupation brought starvation.[74] Under such circumstances, huaqiao men were forced to "climb thousands of mountains and cross tens of thousands of rivers," emigrating "for no other reason than the livelihood and happiness of the family."[75] Qiaofu who wanted to divorce their husbands because remittances had stopped were mistaken, because the true culprit was U.S. imperialism, said the officials. Saying that huaqiao men were "living under the rule of American imperialism in Nanyang [the South Seas]" and "their business operations were running into more difficulties," while the land reform had redistributed land in the village, officials exhorted the women to "oppose dismissive attitudes toward labor" and "achieve self-reliance" by eagerly participating in agricultural production.[76] Since American imperialism was destined to meet its doom, officials told qiaofu, "The day when the world returns to the people, the husbands will come back."[77] Here, by calling on qiaofu to be diligent and patient until the return of their husbands, the officials no longer aligned the women's happiness with liberation through divorce but with victory in a national struggle.

At the same time, the Party-state began to intervene in what it saw as a runaway problem in South China by articulating a similar concern for the neglected needs of huaqiao men. After the completion of the land reform review in 1953, the mobilization of overseas remittances emerged as a national priority in the overall strategy of restoring production in the countryside.[78] The first set of central guidelines came in 1954. It laid out the basic principle that any court ruling about huaqiao marriage and family must "take care of the huaqiao abroad and take care as appropriate of the demands of *qiaojuan* women," implying that there had been an excessive use of the Marriage Law by the latter group.[79] An official handbook that provided information on government policies toward huaqiao in 1956 emphasized the "preservation of huaqiao marriage and family" and prioritized the care of huaqiao before that of qiaojuan women.[80] Clarifying that the Marriage Law was not intended to break up old family relationships, the government declared a new focus on persuasion and education to "improve and consolidate the relationship between husband and wife, and transform disharmonious, undemocratic old families into new families that are democratic, harmonious, and united in production."[81] Here the preferential treatment of huaqiao men and reduction of qiaofu's rights to "appropriate care" (*shidang zhaogu*) were justified under the rubric of family harmony and national production.

After 1955, the new guidelines led to a series of efforts to reform and standardize divorce proceedings in the court system. In a 1957 report, the Guangdong Higher People's Court reprimanded the lower courts for neglecting the legal rights of huaqiao and failing to understand that "whenever possible huaqiao marriage and family should be preserved as the material foundation of the bond between huaqiao and the ancestral nation." The criticisms of the lower courts were stern and many: they were "sloppy" and "irresponsible," rarely bothering to consult and notify the huaqiao involved until there was a court decision, and completely relying on the testimony of the qiaojuan plaintiff. To make things worse, proceedings varied from court to court. Some failed to keep detailed minutes or issue formal notices of adjudication. Periods for defense and appeal submissions differed greatly. Because the qiaojuan was often the only party in attendance, some judges conducted divorce trials behind closed doors and without a jury. Court correspondence mailed to huaqiao abroad frequently appeared in illegible handwriting and on poor-quality paper, with official stamps and appeal information missing, words poorly chosen, and the tone disparaging toward the huaqiao recipient. As "*huaqiao* localities" made up more than 60 percent of counties and cities in the province (76 out of 119 units), the Higher Court found that all these inappropriate occurrences could only "affect the correctness and solemnity of the adjudication," "making it extremely easy to provoke *huaqiao* discontent and enemy attacks."[82]

As attention shifted toward the protection of huaqiao men, stricter limits were issued on the use of the courts by qiaojuan women, particularly those who used adultery to get out of existing marriages. Chastising the lower courts for failing to adhere to basic principles, the report found that they gave in easily "under the pressure and threats from *qiaojuan*" and routinely approved divorce petitions from women who had committed adultery, been cohabiting with another man, or given birth to a child out of wedlock. In the counties of Kaiping, Chaoyang, and Chenghai, officials reported that out of the eighty-seven cases in which qiaojuan women were the plaintiffs, thirty-seven cases or 42.5 percent involved confession of adultery.[83] In particular, younger women between the ages of twenty and thirty were most likely to report a high rate of adultery and press for divorce because they thought that the returns of their husbands were doubtful and so were anxious about "misspending their youth," said the report. These plaintiffs often frequented the courthouse to urge a favorable ruling, threatened to commit suicide, or even remarried without waiting for a final ruling. Thinking that there was no other way for their husbands to agree to a divorce, some women would claim falsely to have committed adultery and given birth to illegitimate children, or say that they were "responding to the government's call to divorce."[84] While officials acknowledged that bigamy also occurred widely among huaqiao, the men lived outside the jurisdiction of the People's Republic, making it impossible for the state to prosecute the offense. Yet qiaojuan adultery was a major source of huaqiao resentment, which was sometimes directed at the authorities, making it politically imperative to censure the female behavior domestically.

Under the broad principle of preserving huaqiao families, the Guangdong Higher Court issued guidelines to tighten the basis for divorce and apply an alternative procedure of mediation, persuasion, and education. If a qiaojuan plaintiff sued a huaqiao for divorce because of his bigamy, he should be persuaded to accept the divorce. However, if he refused but expressed his intention to leave the other wife, the court should then persuade the qiaojuan plaintiff to withdraw the divorce petition. Similarly, in the event of qiaojuan adultery, when the huaqiao sued for divorce and an investigation proved the occurrence of adultery, the court should approve it. If the qiaojuan objected, the huaqiao was persuaded to drop the petition before the court proceeded to grant a divorce.[85] However, if the qiaojuan applied for divorce because of her own adultery, the court should deny the application unless there was a possibility of an "accident," referring to a suicide threat by the qiaojuan, in which case the court should work with the Overseas Chinese Affairs and Women's Federation to express sympathy, but not condemn the qiaojuan. At the same time, court officials should warn the qiaojuan's lover (*jianfu*) to break off the illegitimate relations. In particular, village cadres and militiamen should be educated not to engage in illicit relations with qiaojuan.[86] In other words, women were to accept huaqiao husbands who were bigamous but willing to correct themselves. Those who committed adultery were not automatically entitled to divorce unless their husbands insisted. Any claim for a "lack of affection" between husband and wife must pass through the scrutiny of the court system, now committed to preventing marital breakdowns in huaqiao families.[87]

Given the emphasis on mediation, persuasion, and education, qiaojuan women became the main object of these efforts in the majority of huaqiao marital disputes. With the exception of "unreasonable marriages" involving "wives-in-waiting" (*wanglangxi*) who married absent men through proxies such as roosters (*bai gongji*) and conjugal beds (*bai dachuang*), and whose huaqiao husbands were counterrevolutionaries, where it was still pertinent to rule in favor of the qiaojuan plaintiff, court officials were instructed to preserve the status quo of huaqiao families.[88] This included cases where the scarcity or lack of remittances was the cause of marital disputes. In Wenchang county, officials reported that their intervention paid off. In one example, Li Yue'e, wife of Wang Jingbin, ran away from home and applied for divorce. Wang had been in Southeast Asia for nineteen years and rarely sent any letters or remittances home. Li's relationship with her mother-in-law was also poor. According to the report, the court made several attempts to "educate her about family values, spousal relations and the pros and cons [of staying in or leaving the marriage]." As a result, her basic attitude improved. To resolve the conflict completely, the court helped her conduct a family meeting, during which "everyone brought up the issues, analyzed them, and distinguished between right and wrong." Later, officials wrote to Wang to say that his wife had returned, participated in production eagerly, and enjoyed better relations with his mother at home. But production was still difficult, so officials asked him to help by sending money home. Afterward, Wang sent four remittances in two months. His wife Li came to the court to express her gratitude.[89] Here, divorce was averted because the female plaintiff received proper persuasion and education from the court.

In other cases where divorce was unavoidable and a court settlement became necessary, qiaojuan women seemed to be at greater risk than huaqiao men in claims over property and child custody. As the protection of women and children had been central to the Marriage Law, central guidelines maintained that a qiaojuan in a divorce should recover the property that she possessed prior to marriage, retain a portion of any land received from the land reform, and receive the property obtained through laboring in the huaqiao family. All other property belonging to the huaqiao including houses should remain in his ownership. Nonetheless, it was unclear how the division between property obtained before and after the marriage would be worked out in reality. Given the widely held assumption that the huaqiao must be the primary provider for the household, the qiaojuan plaintiff could be greatly disadvantaged. One case in Shunde county involved a female plaintiff whose husband was a trader in Kuala Lumpur, Malaya. Married for ten years, the two had only lived together for two months and been separated since then. The woman initiated a divorce and the huaqiao agreed, but they could not reach an agreement over property. She demanded compensation of 2000 yuan, a house, and a store, and he did not respond.[90] Arguing that the qiaojuan did not play any role in contributing to the huaqiao's wealth, the court ruled that she should not seek a share of the property but only accept a much reduced amount of compensation of six hundred yuan. In another case, where the female qiaojuan suggested that the majority of the properties in the country had been purchased after her marriage to the huaqiao, entitling her to a share, the court ruled that the properties had been obtained through overseas trade conducted by the huaqiao, and the qiaojuan did not participate in labor. Instead, it persuaded her to accept a sum for living expenses after the divorce.[91]

A similar principle of huaqiao protection also extended to child custody. If huaqiao insisted on raising children resulted from the marriage and such an arrangement "would not cause any harm to the children," the qiaojuan should be persuaded to transfer them to the care of the domestic kin of the huaqiao. One small concession was made to qiaojuan women who were granted a divorce. If a woman had difficulty finding a place to live after the divorce, the court should advise that she be allowed to stay in the huaqiao's residences until her remarriage. But it also added that this arrangement should only be verbal and not be written down in the notice of adjudication to avoid upsetting the huaqiao.[92] As women who filed for divorce often found themselves under strong social and economic pressures to leave and remarry, the concession seemed apologetic and pointless.

Two photographs found in the Guangdong Provincial Archives encapsulate what the Party-state considered to be a proper temporal order. In one

THE WOMEN WHO STAYED BEHIND   139

Figure 4.1 Han Caiguang, head of Puqian remittance bureau and deputy director of the Overseas Chinese Federation, helps two women write a letter to their men abroad. *Source:* Guangdong Provincial Archives.

photograph, the head of Puqian Remittance Bureau in Wenchang county and deputy director of the Overseas Chinese Federation, Han Caiguang, is shown helping two women with small children to write a letter to their men abroad. In a similar photograph, the same government official, Han, dresses up as a mail carrier, delivering a remittance to a mother and her young son. The recipients are smiling with joy and anticipation while standing at the threshold between the family house and the outside world; the carrier wears a sun hat with rolled-up shirt sleeves and trousers, handing over an envelope from afar. In both images, the Party-state is inserting itself into the center of huaqiao life, serving as a guardian of women and children while the men are away, implying that effective communication requires help. Furthermore, the male official is at the forefront of time, bringing the women up to date and looking after the next generation for the time being. The harmonious reordering of temporalities suggests that the Party-state no longer tried to liberate the women from transnational marriage, but led in preserving it.

Women as Intermediaries

The turn toward the preservation of huaqiao families and "care" of huaqiao men signaled a recalibration of central agendas. To open up space for huaqiao groups to remain temporarily outside socialist transformation, central officials not only reevaluated policies but also targeted women in a different way. Not only were the women told to stay in their marriages; they were also expected to devote themselves to farming but also to resume lending activities, strive for remittances from families abroad but also restrict household consumption, and choose freely to invest or not in cooperatives that nonetheless pressured them for contributions. All these were mutually contradictory at the local level because remittances had always served private consumption and rural commercialization in the past but were now being mobilized for agricultural collectivization under the aegis of the Party-state. Captives of these new pressures, the women were recast as actors mediating huaqiao integration with socialism.

The expectation for women to stay married to overseas men was espoused in the central guidelines for handling huaqiao marriages, which described a shared origin, a reluctant separation, and a precarious bond between huaqiao and the nation. No longer pushing the cause of women's liberation, central officials reclaimed huaqiao men as historical subjects who had been oppressed by the "semi-feudal, semi-colonial society," implying that their displacement had been caused by the same conditions leading to the Communist Revolution. "Forced to leave their families behind but send home large amounts of remittances obtained from laboring abroad," the men were "involuntary" exiles of the laboring class that "had always loved the ancestral nation and their parents and wives in the family." Despite their inherent loyalty and patriotism, huaqiao were being tested because they lived in "colonized countries" under the "damaging effects of imperialist and reactionary propaganda." This situation would make it "easy for them to become confused and suspicious." Hinting at the possibility that they could be manipulated by hostile forces abroad, central officials warned that the "correct handling of huaqiao marital disputes" would have a direct impact on the overall huaqiao policy. It was therefore crucial to "unite *huaqiao*, protect their legal interests, and consolidate their connection with the ancestral nation."[93] This began with not finding fault with huaqiao men for "causing long separations in the family," but with "actively reducing marital disputes" by educating qiaojuan women. The task involved helping them "eagerly participate in production, study culture, manage housework, and raise children." The women could also encourage huaqiao to write home, send money, and visit if possible, in order to "strengthen the affection between husband and wife."[94] Coming to terms with emigrant China, the Party-state no longer portrayed women who stayed behind as victimized objects to be liberated immediately but tried to mold them into agents who could help cement the bond between the diaspora and the nation.

The call to strive for remittances reflected the eagerness of the Party-state to put the early campaigns behind it and move the women forward to the next phase of development. Seeking to reverse the continuous decline of remittances after the land reform, officials admitted that the downward trend had to do with international restrictions on the transfer of funds to Communist China, but did not think that it was the main cause. Rather, they posited that many qiaojuan were still resentful over the class struggle and muddled about current conditions. Despite central policies to protect their right to personal income, they feared showing wealth, lending money, and having their remittances confiscated or restricted in use; some even worried that the government would liberate Taiwan and Hong Kong, causing a third world war. Without commenting on whether the rapid changes in government positions contributed to these anxieties, officials claimed that all the women needed to do was to write their husbands about the "progress that had been happening in the ancestral nation" and encourage them to send money home.[95] As remittances were an important source of initial capital for rural collectivization, the high stakes put intense pressure on the women to do their part. Despite the principle of voluntary participation, when credit cooperatives started to form in Taishan after 1953, cadres aggressively recruited qiaojuan women to join and purchase shares. In the reports, when one woman declined to participate, she was immediately chided by a cadre informing her, "You are now asked to join the cooperative but you refuse. In the future, even if you found yourself a whole bunch of guarantors [to support your participation], you wouldn't be allowed to join."[96] Some cadres went so far as going to the banks and obtaining the lists of names of qiaojuan account holders and the amounts of their deposits. When qiaojuan refused to make contributions to the local cooperative, cadres would use the lists to question them, which then frightened some into withdrawing all their money from the bank.[97] At a meeting, cadres lectured huaqiao landlords plainly that it was a "test" to see if they would put money in the cooperative.[98] In response, many qiaojuan complied because they did not want to be seen as backward, thinking that they were "using 30,000 yuan to buy a path to socialism." Some were sneering, "We have given way much more to the peasants in the land reform. To give another 30,000 yuan [to buy shares in the cooperative] is nothing at all."

Facing such intense scrutiny locally, some women decided that it would be best to forsake remittances and concentrate on production. Nonetheless, they also were criticized for "thinking one-sidedly that they only needed to rely on their own production, but did not need to strive for remittances."[99] In one example mentioned in the reports, a woman "had participated eagerly in the land reform and struggle sessions against the landlords." She also recently had joined a production cooperative. But her activism enraged her husband overseas, who sent three consecutive letters to scold her for her transformation. Before that happened, she used to receive 1200 Hong Kong dollars every year. After receiving two hundred Hong Kong dollars in September 1952, she did not receive any more remittances. Thinking that her labor power was too little, having to participate in farming and take care of the family at the same time, she began to share meal costs with a single man in the militia. She said that she had her mind set on improving production and was not keen on striving for remittances.[100] Needless to say, this became a problem for the officials, who wanted qiaojuan like her to fulfill multiple tasks fully and not selectively.

This example revealed how the women who stayed behind were held to a fixed, intermediate position, unable to live up to either set of the expectations as a good socialist or as a good huaqiao wife. In the above story, the political transformation that led one woman to cast off feudal oppression was laudable but her failure to sustain remittances was not. What seemed more problematic was that she successfully rearranged her life and embraced production by linking up with a local man, so that she no longer needed to depend on an angry and distant husband. Yet this was unacceptable to the officials. Similar to how some women had rejected liberation through divorce and how others went for it before, this case demonstrated how pragmatism worked unevenly in the evolution of the women living with socialism.

Still, many others chose to flee the countryside, triggering a mass exodus from the countryside that officials considered "a dominant trend" after the land reform. In Taishan, there were about 1,000 qiaojuan exits in 1952. By the end of 1953, the number increased over tenfold to nearly 11,500. The first four months in 1954 recorded over 2,500 exits. In one subdistrict area, over a hundred qiaojuan households packed and left. In one village, the same happened to nearly 30 percent of all qiaojuan households (twenty-four of eighty-three) by 1954.[101] According to the officials, most qiaojuan moved to Guangzhou city or left the country for Hong Kong with "excuses to reunite with huaqiao husbands or collect remittances." Many women were unable to endure the hardships of agricultural labor, officials said, but "went home crying and writing their husbands to ask to join them overseas." Others who had not yet been mobilized feared that they would be next. Some qiaojuan who were classified as overseas Chinese merchants claimed that their marginalized position made it meaningless to stay in the villages because they were discriminated against and barred from participating in the new cooperatives. In response, officials were unable to make any concrete suggestions, but only recommended "further education of *qiaojuan*" and "promotion of policies among peasants and cadres" to cultivate unity for the sake of production.[102]

Conclusion

The surprising outcomes of the land and marriage reform in South China suggested that socialism in the 1950s was far from a closed system but continued to be influenced by global forces through the deep legacies of mass emigration. The meeting of two paths of development, socialist and huaqiao, led to a series of dramatic turns, as the Party-state was not only inspired to capture transnational resources for socialist construction but was also forced into a sequence of speed-ups, slowdowns, and do-overs. At first, rural South China appeared to officials as distinctly backward and disjointed, where households failed to engage in agricultural production and women were left behind, unproductive and wasteful. But the forceful struggles against huaqiao landlords and marriages backfired, spurring efforts to undo the damage and restore production.

A diaspora moment, the events also provided an opportunity to study the dynamics of emigrant connections through gender. As men moved overseas and sent money home, women filled the absences by sustaining and expanding kinship networks as wives, mothers, and daughters-in-law.

They gave social meaning and power to remittances, not only because they were the intended recipients, but because they used the resources to acquire land and housing, hire labor, run businesses, make loans, and buy other services. These activities contributed to the development of lineage networks and a commercialized rural economy, providing a space for the return of expatriated men. When the men failed to hold up their end of kinship obligations, the women still had to lead the household through adaptation. If they did not, the household would be unlikely to survive. It took the Party-state quite a while to learn that emigrant connections hinged upon gender roles.

In the aftermath, the central leaders declared huaqiao to be a special category, outside of socialist time and free from interference. Men overseas were to receive favorable treatment, but it was also a temporary condition, meant to expire after a certain period of time. Caught between a fractured present and an idealized future, the women who stayed behind were to become go-betweens to assist huaqiao and the nation in a reunification. Fixed in an intermediary role, they juggled contradictory demands, were unable to evolve, and would never arrive. Toward the end of the 1950s, a sudden acceleration of socialist transition under the Great Leap Forward (1958–60) made the preservation of any patterns across the decade and beyond a least probable outcome. While emphatic criticisms in the diaspora had forced the party to revise its initial goals for rural South China, the ambition to reroute a diaspora toward the nation was, for the moment, a lost cause.

CHAPTER 5

Homecomings

During a visit to Burma in 1956, China's Premier and Foreign Minister Zhou Enlai encouraged Chinese living in Rangoon to become local citizens in a famous speech likening them to daughters who "married out" (*jia chuqu*) and sons who "married uxorilocally" (*zhaozhui*). No longer members of the "natal family" but of "another family," they would "bring sons" to Burma and "a new branch of relatives" to China.[1] Evoking the traditional function of marriage in joining two families to portray how migration could join the two nations, Zhou's speech echoed Burma's avowal of a "kinfolk" relationship (*pauk-phaw*) with China in 1954 and China's diplomatic framework of "peaceful coexistence" at the 1955 Bandung Conference.[2] Underneath his political message was the assumption that Chinese emigration, like traditional marriage, was a one-way, permanent transfer of individuals from one entity to another. Capable of producing "sons" for Burma and "relatives" for China, Chinese abroad would be a conduit benefiting both nations.

Conveying a sense of linearity and order, Zhou's marriage metaphor could not describe how a cascade of events during the 1950s and 1960s was uprooting Chinese settled in Southeast Asia and sending them to China. After the end of World War II, Southeast Asia evolved in at least three ways: it transformed from largely colonial territories to new nation-states, emerged as an area of contest between communist and anticommunist insurgencies, and shifted in relation to foreign powers during Cold War struggles. The ever-changing political landscape brought domestic discrimination and violence against many social groups, including the ethnic Chinese who had been a diverse and vital part of local society but were now denounced as outsiders unfit for citizenship. As Malaya, Indonesia, Burma, Cambodia, Thailand, the Philippines, and Vietnam each witnessed anti-Chinese, anticommunist activities at one point or another, Chinese who were displaced formed large exoduses to China, among other places. Between 1950 and 1966, more than 420,000 Chinese from Southeast Asia arrived in the People's Republic of China (PRC), of which nearly 60 percent came before 1958.[3] In Guangdong province alone, local authorities resettled 20,000 from British Malaya between 1950 and 1958, 54,000 from Indonesia in 1960, 5,000 from India in 1963, 3,000 from Burma in 1964, and 107,000 from Vietnam in 1978.[4] Seen in this light, couching Chinese emigration in the nominal terms of marriage only served to amplify the cacophony of the "married-out" suddenly forced to come "home."

These "homecomings" suggest a contingent quality of the diaspora-homeland connection that could occasionally surface, demand reintegration, and provoke serious tensions. Driven out by political and social turmoil in various places across Southeast Asia, the large and sudden reverse migration of Chinese populations caused a "diaspora moment," demonstrating histories of mass emigration in motion, not only because of the changes occurring outside China but also because of those generated by it. Differing widely in geographical origins and social status, many of the new arrivals came as part of a family group that no longer had ties to a Chinese village, had held urban, skilled occupations, and sometimes did not speak a Chinese language or were not ethnically Chinese, as in the case of Southeast Asian women married to Chinese men.[5] To meet the wide-ranging challenges of resettlement, the Communist Party-state labeled the repatriates *guiqiao* (returned overseas Chinese), huaqiao who were defined by their *gui* (return) to the homeland regardless of background.[6] Marked off from the domestic population, guiqiao were to receive privileged treatment in housing and job assignments and be kept free from class struggle, a centralized campaign to abolish class oppression and build an equal society. Nonetheless, as the pace of socialist construction accelerated dramatically after 1955, acute tensions emerged over the process of guiqiao reintegration.

These tensions grew into a crisis during the late 1950s and early 1960s, when the Communist Party-state sought to raise production and mobilize guiqiao resources but also was haunted by guiqiao's exteriority to the nation. As the returning diaspora existed both before and outside the 1949 Chinese Communist Revolution, each encounter raised the question of how the groups would fit into a new China, just as they did in the emerging sovereign states in Southeast Asia. After collectivization kicked into high gear in 1955, party officials became more rigid in differentiating guiqiao by economic means, while remaining publicly silent on class, since it would implicate the central desire to mobilize guiqiao labor and wealth. In both Guangdong and Fujian provinces, they forcefully relocated poor returnees from urban areas to subsidized state farms to join agricultural production, while becoming heavily involved in soliciting rich returnees to invest in private housing projects in the cities known as "overseas Chinese new villages" (*huaqiao xincun*). Internally, the officials criticized guiqiao for their "difficult behavior," "capitalist thinking," and "double nature," all of which implied a dubious class character in the absence of class struggle. As the challenge of balancing high socialism and guiqiao privileges mounted, the officials became fixated on how the newcomers carried with them an unknown foreign past and continued to draw on personal and family ties to evade state control, but avoided discussing whether the discontent of guiqiao was caused by the ever-changing state policies or was broadly shared by other domestic groups in China.

Frustrated by an inability to turn guiqiao into desired subjects in a fast-changing China, officials came to associate the difficulties with the specter of a returning capitalism. Like the two preceding governments in the late Qing and Republican periods, the Communist Party-state acknowledged the special place of huaqiao in the modernizing nation. But its distinct struggle came from a multitrack strategy to cope with a vast and varied diaspora arriving in the homeland, leading to the development of one policy for the domestic citizens and another for the returnees, one policy for the overseas Chinese rich and another for the overseas Chinese poor. These expedients were only supposed to be temporary in the context of a larger socialism still under construction and the desire to incorporate the different social formations into a single time and space. As party leaders had learned from the experience of land and marriage reform that a too-rapid transformation could jeopardize huaqiao support and remittance mobilization (discussed in chapter 4), they were careful to extend similar accommodations to guiqiao. Yet this agenda became unsustainable as the pace and mode of socialist development shifted radically. By the time of the Cultural Revolution (1966–76), the "homecomings" of guiqiao came to be feared as a form of capitalism that might have been displaced but was always returning.

Focusing on guiqiao resettlement in a huaqiao state farm and "new village" near Guangzhou, the sources of this chapter are largely drawn from internal documents produced by the Guangzhou Overseas Chinese Affairs Bureau from 1955 to 1966 and stored at the Guangzhou City Archives. As in chapter 4, I seek to read against the grain of these texts, treating them as Party attempts to communicate and work out the implementation of new policies, which had a real impact on social reality. Reading the information critically, I try to draw out the silences, contradictions, and connections in these official narratives as well as to put them into wider national and regional conversations. Since access to post-1949 archives is not always guaranteed, these sources offer a precious window onto the interactions between cadres and returnees and between state agencies in the context of an evolving understanding of the diaspora. The firsthand accounts suggest that officials were actively engaging and problematizing issues related to the returning groups they knew to be important but found elusive in the absence of applicable class labels. In response to continuous arrivals, guiqiao resistance, and the increasing pressures of socialist transformation, the officials first depicted guiqiao as "difficult people, difficult cases," criticized guiqiao's "capitalist" character during the Great Leap Forward even as they were immune to class struggle, and in its aftermath asserted that a "double nature" made guiqiao a uniquely insidious threat to socialism. At this diaspora moment, these discussions suggest not only the significance and complexity of the returning diaspora, but just as importantly a constant revision of the nation's past, present, and future. The resulting divergences rendered the creation of a unified homeland-nation during socialist construction a powerful yet unfulfilled ideal.

"Difficult People, Difficult Cases"

Part of a broader problem of huaqiao reintegration, guiqiao resettlement was one of the most difficult tasks facing the early PRC state, suggesting how socialist construction emerged in dialogue with an ongoing history of emigration and return. In a recent study, Glen Peterson has suggested that a new overseas Chinese policy after 1953 led to the creation of huaqiao into a special category, making it the most elaborate state initiative to engage the overseas Chinese.[7] Led by prominent national figures He Xiangning, her son Liao Chengzhi, and Fang Fang, the Overseas Chinese Affairs Commission of the central government proposed an extension of preferential treatment (*youdai*) to huaqiao following the damaging effects of the land reform on overseas Chinese properties and support. With some similarities to previous initiatives adopted by the late Qing and Republican governments, the PRC directive expanded them to grant huaqiao special privileges that were unavailable to the general population, such as permission to engage in private consumption, access to extra rations of food grains and other basic necessities, and opportunities to purchase rare consumer goods, thus a significant relief from socialist transformation.[8] This approach was well reflected in the consideration of the returnees, who were entitled to preferential treatment in financial aid, jobs, and housing. Situating guiqiao outside socialist time, the policy operated on the assumption that the returning diaspora, given its social backwardness and strategic distinctiveness, had to be brought into the nation differently and far more gradually than others. Instructed to accommodate the needs of guiqiao, officials in charge of resettlement were forced to address a series of what they called "difficult people, difficult cases" in the archival reports. The difficulties suggest not only that the work of resettlement was enormously complicated but also that the officials had few tools and information with which to negotiate the diverging socialist and huaqiao temporalities.

The officials under discussion worked at the Guangzhou Overseas Chinese Affairs Bureau (Guangzhou qiaowu ju), the first point of contact for many guiqiao who were in need of government assistance.[9] Created in July 1954, the bureau was responsible for the administration of all huaqiao policies in the city of over 1.6 million people, though the diverse and complex challenges of guiqiao resettlement soon consumed most of its attention. Differing vastly in social backgrounds, many guiqiao had never before lived in China, but saw it as a safe haven from political turmoil. Largely urban dwellers, they included petty traders, shopkeepers, technicians, schoolteachers, and journalists. Some spoke regional Chinese languages at home, studied Mandarin in school, or knew only Southeast Asian languages. Some were wives and children accompanying Chinese men in their repatriation and were part Chinese or not Chinese at all.[10] Welded into a single group marked by a collective "return" from abroad, guiqiao were entitled to preferential treatment, but tight resources and competing understandings of the policy made it a source of friction, resulting in an official portrayal of guiqiao as sharing a "difficult" character: members were "economically oriented," "always haggling over wages," had "low quality of thought," and "frequently cried and wrangled"; they were "envious of urban life" and "fearful of physical labor," "acted like ruffians," were "unwilling to labor," and "could not be educated overnight."[11] Though such reports reflect a limited bureaucratic perspective in enforcing compliance more than the true voices of the guiqiao, they offer an important look into the daily interactions between local actors, making the biases, contradictions, and silences available for analysis. Taken together, they shed light on a wide gap between official commitments and guiqiao expectations and signs of rivalry between state agencies over resettlement.

In accordance with central directives, the bureau applied three broad principles of resettlement to the guiqiao seeking help, aside from providing short-term aid. First, it encouraged all guiqiao to "return to their original native places" (*hui yuanji*) under the slogan, "Those who have homes should return home. Those who have relatives should seek shelter with their relatives" (*youjia huijia youqin touqin*). Second, it urged guiqiao to participate in "self-help through production" (*shengchan zijiu*) through job referrals to cooperatives, factories, and other work units within and sometimes outside the province. Third, the bureau tried to mobilize guiqiao to "turn toward the farm villages" (*mianxiang nongcun*), contribute their "surplus labor power" (*shengyu laodongli*) to agricultural production, and help relieve the population burden on the industrializing city. Exempted from relocation were those who received remittances or other regular income enabling them to live in the city without government help, those who were skilled and suitable for industrial work, students and intellectuals, as well as the old, weak, sick, and handicapped.[12] In other words, all those who were poor, able-bodied, and unskilled were deemed a "surplus" and expected to become farmers in the countryside.

It soon became clear that these principles were unpopular and ineffective. Though guiqiao were asked to "return to their original native places," officials noted that the majority of them did not have farmland there, had left a long time ago, and were no longer familiar with the place. Others told officials that they would rather die in Guangzhou than move to the countryside because they thought that government services were more widely available in the city.[13] The work of "self-help through production" was no less complicated. Many insisted on working in factories and government sectors, such as railways and education, and only wanted technical training. Others complained about long hours and low wages in the handicraft industry. Some could not wait for a job referral and left for Hong Kong after having just registered at the bureau. A few were posted to remote provinces such as Qinghai and Xinjiang to support the national call to develop the northwest, but they secretly returned to Guangzhou shortly afterward. To the officials, all these were incorrect behaviors because guiqiao should "obey the assignments and go to places where the ancestral nation wants them."

By far, the call to join agricultural production in the countryside provoked the strongest resistance. To avoid relocation, many repeatedly demanded job referrals, lived on money borrowed from relatives, or took to reselling goods such as bicycles, watches, and luxury fountain pens that they had brought with them from abroad. They argued angrily with officials that they were not criminals and "should not be sent to the farm for labor reform." Others made it clear that they would rather beg in the streets of Guangzhou or move back to Southeast Asia than move to the countryside.[14] But as agricultural collectivization proceeded rapidly after 1955 to help feed a growing population in the cities, the bureau stepped up its efforts to relocate the guiqiao as a chief priority.

These reactions led bureau officials to compile a section in the work reports titled "Difficult People, Difficult Cases" (*nanren nanshi*), but they also refrained from applying class analysis to the groups. Gathered from observations, interviews, and gossip, the cases portrayed guiqiao as utterly recalcitrant, a stark contrast to the officials, who seemed equally unprepared to deal with them. Consequently, the officials made claims about the character of guiqiao on the whole: those who had remittances were few; their thinking was impure; they craved urban life, were unwilling to participate in production, and only wanted quick and easy work that compensated well.[15] Many thought that if the government would not find them a job, it should then provide money for food and rent; when their clothes were torn, they even wanted the government to sew them up.[16] Despite these criticisms, officials were silent about the class backgrounds of guiqiao who had been recently displaced, since they found it impossible to determine their conditions overseas. This made guiqiao simultaneously seem like a group differentiated from domestic Chinese and an undifferentiated group from abroad sharing a "difficult" character.

Heavily filtered through official concerns, the reports nonetheless remain revealing in some of the difficulties facing guiqiao. Most of the cases of "difficult" behavior suggest that rural relocation looked to be the worst probable prospect for guiqiao, causing some to fight the bureaucracy tirelessly to avoid it. In one case, a guiqiao from Malaya had returned in 1952 and was assigned to Xinglong Huaqiao Farm on Hainan Island. In 1954, he came back to the city claiming to be ill, asked the bureau for financial aid, and repeatedly refused to go back to the farm. For more than a month, he kept dropping by the bureau every day or two to demand a new job, bursting out in anger, and insulting the officials for failing to carry out "*huaqiao* work." Appalled, officials found him to be dishonest because he had help from a sister and was being investigated by the police for stealing someone's money.[17]

Another case involved a man and his family who had returned from Malaya in 1953 and opened a sewing machine store in Zhangjiang city. After closing down the store because of poor business, Liu wanted to move his family to Guangzhou. Although bureau officials tried to persuade him to stay in Zhangjiang, he said that he would rather die than agree. Determined to find better options, he approached first the provincial Overseas Chinese Affairs Committee and then the bureau for job referral and financial aid, working the state bureaucracy relentlessly from provincial to city level and from Zhangjiang to Guangzhou. When all he received was persuasion to move to the countryside, he yelled at bureau officials for trying to get rid of his family and said that he would rather exit the country permanently than "face death" on the farm, to which officials added bluntly that he now demanded free medical treatment.[18] These fraught encounters suggest that some guiqiao did not find farming an acceptable solution and feared that they would be worse off relocating, while officials were exasperated by the displays of bad temper and constant dependence on state support.

Other examples of resistance to rural relocation seem to suggest a multitude of tactics from guiqiao who refused to go quietly. When bureau officials asked one guiqiao seeking a job and aid to wait and be patient, the man "acted like a fool, banged his head on the blackboard, and threatened to kill himself."[19] Another man came for more assistance after having received ten yuan only ten days earlier. When officials rejected the application, he lay down on the chairs in the office and refused to leave. Two days later, he was joined by his lover to hector the officials. One married couple alternated between dropping in and writing letters to pressure officials for financial assistance, threatening that "whatever accident or situation happens to us, the government is going to be responsible." Refusing mobilization to go to a farm, another woman spanked her ten-year-old son in front of the officials to make him cry, making a public scene. She later agreed to relocate on the condition that the government adopt her son and let him stay in the city. For others who reluctantly agreed to move to the farms, officials noted that some kept changing their minds and wasting precious resources. For example, one guiqiao from Indonesia had agreed to return to his native Fujian province. After officials bought him a bus ticket, made him sign a letter accepting relocation, and saw him off, they spotted him on the street several days later: he had gotten off the bus and come back to the city. Similarly, another guiqiao from Malaya who had been given a boat ticket to move to a farm did not show up on the scheduled date of departure. The string of unruly behavior led bureau officials to conclude that guiqiao lacked "awareness of collective interests and productive labor."

Sounding as reproachful as they were amazed, officials remained silent on what made guiqiao engage in such spirited acts of resistance. Shot through with the frustration of officials trying to enforce compliance, the defiant voices of guiqiao suggest that members came from urban, nonagricultural backgrounds, and were literate and experienced in technical and retail trades. Some were shopkeepers, factory workers, and repair persons. Newly arrived in China, they had lost their previous homes, communities, and livelihoods, and were terrified of farm life. Difficulty in adjusting was sometimes compounded by personal and family tragedy. One case in the reports involved a woman who returned with her husband and children from Indonesia. Shortly after landing in Guangzhou, her husband died of tuberculosis. The woman was left to take care of four children aged fifteen years and younger. Officials wrote that they issued a monthly subsidy of twenty yuan to the family, but the woman became sexually involved with some men and began to ignore her children. Neighbors were gossiping and her children were upset.[20] Critical of the woman's neglect of her role as a mother, officials apparently thought that the financial aid they had provided was a sufficient solution to the problems, and they were concerned with the woman's alleged sexual promiscuity and the unwelcome prospect of having the young children end up in their care.

Other cases also suggest that dispossessed families with young children made up a significant group of aid seekers and were distraught over how they would survive in a strange land governed by unresponsive bureaucrats. Told to accept relocation to the countryside and mandatory labor on state-run huaqiao farms, many resisted what they perceived as political injustice and downward social mobility in the present, while officials thought the "difficult" behavior originated from a past of living overseas, causing guiqiao to be uniformly crass, immoral, and uncivilized in the homeland.

The troubles confronting bureau officials could also be understood in relation to the political ambiguity of guiqiao in 1950s China vis-à-vis the domestic population. Not only was class analysis of Chinese society inapplicable to the new arrivals, the central authorities had also declared huaqiao groups a subject of national concern because of the importance of huaqiao support and remittances. Tensions between huaqiao mobilization and guiqiao resettlement could be seen in cases in which bureau officials criticized guiqiao aid seekers for being wasteful, and some guiqiao responded by asserting their special status and reminding officials of the central policy of "caring for huaqiao." For example, officials reported that one guiqiao from an unspecified country in the Americas had a mother in the city who earned a rental income of over forty yuan a month, but the man still applied for financial aid to pay for his hotel. When officials tried to convince him to live with his mother, he shot back, saying, "I am a guiqiao. Overseas Chinese authorities must deal with this."[21] Baffled by these brash remarks, bureau officials advised each other to practice patience and calm by referring to the mass line of the party. Training sessions in 1956 advised local cadres to cultivate "three thicks" (*sanhou*), "thick skin, thick soles, and thick forbearance" (*lianpi hou, jiaodi hou, hanyang hou*), meaning the ability to tolerate embarrassment, travel long distances, and hold one's temper. When doing huaqiao work, cadres should serve without complaining, listen, and educate guiqiao patiently, but never "lose one's temper," "give orders," or call the masses "backward and stubborn."[22] Officials did not say whether the instructions brought good results.

The political ambiguity of guiqiao helped explain other challenges facing the bureau that were coming from its counterparts in the state system. Though the reports blamed the difficult character of guiqiao, other state agencies also threw obstacles in the way. In the area of job placement, bureau officials discovered that their requests for help from other work units were frequently met with indifference and even open hostility. Officials wrote that even though they "promoted huaqiao policy to employing units, particularly the distinctiveness and potential of huaqiao for united front work [*tongzhan xing*]," making the employment of returned huaqiao a state priority above "ordinary issues," cadres in other work units "tended to think that the history and overseas social relations of huaqiao are too complicated."[23] Instead, they put out "strict criteria of selection" and "did not want anyone who was older, had family relatives and social relations abroad, were near-sighted, could not speak Cantonese but only Mandarin, were married, had children, or were women."[24] The exhaustive list of criteria based on age, gender, eyesight, language ability, family background, and marital status suggests that the work units were not short of candidates for consideration, given the city's high unemployment following Liberation.[25]

Despite central orders to offer guiqiao preferential treatment in employment, bureau officials found that other work units commonly ignored the policy and sometimes deliberately challenged the mandate of the bureau. For example, some work units discriminated against the returnees, citing the "complicated" political affiliations of the group, referring to the lack of information about guiqiao's political activities overseas. Bureau officials attributed the problem to a "generally low awareness of huaqiao policy," but this explanation failed to address the variety of conflicts in the city. As bureau officials learned, cadres working at local police stations often taunted *qiaojuan* (overseas Chinese dependents) applying for permits to visit Hong Kong, saying that they had "nothing to do after filling their stomachs," getting their "money from exploitation elsewhere," and consulting the bureau for everything as though it were their "father."[26] Incidents like this suggest that the state system was far from a cohesive unit in dealing with huaqiao groups. Instead, some state actors resented guiqiao's special status and thought that they should be restrained rather than encouraged.

Given the difficulty of helping guiqiao find jobs in the city, rural relocation emerged as a promising solution to the problem of resettlement. From the early 1950s onward, successive waves of return migration to the PRC led to the construction of huaqiao state farms throughout South China, with the understanding that state investment would gradually turn guiqiao into self-sufficient and productive agricultural communities. First established to resettle Chinese deported by British authorities in Malaya for suspected communist activities, huaqiao farms were part of a larger centrally managed development to relocate "surplus population" from the cities, including demobilized soldiers, convicted criminals, and unemployed urban residents. As Glen Peterson and Han Xiaorong have pointed out, though a small part of rural economy, state farms were responsible for opening up new farmland, producing specialized crops, and sometimes securing border regions, making their function similar to that performed by the Ming-dynasty soldier-farmer colonies known as *weisuo*.[27] Mainly occupying undeveloped mountainous and coastal areas, huaqiao farms were "state units" (*guojia danwei*) financed by the central government and administrated by the provincial Overseas Chinese Committee. Unlike ordinary peasants who received a share of the collective output of their production units, members of state farms were entitled to monthly salaries and benefits, and thus enjoyed higher living standards than ordinary peasants and were treated like urban factory workers.[28] Between 1951 and 1955, nine huaqiao farms were built in the province, housing a total of 5,618 returnees. From 1958 to 1964, thirteen farms were added, indicating a continuous increase in guiqiao arrival. Even after the Cultural Revolution erupted in 1966, three additional farms were built.[29]

Though huaqiao farms required major state investment, some became known for problems of mismanagement and inefficiency. In these cases, farm residents were often inexperienced in agriculture, dissatisfied with farm life, and did not get along with one another. One early example near Guangzhou was the Huangbeixiang Huaqiao Farm and Ranch, established in September 1955 and located in Menggang district of Panyu county. Placed under the supervision of the Production and Welfare Section of the Panyu county government, the farm had originally housed ten guiqiao families from Indonesia. Unlike other larger farms that were operating at the time, families on the Huangbeixiang farm helped finance the construction as shareholders. They each contributed a sum of five hundred yuan to the construction fund and paid for the building of a house for their own use. In return, each member received a regular fixed income of twelve yuan per month. After becoming an advanced production cooperative in 1956, the farm was enlarged by new members, new funds, and more land, but serious problems started to appear. The farm received nineteen poor guiqiao, each of whom was subsidized with three hundred yuan in production assistance, seventy yuan in living allowance, and a thousand yuan to build a straw hut for their residence. In additional to an initial fund of five thousand yuan contributed by guiqiao shareholders, the farm was supported by additional government funds of 7,960 yuan and allocated 140 *mu* of land, bringing the total farm area to more than 210 mu and the arable land to 190 mu. It was equipped with five plowing cows, one mechanical water pump, one two-wheel two-blade plow, and other farm tools to grow crops such as peanuts, green plums, sweet potatoes, and grain. Thirty-eight of sixty farm members were considered able to contribute labor power.[30]

Despite the resources committed by the state and returnee families, new and old members soon deserted the Huangbeixiang farm en masse. By the end of 1956, officials reported that seventeen of the nineteen new guiqiao and two of the ten shareholding families had fled, leaving only thirteen people participating in actual labor. The new members left at a higher rate because they were not tied down by any previous financial contribution. Even so, officials noted that at least two more guiqiao families wanted out and many others were fretful. One guiqiao said angrily before his departure, "This farm is worse than the Labor Reform Department. We work ourselves half to death and don't receive a penny. Even the Labor Reform Department will feed you," indicating that some members might not have received the guaranteed wages. Others were anxious about their future and felt stuck in a miserable situation: "What is really unlucky is that my family has already built a house and invested on this farm. If this continues, death is the only way out [*silu yitiao*]." Speaking to officials and guiqiao who were visiting, one of the farm members made an offer: "If any of you want to join this farm and ranch, I can sell you my house and shares at a discounted price."[31]

Aside from the flight of farm residents, officials reported that a "low level of work enthusiasm" hampered farm productivity, indicating that the farm struggled to achieve economic self-sufficiency. In their telling, the attitude that everyone was "eating from one big pot," referring to free riding, was common. For example, one new member, who had been on the farm for four months, only reported for ten days of work. Others treated farming as a stopgap measure, saying, "we came to the farm because we are waiting for employment in Guangzhou." As soon as rumor came that there was work in the city, they immediately disappeared without a trace. Second to lack of motivation was lack of skill. Most farm members had never performed any agricultural work in their lives. Coming from largely nonagricultural backgrounds overseas, some had been entertainers and handicraft workers. Lacking skill and experience, they hired peasants to perform the heavy work, each of whom had to be paid 1.2 yuan per day, which quickly exhausted the twelve yuan per month received by a farm member. Knowing little about farming, some members also cared little about the conditions of common property. For example, officials wrote, three plows were left exposed in the heat of the sun for over a month, causing the wood to crack. In the end, the peasants who were hired as farmhands could not stand the sight, so they went to gather up the tools.

Besides low productivity, "mutual contempt" among guiqiao and a lack of political leadership prevented the development of a cohesive social community. Some incidents were relatively minor. For example, officials found that one guiqiao did not get along with anyone: "when a neighbor's chicken appeared at his door, he threatened to beat it to death." But a more serious rift emerged between old and new farm members because of their different economic backgrounds. The old members thought that they had built the entire farm and invested large sums of money as shareholders, whereas the new members were poor and reliant on government handouts. They worried that the new group was taking advantage of them. By the same token, new members were jealous of the old members for having their own houses and seeming to enjoy a comfortable life, despite having low amounts of labor power and many children. Adopting the party language of class, one new member even charged that the shareholding guiqiao were all "capitalists." Such "disunity" was exacerbated by official oversight, causing the farm to become a "three-not-governed" (*san buguan*), implying a sense of immorality: "County officials do not want to govern it. The Overseas Chinese Affairs Bureau does not want to govern it. The farm cannot govern itself." Consequently, officials observed that the mass line was not followed and political awareness among residents was weak. Political meetings were seldom held, so good behavior was not celebrated and bad behavior was not criticized. Finding that "a sense of righteousness failed to be established," officials wrote that many farm members became "nostalgic for a former decadent life in the colonies," alluding to their history of living abroad.[32]

These criticisms about the lack of motivation, skill, and unity in the Huangbeixiang farm suggest that guiqiao were far from being a homogeneous group, in spite of being lumped together for relocation by the Party-state. The poorer guiqiao regarded their residence on the farm as involuntary and temporary, seeing that the best opportunities for advancement were in the city. Others who had put money on the farm expected state protection for their investment, so they viewed the newcomers as freeloaders. Given the class tensions, the only commonality was that both groups were unaccustomed to agricultural activities and had to rely on local peasant expertise. Avoidance and inattention of state agencies contributed to another layer of the problem, as no one seemed ultimately responsible for the management of the Huangbeixiang farm. Although the Production and Welfare Section of the Panyu county government had primary responsibility for the daily operation, the farm was located in a remote area and the cadres of the section had no knowledge of agriculture. Since the farm's many serious problems had already made it a political hot potato, neither the county government nor the Overseas Chinese Affairs Bureau wished to get involved. Finding that farm members were left to their own devices, officials of the Guangzhou government could only comment on the incorrect views toward socialism among guiqiao because of their "nostalgia" for life abroad.

Emerging from the challenges of resettlement, the comments in the reports about the foreign past of guiqiao became a substitute for discussions of class. Although returnees were exempt from class analysis, the construct guiqiao took on a class character of its own. From bureau to farm, members appeared uniformly intractable and unproductive in the descriptions. Furthermore, allegations of nostalgia for life abroad carried overtones of wasteful material indulgences that made guiqiao incompatible with a new collective life. Linking the difficult behavior to a past of living abroad, officials did not probe how resettlement policies further marginalized the dispossessed guiqiao and divided state actors. Rather, the effects of a purported foreign past became a convenient explanation for the ineffectiveness of rural relocation.

"Capitalists" without Class Struggle

Just as rural relocation became standard policy after 1955, a concurrent party agenda to attract overseas Chinese investment led to a very different homecoming for wealthier guiqiao, causing serious tensions during the Great Leap Forward campaign (1958–60). As part of the privileged treatment of huaqiao families in the aftermath of the land reform in rural South China, the central government announced that it would offer opportunities

Figure 5.1 Guangzhou Huaqiao New Village, from *Guangzhou huaqiao xincun*.

for guiqiao and qiaojuan (overseas Chinese dependents) to purchase private housing in the cities.[33] The first such initiative, the Guangzhou Overseas Chinese New Village (*huaqiao xincun*), was an unprecedented undertaking involving multiple levels and branches of the government. Planning was first announced in 1954 to build a community of Western-style single homes, duplexes, and apartments in the northeastern suburbs of Guangzhou. With a total investment of half a million yuan in infrastructure, twenty-five hectares of land, and an extra fifty hectares earmarked for future needs, guiqiao and qiaojuan were invited to build and buy houses on land provided at zero cost and exempted from property taxes for five years. By the end of 1959, the development contained over 120 residential buildings, housing more than 100 households and 1,500 residents from more than twenty countries. The next phase of construction aimed to expand the total number of buildings to 400 and residents to 5,000. A prototype for a larger endeavor to attract return investment, this unusual project brought a total of twenty-four huaqiao new villages across Guangdong and Fujian provinces, just when China was about to enter a radical phase of collectivization to raise national productivity in 1958.

A central effort to integrate overseas Chinese resources, the Guangzhou Huaqiao New Village represented the creation of a special space-time for the returning rich within a broader scheme of socialist transformation. A 1959 promotional brochure opens with a congratulatory message from He Xiangning, chair of the Central Overseas Chinese Commission, who describes the new village as "a joyful paradise for guiqiao and qiaojuan" (*guiqiao qiaojuan de xingfu leyuan*). The image of paradise resonates in the rest of the brochure, which portrays the housing construction as a dream come true for the Chinese abroad. "Being away from home a thousand miles makes one long for home even more," says the preface, Chinese abroad have "profound sentiments toward their ancestral nation and native places," and the bonds are "as tight as the one between flesh and bones." For a long time, they have "invested high hopes in the prosperity, wealth, and power of the ancestral nation, and in the success and growth of their native places." They yearned for the "protection of a strong ancestral nation" and "for the day of return after being a guest [in a foreign land]." "With the birth of New China," the brochure claims, "this beautiful wish has been fulfilled."[34] Adding to the progress already made in public morality, culture, education, and hygiene since Liberation, the new village would "benefit, accommodate, and take care of an increasing number of guiqiao wishing to help build socialism." Here, the link between a fixed homeland and a displaced diaspora is revived, even as Communist Liberation is said to have thoroughly transformed old China.

A paradise on earth and a wish come true, the new village was presented as a fairytale ending to the emigrant bound to return. In this construct, the "ancestral nation" is synonymous with "home" and the emigrant "being a guest" elsewhere is only temporarily away. At once ancient but still under completion, the "ancestral nation" is the object of a lifelong desire of the emigrant, who lives in its service and risks permanent exile. Reunited by the development of the new village, the emigrant returns to the care of the ancestral nation, while the ancestral nation takes control of the resources that it needs to bring socialism to fruition. The intervening years of separation are left outside the frame, unseen and undiscussed. Also bypassed are the recent land and marriage reforms, and the campaigns of class struggle and women's liberation that alienated many Chinese abroad (discussed in chapter 4); instead, the brochure invokes the dream of a strong and modern China, which it claims has been fulfilled by the Communist leadership.

Though the new village was to be the "home" to which the emigrant dreamed to "return," it nonetheless had to be artificially created to address an imperfect reality. Staged in attractive detail, the brochure features residents getting around in cars, eating Western and Southeast Asian foods, playing the piano, tending to gardens and pets, enjoying little grandchildren, and having measurements taken to make new clothes. Cast as a "return," such a life of material pleasure was unlikely to be one that had been lived by the emigrants before they left China or that could be lived by the general population at the time; rather, it was meant to give shape to a traditional desire among many emigrants for a triumphant homecoming. Given that this kind of private fulfillment through consumption had become ideologically incorrect by the late 1950s, it required a significant rearrangement of political and financial commitments by the Party-state. In fact, the name of the development, Guangzhou Huaqiao New Village, reflected a conscious making of time and space—huaqiao returnees would enjoy retirement in a "village" filled with urban comforts and at home under the broad structure of socialist modernity. Aimed to bridge the real gap between a new China and a returning diaspora in an imagined reintegration, this principle of special treatment also anticipated the future, as it lay at the core of the Special Economic Zones such as Shenzhen, and the Special Administrative Regions such as Hong Kong—special places where bold political and economic experiments were carried out under the leadership of Deng Xiaoping in the 1980s and 1990s.

Carefully designed to attract guiqiao capital, the new village also served as a showcase to demonstrate the superiority of Chinese socialism. Featuring state-of-the-art architectural design, engineering know-how, and scientific management, the 1959 brochure projects the soft power of a centrally planned nation taking care of all possible needs, a message that could be compared with the 1959 "kitchen debate" between Nixon and Khrushchev. Filling the pages of the brochure are an extensive range of floor plans, landscaping sketches, and photographs of model units where the interiors are fully stocked with modern furniture, electrical appliances such as radios and refrigerators, and traditional art objects. Descriptions boast of streets lined with trees and a community serviced by a wide range of amenities, including a sports ground, an assembly hall, a recreational club, a library, a bank, a hospital, a staff dormitory, a nursery, and an elementary school attended by more than eight hundred students. It was said that future development would add a theater and a secondary school.[35]

Designed to be self-contained, life in the new village was also meant to accommodate the delicate pleasures, exotic tastes, and traditional customs

Figure 5.2 These images in the *Guangzhou huaqiao xincun* brochure aim to suggest that renowned Cantonese opera performers Ma Shizeng and his former wife Hong Xiannü are both well adjusted after their return to China. Ma is shown writing a new play about the ancient poet Qu Yuan and enjoying a conversation with his mother and children about daffodils. Hong Xiannü is featured walking a bicycle accompanied by a child in front of her two-level home and practicing operatic moves with flowing sleeves in her private studio.

of the residents. Appearing mainly as women, children, youth, and the elderly, residents in the brochure are pictured giving singing performances as "Nanyang [South Seas] girls," dancing, riding bicycles, and celebrating Chinese New Year. Perhaps the most notable are the images of the famous Cantonese opera stars Ma Shizeng and Hong Xiannü, whose high-profile return in 1955 set off a flurry of speculation in the overseas Chinese media. The brochure provides a glimpse of the well-adjusted lives of Ma and Hong, a formerly married couple who vowed to devote themselves to the development of the arts in New China. In side-by-side pictures, Ma "chats with his elderly mother, son, and daughter about the art of growing daffodils" and "contemplates a play centered on Qu Yuan to introduce the patriotic ancient poet to the stage of Cantonese opera," while Hong, accompanied by a child, walks her bicycle in front of a two-level home and practices an operatic performance with flowing sleeves in a studio with mirrored walls. The theme of easy interplay between life and art and between a former existence abroad and a new one after return suggests that both Ma and Hong found "home" in the patronage of socialism. They also helped establish that the Communist Party-state was the greatest huaqiao protector of all.

Intersecting with the Great Leap Forward, led by Mao Zedong, the new village could be seen as an aberration in the history of the early PRC, but it was also a sign of multiple, coexisting times and spaces during rapid collectivization. Given that the rest of the population was under great pressure to produce "more, faster, better, and cheaper," the village—with its exclusive membership and support of a bourgeois lifestyle—seemed to fly in the face of the national call to cut waste, endure sacrifice, and surpass Western capitalism in the late 1950s. But one needs to look no further than the contemporaneous images of extraordinary productivity in the factories and fields to find important parallels. A model home for the returning rich, the new village was purposely designed to lure investment from Chinese around the world, and to yield "more, faster, better, and cheaper" no less than the experimental wheat field or the backyard steel furnace in the political messages targeting a domestic audience. In this careful staging to engage the diaspora, the returned emigrant was not in conflict with the peasant or the worker, but marched to the beat of the same drum.

Nonetheless, the sudden acceleration of socialist transformation under Mao's orders did have the effect of bringing the tensions between coexisting party agendas to the fore, as indicated by the archival record. Since guiqiao were mobilized to contribute investment and were kept free from class struggle, this raised the question of how well they could be reintegrated into the imminent future. Indeed, the 1959 overseas brochure could be read in juxtaposition to the internal reports, which reveal that residents in real life were not exempt from the call for frugality, labor, and self-sacrifice, but were subject to intense scrutiny. These discussions suggest that the new village was not only a showcase but also a transitional tool to remake "capitalist" returnees into socialist subjects. As the Great Leap Forward unfolded, party officials filed one criticism after another about the residents elected to serve on the village work committee for their "capitalist-class management," "serious waste," "rightist conservative tendencies," and being "overly accommodating toward the property owners." Too many whined about political meetings and study sessions that "kept happening all day" and "got on their nerves," and about the shortages of supplies. Some said the "three most inconvenient things" about living in the new village were "access to transportation, receiving medical treatment, and going to operas." A few were openly regretful that they had returned and would rather leave China again.[36] Taken together, the reports suggest that party officials regarded all rich guiqiao as "capitalists" in daily practice and were troubled by their attitudes and concentration in the same environment, a concentration that was meant to facilitate control.

The barrage of criticisms about the "capitalist" guiqiao during the Great Leap Forward registered a growing disquiet over an expanded engagement with the diaspora. As seen in the last chapter, the land reform proved that applying class struggle to huaqiao groups was not only enormously difficult and unpopular, but also risked closing off a vital source of foreign exchange to help build socialism. This led the Party-state to proclaim a series of measures to protect the right of huaqiao families to receive and spend remittances and extend a set of privileges to them. After 1955, to meet the ever-increasing demands of socialist transformation, the Party-state ramped up its efforts to attract overseas Chinese investment by undertaking the construction of the new village. Encouraging rich huaqiao to return but protecting them from class struggle, party officials might have hoped that the mobilization of their wealth toward socialist goals would justify the means. But they became haunted by these measures along the way. Labeling the problem "capitalist," officials nonetheless remained silent about whether guiqiao had been an "exploitative" class like the domestic kinds, since this would have forced them to confront the paradox of mobilizing the overseas Chinese rich. "Capitalists" without class struggle, guiqiao embodied an anxiety over the future of socialism.

To manage the discord emerging from the Great Leap Forward, party officials began to articulate how a former life under capitalism made guiqiao ill-disposed toward socialism. A capacious criticism, the "capitalist" tendencies of village residents did not simply mean that they were rich but also that they had become averse to collective labor. Noting that the vast majority of guiqiao residents had only returned after 1956, Party officials observed that they "had lived overseas for long periods of time or were born there," worked in trading, and went "frequently to Hong Kong and Macao," the Western colonies across the border. As a result, they were "more deeply affected by capitalism" than the domestic population and had "strong capitalist thinking." Furthermore, most "relied on remittances and interests from investment for livelihood," and few engaged in "productive labor." According to this understanding, foreign birth and life prior to returning, involvement in trade, shuttling back and forth between socialist China and Western capitalist colonies, and reliance on remittances were "capitalist" because such border-crossing activities, past and continuous, caused guiqiao to shun labor. To the dismay of officials, most residents came back to the country intending merely to "enjoy [their] fortune" (*xiangfu*) and "return to their roots" (*luoye guigen*), and therefore "political awareness was low." Those who participated in some amount of labor did so only because it brought extra income or they were getting too old to take up more profitable work. In other words, officials thought that previous lives of emigration and settlement led guiqiao to disengage from socialist transformation.

Focusing on how foreign experiences in the past predetermined guiqiao resistance, officials made no mention of how the central policies of special treatment could have influenced their formation as socialist subjects. Instead, they stressed that those who avoided labor were "in doubt," "indecisive," and had "wait-and-see, middle-of-the-road attitudes," meaning they were unable to fully evolve. Even when some responded to reform, officials found the transformation half-hearted. Using the story of two "capitalist matrons" surnamed Wu and Lin as an example, officials told a story of how the women residents came to work in a construction project involving a sewage pipe. Being the wives of rich huaqiao men returning from abroad, the two "had always used a car for transportation while overseas" and "never participated in labor, not even the slightest kind." After receiving education, Wu and Lin "labored for the very first time" but not without showing up in dresses, diamond rings, and lipstick. Thus, the women's "capitalist" nature appeared resistant to change and ludicrously out of place, for even work as tough as building a sewage pipe could not dent their superfluous concern with beauty and status. In the end, the remaking of "capitalist matrons" into socialist subjects was successful only in eliciting labor from the body, but not in altering the soul.

In addition to references to resistance to productive labor, official criticisms of "capitalist" tendencies were a larger commentary on guiqiao's ability to circumvent the state system through transnational means. Sustained by private networks across the nation's borders, guiqiao sometimes had access to sources of income, goods, and information through Hong Kong and Macao or via family and other personal connections elsewhere. These back channels enabled guiqiao to escape the constraints of collective life, troubling party officials who took pains to enforce them. Moreover, though the Party-state had hoped that the extension of rights and privileges would help encourage the inflow of remittances, the resources exchanged were not always remittances. Officials noted that many residents in the new village regularly received packages of goods from relatives overseas, so that they did not always have to purchase them from government-run huaqiao stores at inflated prices or depend on rations that limited selection and quantity. Often mailed from Hong Kong, the packages consisted of milk powder, bread, oatmeal, flour, biscuits, peanut oil, soy products, and sugar. Other manufactured items, such as cloth, clothing, and watches, were also sent from Indonesia and Malaya.[37] During the Great Leap, remittances sent to the mainland declined, but the volume of packages rose because news of food shortages prompted families abroad to substitute food items for cash. Officials estimated that the shift was responsible for causing remittances to fall from an annual total of 100–140 million to 50–110 million U.S. dollars during the duration of the campaign.[38] Apart from being consumed, scarce commodities were sometimes sold on the black market or used to bribe officials. These uses undermined the official goal of attracting remittances to stimulate national production rather than private consumption and speculation, suggesting the incompleteness of party control over guiqiao.

Furthermore, criticisms of "capitalist" tendencies referred to the ways in which guiqiao openly challenged the authority of the Party-state, another unwelcome phenomenon defying control. Speaking with an air of worldliness, some guiqiao were heard questioning socialist claims to superiority: "Hong Kong is better than Guangzhou. Things in Hong Kong are cheap and good. Once you are in Hong Kong, you won't want to go back to Guangzhou"; "[the government policies of] united purchase and marketing are united murder. Firewood, grain, oil and cloth are all restricted. Everything is so inconvenient." Others defended the special status of huaqiao groups: "The children of huaqiao should not be asked to go up to the mountain and down to the countryside. Otherwise it will scare huaqiao from returning and sending more money"; "not taking care of huaqiao is to discriminate against huaqiao."³⁹ Perhaps most revealing was how some guiqiao spoke disparagingly about their treatment in resettlement, according to the reports:

> *Huaqiao* policy gets created at five o'clock and revised at six o'clock [changes constantly]. It is like flowers reflected in a mirror, moon reflected in the water [i.e., it cannot be grasped].
>
> *Huaqiao* retail stores exploit *huaqiao*. They treat *huaqiao* like "Gold Mountain men" [*jinshan ding*] and "Nanyang uncles" [*Nanyang bo*].
>
> When helping *guiqiao* to find employment, the government only sees the rich but ignores the poor [meaning that it always helps the rich first].⁴⁰

In these expressions of dissatisfaction that officials collected but did not comment on, guiqiao voices sought to expose the Party-state as inconsistent, inscrutable, and unfair. In the area of resettlement, guiqiao protested that the government squeezed them for their wealth but ignored their hardships. Despite the official view, these guiqiao seemed to insist that current injustices under socialism at home, rather than a past of influences by capitalism abroad, provoked their resistance. In fact, if their pasts meant something important in the late 1950s, it was that they gave some guiqiao the confidence to claim an outside perspective and remind the Party-state that it had fallen short of its promises and ideals.

Described as "capitalist," the dissenting voices in the archival record told of a wider political struggle to speed up the pace of national transformation and maintain a coherent response to the opportunities and challenges presented by guiqiao groups. The tension was captured in a speech given by Guangzhou Mayor Zhu Guang at a meeting on huaqiao affairs in April 1958 at the beginning of the Great Leap Forward. He urged guiqiao to cast off the old ways of living abroad by committing to the following: "cease to engage in smuggling [of goods bought from Hong Kong] and market speculation [on foreign exchange]; strive for remittances; manage the household by diligence [*qin*] and thrift [*jian*]; participate in socialist construction whenever possible; educate their children to take up labor and don't spoil them; and urge their relatives overseas to obey the laws of their countries of residence." Moreover, guiqiao should encourage their relatives living in Hong Kong and Macao to move back to the mainland, while they themselves should avoid visiting those two places. In other words, guiqiao were asked to transform into laborers bound to the collective and leave behind transnational habits of living, but they were also expected to preserve the necessary ties to receive remittances from abroad. While the party was silent on the political implications of mobilizing overseas Chinese wealth, it actively portrayed guiqiao as an unproductive class of smugglers, speculators, and consumers that should be reformed. This conflicting demand to move past but not beyond a transnational existence was at once avoiding class analysis and deeply infused with it.

"Double Nature"

In 1960, the political disarray resulting from the catastrophic failure of the Great Leap Forward converged with a crisis in Indonesia implicating China, leading to serious doubt about guiqiao reintegration. As plummeting industrial and agricultural production and widespread rural famine rattled the socialist order, the year 1960 also marked a mutual deadline for the PRC and Indonesian governments to resolve the question of the "dual nationality" of the ethnic Chinese in Indonesia.[41] According to an earlier agreement, Chinese who wished to remain in Indonesia were supposed to go through an official process to relinquish Chinese nationality and apply for Indonesian citizenship. However, in 1959, a series of events instigated by the Indonesian army to ban "alien retail traders" and Chinese residence in West Java disrupted plans for an orderly transition.[42] Given the tense atmosphere and outbreaks of violence, Chinese who were already applying for Indonesian citizenship felt the need to seek immediate repatriation to the PRC.[43]

By the end of 1960, under the grand slogan "the great ancestral nation is the most powerful protector of huaqiao" (*weida zuguo shi huaqiao zui youli de kaoshan*), the PRC government brought 94,000 guiqiao to China, 54,000 of whom were resettled in Guangdong province. Over 7,000 of these remained in Guangzhou city. A significant number of others funded their own relocations to China.[44] With the final number of arrivals reaching 120,000, this massive repatriation unexpectedly coincided with attempts led by the Chinese Communist Party to regain its footing and restore production after the Great Leap. One way was through renewing class struggle to recommit the nation to socialism, which brought a hard shift in tone about guiqiao capitalists and the expiration of their special status.

Negatively cast as "double-natured" after 1960, guiqiao was one of the most important registers in the dramatic shifts of Mao's China during the late

1950s and early 1960s. Having led the building of state farms and private housing in the 1950s, party leadership suspended class struggle and constructed a separate space-time to accommodate the reintegration of guiqiao during the transition to socialism. This ambiguity allowed the government to incorporate and differentiate groups according to their labor power and monetary resources, but it also required a significant flexibility to tolerate the privileged treatment of guiqiao within the larger project of socialist construction. This flexibility ended during the disaster of the Great Leap Forward and in the long shadow it cast over the rest of the Mao period. To reestablish the absolute certainty of socialist values, the party began to attack guiqiao and other huaqiao groups, along with other class enemies, for a perceived political unreliability and continuing exteriority to the nation despite their return. Moreover, it imagined that they harbored a deep, insidious attachment to capitalism that could undermine socialism from within.

This dramatic development began with a sharp deterioration of the state's ability to balance different coexisting times and spaces during the early 1960s. In Guangzhou, official reports suggest that the sudden return of Chinese from Indonesia in 1960 heavily strained resources and relations in the city, where local authorities had already been battling severe shortages on all fronts in the aftermath of the Great Leap. Long lines started appearing outside restaurants and shops, as the new guiqiao carrying foreign-issued passports and PRC-issued remittance certificates tried to buy meals and other necessities.[45] Some engaged in speculation in the black market, buying and selling goods such as biscuits, cigarettes, watches, and bicycles that they had brought from abroad. Guiqiao reception offices reported the theft of food items.[46] Although the central policy was to relocate the new arrivals to either their "original native places" or the nine national huaqiao farms throughout the province, most of the guiqiao, like those who came before them, fought hard to stay in the city. Widespread resistance to rural relocation was reported early in March 1960. Officials found that guiqiao who had money lodged with family relatives in Guangzhou or relied on interest from investment and savings to survive. Some relentlessly tried to find work locally to avoid moving to the countryside.[47] All these activities suggest that the 1960 arrivals heightened competition for the already scarce resources in the city.

Guiqiao interactions with state actors and ordinary citizens combined to create old and new problems of resettlement. Although all employment assignments and household registrations of guiqiao were to be handled through the Overseas Chinese Affairs Bureau and several reception services offices under the Provincial Receiving Committee, some returnees found ways to get around the bureaucracy. Some bypassed the bureau and applied directly to the Public Security Bureau for household registrations in hopes of gaining faster approval.[48] Others were able to find work in factories through personal connections, even though private recruitment was forbidden by the state. When a chemical fertilizer factory in the suburbs had to lay off its workers, a group of new guiqiao who had been employed there illegally went to petition the officials for assistance. Those who had already been relocated in the countryside reappeared in the city, searching for work, roaming around in groups, and protesting their conditions.[49] There were reports of housing scams preying on guiqiao, as some of the newcomers bought wooden shacks that were in fact government property and slated for demolition. Others bought houses at much-inflated prices or of smaller sizes than they had been led to believe.[50] Returning at the juncture of a national crisis and the fallout of a foreign one, guiqiao seemed to have found themselves doubly displaced.

Not surprisingly, the majority of Indonesian guiqiao covered by the government repatriation program ended up being relocated to state farms, a treatment that once again provoked vigorous resistance. According to Han Xiaorong, about 60 percent of the Indonesian returnees in 1960 were assigned to state farms, in contrast to the 1956 figure of only 4 percent in Guangdong.[51] In the two farms, Lufeng and Huaxian, that were established in the first half of the 1950s, about 70 percent of all inhabitants arrived during the year 1960. There, receiving the most party attention were the youthful, able-bodied guiqiao, who officials said were only about one-fifth to one-fourth of all new arrivals but represented one-third to one-half of the labor force on the farms, making their contribution to productivity crucial. Nonetheless, officials found that instead of devoting their energies to farming, the returned youth were boisterous troublemakers. In a 1961 report by the Communist Youth League, officials observed that while the youth had hoped to help build the nation, most had not imagined becoming farmers. This "psychological unpreparedness" led to resentment and open conflicts. Though officials believed that the youth were "unprepared," some youth insisted that they had been "deceived" because the government seemed interested only in exploiting their labor to develop resources and had little concern for their welfare. Some were shocked that the huaqiao farms were nothing like the mechanized Soviet farms seen in films, but were actually "deserts." Others boldly suggested that the anti-Chinese movement in Indonesia might have been instigated by the Chinese embassy to trick them into repatriation. Many demanded to go to schools in the city or to return to Indonesia immediately.[52]

From the standpoint of the party officials, these were objectionable comments about a privileged treatment, the result of special consideration for the returnees. For example, officials explained that every new guiqiao was entitled to thirty catties of grain each month, about one-third to one-half more than the ration for an ordinary peasant. Without indicating whether the guiqiao actually received the rations, officials noted that everybody was complaining incessantly about not having enough to eat, even sneering that "all the things available in the country can be bought overseas, but you cannot buy anything once you return. The ancestral nation is bragging to foreigners." Instead of keeping the peace, young guiqiao "caused disturbances," "assaulted kitchen cooks," and "stole sweet potatoes from the collective." Finding that the youth lacked agricultural skills, officials briefly acknowledged that they in fact came from educated backgrounds.[53] This recognition suggested a probable sense of displacement among these guiqiao, who felt trapped in the harsh conditions of farm life.

Meanwhile, the Indonesian crisis also brought new residents to the Guangzhou Huaqiao New Village. Twenty families were added, bringing the total number to 159 households and 805 residents. The archives from 1960 to 1966 suggest that surveillance of village residents tightened, despite images of a free and comfortable life in the 1959 publication discussed earlier. As a small but wealthy sector of the city's population, the village was deemed to have a "high concentration of capitalists," suggesting the visibility of guiqiao residents to party authorities. A 1960 report showed detailed records of the residents, classifying 82.3 percent or 131 households as "capitalist elements," of which 80 percent were "upper-middle class capitalists" and the remaining were "upper class." Over 70 percent of all residents (600 people or 117 households) were guiqiao, while others were qiaojuan (domestic dependents of huaqiao). Ninety-five per cent of all households were from Southeast Asia, especially Indonesia. Most of them had recently arrived in China (i.e., after 1956) and still had properties and immediate kin overseas.[54] As the most recent arrivals, the new guiqiao were kept under close watch.

Apart from receiving new residents, the new village was the site of a recently established People's Commune aimed at rallying people around production, but which brought sharp critiques of the unreliability of the guiqiao. Reporting in 1960 that there were 272 people "idling at home," party officials calculated that there were two people per household who did not participate in any labor. In a group of sixty "capitalist elements," only fourteen people "expressed support" for the commune; thirty-seven were "in doubt but got on the bandwagon"; the remaining nine "expressed discontent." As the report noted, since a chief purpose of the People's Commune was to "destroy the capitalist class at its foundation," these guiqiao acted like "gentlemen stealing chickens, calm on the surface but nervous within."[55] The centrist faction was the most superficial and unreliable. According to officials, members had "five great fears": "fear of restriction and lack of freedom, fear of labor and production, fear of joining collective life (including dining halls), fear of being separated from family members, fear of not being able to spend money," all of which in their minds would cause their quality of life to deteriorate. Some in the "center-left" group thought conditions in the village were premature to set up a commune. Others in the "center-right" group could not care less, since "everyone already had money and could take care of themselves." Yet, in order to "create political capital" and "appear progressive," these guiqiao tried to act eager and supportive on the outside. In one example, officials wrote that two of the "big capitalists" went to every single political meeting, but said "nothing got through their ears." They only went so as to "not get criticized for being backward." Their wives did not participate in the meetings at all and often bought food on the black market, which officials thought an indication of the imperviousness of guiqiao.[56]

Though the archival record did not specify the gender ratio in the new village, officials tended to focus exclusively on the productivity of women residents. While the 1959 publication discussed earlier featured photographs of women laboring diligently in a sewing workshop, officials reported that only eight to ten people actually worked there, though more than twenty had signed up. The low level of participation forced the workshop to close in 1959. After the People's Commune was established in 1960, three new cooperatives were set up: sewing, knitting, and embroidery. About twenty-five women, mostly "wives of the capitalist class," joined. Soon the complaints came pouring in. Those in the sewing group complained about back and leg pains, which they claimed could cause physical deformity and loss of beauty. Those in the knitting group complained about headaches, dizziness, and tired hands, saying that these problems caused them to develop neurasthenia and even mental illness. Those in the embroidery group complained about low wages. They were discouraged that after spending several days toiling, they still could not produce a finished product. Furthermore, each piece would only generate an income of eight cents. With such low returns for their hard work, one woman said, "Even when my children ask [for pocket money], I have to give them at least a dollar or eighty cents. Participating in production is just not worth it." In the end, only fifteen women remained in the cooperatives.[57] These unsuccessful examples led party officials to conclude that participation in the commune was almost nonexistent in the village.

According to the reports, other aspects of collective life in the commune suffered similar setbacks. In the health services group, which consisted of eleven "wives of the upper-middle class," members were educated in hygiene with the expectation that they would serve others in the future. However, the wife of one "big capitalist" stated, "It is useful to apply the knowledge to one's children. But to wash someone else's rotten feet is a scary thought."[58] The dining hall also failed to attract much interest. Only twenty-six people regularly ate there, most of them students and workers. Though only eight to ten catties of rice were cooked a day, there were always leftovers because most of the "capitalist class" did not go there: "when the food looked good, they would buy a little with the meal tickets." Village residents also seemed wary of having their children attend the nursery. Although a total of 110 young children lived in the new village, only twenty-one went to day care. This was because "most of the families did not trust the standards of food, sanitation, facilities, and teachers there," said the officials.[59]

These reports illustrate a profound frustration among the officials that efforts to hasten socialist transition in the new village amounted to nothing. In search of a deeper answer, they drew a new distinction between returning and domestic capitalists by highlighting the former's foreign origins and lack of political reform. Asserting that all capitalists were similarly "two-faced," officials wrote that guiqiao were a much more stubborn variety because "they had lived overseas for long periods of time, whereas their time spent in China had been short." Their political and economic relations with "capitalist society" involved "hundreds of threads and thousands of strands" (*qiansi wanlü*), meaning they were impossible to know and disentangle. After their return, guiqiao were concentrated in the village and separated from the laboring masses. As "overseas orphans" (*haiwai guer*), they had been subject to abuse and discrimination abroad. Yet they had not been exposed to reform, as had the domestic capitalists, claiming that they were "patriotic," "no different from the masses," and had "no need for political education."[60] Here the foreign past of guiqiao was represented as a form of "capitalist" contamination far more deep-seated than the domestic type.

A remarkable turning point, this commentary on guiqiao in 1960 stressed that past exposures to "capitalism" undercut their receptiveness to socialism, sowing the seeds of a deterioration of their political status in the aftermath of the Great Leap Forward. In the commentary, officials sought for the first time to separate guiqiao capitalists from domestic capitalists by tracing the history of the former and underlining their foreignness. They used "capitalist society" to refer to the original homes of guiqiao in Southeast Asia but were vague about its actual meaning. They criticized the special status of guiqiao, from their residential separation to their political exemptions and their patriotic assertions, for making them resistant to change, though they avoided mentioning that this status was created by Party-state policies. In 1963, a new campaign to reinvigorate the class struggle unfolded. Known as the Socialist Education Movement, this effort was associated with Mao Zedong, who had stepped down as head of state because of the Great Leap but remained as chair of the Communist Party. Following the Sino-Soviet split, Mao and his associates sought to fight a trend of "revisionism" that they saw in the Soviet Union and that they thought was unfolding in China in the form of an entrenched party bureaucracy and recurring bourgeois elements in society.[61] As they called upon the nation to "never forget class struggle," the political status of all huaqiao groups took a sharp turn for the worse.

Already criticized for being "capitalist" and "two-faced," guiqiao in the Socialist Education Movement were described as having a "double nature" (*shuangchong xingzhi*). Writing broadly about "*huaqiao* capitalists," an analysis by the United Front Department of the Foshan District Committee in 1963 posited that even though they shared many similarities with the domestic capitalists, who made "a livelihood by controlling the means of production and exploiting the working class," huaqiao were indecisive as to whether to commit to the socialist or capitalist path.[62] This was because, on the one hand, huaqiao had suffered oppression and discrimination under foreign imperialism and ethno-nationalism while abroad. As a result, they looked to the ancestral nation for protection and hoped that it would become wealthy and powerful, which demonstrated their patriotism. On the other hand, the interests of huaqiao as a capitalist class led them to harbor misgivings about socialism. They could also be easily swayed by reactionary propaganda overseas. As a consequence, this "double nature" of huaqiao capitalists drove them to "wander around the intersection of two very different social systems, socialism and capitalism" and to "have one foot in each of two different boats at the same time," making the class struggle against them a "long and tortuous battle."

A full-fledged development of the "two-faced" portrayal, this analysis in 1963 provided underpinnings for a renewed class struggle by implying that huaqiao groups were politically deviant. While party cadres had been vague about what made huaqiao "capitalist," they now asserted that huaqiao engaged in the exploitation of the working class abroad. This history made them similar to domestic capitalists within China, and hence class struggle was relevant. More significantly, party cadres pointed out that what made huaqiao distinct was that they were unable to fully invest in either capitalism or socialism, as in the expression, "having one foot in each of two different boats." It is worth mentioning that this Cantonese slang, often used to describe sexual infidelity, was being borrowed to suggest political infidelity. As class struggle—first applied to huaqiao families during the land reform and subsequently downplayed but never applied to guiqiao—was back on the table, diaspora connections became a liability. To fight a feared revisionism, the party not only tried to correct the assumption that there was no need for class struggle among huaqiao; it now opined that the class struggle of huaqiao was far more complicated and severe than the ordinary kind because too much attention in the past had been focused on accommodating the special characteristics of huaqiao. Henceforth, "politics" must be in command to reeducate huaqiao through the study of Mao Zedong Thought.

To revive class struggle, the Socialist Education Movement in Guangzhou took the form of a mass recounting and studying of "three histories" (*sanshi*) under the leadership of street neighborhood associations in 1963–64. In communities with high guiqiao and qiaojuan concentrations, older residents were told to narrate the "history of the street neighborhood" (*jiedao lishi*), the "history of the laboring people" (*laodong renmin lishi*), and the "history of the blood and tears of *huaqiao*" (*huaqiao xielei shi*), the last of which was directed at guiqiao and qiaojuan who could remember the pre-Liberation days. All narrators were instructed to divide people into exploiter class and exploited class and to separate socialism from capitalism. They were also reminded that "it is only through revisiting the bitterness of the past that one could understand the sweetness of the present." After these sessions, street neighborhood associations reported that class consciousness among guiqiao and qiaojuan was raised spectacularly. Commitment to socialism was firmly established.[63]

Examples from the Er Long Street Association in the city's Haizhu district illustrate how the movement helped huaqiao groups enact socialist subjectivity. In one story, a woman surnamed Zhang returned to China from Malaya in 1956. She was unhappy about the status quo, took to complaining that her return was a mistake, and contemplated an exit to Hong Kong. But after hearing about "poverty in the old society" and the story of a slave girl sold to "the king of Er Long Street" at the photographic exhibition "How Did She Become Crazy?" Zhang was instantly transformed. She remembered the days when she had also suffered poverty in the old society and was "forced to abandon her two-year-old daughter" before emigrating overseas. She recalled her experience of "living abroad and witnessing how patriotic huaqiao were persecuted by the British colonial authorities in Malaya." After that, she thought of "her happy life after returning to the ancestral country, reflected upon her mistakes, and dropped the idea of moving to Hong Kong."[64] In this account, the "old society" referred to China before Liberation, when poverty had forced Zhang to leave home and become a huaqiao. The story of the slave girl in the exhibition was a reminder of the ills of the nation's feudal past, allowing Zhang to travel through her own past and recover a parallel memory of a young daughter whom she had given up before emigration. Transported back to her days in Malaya, she relived the oppression of British colonial rule and rediscovered happiness in her present life since returning to the new China. Because of this momentous revelation, Zhang chose to stay and rejected the lure of another colonial society that would once again make her a huaqiao.

Another story centered on an older qiaojuan surnamed Li, who had family members living in the United States and was a religious devotee.

She recalled that in the drought year of 1943, she "went to seven different temples to pray for protection, bowed her head numerous times, and got cheated out of her money by swindlers." Yet her family still went hungry and lost their home, just as "dead bodies were lying around in Taishan," a famous home area of the overseas Chinese. Li went on to contrast this dark memory with the present since Liberation. Despite being in another drought year, she "saw no signs of it," noting that "supplies were abundant" and "people were happy." Whereas religion had not kept her free from hunger, Li realized that the Communist Party finally provided the material and spiritual riches that she had always craved.[65] However, the starvation emphasized in the narrative dated from a time of war against Japan, which cut off remittances to China in 1942, while the more recent famine during the Great Leap Forward was occluded.

Not to be taken at face value, the accounts of Zhang and Li marked the abolition of the special treatment of guiqiao and qiaojuan that had been in place since 1953. As emigration appeared as a stream of evil—poverty, slavery, family breakdown, colonialism, hunger, death, and religious superstition—that could only be terminated by Liberation, it stood for an endless cycle of feudal oppression that was eventually broken by the linear, progressive march of socialist time. Zhang was in the loop of going abroad, returning, and wishing to go again. Li was visiting one temple after another, succumbing to rounds of prayers and delusion. By reliving the cycle of separation and victimization, both women were reborn as socialist subjects. The striking redefinition of temporalities indicated a fundamental change in the place of the diaspora in 1960s China. Under the central policy of special accommodation, huaqiao groups were allowed to remain temporarily outside but not above an ultimate transition to socialism. Though the actual implementation was rife with tension, there remained a basic tenet that emigrant pasts and national history were different and coexisting, requiring a final but incremental process of integration. By the time of the Socialist Education Movement, the temporary status of huaqiao had expired. Instead, they became part of China's past ended by the Communist Revolution.

This reinterpretation of emigrant histories as cyclical but brought into linear time by Liberation was an instruction for huaqiao groups to complete socialist transformation immediately, but it also carried a paradox. Trotted out to perform the "old society," guiqiao and qiaojuan walked a thin line between the past and the present. They enabled a response to a feared revisionism, but they also became a living proof that feudal, bourgeois, and capitalist elements had not yet departed. On the eve of the Cultural Revolution, a final act to smash the old ways, autobiographies written in the voices of young qiaojuan and guiqiao attempted to resolve the paradox. Through a common theme of devotion to Mao Zedong, these accounts trace a deep awakening to one's family background, ending in a purifying repudiation of diaspora connections. Typical was the following example, entitled "Listen to the words of Chairman Mao. Dedicate one's youth to the ancestral nation" (May 12, 1966), attributed to a qiaojuan woman named Zhang Xiufen:

> I was born into a *huaqiao* family. My father and uncles all live abroad. After graduating from high school in 1963, I was not admitted into a university. I stayed at home and did nothing for three years. From a young age, I was under the influence of capitalist thought. I grew envious of the indulgences of my relatives abroad who wore high-heeled shoes and stylish clothes.... At the end of 1963, my uncle overseas introduced me to a *huaqiao* youth named Cai XX. Cai owned two restaurants in Colombia. I thought that after leaving the country, I would be rich, live in a foreign-style house, and get around in a car. At that time, I was assigned to do some substitute teaching in a primary school. I kept counting the days [to my departure]. My individualistic and selfish thoughts were many. I thought that I was applying my talents to trivial tasks.... Later, I joined the street neighborhood youth association and studied the thought of Chairman Mao. I learned to analyze things through "class." What is the class background of Cai? After marrying him, wouldn't I become the housewife of a capitalist? I would then look after the children, cook, and depend on another person for a living for the rest of my life. What's more, in a capitalist society, men have the right to have "three wives or four concubines." Therefore I abandoned my wish to leave the country. I applied to work in a farm village.[66]

In this account, Zhang Xiufen recounted how her birth and upbringing in a huaqiao family had exposed her to "capitalist thought," causing her to idle at home and fantasize a materialist life abroad. The prospects of marrying a huaqiao in Colombia epitomized her "individualistic" and "selfish" desires for wealth and pleasure. After receiving education in Mao Zedong thought, Zhang developed a critique of huaqiao marriage for leading her to a future of economic dependence and gender inequality. Seeking release from the ruinous cycle of emigration and diaspora, Zhang rejected the marriage arrangements and rededicated herself to socialism by becoming a rural peasant.

Another example of self-criticism and transformation was associated with Zhang Yingguang, a male guiqiao who lived on the Huaxian Hong Xiuquan Fruit and Fertilizer Farm, named after the leader of the mid-nineteenth-century Taiping Rebellion. Like the previous story, Zhang Yingguang recalled how he became a "new peasant" and joined the Communist Youth League in a piece entitled "Always listen to the words of Chairman Mao. Make a lifetime of revolution in the village" (April 19, 1966):

> I came from a *huaqiao* merchant family. In 1960, I came back to study. I wanted to become an expert, an engineer. I was afraid of going to the countryside. Salaries are low and you have to endure sun and rain. Work is dirty. Life is dull. After reading Mao's essay about the spirit of the "Foolish Man [Moving the Mountain]," I joined agricultural production. My parents objected [to my decision] and terminated their remittances. They said that I needed to inherit the family business. I was determined to be an heir of the proletariat, not of the capitalists. . . . They considered farming a lowly business. If [they turned me into] an heir of capitalism, that would not be showing me their love, but doing me harm. It would be to destroy my revolutionary career.[67]

In this narrative, overseas upbringing and merchant family background predetermined Zhang Yingguang's "capitalist" outlook and fear of farm work, but he was redeemed after returning to China and studying Mao Zedong Thought. Viewing through the lens of class politics his personal desire to become an engineer and that of his parents for him to inherit the family business abroad, Zhang rejected all that would make him a huaqiao, a capitalist, and an intellectual. In doing so, he turned against his father, took up farming, and broke the lineage of capitalism. Reborn as a native member of the proletariat, Zhang was set for a revolutionary future under the guidance of Chairman Mao.

Written in the first person, both accounts suggest the extreme reform required of huaqiao groups by the late 1960s. Multiple conflations made possible the appearance of fixed, bounded opposites. On one end was a capitalist life abroad. On the opposite end was a socialist life at home. In this new narrative, huaqiao fell on the wrong side of history, and the only path to redemption was a total annihilation of one's emigrant past and transnational ties. Building on the momentum of the Socialist Education Movement, the Cultural Revolution (1966–76) brought wholesale and vehement attacks on huaqiao groups and practices. Branded as one of the "seven black elements" (*hei qi lei*), overseas Chinese (*qiao*) shared the charge of being class enemies with landlords (*di*), the rich (*fu*), counterrevolutionaries (*fan*), criminals (*huai*), rightists (*you*), and spies (*te*). All transnational ties were denounced as "overseas relations" (*haiwai guanxi*), a term suggesting reactionary and subversive activities. Open violence against huaqiao groups became commonplace. Following the utter collapse of the central bureaucracy across the nation, new regulations forbade guiqiao and qiaojuan to leave the country, visit relatives overseas, send letters overseas, or receive remittances. Chinese of foreign nationality were prohibited from entering the country and gaining permanent settlement and citizenship.[68] Yet this assault on emigration coincided with multiple waves of return migration, including a new stream from Indonesia after Suharto's rise to power in 1965, and another from Vietnam because of a growing conflict with China during the late 1970s. The returns later forced a further expansion of state farms and a new relaxation of policy allowing the returnees to leave for Hong Kong and remigrate elsewhere.[69] Seen in this context, the dramatic accounts attributed to huaqiao youth suggest an ever-changing autobiography of the nation, as it struggled to cope with an unpredictable diaspora and maintain a linear order of the past, present, and future.

Conclusion

During the "homecomings" of Chinese abroad, Party-state discussions about guiqiao told of an evolving engagement with a returning diaspora while seeking to build a socialist China. From the beginning, officials treated the returnees as a single group and did not apply class analysis to them. Yet, for pragmatic reasons, officials also differentiated guiqiao according to their economic status to determine policy and treatment. They solicited the return of the overseas Chinese rich and their investment in urban housing. They tried to turn poor refugees into a productive, self-sufficient workforce on state farms. This split strategy, one for the domestic and another for the returned, one for the rich and another for the poor, created a paradox at the heart of party ideology, in which class was a core element. The fragmentation required significant room for ambiguity, but it vanished under the sweeping call for change during the 1960s.

Though class was initially displaced from the official language about guiqiao, this chapter has shown that it crept back through criticisms of a "foreign past." In these criticisms, guiqiao had a "difficult" character because of an enduring history of living overseas. They were nostalgic for life in "capitalist society." Two-faced and double-natured, they could not decide whether to follow socialism or capitalism. In the end, they were instructed to put absolute faith in socialism by banishing their former existence and relations once and for all. As guiqiao in fact came from vastly different social backgrounds and life histories, the criticisms not only concealed the internal diversity of members, but also overstated their foreignness and immutability compared to other social groups in China. Invented as a temporal atavism at a time of increasingly rigid politics, the figure of guiqiao came to represent the specter of a returning capitalism in Mao's China.

To sum up this "diaspora moment" in the terms of Zhou Enlai's marriage metaphor, China's "married-out" children returned to the natal family without warning. Searching for an idealized homeland, they represent how the histories of mass emigration impinged on the present and demanded a reintegration. Yet, while they had been absent, the masters of the house had also changed. Determined to break with the past, the new masters then vowed to build utopia. As the visions of time not only failed to line up but never stood still on either side, "home" turned out to be a constant state of seeking rather than one of having.

Conclusion and Epilogue

During the nineteenth and twentieth centuries, Chinese emigrants not only helped transform the world's new frontiers and old homesteads, but also turned China into a diaspora's homeland. Combining the twenty million who moved overseas with another thirty million who traveled overland to North Asia, modern Chinese migrations were nearly as great in size as the European migrations across the Atlantic Ocean. Mass emigration also made South China comparable to other world regions, such as South Asia and Eastern and Southern Europe, which also witnessed large exoduses of their populations during the same period.[1] Like their counterparts elsewhere, Chinese emigrants helped weave the old country into webs of exchange, advancing the forces of mass production, consumption, urbanization, communication, and transportation. They also injected new blends of culture and politics into Chinese life, bringing the world home. By the second half of the twentieth century, many former colonial and settler societies in the New World had come to embrace their founding as "nations of immigrants."[2] A related but distinctive phenomenon occurred in the Old World: China became a homeland-nation, at once fragmented and networked. Century-long and worldwide, Chinese mass migration deserves greater recognition as a touchstone of China's development in a global system.

Appearing in different guises, the "diaspora moments" explored in this book reveal a pattern of rupture, transformation, and recombination during a century of Chinese movements. Collectively, they make up a chronicle of "diaspora time," intersecting with other temporalities of human action and creating spaces for productive engagement. By approaching Chinese history through diaspora moments, the point is not to decenter China or the nation, but simply to view it through the webs of entanglement and interdependency where it has belonged. Coming into focus are times when the evolving nation was stopped by a wider field of activity, responded purposefully, or simply muddled through. Various actors, including emigrants and returnees, as well as Chinese and non-Chinese players, jostled in these working spaces, causing unintended, long-term consequences. One of the most enduring creations was the idea of a "temporary" diaspora (*huaqiao*) in contrast with an "eternal" homeland (*zuguo*). From the great departures to continuous ties to unexpected returns, diaspora was something to act with.

As we have seen, the first diaspora moment in modern Chinese history concerns the indentured "coolie" migration to the Americas. Long misunderstood as a belated gesture to legalize emigration, the 1893 edict—which actually called for returns—helps uncover a longer arc of historical development since the 1840s, one in which Chinese indentured laborers to the British West Indies, Cuba, and Peru contributed significantly to China's evolution from empire to nation. From 1847 to 1874, the coolie emigrants enmeshed the Qing with other production and labor regimes, spheres of public debate, and a system of sovereign states. Here, diaspora time met with the temporalities of Western capitalism, colonialism, and imperialism, facilitating a crucial transition from slavery to free labor in the Americas. Just as importantly, the rupture heralded the beginning of Chinese sovereignty and a new diaspora–homeland dynamic. Lying in the wake of the indenture trade was a rapid expansion of diplomacy and a new attention to huaqiao, a diaspora understood to be widely dispersed but always returning.

Accompanying the rupture was a series of transformation integral to the founding of modern China. The second diaspora moment in this book emerged in tension with the temporalities of Nationalist China and the Japanese empire during the 1920s and 1930s. Drawn to prosperous Chinese migrant settlements in the port cities of Southeast Asia, Chinese intellectuals at Shanghai's Jinan University produced a massive scholarship on Chinese in the South Seas or Nanyang. Deeply engaged with European and Japanese thought traversing maritime Asia, their work was an act of negotiation with colonial knowledge. Inhabiting the oceanic circuits of print, education, and research enabled by Chinese emigrants, the Jinan researchers narrated China's future resurgence as a global power through uniting with the diaspora. In terms of their impact on scholarship, their discovery of Chinese emigrants as central subjects of a larger maritime history and geography also helped inaugurate the field of overseas Chinese history.

Apart from rupture and transformation, recombination was another mode in which diaspora time operated in modern Chinese history. Turning to a Chinese creole intellectual from Singapore, the third moment involves Lim Boon Keng, whose Confucian revivalism was one of many variations across the twentieth century. By situating Lim in the forces of colonial power and religion-making across Asia, his famous conflict with the anti-Confucian Chinese writer Lu Xun fades as a clash of opposites. To make Confucianism compatible with modernity, Lim attempted to recover its authenticity, but the process also involved combining it with global ideologies of race, gender, Christianity, and science. These forces were simultaneously reshaping China. Therefore, Lim's "authentic" neo-Confucianism suggests that Chinese traditional culture is an open, shared enterprise, where members of the Chinese nation and diaspora have repeatedly competed with and built on each other's claims to assert a global Chinese identity.

The fourth and fifth moments in this study feature two distinct encounters with the temporalities of diaspora in Mao's China, leading to a reconfiguration and a reassertion of national time. The different temporalities include one traditionally residing in rural South China and one newly arriving as a vast reverse migration fleeing Southeast Asia. During efforts to liberate production and women from feudalism in Guangdong province, the Communist Party encountered a social fabric of interdependent relations between overseas men and domestic women, and between emigrant and nonemigrant households. Threading through was a multitude of economic activities locally, transnationally, and ultimately too important to socialist building in an ascendant Cold War. Consequently, party officials temporarily moved huaqiao families outside socialist time and envisioned women who stayed behind as bridges toward a reintegrated future. However, this temporary status of huaqiao groups crumbled during a dramatic compression of socialist time and continuous waves of return migration. As the diaspora's homeland and a new communist nation, China in the 1950s and 1960s faced the double tasks of resettlement and revolution, which appeared to be not only divergent but also increasingly at odds with each other. In the headlong rush toward a utopian future, the Party-state denounced the returning diaspora as an unknown foreign past threatening to bring capitalism back into the present. In 1978, things came full circle. When Deng Xiaoping assumed power and shifted China away from the

Maoist course, one of the first things he did was to reach out to capitalists in the diaspora.

Moving in time as well as in space, diaspora puts into focus mass migration as a historical force traversing China and the world. Receding from view is a smooth, orderly periodization of states that has supported a self-confirming telos of the nation, shrouding a journey enriched by sharp turns, long arcs, full circles, and unexpected shortcuts.

New Migrants, Rising China, and Greater China

A volatile mix, "diaspora moments" demonstrate a shifting dialectic of times, spaces, and actors that will go on to shape China in the twenty-first century. Indeed, some broad trends can be observed after Chinese emigration resumed and accelerated in the 1980s and 1990s. During the Mao period—aside from reverse migration, trickles from South China through Hong Kong, and a permitted exit for returnees and resident family members of Chinese overseas in the early 1970s—emigration was not allowed for the general population. Deng Xiaoping's economic reform changed the picture beginning in the late 1970s. Under his leadership, central and local governments also led efforts to reconnect with the diaspora in Hong Kong, Taiwan, Southeast Asia, and the Americas, which encouraged economic investment and cultural reidentification.[3] Besides those living in traditional sending areas, Chinese students and contract workers were the first to rejoin the global migration. The end of the Cold War in 1989 further contributed to increased outflows. The collapse of the Soviet Union led to a loosening of emigration controls in Eastern Europe and a lengthy political and economic transition around the world. In China, after the violent suppression of the 1989 Tian'anmen Democracy Movement, the Chinese Communist government deepened market reforms and further liberalized exit.

The far-reaching effects are well known: a rising consumer society, a widening rural–urban gap, and a political system oscillating between staying open and being in control. Finding new markets, global capitalism expands. Finding new opportunities elsewhere, people leave again.

A growing outflow of about six million people since 1978, the emigrants are officially described as "new migrants" (*xin yimin*) to distinguish them from the older huaqiao. Apart from traditional destinations in the West and Southeast Asia, many of the new migrants relocated to countries in

Eastern and Southern Europe, the Middle East, Latin America, and Africa.[4] Since the 1990s, dominating Chinese state and media attention has been a mobile elite with foreign citizenship or resident status, business experience, and university degrees. The potential influence of this small group led to a shift of government exhortations—from "return to serve the country" (*huiguo fuwu*) to "serve the country" (*weiguo fuwu*).[5] The imperative to return was dropped. The bulk of the new migrants have continued to be workers and small merchants in low-cost retail, construction, and manufacturing sectors of developing and developed economies. At the same time, an increasing number of middle- and upper-class families are pursuing education and investment opportunities abroad, while more large-scale corporations are becoming active internationally, partly under Xi Jinping's economic strategy of "One Belt, One Road." Given these developments, Chinese circulations—including emigration, settlement, and return—will likely gain greater importance in the years to come.[6]

Has China, therefore, arrived at a new diaspora moment in the twenty-first century? Are we witnessing yet another pattern of rupture, transformation, and recombination?

If diaspora is a series of temporal disjunctions suggesting a fragmented and networked homeland, as my argument posits, there are signs of it resurfacing and revealing the fissures of a rising China. On the road to "national rejuvenation" in the current state narrative, what seems clear is that decades of bold, experimental market reform have caused Chinese spaces and times to proliferate. One of the unmistakable splits lies in the urban versus the rural. In numerous cities, rural migrants have occupied a "temporary" status that is here to stay.[7] Leaving behind the elderly and children, they have linked their native towns and villages to other spaces beyond, creating new, uneven interdependencies. They have also laid the foundation for the global aspirations of urban Chinese, who have responded to the reintegration with the world economy by migrating overseas, a sign of "desiring China," as observed by Lisa Rofel.[8]

Yet the two kinds of interrelated mobility, domestic and global, are rarely discussed together in official and scholarly discourses. Though much smaller than the domestic migration from rural areas in size and social impact, the global migration from urban areas exerts far greater influence on the national self-understanding. Compared to the six million new migrants, Chinese rural migrants are currently estimated at 200 million people, one of the largest movements ever in human history. While rural migrants face institutional and social discrimination, the new migrants are broadly admired as the returning "sea turtle" (*haigui*) or the soaring "seagull" (*hai'ou*), embodying the transformative potential of transoceanic and airborne journeys beyond the nation.[9] By contrast, the rural migrant is often associated with a "blind flow" (*mengliu*) or "floating population" (*liudong renkou*), rarely an object of national envy or a worldly subject in its own right. As Pál Nyíri finds, the new migrant is a "symbolic figure of the globally modern and yet authentically national, even racial way of being Chinese,"[10] suggesting how emigrant success in a global arena contributes to a new sense of Chinese identity and power. Here, the phenomenon of new migrants carries unusual weight as a cornerstone of China's new engagement with the world.

This developing trend has not been lost on contemporary scholars, who have put out timely and insightful work on the new migrants, a heterogeneous group that could also be understood through a wider lens of diaspora. Focusing on the displays of nationalism, scholars have stressed how the new migrants have resisted assimilation into local society, cultivated close ties with Chinese corporations and government, trumpeted the official stance on Taiwan and Tibet, and marched internationally to defend China during the 2008 Olympic torch relay.[11] If diaspora uncovers both the fragmentation and interconnections of seemingly discrete groups, as I have argued, the flare-ups of nationalism also reveal the multiple facets of an emergent China. Recalling the turbulent history between China and Indonesia in the 1950s and 1960s, Liu Hong cautions against the perception that Chinese overseas can be an effective vehicle of China's national interests, as national interests have tended to take precedence when they are in conflict with those of Chinese overseas.[12] Just as importantly, even as certain elite and state interests seem to align for the time being, it remains unclear whether the patriotic expressions among the new migrants are meant to safeguard the well-being of the Chinese nation or their own.[13] Whether it is the costly relocation to acquire a Western education and a foreign citizenship or the worried flight of private wealth to overseas capital and real estate markets, the practices seem too class-specific and contradictory to fit neatly under the rubric of "nationalism." Rather, they suggest textures of a flexible strategy, as described by Aihwa Ong.[14]

In addition, without forgetting that emigration has historically been a family-based strategy of survival and accumulation, the new migrants attest to the economic power of China as forcefully as to the social anxieties beneath it. For China's urban classes, heated growth and increased susceptibility to domestic and global fluctuations have contributed to the specter of an imminent crisis. While some of the new migrants show a new confidence in speaking on China's behalf, as many have before them, there is by no means a perfect or permanent unity. Instead, splits along the lines of generation, class, and location suggest not one but many faces of recent Chinese emigrants: intellectuals who grew up in the early reform era and moved to the West prior to 1989, small entrepreneurs and low-income laborers who moved to Eastern Europe and Southeast Asia after the early 1990s, and more recently youth and members of a rising middle class and "new rich" who are mainly students, professionals, and consumers living in Western cities. These social layers point up not just a common origin and different degrees of localization, but more importantly a constellation of moving, interdependent forces. Among the most crucial forces were the global expansion of the neoliberal economy and dramatic shifts in geopolitics after the Cold War. Together they have reshaped mobility and its perceptions in profound ways.

Given a capacity to engage a vast historical geography of seemingly disparate elements, diaspora can also offer a useful reframing if we juxtapose the new migrants with contemporary Taiwan and Hong Kong. There, in the deeply entwined and contested "Greater China," little nationalism toward mainland China can be found. Instead, the region lays bare many overlapping and competing claims to Chinese identity and power that have evolved since the mid-twentieth century. After 1945, Taiwan was a displaced nationalist state grafted onto a former Japanese colony, governing a mixed population of refugees, settlers, and aborigines, and held within the sphere of U.S. power. A British colony since 1842, Hong Kong became a safe haven for millions from varying class, regional, and linguistic backgrounds fleeing war and communism on the mainland. Both turned into crucial battlefronts for political ideologies, homes for Chinese exiles, and highly successful capitalist economies.[15] Nonetheless, China's rapprochement with the United States beginning in 1972, the joint declaration with Britain in 1984, and a historic meeting with the Taiwanese leadership in

1992, together with a rapid opening to Western capitalism, introduced prospects for a deferred reunion—"one China, different interpretations" on the question of Taiwan (*yige Zhongguo, gezi biaoshu*), and "one country, two systems" in the case of Hong Kong (*yiguo liangzhi*). Since its handover to Chinese rule in 1997, Hong Kong has been a "special administrative region," a status joined by Macao in 1999. Hong Kong has also entered a transitional period of "no change for fifty years" (*wushi nian bubian*), a freezing of basic political and social structures formulated during the colonial era.[16]

While an ambiguous framework for future reintegration unfolds, momentous struggles have sprung up in the changing political economy of the region. During Deng Xiaoping's market reforms, both Taiwan and Hong Kong evolved into international business gateways to a reopening China. As the Tian'anmen Democracy Movement gave way to a neoliberal turn, great prosperity and confusion pervaded the 1980s and 1990s. In Taiwan, democratization since 1987 had already unleashed a wide array of political and cultural projects, including a nascent Taiwanese nationalism and new native identities such as mainlander (*waishengren*) and local (*benshengren*).[17] In Hong Kong, a forced "return" to Chinese rule sparked a painful search for stability amid a mass exit of middle- and upper-class families to Western countries. In both societies, large-scale protests have proliferated, demanding greater autonomy, self-government, and independence from China, triggering stern warnings from Beijing and defiant movements to forge a separate identity.[18]

Collectively, these events suggest a broader shift of power in the region, altering relations between multiple Chinese times and spaces. At the height of the Cold War, both Taiwan and Hong Kong occupied privileged positions in a U.S.-led capitalist economy lying outside Communist China, positions that were shared with Japan, South Korea, and Singapore. At the turn of the twenty-first century, vastly expanded neoliberal policies, terrorism and counterterrorism, and a more globally engaged and self-assured China have combined to unsettle the geopolitical order in Asia and beyond. In this sense, the recent eruption of discord in Taiwan and Hong Kong reflects a deeper restructuring since the 1970s.

Here, by recognizing new migrants, Greater China, and a rising China as split and intertwined through migrant flows, diaspora offers a view of networked histories in the present. Unlike a tentative consolidation of identities for some of the new migrants, the meanings of being "Chinese" in Taiwan and Hong Kong have splintered and grown further apart. This suggests that, despite some alarming narratives portraying China as a juggernaut taking over the world, the implications of a vast and deepening Chinese global engagement would not only aid but also limit its assertions of power. Unexpected tensions and conflicts can find their way through China's dense web of entanglements. Episodes of fluctuation in Chinese society may also reverberate outward in an ever more connected world. Given the proliferation of time and space in which China acts, the Chinese state may face mounting pressure to meet commitments and challenges on a larger scale. This endless task of juggling and reorganizing fragments could very well transform China. As for how, that lies in what openings will emerge, how future actors will encounter them, and how they deal with the past—not as a form of path dependency but as a possibility for recombination. A shifting dialectic of actors, times, and spaces, diaspora will remain such a possibility.

The Futures of Transnational History

A new interpretation of China's development through "diaspora moments," this book insists on a historical perspective but also rethinks the practice of history in light of the transnational turn. Calling attention to movements in time, it seeks to advance ongoing discussions of movements in space. Eschewing the singularity of fields, it puts in dialogue the study of modern China, Chinese overseas, and Chinese Americas. If diaspora is a useful way of writing transnational history, so goes my claim, let us also consider the meanings and possible implications of this approach.

As suggested earlier in this book, a more robust emphasis on time is not meant to negate space or even place; rather, it means picking up the work of the transnational turn. In a brief yet incisive commentary, the American studies scholar Matthew Pratt Guterl writes that "while the historical storyscapes get bigger, wider, and more richly detailed, the temporal plot points generally stay the same. Or, put another way, to bend space, to 'go' transnational, historians often recommit to the hegemony of time."[19] What he refers to is a general adherence to the conventional eras and periodizations in national history, despite numerous attempts to revise them. Instead of acting "like a transparency laid over a familiar map" or yet another "dimension" of national narratives, a second generation of transnational history, argues Guterl, should be "rooted in new conventions of time and space."[20]

What could be the meaning and payoff of this approach? Rooted in the age of global migration, my attempt at a new chronology not only challenges a linear state-centric periodization but also provides a fresh look at the diaspora–homeland dynamic as a bottom-up process. By questioning the absolute certainty of "national time," I find it possible to detect moments of tension that elude a full and long-lasting orchestration by the nation. Instead, these moments nudge, shun, and sometimes rip through linear plotlines. Often overlooked or misunderstood, the encounters make clear that diasporas and homelands do not necessarily exist in terms of center and periphery, however changing the meanings, but participate in a dance of appearance, disappearance, and reappearance. As we have seen, China's links and fissures with the diaspora mark the complex global connections it has both inherited and shaped. In the present-day identification with a rising China among some of the new migrants, a new diaspora moment has arisen in emergent political and economic geographies. Residing not outside but underneath, another diaspora moment has also impinged on the telos of the homeland-nation, as in the popular movements against reintegration in both Taiwan and Hong Kong, at a time of increasing interdependence with mainland China. Shaking up the center–periphery model in understanding China and Chinese in the world, the bottom-up description suggests an entirely different way of understanding how diasporas and nations can be mutually imbricated.

Another possible payoff is to better understand the nation not as enclosed but as evolving within a broader historical geography. If we accept that multiple temporalities and spatialities coexist, the nation will look more like a bricolage of global and local elements than a fixed and predetermined whole. The examples I have discussed indicate that diaspora did not consist of the same venues and actors in the long century of Chinese mass emigration, but was always contextual, emerging not from the sum of its parts but from their interactions. This is not to say that Chinese time and space were ever synchronized before; nor was emigration the only source of differentiation or connection. Rather, technological advances in the modern age have made it imaginable to create a single time and space for control, while the unprecedented movements of goods, ideas, money, and people have repeatedly inspired and thwarted that dream. Seen through a global lens of diaspora, the nation is multispatial, polyrhythmic, and always incomplete.

A more expansive framing of time and space also means opportunities to bring together multiple historiographies for a new global history. For the scholarly fields that I have engaged, some of the most provocative explorations of the transnational turn have come from Asian American studies. Since the 1990s, and even more impressively in the last decade, such efforts include the concept of "worlding," Asian America across the Pacific involving "returned," transient, and adopted Asians and Asian Americans, the homeward impact of the Cold War in Asia on the United States and Canada, a new look at Chinese transnationalism in Latin America and the Caribbean beyond indentured labor migration, and critical refugee studies focusing on the displacement of Hmong, Cambodian, and Vietnamese peoples and their descendants in the United States.[21] Taken together, these inquiries provide compelling critiques of U.S. exceptionalism and multiculturalism, refusing to reify "America" as a fixed and bounded nation. While it lies beyond the scope of my project to explore whether and how diaspora moments could be usefully applied to the United States or elsewhere, Asian American studies are undergoing an unmistakably massive reframing of time and space. Such a rewriting of the Americas, I believe, lends itself to a greater appreciation of the relevance of China and other parts of Asia. By inviting multiple geographies and chronologies into our practice, not only will we push along the transnational turn; we will also get closer to a global history recognizing what Lisa Lowe calls "the intimacies of four continents."[22]

This book strives to let in a larger and more fluid social universe in which modern China took shape and continues to evolve. It puts in conversation the study of China, Chinese overseas, and Chinese Americas, building a case for an interconnected archive. It takes a fresh look at mass emigration that ends up altering China and weaving it with other lands. It also reinterprets diaspora as a concept for studying movements between times and spaces in a global frame. A creature of Chinese engagement with the world since the nineteenth century, the idea of a "temporary" diaspora bound to a "permanent" homeland turns out to be a futile attempt to fix both in time, as neither of them stood still. Yet the appeal of "diaspora"—as a means to unify and transcend times and spaces—endures. So long as reintegration is not to confirm a single center, but to recognize a plural inheritance that requires constant adaptation, some success can be expected. Yet reconnection can lead to new uncertainties, making any success provisional. After a messy, complicated history of encounters, how is it possible to remake disparate entities into a single whole? Any answer to this question is bound to be partial and deeply contested.

Finally, the task of writing a global history through diaspora comes with real challenges. Even if the point is not to capture the past in its full breadth but to yield flashes of insight, it remains a struggle to cope with the massive primary and secondary sources at different sites and the diverse set of skills required for timely delivery. While the result can be uncertain, one may keep an eye on the potential rewards. The case for diaspora, as I have discovered, is to inspect the endless construction of the past, present, and future in a series of coming, going, and seeking, for each moment demands yet another reconciliation of memories and dreams.

NOTES

Introduction

1. For an overview of global migration, see Jose C. Moya and Adam McKeown, *World Migration in the Long Twentieth Century* (Washington, DC: American Historical Association, 2011), and Patrick Manning, *Migration in World History* (London: Routledge, 2013). For one of the latest empirical studies of Chinese emigration, see Adam McKeown, "Chinese Emigration in Global Context, 1850–1940," *Journal of Global History* 5, no. 1 (2010). There was a larger Chinese overland migration to Manchuria, but it is not the focus of this study. See Thomas R. Gottschang and Diana Lary, *Swallows and Settlers: The Great Migration from North China to Manchuria* (Ann Arbor: Center for Chinese Studies, University of Michigan, 2000).

2. Examples of the vast literature include Chin-Keong Ng, *Trade and Society: The Amoy Network on the China Coast, 1683–1735* (Singapore: Singapore University Press, National University of Singapore, 1983); Billy K. L. So, *Prosperity, Region, and Institutions in Maritime China: The South Fukien Pattern, 946–1368* (Cambridge, MA: Harvard University Asia Center, 2000); Wang Gungwu, *The Chinese Overseas: From Earthbound China to the Quest for Autonomy* (Cambridge, MA: Harvard University Press, 2000); and *The Nanhai Trade: The Early History of Chinese Trade in the South China Sea* (Singapore: Times Academic Press, 1998).

3. See Anthony Reid, *Southeast Asia in the Age of Commerce, 1450–1680* (New Haven, CT: Yale University Press, 1988); Philip A. Kuhn, *Chinese among Others: Emigration in Modern Times* (Lanham, MD: Rowman and Littlefield, 2008).

4. Adam McKeown, *Melancholy Order: Asian Migration and the Globalization of Borders* (New York: Columbia University Press, 2008).

5. Adam McKeown has estimated that the return rate of Chinese emigrants from 1870 to 1930 averaged over 70 percent. See "Chinese Emigration in Global Context," 111.

6. Giovanni Arrighi, Takeshi Hamashita, and Mark Selden, *The Resurgence of East Asia: 500, 150 and 50 Year Perspectives* (London: Routledge, 2003); Reid, *Southeast Asia in the Age of Commerce*.

7. Wang Gungwu, "Merchants without Empire: The Hokkien Sojourning Communities," in *The Rise of Merchant Empires: Long-Distance Trade in the Early*

Modern World, ed. James D. Tracy (Cambridge: Cambridge University Press, 1990), 400–421.

8. See Yen Ching-huang, *The Overseas Chinese and the 1911 Revolution, with Special Reference to Singapore and Malaya* (Kuala Lumpur: Oxford University Press, 1976); Michael R. Godley, *The Mandarin-Capitalists from Nanyang: Overseas Chinese Enterprise in the Modernization of China, 1893–1911* (Cambridge: Cambridge University Press, 1981); Wang Gungwu, *China and the Chinese Overseas* (Singapore: Times Academic Press, 1991); and Kuhn, *Chinese among Others*.

9. Major works include Sucheng Chan, *Asian Americans: An Interpretive History* (Boston: Twayne, 1991); Judy Yung, *Unbound Feet: A Social History of Chinese Women in San Francisco* (Berkeley: University of California Press, 1995); and Him Mark Lai, *Becoming Chinese American: A History of Communities and Institutions* (Walnut Creek, CA: AltaMira, 2004).

10. See critiques of the implications by Adam McKeown, *Chinese Migrant Networks and Cultural Change: Peru, Chicago, Hawaii, 1900–1936* (Chicago: University of Chicago Press, 2001), and Lisa Lowe, *Immigrant Acts: On Asian American Cultural Politics* (Durham, NC: Duke University Press, 1996).

11. See Wang Gungwu's various essays in *China and the Chinese Overseas* (Singapore: Times Academic Press, 1991). His thinking on the subject has been most influential in the field of Chinese overseas history. For a thoughtful discussion on Wang's use of different terms, see Huang Jianli, "Conceptualizing Chinese Migration and Chinese Overseas: The Contributions of Wang Gungwu," *Journal of Chinese Overseas* 6 (2010): 1–21.

12. Here I borrow Prasenjit Duara's idea of "hardening" and "softening" of boundaries in "Nationalists and Transnationals: Overseas Chinese and the Idea of China, 1900–1911," in *Ungrounded Empires: The Cultural Politics of Modern Chinese Transnationalism*, ed. Aihwa Ong and Donald Nonini (New York: Routledge, 1997), 40–41.

13. Some examples are Aihwa Ong, *Flexible Citizenship: The Cultural Logics of Transnationality* (Durham, NC: Duke University Press, 1999); Aihwa Ong and Donald M. Nonini, eds., *Ungrounded Empires: The Cultural Politics of Modern Chinese Transnationalism* (New York: Routledge, 1997); Michael W. Charney, Brenda S. A. Yeoh, and Chee Kiong Tong, eds., *Chinese Migrants Abroad: Cultural, Educational, and Social Dimensions of the Chinese Diaspora* (Singapore: Singapore University Press, 2003); Maria Ng and Philip Holden, *Reading Chinese Transnationalisms: Society, Literature, Film* (Hong Kong: Hong Kong University Press, 2006); Elaine Yee Lin Ho and Julia Kuehn, eds., *China Abroad: Travels, Subjects, Spaces* (Hong Kong: Hong Kong University Press, 2009); Andrea Riemenschnitter and Deborah L. Madsen, eds., *Diasporic Histories: Cultural Archives of Chinese Transnationalism* (Hong Kong: Hong Kong University Press, 2009); Kam Louie, David M. Pomfret, and Julia Kuehn, eds., *Diasporic Chineseness after the Rise of China: Communities and Cultural Production* (Vancouver: University of British Columbia Press, 2013).

14. The pioneering works include Arif Dirlik and Rob Wilson, eds., *Asia/Pacific as Space of Cultural Production* (Durham, NC: Duke University Press, 1995); Evelyn Hu-Dehart, ed., *Across the Pacific: Asian Americans and Globalization* (Philadelphia: Temple University Press, 1999); Madeline Hsu, *Dreaming of Gold, Dreaming of Home: Transnationalism and Migration between the United States and South China, 1882–1943* (Stanford, CA: Stanford University Press, 2000); and Eiichiro Azuma, *Between Two Empires: Race, History, and Transnationalism in Japanese America* (New York: Oxford University Press, 2005).

15. This includes Erika Lee, "Orientalisms in the Americas: A Hemispheric Approach to Asian American History," *Journal of Asian American Studies* 8, no. 3 (2005): 235–56; Moon-Ho Jung, *Coolies and Cane: Race, Labor, and Sugar in the Age of Emancipation* (Baltimore: Johns Hopkins University Press, 2006); Henry Yu, "The Intermittent Rhythms of the Cantonese Pacific," in *Connecting Seas and Connected Ocean Rims: Indian, Atlantic, and Pacific Oceans and China Seas Migrations from the 1830s to the 1930s*, ed. Donna R. Gabaccia and Dirk Hoerder (Leiden: Brill, 2011); John Price, *Orienting Canada: Race, Empire, and the Transpacific* (Vancouver: University of British Columbia Press, 2011); Kornel S. Chang, *Pacific Connections: The Making of the Western U.S.-Canadian Borderlands* (Berkeley: University of California Press, 2012); Elliott Young, *Alien Nation: Chinese Migration in the Americas from the Coolie Era through World War II* (Chapel Hill: University of North Carolina Press, 2014); Chih-ming Wang, *Transpacific Articulations: Student Migration and the Remaking of Asian America* (Honolulu: University of Hawai'i Press, 2013); and Michael Jin, "Americans in the Pacific: Rethinking Race, Gender, Citizenship, and Diaspora at the Crossroads of Asian and Asian American Studies," *Critical Ethnic Studies* 2, no. 1 (2016): 128–47.

16. I thank an anonymous reader of this manuscript and Cindy I-fen Cheng for urging me to be more careful and precise about the differences between Chinese American history and the larger Asian American studies. For Chinese American history in wider contexts and Chinese in the Americas, see Beth Lew-Williams, "The Chinese Must Go: Immigration, Deportation and Violence in the 19th Century Pacific Northwest" (Ph.D. diss., Stanford University, 2011); Evelyn Hu-Dehart, "Chinatowns and Borderlands: Inter-Asian Encounters in the Diaspora," *Modern Asian Studies* 46, no. 2 (2012): 425–51; Kathleen López, *Chinese Cubans: A Transnational History* (Chapel Hill: University of North Carolina Press, 2013); Grace Peña Delgado, *Making the Chinese Mexican: Global Migration, Exclusion, and Localism in the U.S.-Mexico Borderlands* (Stanford, CA: Stanford University Press, 2012); Fredy González, "We Won't Be Bullied Anymore: Chinese-Mexican Relations and the Chinese Community in Mexico, 1931–1971" (Ph.D. diss., Yale University, 2013); Ana Maria Candela, "Nation, Migration and Governance: Cantonese Migrants to Peru and the Making of Overseas Chinese Nationalism, 1849–2013" (Ph.D. diss., University of California, Santa Cruz, 2013).

17. For "China-centered history," see Paul Cohen, *Discovering History in China: American Historical Writing on the Recent Chinese Past* (New York: Columbia

University Press, 1984). For critiques of China-centered history, see Prasenjit Duara, *Rescuing History from the Nation: Questioning Narratives of Modern China* (Chicago: University of Chicago Press, 1996), and Rebecca E. Karl, *Staging the World: Chinese Nationalism at the Turn of the Twentieth Century* (Durham, NC: Duke University Press, 2002).

18. Important examples are Diana Lary, *Region and Nation: The Kwangsi Clique in Chinese Politics, 1925–1937* (Cambridge: Cambridge University Press, 1974); G. William Skinner and Hugh D. R. Baker, eds., *The City in Late Imperial China* (Stanford, CA: Stanford University Press, 1977); Lyman P. Van Slyke, *Yangtze: Nature, History, and the River* (Reading, MA: Addison-Wesley, 1988); Roy Bin Wong, *China Transformed: Historical Change and the Limits of European Experience* (Ithaca, NY: Cornell University Press, 1997); Kenneth Pomeranz, *The Great Divergence: China, Europe, and the Making of the Modern World Economy* (Princeton, NJ: Princeton University Press, 2000); Robert Marks, *Tigers, Rice, Silk, and Silt: Environment and Economy in Late Imperial South China* (Cambridge: Cambridge University Press, 1998).

19. Lynn Pan, ed., *The Encyclopedia of the Chinese Overseas* (Cambridge, MA: Harvard University Press, 1999).

20. Ien Ang has also cogently criticized the assumptions of the illustration. See Ang, *On Not Speaking Chinese: Living between Asia and the West* (London: Routledge, 2001), 85–88.

21. For example, see Thomas S. Mullaney, *Critical Han Studies: The History, Representation, and Identity of China's Majority* (Berkeley: University of California Press, 2012), and Peter J. Katzenstein, ed., *Sinicization and the Rise of China: Civilizational Processes beyond East and West* (Milton Park, UK: Routledge, 2012).

22. See, for example, figure 7.2 in James A. Cook, "Rethinking 'China': Overseas Chinese and China's Modernity," in *Visualizing Modern China: Image, History, and Memory, 1750–Present*, ed. James A. Cook, Joshua L. Goldstein, Matthew D. Johnson, and Sigrid Schmalzer (Lanham, MD: Lexington, 2014), 133. Various tables in Pan, ed., *The Encyclopedia of the Chinese Overseas* also provide different numbers of total populations of Chinese descent around the world.

23. See McKeown, *Melancholy Order*, and Young, *Alien Nation*, for excellent analyses of how immigration control helped expand the state bureaucracy.

24. Representatives include Hsu, *Dreaming of Gold, Dreaming of Home*; McKeown, *Chinese Migrant Networks and Cultural Change*; Kuhn, *Chinese among Others*; Glen Peterson, *Overseas Chinese in the People's Republic of China* (Milton Park, UK: Routledge, 2012); Eric Tagliacozzo and Wen-Chin Chang, eds., *Chinese Circulations: Capital, Commodities, and Networks in Southeast Asia* (Durham, NC: Duke University Press, 2011); and McKeown, *Melancholy Order*.

25. See, for example, Paul Gilroy, *The Black Atlantic: Modernity and Double Consciousness* (Cambridge, MA: Harvard University Press, 1993), and Stuart Hall, "Cultural Identity and Diaspora," in *Identity: Community, Culture, Difference*, ed. Jonathan Rutherford, 222–37 (London: Lawrence and Wishart, 1990).

26. See, for example, Ling-chi Wang and Wang Gungwu, eds., *The Chinese Diaspora: Selected Essays* (Singapore: Times Academic Press, 1998). For a critique and a suggestion of a "diasporic perspective," see Adam McKeown, "Conceptualizing Chinese Diasporas, 1842 to 1949," *Journal of Asian Studies* 58, no. 2 (1999): 311.

27. Wang Gungwu, "A Single Chinese Diaspora? Some Historical Reflections," in *Imagining the Chinese Diaspora: Two Australian Perspectives*, ed. Annette Shun Wah and Wang Gungwu (Canberra: Centre for the Study of the Chinese Diaspora, Australian National University, 1999), 1–17; Ang, *On Not Speaking Chinese*; and Shu-mei Shih, *Visuality and Identity: Sinophone Articulations across the Pacific* (Berkeley: University of California Press, 2007). I have also discussed their criticisms of diaspora elsewhere. See Shelly Chan, "The Case for Diaspora: A Temporal Approach to the Chinese Experience," *Journal of Asian Studies* 74, no. 1 (February 2015): 107–28.

28. For the contemporary phenomena of "re-Sinification" in Southeast Asia and "roots-searching" in multicultural United States that challenge a linear narrative of assimilation and localization, see Caroline S. Hau, *The Chinese Question: Ethnicity, Nation, and Region in and beyond the Philippines* (Singapore: National University of Singapore Press, 2014), and Andrea Louie, *Chineseness across Borders: Renegotiating Chinese Identities in China and the United States* (Durham, NC: Duke University Press, 2004).

29. Avtar Brah, *Cartographies of Diaspora: Contesting Identities* (London: Routledge, 1996); Khachig Tölölyan, "Rethinking Diaspora(s): Stateless Power in the Transnational Moment," *Diaspora* 5, no. 1 (1996): 3–36.

30. See Lisa Lowe, *Immigrant Acts: On Asian American Cultural Politics* (Durham, NC: Duke University Press, 1996); James Clifford, *Routes: Travel and Translation in the Late Twentieth Century* (Cambridge, MA: Harvard University Press, 1997); and Rogers Brubaker, "The 'Diaspora' Diaspora," *Ethnic and Racial Studies* 28, no. 1 (January 2005): 1–19.

31. Wang Gungwu, "A Note on the Origins of Hua-Ch'iao," in *Community and Nation: Essays on Southeast Asia and the Chinese*, ed. Anthony Reid (Singapore: Heinemann Educational, 1981), 118–27.

32. Wang Gungwu, "A Note on the Origins of Hua-Ch'iao," 119.

33. James A. Cook also argues that the term *huaqiao* or "Chinese sojourner," emphasizing the "permanence of Chinese citizenship," would "transform the way in which many overseas Chinese imagined the Chinese nation, extending the country's influence far beyond the geographical confines of China proper to include all residents in Chinese communities abroad." See Cook, "Rethinking 'China,'" 128.

34. Examples of a spatial focus include Laurence J. C. Ma and Carolyn L. Cartier, *The Chinese Diaspora: Space, Place, Mobility, and Identity* (Lanham, MD: Rowman and Littlefield, 2003); Wang Gungwu, "Chineseness: The Dilemmas of Place and Practice," in *Don't Leave Home: Migration and the Chinese* (Singapore: Times

Academic Press, 2001); and Tu Wei-ming, "Cultural China: The Periphery as the Center," in *The Living Tree: The Changing Meaning of Being Chinese Today* (Stanford, CA: Stanford University Press, 1994).

35. Few scholars have written extensively about time in diaspora. The most important example I could find is Brian Keith Axel. Focusing on the Sikh diaspora, Axel has argued that context is not only spatial but temporal in "The Context of Diaspora," *Cultural Anthropology* 19, no. 1 (2004): 26–60. He also discusses the relationship between temporality and corporeality in "The Diasporic Imaginary," *Public Culture* 14, no. 2 (2002): 411. For the unique contributions historians could make to migration studies vis-à-vis social scientists, see Donna Gabaccia, "Time and Temporality in Migration Studies," in *Migration Theory: Talking across Disciplines*, ed. Caroline Brettell and James Frank Hollifield (New York: Routledge, 2015), 37–66.

36. Some of the key works influencing the "spatial turn" are Henri Lefebvre, *The Production of Space* (Oxford: Blackwell, 1991), and Edward W. Soja, *Postmodern Geographies: The Reassertion of Space in Critical Social Theory* (London: Verso, 1989). On the social and cultural production of time, see Stephen Kern, *The Culture of Time and Space 1880–1918* (Cambridge, MA: Harvard University Press, 1983), and Reinhart Koselleck, *Futures Past: On the Semantics of Historical Time* (New York: Columbia University Press, 2004).

37. See Duara, *Rescuing History from the Nation*; Dipesh Chakrabarty, *Provincializing Europe: Postcolonial Thought and Historical Difference* (Princeton, NJ: Princeton University Press, 2000); Harry Harrotunian, "Some Thoughts on Comparability and the Space-Time Problem," *boundary 2* 32, no. 2 (summer 2005): 23–52.

38. Steve J. Stern, "The Tricks of Time: Colonial Legacies and Historical Sensibilities in Latin America," in *Colonial Legacies: The Problem of Persistence in Latin American History*, ed. Jeremy Adelman (New York: Routledge, 1999), 139.

39. Stefan Tanaka, *New Times in Modern Japan* (Princeton, NJ: Princeton University Press, 2004).

40. Louise Young, *Beyond the Metropolis: Second Cities and Modern Life in Interwar Japan* (Berkeley: University of California Press, 2013).

41. Gail Hershatter, *The Gender of Memory: Rural Women and China's Collective Past* (Berkeley: University of California Press, 2011).

42. I thank Rebecca Karl for referring me to Henri Lefebvre's chapter, "The Theory of Moments," in *Critiques of Everyday Life*, vol. 2 (London: Verso, 2002), 340–58. His ideas of "repetition" and "the newness that springs from repetition" help me articulate the series of rupture and recombination that I found in the Chinese homeland–diaspora dynamic. An anonymous reader of this manuscript has also pointed out the relevance of Anna Lowenhaupt Tsing's concept of "friction" to my observation of interacting temporalities, a point with which I heartily agree. See Tsing, *Friction: An Ethnography of Global Connection* (Princeton, NJ: Princeton University Press, 2005).

Chapter 1: A Great Convergence

1. Wang Gungwu, *The Chinese Overseas: From Earthbound China to the Quest for Autonomy* (Cambridge, MA: Harvard University Press, 2000), 46.

2. Philip A. Kuhn, *Chinese among Others: Emigration in Modern Times* (Lanham, MD: Rowman and Littlefield, 2008), 240.

3. Michael R. Godley, *The Mandarin-Capitalists from Nanyang: Overseas Chinese Enterprise in the Modernization of China, 1893-1911* (Cambridge: Cambridge University Press, 1981), 1.

4. "Xue Fucheng zouqing huoxu nanyang haijin" (1893), in *Huagong chuguo shiliao*, ed. Chen Hansheng, vol. 1 (Beijing: Zhonghua shuju, 1984), 292-98. See also a discussion in Yen Ching-Hwang, *Coolies and Mandarins: China's Protection of Overseas Chinese during the Late Ch'ing Period, 1851-1911* (Singapore: Singapore University Press, 1985), 262-66.

5. See Moon-Ho Jung, *Coolies and Cane: Race, Labor, and Sugar in the Age of Emancipation* (Baltimore: Johns Hopkins University Press, 2006); Evelyn Hu-Dehart, "La Trata Amarilla: The 'Yellow Trade' and the Middle Passage, 1847-1884," in *Many Middle Passages: Forced Migration and the Making of the Modern World*, ed. Emma Christopher, Cassandra Pybus, and Marcus Rediker (Berkeley: University of California Press, 2007), 166-83; and John King Fairbank, *Trade and Diplomacy on the China Coast: The Opening of the Treaty Ports, 1842-1854* (Cambridge, MA: Harvard University Press, 1953), 217. For a recent study of human trafficking in late Qing and Republican China, see Johanna S. Ransmeier, *Sold People: Traffickers and Family Life in North China* (Cambridge, MA: Harvard University Press, 2017).

6. The historical literature on Chinese coolies is enormous. See Persia Crawford Campbell, *Chinese Coolie Emigration to Countries within the British Empire* (London: P. S. King and Son, 1923); Watt Stewart, *Chinese Bondage in Peru* (Durham, NC: Duke University Press, 1951); Robert L. Irick, *Ch'ing Policy toward the Coolie Trade, 1847-1878* (Taipei: Chinese Materials Center, 1982); Yen Ch'ing-huang, *Coolies and Mandarins: China's Protection of Overseas Chinese during the Late Ch'ing Period, 1851-1911* (Singapore: Singapore University Press, 1985); Arnold J. Meagher, *The Coolie Trade: The Traffic in Chinese Laborers to Latin America, 1847-1874* (Philadelphia: Xlibris, 2008); Walton Look Lai, *Indentured Labor, Caribbean Sugar: Chinese and Indian Migrants to the British West Indies, 1838-1918* (Baltimore: Johns Hopkins University Press, 1993); Evelyn Hu-Dehart, "Chinese Coolie Labour in Cuba in the Nineteenth Century: Free Labour or Neo-Slavery?" *Slavery and Abolition* 14, no. 1 (1993): 67-86.

7. See Jung, *Coolies and Cane*, and Lisa Yun, *The Coolie Speaks: Chinese Indentured Laborers and African Slaves in Cuba* (Philadelphia: Temple University Press, 2008).

8. Elliott Young, *Alien Nation: Chinese Migration in the Americas from the Coolie Era through World War II* (Chapel Hill: University of North Carolina Press,

2014), and Adam McKeown, *Melancholy Order: Asian Migration and the Globalization of Borders* (New York: Columbia University Press, 2008).

9. Fairbank, *Trade and Diplomacy on the China Coast*, 217.

10. A number of recent works have explored the nexus of migration, diplomacy, and citizenship in other contexts. See Cindy I-Fen Cheng, *Citizens of Asian America: Democracy and Race during the Cold War* (New York: New York University Press, 2013); Madeline Hsu, *The Good Immigrants: How the Yellow Peril Became the Model Minority* (Princeton, NJ: Princeton University Press, 2015); Yucheng Qin, *The Diplomacy of Nationalism: The Six Companies and China's Policy toward Exclusion* (Honolulu: University of Hawai'i Press, 2009); and Meredith Oyen, *The Diplomacy of Migration: Transnational Lives and the Making of U.S.-Chinese Relations in the Cold War* (Ithaca, NY: Cornell University Press, 2015).

11. Irick, *Ch'ing Policy toward the Coolie Trade*, 2. One example of works stressing Qing inertia is Immanuel C. Y. Hsü, *China's Entrance into the Family of Nations: The Diplomatic Phase, 1858–1880* (Cambridge, MA: Harvard University Press, 1960).

12. Pär Kristoffer Cassel, *Grounds of Judgment: Extraterritoriality and Imperial Power in Nineteenth-Century China and Japan* (Oxford: Oxford University Press, 2012), 6.

13. See Xue Fucheng's diary written during his diplomatic service in Europe, *Chushi Ying Fa Yi Bi siguo riji* (Changsha shi Yuelu shushe: Hunan sheng xinhua shudian, 1985). For an English translation, see Xue Fucheng, *The European Diary of Hsieh Fucheng: Envoy Extraordinary of Imperial China*, translated by Helen Hsieh Chien, introduced and annotated by Douglas Howland (New York: St. Martin's, 1993).

14. "Governor Barkly to the Right Hon. Earl Grey," August 26, 1851, in "Papers Related to Chinese Immigrants Recently Introduced into British Guiana and Trinidad," House of Commons Parliamentary Papers Online, 1–2.

15. Lisa Lowe, *The Intimacies of Four Continents* (Durham, NC: Duke University Press, 2015), 24.

16. McKeown, *Melancholy Order*, 78.

17. On intra-Asian trade networks and Chinese emigration, see Takeshita Hamashita, "The Intra-Regional System in East Asia in Modern Times," in *Network Power: Japan and Asia*, ed. Peter J. Katzenstein and Takashi Shiraishi (Ithaca, NY: Cornell University Press, 1996), 113–35.

18. Lowe, *The Intimacies of Four Continents*, 27.

19. "Despatches from the Secretary of State," Sub-Enclosure 1, in Enclosure in No. 1, Macao, June 21, 1851, in "Papers Related to Chinese Immigrants," 72–75.

20. Sub-Enclosure 2, in Enclosure in No. 1, Hong Kong, July 19, 1851, in "Papers Related to Chinese Immigrants," 78.

21. Sub-Enclosure 2, in Enclosure in No. 1, Hong Kong, July 19, 1851, in "Papers Related to Chinese Immigrants," 79.

22. Sub-Enclosure 4, in Enclosure in No. 1, Hong Kong, August 21, 1851, in "Papers Related to Chinese Immigrants," 85, 87.

23. Sub-Enclosure 4, in Enclosure in No. 1, Hong Kong, August 21, 1851, in "Papers Related to Chinese Immigrants," 88.

24. Sub-Enclosure 4, in Enclosure in No. 1, Hong Kong, August 21, 1851, in "Papers Related to Chinese Immigrants," 89.

25. Governor Barkly to the Duke of Newcastle, February 26, 1853, in "Papers Relating to Chinese Immigrants," 34–36.

26. Copy of a Despatch from Acting-Governor Walker to His Grace the Duke of Newcastle, Demerara, July 8, 1853, in "Papers Relating to Chinese Immigrants," 65–66.

27. Enclosure 3, in No. 16, Blankenburg, June 23, 1853, in "Papers Relating to Chinese Immigrants," 68.

28. Enclosure 4, in No. 16, Queen's Town, July 2, 1853, in "Papers Relating to Chinese Immigrants," 69.

29. Enclosure 3 in No. 8, Note by Dr. Winchester, August 26, 1852, in "Correspondence with the Superintendent of British Trade in China, upon the Subject of Emigration from That Country." House of Commons Papers, 10.

30. Copy of a Despatch from Governor Barkly to the Right Hon. Sir J. S. Pakington, Bart, January 24, 1853, in "Papers Relating to Chinese Immigrants," 10.

31. Dr. Bowring to the Earl of Malmesbury, Hong Kong, September 7, 1852, in "Correspondence with the Superintendent of British Trade in China," 5.

32. See also McKeown, *Melancholy Order*, 68. He has also argued that the free migrant was one isolated from "nonregulated brokers, ethnic labor recruiting, informal credit arrangements, and village and family networks," but subject to the control of government institutions.

33. See also Young, *Alien Nation*, for a discussion of mutinies.

34. Fairbank, *Trade and Diplomacy*, 216.

35. Irick, *Ch'ing Policy toward the Coolie Trade*, 32–35.

36. Irick, *Ch'ing Policy toward the Coolie Trade*, 28.

37. The British court later found Syme guilty of a breach of the treaty between Britain and China and imposed a fine of two hundred dollars, not for engaging in the coolie trade but for superseding the authority of the British consul and visiting a Chinese police court to obtain the release of his broker.

38. Enclosure 1, in No. 10, Acting-Consul Backhouse to Dr. Bowing, Amoy, January 11, 1853, in "Correspondence with the Superintendent of British Trade in China," 96.

39. Cited in Irick, *Ch'ing Policy toward the Coolie Trade*, 29.

40. Commander Fishbourne to Captain Massie, Hermes, Amoy, December 15, 1852, in "Correspondence with the Superintendent of British Trade in China," 90.

41. Sir George Bonham to Mr. Hammond, London, July [day illegible], 1854, in "Correspondence upon the Subject of Emigration from China," House of Commons Papers, 24.

42. "He Guiqing nacheng daiyi guibian neidi minren feitu ji wushang yiren zhi ren bing chao xianyi banfa yu yi jiaoshe shangyu" [A memorial by He Guiqing stating the arrest and punishment of criminals who kidnapped the people and wrongly harmed the barbarians as well as a proposal for future proceedings with the barbarians]. In *Huagong chuguo shiliao huibian*, ed. Chen Hansheng, vol. 1, pt. 1 (Beijing: Zhonghua Shuju, 1985), 20–21.

43. For example, see Hosea Ballou Morse, chap. 8, "Emigration," in *The International Relations of the Chinese Empire (1910–18)*, vol. 2 (New York: Longmans, Green, 1900), 163–64, and Alexander Michie, *The Englishman in China during the Victorian Era*, vol. 2 (Edinburgh: William Blackwood and Sons, 1900), 171–74, as cited in Irick, *Ch'ing Policy toward the Coolie Trade*, 161.

44. W. A. P. Martin, *A Cycle of Cathay or China, South and North with Personal Reminiscences*, 3rd ed. (Taipei: Ch'eng-wen Publishing, 1966), 160 (original edition, New York: Fleming H. Revell Company, 1900).

45. See Mary Clabaugh Wright, *The Last Stand of Chinese Conservatism: The T'ung-Chih Restoration, 1862–1874* (Stanford, CA: Stanford University Press, 1957).

46. Quoted in Irick, *Ch'ing Policy toward the Coolie Trade*, 149.

47. See, for example, Wong Sin Keong, *China's Anti-American Boycott Movement in 1905: A Study in Urban Protest* (New York: Peter Lang, 2002), and Qin, *The Diplomacy of Nationalism*

48. For criticisms of the Tongzhi leaders, see Wright, *The Last Stand of Chinese Conservatism*, 231.

49. Wright, *The Last Stand of Chinese Conservatism*, 228–31.

50. Quoted in Irick, *Ch'ing Policy toward the Coolie Trade*, 163.

51. Irick, *Ch'ing Policy toward the Coolie Trade*, 151, 154–55.

52. Persia Crawford Campbell, *Chinese Coolie Emigration to Countries within the British Empire* (New York: Negro Universities Press, 1969), 141–43.

53. Arnold J. Meagher, *The Coolie Trade: The Traffic in Chinese Laborers to Latin America, 1847–1874* (Philadelphia: Xlibris, 2008), 174, table 17 (176–77), 286–89.

54. Irick, *Ch'ing Policy toward the Coolie Trade*, 218–19.

55. Meagher, *The Coolie Trade*, 288.

56. Stewart, *Chinese Bondage in Peru*, 148.

57. See Stewart, *Chinese Bondage in Peru*, 149, and Irick, *Ch'ing Policy toward the Coolie Trade*, 213–14.

58. See Irick, *Ch'ing Policy toward the Coolie Trade*, 221–38; Stewart, *Chinese Bondage in Peru*, 152–59. The affair had broad implications on Japan in the areas of emancipation of female prostitutes, international law, state sovereignty, and contributions to "freedom" as a global idea. See Daniel V. Botsman, "Freedom without Slavery? 'Coolies,' Prostitutes, and Outcastes in Meiji Japan's 'Emancipation Moment,'" *American Historical Review* 116, no. 5 (2011): 1323–47; Bill Mihalopoulos, *Sex in Japan's Globalization, 1870–1930: Prostitutes, Emigration and Nation Building*

(London: Pickering and Chatto, 2011); and Douglas Howland, "The *Maria Luz* Incident: Personal Rights and International Justice for Chinese Coolies and Japanese Prostitutes," in *Gender and Law in the Japanese Imperium*, ed. Susan L. Burns and Barbara J. Brooks (Honolulu: University of Hawai'i Press, 2014), 21–47.

59. "Nanyang dachen He Jing wei paiyuan wang Ri chaban Bilun huagong shiye yi banjun linghui huaren dao hu zhi zongshu ziwen" [The final report by the Nanyang superintendent He Jing on the sending of officials to Japan to investigate the incident involving Chinese laborers on the Peruvian vessel, the end of the investigation, and the return of the Chinese to Shanghai], in *Huagong chuguo shiliao huibian*, ed. Chen Hansheng, vol. 1, pt. 3, 993.

60. Stewart, *Chinese Bondage in Peru*, 159.

61. Quoted in Irick, *Ch'ing Policy toward the Coolie Trade*, 263.

62. "Bilu huagong xiang meiguo zhumi gongshi xushuo kuqing qiuhuan bingwen" [A petition of hardship submitted by Chinese laborers in Peru to the U.S. consul], in *Huagong chuguo shiliao huibian*, ed. Chen Hansheng, vol. 1, pt. 3, 965–66.

63. My translation of the original Chinese text. See another translation in Stewart, *Chinese Bondage in Peru*, 139–40n4.

64. Stewart, *Chinese Bondage in Peru*, 139.

65. Stewart, *Chinese Bondage in Peru*, 142.

66. See *The Cuba Commission Report: A Hidden History of the Chinese in Cuba: The Original English-Language Text of 1876* (Baltimore: Johns Hopkins University Press, 1993).

67. See Edward Rhoads, *Stepping Forth into the World: The Chinese Educational Mission to the United States, 1872–81* (Hong Kong: Hong Kong University Press, 2011), and Chih-ming Wang, *Transpacific Articulations: Student Migration and the Remaking of Asian America* (Honolulu: University of Hawai'i Press, 2013), 21–49.

68. "Li Hongzhang lun paiyuan chaban Bilu huagong" [A commentary by Li Hongzhang on the sending of officials to investigate Chinese laborers in Peru], *Huagong chuguo shiliao huibian*, ed. Chen Hansheng, vol. 1, pt. 3, 1041–42.

69. Yung Wing, *My Life in China and America* (New York: Henry Holt, 1909), 195.

70. "Zhaolu Rong Hong suo cha huagoong gongci jianzheng" [Document on Yung Wing's investigation of the testimonies from Chinese laborers], in *Huagong chuguo shiliao huibian*, ed. Chen Hansheng, vol. 1, pt. 3, 1055–59.

71. "Xu Qianshen zhichi Xibanya zhaogong youwei xuding zhaogong zhangcheng tiaoyue cheng zhongchu wen" [A report submitted by Xu Qianshen to the Zongli Yamen that condemns Spain's violation of the regulations in the recruitment of labor], in *Huagong chuguo shiliao huibian*, ed. Chen Hansheng, vol. 1, pt. 3, 880.

72. "Xu Qianshen zhichi Xibanya zhaogong youwei xuding zhaogong zhangcheng tiaoyue cheng zhongchu wen," 892–93.

73. McKeown, *Melancholy Order*, 77.

74. David Northrup, *Indentured Labor in the Age of Imperialism, 1834–1922* (Cambridge: Cambridge University Press, 1995), 112.

75. Hsü, *China's Entrance into the Family of Nations*, 185.

76. Rebecca Karl, *Staging the World: Chinese Nationalism at the Turn of the Twentieth Century* (Durham, NC: Duke University Press, 2002), 55.

Chapter 2: Colonists of the South Seas

I would like to thank Ana Maria Candela for her valuable comments and suggestions for an earlier version of this chapter.

1. Luo Huangchao, "Liu Shimu yu Huaqiao shiye he Nanyang yanjiu" [Liu Shimu and overseas Chinese affairs as well as South Seas studies], *Jinan Xuebao* 3 (1983): 13–16. For other examples of Chinese intellectuals traveling and working in Nanyang and their conceptions of Nanyang, see Bin Yang, "Under and beyond the Pen of Eileen Chang: Shanghai, Nanyang, Huaqiao, and Greater China," *Frontiers of History in China* 11, no. 3 (2016): 458–84; Glen Peterson, "Migration and China's Urban Reading Public: Shifting Representations of 'Overseas Chinese' in Shanghai's *Dongfang Zazhi* (Eastern Miscellany), 1904–1948," in *Migration, Indigenization and Interaction: Chinese Overseas and Globalization*, ed. Leo Suryadinata (Singapore: World Scientific, 2011), 277–96; and Brian Bernards, *Writing the South Seas: Imagining the Nanyang in Chinese and Southeast Asian Postcolonial Literature* (Seattle: University of Washington Press, 2015).

2. Nanyang zhi bazhe [Hegemons of the South Seas], speech by Umetani Mitsusada, translated by Liu Shimu (Shanghai: Zhonghua Nanyang xiehui choubei chu, 1923).

3. The Jinan University in Shanghai should not be confused with the Jinan University in Shandong province. The one under discussion was originally founded in Nanjing as Jinan Academy in 1906 to educate children of the overseas Chinese, moved to Shanghai's Zhengru in 1918, and was reorganized into Jinan University in 1927. It was later relocated to Jianyang, Fujian province, in 1941; returned to Shanghai and merged with two other universities, Fudan and Jiaotong, in 1949; and reopened as an independent institution in Guangzhou in 1958. See Jinan Daxue xiaoshi bianxie zu [Jinan University history editorial group], *Jinan Xiaoshi, 1906–1986* [The history of Jinan University, 1906–1986] (Guangzhou: Jinan Daxue, 1986); Leander Seah, "Conceptualizing the Chinese World: Jinan University, Nanyang Migrants, and Trans-Regionalism, 1900–1941" (Ph.D. diss., University of Pennsylvania, 2011). For a survey of overseas Chinese studies published in the Guomindang period, see Li Anshan, "Zhonghua minguo shiqi Nanyang yanjiu shuping," *Jindaishi Yanjiu* 4 (2002): 290–314.

4. See Li Jierong, "Jinan daxue Nanyang wenhua jiaoyu shiye bu de lishi chengjiu yu gongxian" [The historical achievements and contributions of the Department of Nanyang Cultural and Educational Affairs at Jinan University], *Jinan Xuebao* 23, no. 5 (September 2001): 110–16; Zhao Canpeng, "Jinan daxue Nanyang

wenhua shiye bu de lishi yange" [The historical development of the Nanyang Cultural Affairs Department at Jinan University], *Dongnanya yanjiu* 6 (2007): 5–12.

5. The Jinan publications that were later translated into Japanese include Chen Da, *Nanyang huaqiao yu Min Yue shehui* [Nanyang overseas Chinese and society in Fujian and Guangdong] (Changsha: Shangwu yinshu guan, 1938), or the English version, *Emigrant Communities in South China: A Study of Overseas Migration and Its Influence on Standards of Living and Social Change* (New York: Institute of Pacific Relations, 1940); Qiu Hanping, *Huaqiao wenti* [The question of the overseas Chinese] (Shanghai: Shangwu yinshu guan, 1939); Li Changfu, *Zhongguo zhimin shi* [History of China's colonization] (Shanghai: Shangwu yinshu guan, 1937); Huang Jingwan, *Huaqiao dui zuguo de gongxian* [The contributions of the overseas Chinese to the ancestral nation] (Shanghai: Tangdi she, 1941); and Liu Jixuan and Shu Shicheng, *Zhonghua minzu tuozhi Nanyang shi* [The development and colonization by the Chinese nation in Nanyang] (Shanghai: Shanghai yinshu guan, 1934). See Tan Yeok Seong (Chen Yusong), "Riben de huaqiao yanjiu lice" [A study of the Japanese studies of the overseas Chinese], in *Yeyinguan wencun* [Collected writings from the Yeyin Studio] (Singapore: South Seas Society, ca. 1983), 205–9. See also George L. Hicks, *A Bibliography of Japanese Works on Southeast Asia, 1914–45* (Hong Kong: Asian Research Service, 1992). According to Hicks, the Mantetsu East Asian Economic Research Bureau has published a six-volume Nanyang Chinese Series (Nanyō Kakyō Sōsho) from 1937, while the government-general of Taiwan Foreign Affairs Department published two volumes of field surveys of Chinese society in Guangdong and Fujian provinces and over two hundred regular general reports on Chinese in Southeast Asia during the Pacific War (xii). It peaked during 1940–41 on the eve of the Japanese invasion of Southeast Asia (xiv).

6. Examples of newspapers include *Nanyang Siang Pau* [Nanyang Shangbao, 1923–56] and *Sin Chew Jit Poh* [Xingzhou Ribao, 1929–41, 1951–56].

7. Tan, "Riben de huaqiao yanjiu lice." See Victor Purcell, *The Chinese in Southeast Asia* (London: Oxford University Press, 1965), and Suyama, Taku, "Pang Societies and the Economy of Chinese Immigrants in Southeast Asia," in *Papers on Malayan History*, ed. K. G. Tregonning (Singapore: Department of History, University of Singapore, 1962), 193–213.

8. One example of the reprints is Yang Jiancheng, ed., *Nanyang Yanjiu Shiliao Chongkan* [Nanyang studies series] (Taipei: Zhonghua xueshuyuan Nanyang yanjiusuo, 1984). See also Wang Gungwu, "Southeast Asian Huaqiao in Chinese History-Writing," in *China and the Chinese Overseas* (Singapore: Times Academic Press, 1991), 22–40.

9. I draw on the insightful discussions on the region's broader transformations in these works: Mark Ravinder Frost, "Asia's Maritime Networks and the Colonial Public Sphere, 1840–1920," *New Zealand Journal of Asian Studies* 6, no. 2 (December 2004): 63–94; Sunil Amrith, *Migration and Diaspora in Modern Asia* (New York:

Cambridge University Press, 2011); and Su Lin Lewis, "Print Culture and the New Maritime Frontier in Rangoon and Penang," *Moussons* 17 (2011): 127–44.

10. For a discussion of Chinese schools and newspapers in early twentieth-century Southeast Asia, see C. F. Yong and R. B. McKenna, *The Kuomintang Movement in British Malaya, 1912–1949* (Singapore: Singapore University Press, 1990), 1–21.

11. A brief discussion can be found in Wang Gungwu, "Southeast Asian Huaqiao in Chinese History-Writing," 27–30.

12. Prasenjit Duara, *Rescuing History from the Nation: Questioning Narratives of Modern China* (Chicago: University of Chicago Press, 1996), 5.

13. There was a smaller group of Chinese intellectuals specializing in Nanyang who were trained in Europe and the United States, taught at universities in Beijing, and did not seem to share the same cultural circuits as the Jinan intellectuals. See Yao Nan, "Zhongguo dui dongnanya shi de yanjiu" [Southeast Asian studies in China], in *Xinyun Yeyu Ji* [A collection of stars, wind, coconuts, and rain] (Singapore: Singapore News and Publications, 1984), 229–31.

14. Frost, "Asia's Maritime Networks and the Colonial Public Sphere." Similar arguments about East Asia as an integrated region can be found in Giovanni Arrighi, Takeshi Hamashita, and Mark Selden, eds., *The Resurgence of East Asia: 500, 150 and 50 Year Perspectives* (London: Routledge, 2003).

15. See, for example, Eric Tagliacozzo and Wen-Chin Chang, eds., *Chinese Circulations: Capital, Commodities, and Networks in Southeast Asia* (Durham, NC: Duke University Press, 2011).

16. Wang Gungwu, *The Nanhai Trade: The Early History of Chinese Trade in the South China Sea* (Singapore: Times Academic Press, 1998).

17. Li Jinsheng, "Yige Nanyang, gezi jieshuo: 'Nanyang' gainian de lishi yanbian" [One Nanyang, different interpretations: The historical evolution of the "Nanyang" concept], *Yazhou wenhua* (Asian culture) 30 (June 2006): 113–23.

18. See Lysa Hong and Jianli Huang, *The Scripting of a National History: Singapore and Its Pasts* (Hong Kong: Hong Kong University Press, 2008), 124n48.

19. Wang Gungwu, *Don't Leave Home: Migration and the Chinese* (Singapore: Times Academic Press, 2001), 298–99.

20. Takeshi Hamashita, "The Intra-Regional System in East Asia in Modern Times," in *Network Power: Japan and Asia*, ed. Peter J. Katzenstein and Takashi Shiraishi (Ithaca, NY: Cornell University Press, 1996), 113–35, and "Tribute and Treaties: Maritime Asia and Treaty Port Networks in the Era of Negotiation, 1800–1900," in *The Resurgence of East Asia*, ed. Arrighi, Hamashita, and Selden, 17–50.

21. Jane Kate Leonard, *Wei Yuan and China's Rediscovery of the Maritime World* (Cambridge, MA: Harvard University Press, 1984), and Fred W. Drake, *China Charts the World: Hsu Chi-yü and His Geography of 1848* (Cambridge, MA: Harvard University Press, 1975).

22. Leonard, *Wei Yuan and China's Rediscovery of the Maritime World*, 97.

23. Japanese translations of Wei's Treatise and Xu's Record are titled *Kaikoku zushi* (1854–56) and *Eikai shiryaku* (1861).

24. Cited in Leonard, *Wei Yuan and China's Rediscovery of the Maritime World*, 100.

25. See Ken'ichi Gotō, *Tensions of Empire: Japan and Southeast Asia in the Colonial and Postcolonial World* (Athens: Ohio University Press, 2003), 3–23, and Mark R. Peattie, "The Nan'yō: Japan in the South Pacific, 1885–1945," in *The Japanese Colonial Empire, 1895–1945*, ed. Ramon Hawley Myers, Mark R. Peattie, and Jingzhi Zhen (Princeton, NJ: Princeton University Press, 1984), and Mark R. Peattie, *Nan'yo: The Rise and Fall of the Japanese in Micronesia, 1885–1945* (Honolulu: University of Hawai'i Press, 1988).

26. Ken'ichi Gotō, "Japan's Southern Advance and Colonial Taiwan," *European Journal of East Asian Studies* 3, no. 1 (2004): 15–44.

27. Yang Jiancheng, "Dongnanya huaqiao yanjiu riwen mingzhu yicong jianjie" [An introduction to the translated works of important Japanese studies on Chinese in the South Seas], in *Sanshi niandai Nanyang huaqiao qiaohui touzi diaocha baogao shu* [An investigative report on the remittance investment of Chinese in the South Seas in the 1930s] (Taipei: Zhonghua xueshu yuan Nanyang yanjiusuo [Chinese Academy, Institute for South Seas Studies], 1983), 4.

28. Syed Hussein Alatas, *The Myth of the Lazy Native: A Study of the Image of the Malays, Filipinos, and Javanese from the 16th to the 20th Century and Its Function in the Ideology of Colonial Capitalism* (London: Frank Cass, 1977).

29. See Huei-Ying Kuo, "Social Discourse and Economic Functions: The Singapore Chinese in Japan's Southward Expansion between 1914 and 1941," in *Singapore in Global History*, ed. Derek Heng and Syed Muhd Khairudin Aljunied (Amsterdam: Amsterdam University Press, 2011), 111–34.

30. Kuo, "Social Discourse and Economic Functions," 113.

31. See Emma Teng, *Taiwan's Imagined Geography: Chinese Colonial Travel Writing and Pictures, 1683–1895* (Cambridge, MA: Harvard University Asia Center, 2004), and Faye Yuan Keeman, *Under an Imperial Sun: Japanese Colonial Literature of Taiwan and the South* (Honolulu: University of Hawai'i Press, 2003).

32. Li Changfu, "Nanyang huaqiao yizhi shi niaokan" [A bird's-eye view of the history of overseas Chinese migration to Nanyang], in *Nanyang shidi yu huaqiao huaren yanjiu: Li Changfu xiansheng lunwen xuanji* [The history and geography of Nanyang and the study of the overseas Chinese: A collection of Mr. Li Changfu's essays] (Guangzhou: Jinan daxue chubanshe, 2001), 62–63.

33. Martin W. Lewis and Kären Wigen, *The Myth of Continents: A Critique of Metageography* (Berkeley: University of California Press, 1997), 42.

34. Zhang Xiangshi, *Huaqiao zhongxin zhi Nanyang* [A huaqiao-centered Nanyang] (Haikou: Hainan shuju, 1927), 3.

35. Li Changfu, "Huaqiao yanjiu zhi jicu wenti" [The basic problems in overseas Chinese studies], in *Nanyang shidi yu huaqiao huaren yanjiu*, 20–21. See a discussion of geographical and historical materialism in Kuan-Hsing Chen, *Asia as Method: Toward Deimperialization* (Durham, NC: Duke University Press, 2010), 102–4.

36. Quoted in Li Changfu, "Shijie de huaqiao" [The overseas Chinese of the world], in *Nanyang shidi yu huaqiao huaren yanjiu*, 24.

37. Quoted in Li Changfu, "Shijie de huaqiao," 41.

38. Li Changfu, "Shijie de huaqiao," 24.

39. Li Changfu, "Huaqiao yanjiu zhi jicu wenti," 8.

40. Li Changfu, "Huaqiao yanjiu zhi jicu wenti," 6.

41. Li Changfu, "Huaqiao yanjiu zhi jicu wenti," 5.

42. Liu Shimu, *Zhonghua minzu zhi haiwai fazhan* [The overseas development of the Chinese nation] (Taipei: Minshizhe chubanshe, 1983, reprint), preface, 1.

43. Liu Shimu, *Zhonghua minzu zhi haiwai fazhan*. For an insightful discussion of the phrase *mother of the revolution*, see Huang Jianli, "Umbilical Ties: The Framing of the Overseas Chinese as the Mother of the Revolution," *Frontiers of History in China* 6, no. 2 (June 2011): 183–228.

44. Liu Shimu, *Zhonghua minzu zhi haiwai fazhan*, 2.

45. See Li Changfu, *Zhongguo zhimin shi*.

46. See, for example, Yen Ching-huang, *A Social History of the Chinese in Singapore and Malaya, 1800–1911* (Singapore: Times Academic Press, 1995).

47. Tang Xiaobing, "'Poetic Revolution,' Colonization and Form at the Beginning of Chinese Literature," in *Rethinking the 1898 Reform Period: Political and Cultural Change in Late Qing China*, ed. Rebecca Karl and Peter Zarrow (Cambridge, MA: Harvard University Press, 2002), 245–65, quote from 249. I thank Ana Maria Candela for pointing me to this piece.

48. Philip A. Kuhn, *Chinese among Others: Emigration in Modern Times* (Lanham, MD: Rowman and Littlefield, 2008), 244–46.

49. Liang Qichao, "Zhongguo zhimin ba da weiren zhuan," in *Yihnbingshi heji, zhuanji*, vol. 19 (Shanghai: Zhonghua shuju, 1941).

50. See Liang Qichao, *Xindalu youji jielu* [Selected notes on travels to the New World] (Changsha: Hunan renmin chubanshe, 1981).

51. Zhang, *Huaqiao zhongxin de Nanyang*, 7–8.

52. Li Changfu, "Nanyang huaqiao yizhi shi niaokan," 63.

53. See Li Changfu, *Zhongguo zhimin shi*.

54. Li Changfu, "Shijie de huaqiao," 40–41.

55. See Wen Xiongfei, *Nanyang huaqiao tongshi* [A general history of the overseas Chinese in Nanyang] (Shanghai: Dongfang yinshu guan, 1929).

56. Wen Xiongfei, *Nanyang huaqiao tongshi*, preface, 1–2.

57. Zhang, *Huaqiao zhongxin de Nanyang*, 3–7.

58. See Kaoru Sugihara, "Patterns of Chinese Emigration to Southeast Asia, 1869–1939," *Japan, China, and the Growth of the Asian International Economy, 1850–1949*, ed. Kaoru Sugihara (Oxford: Oxford University Press, 2005), 244–74.

59. Disunity is a common theme in the memoirs of Tan Kah Kee about the Nanyang Chinese, see *Nanqiao huiyi lu* [Memoirs of a Nanyang overseas Chinese] (Singapore: Yihe xuan, 1946).

60. See Guoli Jinan Daxue Nanyang wenhua shiye bu [National Jinan University Nanyang Cultural Affairs Department], *Nanyang huaqiao jiaoyu huiyi baogao* [A report on the Nanyang overseas Chinese education meeting] (Shanghai: Guoli Jinan Daxue Nanyang wenhua shiye bu, 1930).

61. Yang Jiancheng, ed., *Zhongguo Guomindang yu Huaqiao wenxian chubian, 1908–1945* [A preliminary selection of documents on China's Guomindang and huaqiao, 1908–1945] (Taipei: Zhonghua zueshu yuan Nanyang yanjiusuo, 1984).

62. Yang Jiancheng, ed., *Zhongguo Guomindang yu Huaqiao wenxian chubian*, 18–19.

63. Yang Jiancheng, ed., *Zhongguo Guomindang yu Huaqiao wenxian chubian*, 25.

64. See Philip D. Curtin, *Cross-Cultural Trade in World History* (Cambridge: Cambridge University Press, 1984).

Chapter 3: Confucius from Afar

1. "Liang di shu" [Letters between two places], vol. 2 (Xiamen-Guangzhou, September 1926–January 1927), in *Lu Xun quanji*, vol. 11 (Beijing: Renmin wenxue chuban she, 1981), 103–278.

2. "Haishang tongxin" [Communications from the sea], *Lu Xun quanji*, vol. 3, 398–403. This letter was originally written on January 16, 1927, and published in the monthly magazine, *Yu Si* [Words and strands], no. 118, on February 12, 1927.

3. The May Thirtieth Tragedy refers to British and Japanese firings on Chinese protestors and strikers in Shanghai on May 30, 1925. The March Eighteenth Tragedy refers to Japanese attacks on Tianjin on March 18, 1926. According to Wang Gungwu, Lu Xun's lecture was only half recorded in *Xiada Weekly*, the university magazine. Therefore he mainly uses a version written by Yu Di, who recalled the talk thirty years later in "Huiyi Lu Xun xiansheng zai Xiamen Daxue," *Wenyi Yuebao*, October 10, 1956, reprinted in *Lu Xun huiyi lu* (Shanghai: Shanghai wen yi chu ban she, 1979). Although it may not be fully accurate, Wang finds that the main thrust of the argument is true to Lu Xun's views on the same topic as he expressed them elsewhere. See Wang Gungwu, "Lu Xun, Lim Boon Keng and Confucianism," in *China and the Chinese Overseas* (Singapore: Times Academic Press, 1991), 163–84. The Chinese text of Yu Di's recollections appears in Lee Guan Kin [Li Yuanjin], *Lin Wenqing di sixiang: Zhongxi wenhua di huiliu yu maodun* [The thought of Lim Boon Keng: The contradictions and convergence of Chinese and Western cultures] (Singapore: Xinjiapo Yazhou yanjiu xuehui, 1991), 133.

4. "Liang di shu," 156–59. See also Wang, "Lu Xun, Lim Boon Keng and Confucianism," 170–71.

5. "Liang di shu," 156–59.

6. The foremost scholar of Lim Boon Keng's intellectual thought is Lee Guan Kin; see *Lin Wenqing di sixiang*, and *Dongxi wenhua de zhuangji yu Xinhua zhishi fenzi de san zhong huiying: Qiu Shuyuan, Lin Wenqing, Song Wangxiang de bijiao yan jiu* [The clash of cultures and three responses from Singapore-Malayan intellectuals: Qiu Shuyuan, Lim Boon Keng, Song Ongsiang] (Singapore: Xinjiapo guoli daxue zhongwen xi, 2001). Other discussions of Lim's biography include Jean DeBernardi, "Lim Boon Keng and the Invention of Cosmopolitanism in the Straits Settlements," in *Managing Change in Southeast Asia: Local Identities, Global Connections*, ed. Jean Elizabeth DeBernardi, Gregory L. Forth, and Sandra A. Niessen (Montreal: CASA Secretariat, 1995), and Tu Weiming, "Foreword: Lim Boon Keng—An English-Speaking Confucian," in *Essays of Lim Boon Keng on Confucianism: With Chinese Translations*, ed. Yan Chunbao (Singapore: World Scientific, 2014), vii–x.

7. For portrayals of Lim Boon Keng as a bicultural model in the twenty-first century by Lee Guan Kin, see interviews in "Good Model for Bilingual Elite," *Straits Times*, December 19, 1998; "Three Men, Three Models: The Chinese Divide," *Straits Times*, April 8, 2001; and "The Pull of Two Worlds," *Straits Times*, April 8, 2001.

8. See "Go beyond Mandarin to Connect with China" and "Many Cultures, One Common Aim," *Straits Times*, June 24, 2004.

9. Among the most important U.S. academic contributions to the Confucian revival in Singapore and China during the 1980s and 1990s, see Tu Wei-ming, *The Living Tree: The Changing Meaning of Being Chinese Today* (Stanford, CA: Stanford University Press, 1994), and *Confucian Traditions in East Asian Modernity: Moral Education and Economic Culture in Japan and the Four Mini-Dragons* (Cambridge, MA: Harvard University Press, 1996). For discussions of the phenomenon, see Arif Dirlik, "Confucius in the Borderlands: Global Capitalism and the Reinvention of Confucianism," *boundary 2* 22, no. 3 (autumn 1995): 229–73, and Sébastien Billioud and Joël Thoraval, *The Sage and the People: The Confucian Revival in China* (Oxford: Oxford University Press, 2015).

10. See Yan Chunbao, *Yisheng zhenwei you shui zhi: Daxue xiaozhang Lin Wenqing* [Who can tell the truth from falsehood in one's life: University president Lim Boon Keng] (Fuzhou: Fujian jiaoyu chuban she, 2010), 177–203. Other new biographies include Zhang Yaqun, *Zi qiang bu xi, zhi yu zhi shan: Xiamen da xue xiao zhang Lin Wenqing* (Jinan Shi: Shandong jiao yu chu ban she, 2012), and Lin Jian, *Furonghupan yi sanlin: Linwenqing Linyutang Lin Huixiang de Xiadasuiyue* [Remembering the three Lin by the Furong Lake: The Xiada days of Lim Boon Keng, Lin Yutang, and Lin Huixiang] (Xiamen: Xiamen daxue chuban she, 2011).

11. An earlier iteration of my argument appears in Shelly Chan, "The Case for Diaspora: A Temporal Approach to the Chinese Experience," *Journal of Asian Studies* 74, no. 1 (February 2015): 107–28.

12. I am deeply grateful to Anne Hansen for introducing me to the vast scholarship of comparative religions and religion-making in Southeast Asia. See, for

example, Tomoko Masuzawa, *The Invention of World Religions or How European Universalism Was Preserved in the Language of Pluralism* (Chicago: University of Chicago Press, 2005); Shawn Frederick McHale, *Print and Power: Confucianism, Communism, and Buddhism in the Making of Modern Vietnam* (Honolulu: University of Hawai'i Press, 2004); Anne Hansen, *How to Behave: Buddhism and Modernity in Colonial Cambodia, 1860–1930* (Honolulu: University of Hawai'i Press, 2007); Markus Dressler and Arvind-pal Singh Mandair, eds., *Secularism and Religion-Making* (New York: Oxford University Press, 2011); Thongchai Winichakul, "Buddhist Apologetics and a Genealogy of Comparative Religion in Siam," *Numen* 62, no. 1 (December 2015): 76–99. For discussions of Chinese religions, see Prasenjit Duara, *Sovereignty and Authenticity: Manchukuo and the East Asian Modern* (Lanham, MD: Rowman and Littlefield, 2003); Mayfair Mei-hui Yang, *Chinese Religiosities: Afflictions of Modernity and State Formation* (Berkeley: University of California Press, 2008); and Vincent Goossaert and David A. Palmer, *The Religious Question in Modern China* (Chicago: University of Chicago Press, 2011).

13. Prasenjit Duara, "Religion and Citizenship in China and the Diaspora," in *Chinese Religiosities*, ed. Yang, 43–64.

14. Song Ong Siang, *One Hundred Years' History of the Chinese in Singapore* (Singapore: Oxford University Press, 1984 [1922]), 22–25.

15. For Chinese travel narratives on Southeast Asia in the nineteenth century, see, for example, Fujian Shifan Daxue, ed., *Wanqing haiwai biji xuan* [Notes from overseas during the late Qing] (Beijing: Haiyang chubanshe: Xinhua shudian Beijing faxingsuo faxing, 1983). For European colonial narratives, see J. D. Vaughan, *The Manners and Customs of the Chinese of the Straits Settlements* (Singapore: Mission, 1879; reprint, 1971), and Charles Burton Buckley, *An Anecdotal History of Old Times in Singapore: From the Foundation of the Settlement under the Honourable the East India Company on February 6th, 1819 to the Transfer to the Colonial Office as Part of the Colonial Possessions of the Crown on April 1st, 1867* (Singapore Fraser and Neave, 1902; reprint, 1984). See also Tan Chee Beng, *The Baba of Melaka: Culture and Identity of a Chinese Peranakan Community in Malaysia* (Petaling Jaya: Selangor, 1988).

16. Yen Ching-hwang, *A Social History of the Chinese in Singapore and Malaya, 1800–1911* (Singapore: Oxford University Press, 1986), 295.

17. See Yen Ching-hwang, "The Confucian Revival Movement in Singapore and Malaya, 1899–1911," *Journal of Southeast Asian Studies* 7, no. 1 (March 1976): 53.

18. Lee Guan Kin, *Lin Wenqing de sixiang*, 78–86, details Lim's warm relationships with China-born reformers Khoo Seok Wan (Qiu Shuyuan, 1874–1941) and Lim's own father-in-law, Wong Nai Siong (Huang Naishang, 1894–1924), but offers no direct evidence of Wong's or Khoo's direct influence on Lim's reformism.

19. Established in 1885 by Governor Cecil Smith, two Queen's scholarships were awarded every year to British subjects in the Straits Settlements for university education in Britain. The scholarships were abolished temporarily in 1910 and

resumed in 1924. Between 1885 and 1910, forty-five scholarships were awarded. See Wu Lien-teh, *Plague Fighter: The Autobiography of a Modern Chinese Physician* (Cambridge: Heffer, 1959), 156–57.

20. Lee Guan Kin, *Lin Wenqing de sixiang*, and Khor Eng Hee, "A Biography of Lim Boon Keng," trans. Li Yelin, B.A. honors thesis, University of Malaya, 1985–86.

21. Inaugural issue, *Straits Chinese Magazine* 1, no. 1 (1897).

22. Lim Boon Keng, "Our Enemies," *Straits Chinese Magazine* 1, no. 2 (1897): 52–58.

23. W. C. Lin [Lim Boon Keng], "Straits Chinese Hedonism," *Straits Chinese Magazine* 4, no. 15 (1900): 108–11.

24. Song Ong Siang, "The Position of Chinese Women," *Straits Chinese Magazine* 1, no. 1 (1897): 16–23.

25. For discussions on Victorian gender ideology, see, for example, Anne McClintock, *Imperial Leather: Race, Gender, and Sexuality in the Colonial Contest* (New York: Routledge, 1995), and Catherine Hall, *Civilising Subjects: Metropole and Colony in the English Imagination* (Chicago: University of Chicago Press, 2002).

26. On Lim's rendering of Mandarin Chinese as the "father tongue" of baba Chinese, see Lee Guan Kin, "Lin Wenqing zou xiang Xiamen daxue: Yi ge Xinjiapo haixia huaren de xungen licheng" [Lim Boon Keng's road to Xiamen University: A root-searching journey of a Singapore Straits Chinese], in *Shiji zhi jiao de haiwai huaren* [Chinese overseas at the turn of the century], ed. Zhuang Guotu et al. (Fuzhou, 1998), 514.

27. See December 2, 1898, in *Straits Times*, and Lim Boon Keng, "Straits Chinese Reform: I. The Queue Question," *Straits Chinese Magazine* 3, no. 9 (1899): 22–25.

28. See December 2, 1898, in *Straits Times*, and Lim Boon Keng, "Straits Chinese Reform: I. The Queue Question," *Straits Chinese Magazine* 3, no. 9 (1899): 22–25.

29. Vaughan, *Manners and Customs*, 3.

30. Wu Lien-teh, *Plague Fighter*, 160.

31. G. T. Hare, "The Straits-Born Chinese," *Straits Chinese Magazine* 1, no. 1 (1897): 3–8.

32. Yong, *Chinese Leadership and Power in Colonial Singapore* (Singapore: Times Academic Press, 1992), 52–61.

33. Lim Boon Keng, "Straits Chinese Reform: V. Filial Piety," *Straits Chinese Magazine* 4, no. 13 (1900): 24–25.

34. Lim Boon Keng, "Straits Chinese Reform: V. Filial Piety."

35. Lim Boon Keng, "Straits Chinese Reform: VI. Funeral Rites," *Straits Chinese Magazine* 4, no. 14 (1900): 49–47.

36. Lim Boon Keng, "Suggested Reforms of the Chinese Marriage Customs," *Straits Chinese Magazine* 5, no. 18 (1901): 58–60.

37. Lim Boon Keng, "Straits Chinese Reform: III. The Education of Children," *Straits Chinese Magazine* 3, no. 11 (1899): 102–5.

38. Focusing on the life of Lim Boon Keng, Lee Guan Kin, in *Lin Wenqing de sixiang*, portrays him as a bicultural negotiator who successfully reconciled the

"convergence and contradiction of Chinese and Western cultures" but offers little analysis of his views on Malayness. Mark Frost, in "Asia's Maritime Networks and the Colonial Public Sphere, 1840–1920," *New Zealand Journal of Asian Studies* 6, no. 2 (December 2004), notes the "continued efforts by Baba to represent themselves as authentically Chinese in public," a fact that Frost finds intriguing in light of their "permanent settlement" in the Straits, unlike the China-oriented "sojourners," but he too offers no analysis of their attitudes about the Malay culture they shared.

39. Lim Boon Keng himself acknowledged the fact that Malay wives were often put in charge of the family business while their Chinese husbands had to be away trading in China for months every year. See Lim Boon Keng, "The Chinese in Malaya," in *Present Impressions of the Far East and Prominent and Progressive Chinese at Home and Abroad*, ed. W. Feldwick (London: Globe Encyclopedia, 1917), 875–82. This historical fact and tradition, however, did not prevent Lim and his circle from criticizing Malay women and their offspring for their ignorance and indolence in the nineteenth century, particularly for being publicly mobile and visible, following some high-profile police arrests of Chinese nyonyas gamblers in the late 1890s reported in *Straits Chinese Magazine*. In their view, these women did not seem to conform well to Victorian-style gender norms. One can point to baba internalization of the colonial myth that the natives were always lazy and rowdy. However, as Mark Frost ("Asia's Maritime Networks") has pointed out, at least some baba families, financially established in Singapore, did not have to toil like the immigrant Chinese, and were therefore regarded as a more intelligent, but much less "robust" and "energetic," species of the Chinese in colonial eyes.

40. Arguments about the undesirability of "Malay tendencies" and the superiority of Chinese values thread through the social commentaries in *Straits Chinese Magazine*, but have largely escaped the notice of historians. These can be found in "We Are a Peculiar People," *Straits Chinese Magazine* 6, no. 24 (1902): 167–68; Lim Boon Keng, "Straits Chinese Reform II: Dress and Custom," *Straits Chinese Magazine* 3, no. 10 (1899): 57–59; Lim Boon Keng, "The Role of the Babas in the Development of China," *Straits Chinese Magazine* 7, no. 3 (1903): 94–100; Lim Boon Keng, "Our Nyonyas, by a Baba," *Straits Chinese Magazine* 7, no. 4 (1903): 129–30; and Song Ong Siang, "The Position of Chinese Women," *Straits Chinese Magazine* 1, no. 1 (1897): 16–23.

41. See Vaughan, *Manners and Customs*, 1–2. Vaughan lived in the Straits Settlements for forty-five years and worked as a colonial official.

42. Vaughan, *Manners and Customs*, 43.

43. "China—A New Field for Straits Enterprise. An Interview with Mr. Lew Yuk Lin, Acting Consul for China at Singapore," *Straits Chinese Magazine* 2, no. 7 (1898): 102–4.

44. See Michael Godley, *The Mandarin-Capitalists from Nanyang: Overseas Chinese Enterprise in the Modernization of China, 1893–1911* (New York: Cambridge University Press, 1981).

45. Lim Boon Keng, "The Role of the Babas," 94–100.
46. Lim Boon Keng, "The Role of the Babas," 94–100.
47. Lim Boon Keng, "The Renovation of China," *Straits Chinese Magazine* 2, no. 7 (1898): 88–99.
48. Arthur Smith, *Chinese Characteristics* (New York: Fleming H. Revell, 1894), 330.
49. Smith, *Chinese Characteristics*, 325.
50. Lydia H. Liu, *Translingual Practice: Literature, National Culture, and Translated Modernity—China, 1900–1937* (Stanford, CA: Stanford University Press, 1995), 76.
51. See Yang, "Introduction," in *Chinese Religiosities*, 1–40, and Arvind-Pal S. Mandair and Markus Dressler, "Introduction: Modernity, Religion-Making, and the Postsecular," in *Secularism and Religion-Making* (New York: Oxford University Press, 2011), 3–36.
52. Yang, *Chinese Religiosities*, 3.
53. Lim Boon Keng, "Ethical Education for the Straits Chinese," *Straits Chinese Magazine* 8, no. 1 (1904): 25–30.
54. Lim Boon Keng, "The Role of the Babas."
55. One of Them [Lim Boon Keng], "The Reform Movement among the Straits Chinese," *Straits Chinese Magazine* 2, no. 8 (1898): 172–75.
56. Wen Ching [Lim Boon Keng], "The White Peril: From the Imperial and Official Standpoint," and "The White Peril from the Popular Standpoint," in *The Chinese Crisis from Within* (Singapore: Select Publishing, 2007 [1901]), 177–89, 190–204.
57. Lim Boon Keng, "Ethical Education."
58. Lim Boon Keng, "Ethical Education."
59. Lim Boon Keng, "The Status of Women under a Confucian Regime," *Straits Chinese Magazine* 10, no. 4 (1906): 170–78.
60. Lim Boon Keng, "The Status of Women."
61. Lim Boon Keng, "The Status of Women."
62. Lim Boon Keng, "The Confucian Ideal," *Straits Chinese Magazine* 9, no. 3 (1905), 115–19.
63. C. F. Yong, *Tan Kah-Kee: The Making of an Overseas Chinese Legend* (Singapore: Oxford University Press, 1987), 98–106.
64. Yong, *Tan Kah-Kee*; Lee Guan Kin, *Lin Wenqing de sixiang*, 34–35, 197, 209–13.
65. Lee Guan Kin, *Lin Wenqing de sixiang*, 34–35, 197, 209–13.
66. Yong, *Tan Kah-Kee*, 98–106.
67. See note 6; "Xiamen tongxin 3" [Letters from Xiamen 3], *Lu Xun quanji*, vol. 3, 396–97.
68. Arif Dirlik, "Guoxue/National Learning in the Age of Global Modernity," *China Perspectives* 1 (2011): 8.
69. Lim Boon Keng, *The City of Amoy, Now Named Sze-Min, or, the Island that Remembers the Ming* (Amoy: Amoy University Press, 1936), 49–54.
70. See note 18 in Lee Guan Kin, *Lin Wenqing de Sixiang*, 218.

71. Wang Gungwu, "Lu Xun, Lim Boon Keng, and Confucianism," 166–68. See also notes 17–20.

72. Lian Shisheng, *Xian ren za ji* [The miscellaneous notes of an idler] (Singapore, 1955), quoted in Bi Guanhua, "Lin Wenqing" (Lim Boon Keng), in *Souvenir Magazine of the 90th Anniversary of Ee Hoe Hian Club, Singapore* (Singapore: Ee Hoe Hian Club, 1985).

73. For example, one of the first complete biographies of Lim from the 1980s says: "After the May Fourth movement, the social thought of China underwent rapid change. Heavily influenced by Kang Youwei and Liang Qichao, Lim Boon Keng was attacked by the younger generation. Moreover, Japan's increasing aggression caused enormous strife in China. The waves in Changjiang River always push forward one after the other. An aging man, Lim Boon Keng had become an obsolete figure. . . . How could a pure-hearted and honest third-generation overseas person of Chinese descent withstand such a cruel trial?" See Khor Eng Hee, "A Biography of Lim Boon Keng," 51. Similar portrayals can be found in Tan Yeok Seong, "Lin Wenqing lun," and Lee Guan Kin, *Lin Wenqing de sixiang*.

74. Lim Boon Keng, "Who Is Ch'ü Yüan?" *The Li Sao: An Elegy on Encountering Sorrows* (Reprinted, Taipei: Ch'eng Wen, 1974), 48–49.

75. Lim Boon Keng, "Who Is Ch'ü Yüan?" 170–71.

76. See Tan Kah Kee's accounts of failure to raise funds for Xiada in Southeast Asia in A. H. C. Ward, Raymond W. Chu, and Janet Salaff, eds. and trans., *The Memoirs of Tan Kah Kee* (Singapore: Singapore University Press, 1994), 30–34.

77. Ward et al., *The Memoirs of Tan Kah Kee*, 25–39. See also Yong, *Tan Kah-Kee*, 98–106. According to Tan, during a fund-raising trip led by Lim Boon Keng, a total of 150,000 Straits dollars had been pledged in Malaya. In the end, only $100,000 was received (equivalent to about 200,000 Chinese yuan). At this point, the annual operating costs of Xiada had already shrunk to $240,000, compared to $300,000 earlier and between $1 million and $2 million at Zhongshan University (Guangzhou) and Central University (Nanjing). Tan concluded that although Xiada could continue under those difficult circumstances, there would be no prospects for further development.

78. Ward et al., *The Memoirs of Tan Kah Kee*, 34–36.

79. Khor Eng Hee, "A Biography of Lim Boon Keng," 56–64. Lee Guan Kin, *Lin Wenqing de sixiang*, 166–67, 197–98, 214.

80. See Cai Shijun and Xu Yunqiao, eds., *Xinma huaren kangri shiliao, 1937–1945* [Historical materials of the anti-Japanese resistance of the Singapore-Malayan Chinese] (Singapore: Wenshi chuban siren gongsi, 1984).

81. Cai Shijun and Xu Yunqiao, eds., *Xinma huaren kangri shiliao*, 868–71. The number of Chinese deaths in the 1942 massacre cited by Japanese sources ranged between 5,000 and 20,000. Singapore sources reported higher figures, between 50,000 and 100,000.

82. Bi Guanhua, "Lin Wenqing," 75–80. See also Lee Guan Kin, *Lin Wenqing de sixiang*, 197–98.

Chapter 4: The Women Who Stayed Behind

1. See, for example, Maurice J. Meisner, *Mao's China and After: A History of the People's Republic* (New York: Free Press, 1999); C. K. Yang, *A Chinese Village in Early Communist Transition* (Cambridge, MA: Technology Press, Massachusetts Institute of Technology, 1959); Judith Stacey, *Patriarchy and Socialist Revolution in China* (Berkeley: University of California Press, 1983); Kay Ann Johnson, *Women, the Family, and Peasant Revolution in China* (Chicago: University of Chicago Press, 1983); Pauline B. Keating, *Two Revolutions: Village Reconstruction and the Cooperative Movement in Northern Shaanxi, 1934–1945* (Stanford, CA: Stanford University Press, 1997).

2. Neil Diamant, *Revolutionizing the Family: Politics, Love, and Divorce in Urban and Rural China, 1949–1968* (Berkeley: University of California Press, 2000), and Gail Hershatter, *The Gender of Memory: Rural Women and China's Collective Past* (Berkeley: University of California Press, 2011), 127.

3. See Ezra F. Vogel, *Canton under Communism: Programs and Politics in a Provincial Capital, 1949–1968* (Cambridge, MA: Harvard University Press, 1969), 41–90. On how the overseas Chinese and Chinese migration became an important concern in national politics and international diplomacy during the Cold War in Chinese and U.S. contexts, see Stephen Fitzgerald, *China and the Overseas Chinese: A Study of Peking's Changing Policy, 1949–1970* (Cambridge: Cambridge University Press, 1972); Cindy I-Fen Cheng, *Citizens of Asian America: Democracy and Race During the Cold War* (New York: New York University Press, 2013); Madeline Hsu, *The Good Immigrants: How the Yellow Peril Became the Model Minority* (Princeton, NJ: Princeton University Press, 2015); and Meredith Oyen, *The Diplomacy of Migration: Transnational Lives and the Making of U.S.-Chinese Relations in the Cold War* (Ithaca, NY: Cornell University Press, 2015).

4. See Maurice Freedman, *Lineage Organization in Southeastern China* (London: University of London: Athlone, 1965) and *Chinese Lineage and Society: Fukien and Kwangtung* (London: Athlone, 1966); and James L. Watson, *Emigration and the Chinese Lineage: The Mans in Hong Kong and London* (Berkeley: University of California Press, 1975).

5. See Yuen-fong Woon, *Social Organization in South China, 1911–1949: The Case of the Kuan Lineage of K'ai-P'ing County* (Ann Arbor: Center for Chinese Studies, University of Michigan, 1984), and *The Excluded Wife* (Montreal: McGill-Queen's University Press, 1998).

6. Madeline Hsu, *Dreaming of Gold, Dreaming of Home: Transnationalism and Migration between the United States and South China, 1882–1943* (Stanford, CA: Stanford University Press, 2000), 91–92.

7. See Huifen Shen, *China's Left-Behind Wives: Families of Migrants from Fujian to Southeast Asia, 1930s–1950s* (Honolulu: University of Hawai'i Press, 2012).

8. For the importance of remittances to the Chinese economy, see C. F. Remer, *Foreign Investments in China* (New York: H. Fertig, 1968); Chun-hsi Wu, *Dollars,*

Dependents, and Dogma: Overseas Chinese Remittances to Communist China (Stanford, CA: Hoover Institution on War, Revolution, and Peace, 1967); and Lane J. Harris, "Overseas Chinese Remittance Firms, the Limits of State Sovereignty, and Transnational Capitalism in East and Southeast Asia, 1850s–1930s," *Journal of Asian Studies* 74, no. 1 (February 2016): 129–51.

9. Glen Peterson, *Overseas Chinese in the People's Republic of China* (Milton Park, UK: Routledge, 2012).

10. See Tani E. Barlow, *The Question of Women in Chinese Feminism* (Durham, NC: Duke University Press, 2004), for an insightful discussion of "woman."

11. See Hsu, *Dreaming of Home, Dreaming of Gold*.

12. Overseas Chinese Affairs Section (OCAS), Taishan City Archives (TCA): 5-1-45 (1952), 21.

13. OCAS, TCA: 5-1-45, 3.

14. Letter, date unknown, OCAS, TCA: 5-1-44 (1951), 2.

15. 1 *mu* is equal to 0.0667 hectares or 0.1647 acres.

16. Letter dated November 19, 1951, OCAS, TCA: 5-1-44, 54–55.

17. Guangdong sheng difang shizhi biancuan weiyuanhui, ed., *Guangdong sheng zhi—huaqiao zhi* [Guangdong provincial gazetteer: Overseas Chinese gazetteer] (Guangzhou: Guangdong sheng renmin chubanshe, 1996), 217–18. See also Stephen Fitzgerald, *China and the Overseas Chinese*, 55, and Peterson, *Overseas Chinese*, 46–47.

18. Letter dated November 19, 1951, OCAS, TCA: 5-1-44, 54–55.

19. Letter dated October 16, 1951, OCAS, TCA: 5-1-44, 51.

20. Letter dated October 11, 1951, OCAS, TCA: 5-1-44, 34–35.

21. Report dated December 21, 1951, OCAS, TCA: 5-1-44, 6–8.

22. Report, date unknown, OCAS, TCA: 5-1-44, 40.

23. Report dated December 13, 1951, OCAS, TCA: 5-1-44, 49.

24. Report dated December 28, 1951, OCAS, TCA: 5-1-44, 58–60.

25. Report dated December 28, 1951.

26. Examples include Zhen Dong, *Zhonggong zenyang duidai huaqiao?* [How did the Chinese Communist Party treat the overseas Chinese?] (Hong Kong: Youlian chubanshe, 1953), and *Zhonggong zenyang jieduo huaqiao* [How the Chinese Communist Party rob the overseas Chinese] (Taipei: Haiwai chubanshe, 1955).

27. Hei Yan (Ren Jinghe), *Taishan qiaoxiang xuelei shi: Zhonggong baoxing lu* [The history of blood and fears in the overseas Chinese home village Taishan: The atrocities of the Chinese Communist Party], pt. 1–3 (Hong Kong: Shenzhou tushu gongsi, 1953). See also front matter, pt. 3, page number unmarked.

28. "Taishan xian meizhou qiaohui qingkuang diaocha baogao," September 21, 1954, OCAS, TCA: 5-1-51 (1955), 58–66.

29. Zhuang Guotu, "Zhongguo zhengfu dui guiqiao, qiaojuan zhengce de yanbian, 1949–1966" [The evolution of Chinese government policy toward returned overseas Chinese and overseas Chinese dependents, 1949–1966], *Nanyang wenti yanjiu* [Study of issues in Southeast Asia] 3 (July 1992): 51.

30. Liao Chengzhi, "Qiaoxiang de tudi gaige" [Land reform in the overseas Chinese home villages], in *Liao Chengzhi wenji* [The collected writings of Liao Chengzhi], ed. Laio Chengzhi wenji, zhuangji bianji bangaongshi, vol. 1 (Beijing: Renmin chubanshe, 1990), 233–38. See also Peterson, *Overseas Chinese*, 52–53.

31. "Taishan fucha zhong dui ge jieceng youguan zhengce he shangji zhishi de zhaiyao zhong 'huaqiao bufen'" [A digest of policies and directives related to the reexamination of different class labels of the overseas Chinese in Taishan], August 22, 1953, TCA, OCAS: 5-1-51 (1955), 10–13.

32. Zhuang Guotu, "Zhongguo zhengfu dui guiqiao, qiaojuan zhengce de yanbian, 1949–1966," 57.

33. Mao Qixiong and Lin Xiaodong, eds., *Zhongguo qiaowu zhengce gaishu* [A discussion of China's overseas Chinese policies] (Beijing: Zhongguo qiaowu chubanshe, 1994), 71–72. According to regulations in 1950, class status could only be changed after labor reform of five years for landlords and three years for rich peasants.

34. "Taishan xian remin zhengfu huaqiao shiwu ke 1953 nian gongzuo zongjie" [A 1953 work summary of the Overseas Chinese Section at the Taishan County People's Government," February 20, 1954, TCA, OCAS: 5-1-51 (1955), 28–29. The term *fanshen* literally means "to turn over the body." For its significance to rural transformation during the Chinese Communist revolution, see William Hinton, *Fanshen: A Documentary of Revolution in a Chinese Village* (Berkeley: University of California Press, 1997).

35. "Taishan xian remin zhengfu huaqiao shiwu ke 1953 nian gongzuo zongjie," 25.

36. "Taishan xian remin zhengfu huaqiao shiwu ke 1953 nian gongzuo zongjie," 26.

37. "Taishan tugai fucha hou cunzai de yixie huaqiao wenti diaocha baogao he jianyi" [An investigative report and some suggestions on the overseas Chinese problems remaining after the land reform review in Taishan], May 22, 1953, TCA, OCAS: 5-1-51 (1955), 24–26.

38. "Taishan xian renmin zhengfu qiaowu baogao" [A report on the overseas Chinese affair of the Taishan County People's Government], January 15, 1954, TCA, OCAS: 5-1-51, 27–40.

39. "Taishan xian renmin zhengfu qiaowu baogao."

40. "Muqian Taishan cunzai de yixie youguan huaqiao zhengce wenti baogao" [A report on some problems related to overseas Chinese policies in Taishan right now], May 20, 1954, TCA, OCAS: 5-1-47.

41. "Taishan tugai fucha hou cunzai de yixie huaqiao wenti diaocha baogao ji jianji."

42. "Muqian Taishan cunzai de yixie youguyan huaqiao zhengce wenti baogao."

43. "Muqian Taishan cunzai de yixie youguyan huaqiao zhengce wenti baogao."

44. "Taishan xian renmin zhengfu qiaowu baogao."

45. "Taishan xian meizhou qiaohui qingkuang diaocha baogao."

46. "Taishan xian meizhou qiaohui qingkuang diaocha baogao."
47. "Taishan tugai fucha hou cunzai de yixie huaqiao wenti diaocha baogao ji jianji."
48. "Taishan xian renmin zhengfu qiaowu baogao."
49. M. J. Meijer, *Marriage Law and Policy in the Chinese People's Republic* (Hong Kong: Hong Kong University Press, 1971), 77–78. See also 300–301, app. 8, "The Marriage Law of the People's Republic of China," chap. 3, Rights and Duties of Husband and Wife.
50. See Fitzgerald, *China and the Overseas Chinese*, and Peterson, *Overseas Chinese*.
51. Jacob Eyferth has also written about the party's inability to grasp the economic dynamics concerning highly skilled papermakers in rural Sichuan, as it pushed through the rebuilding of the countryside into self-sufficient units. See *Eating Rice from Bamboo Roots: The Social History of a Community of Handicraft Papermakers in Rural Sichuan, 1920–2000* (Cambridge, MA: Harvard University Asia Center, 2009).
52. For a discussion on the works about the 1950 Marriage Law, see Gail Hershatter, *Women in China's Long Twentieth Century* (Berkeley: University of California Press, 2007), 15–20.
53. Guangdong Provincial Archives (GDPA): 237-1-3 (1953).
54. Zhongshan County, District 12, Zhongxing Township, 3 villages (1953), GDPA: 237-1-3; Chaoyang County, District 14, Tiandong Township (1953), GDPA: 237-1-3; Guangzhou City (1953), GDPA: 237-1-3.
55. Dinghai County, Longdu District, Qianmei Township (1953), GDPA: 237-1-3.
56. Guangzhou City (1953), GDPA: 237-1-3.
57. Zhongshan County, District 12, Zhongxing township, 3 villages (1953), GDPA: 237-1-3.
58. Guangzhou City (1953), GDPA: 237-1-3.
59. Bao'an County, Songliang Township, Ao'hu Township (1953), GDPA: 237-1-3.
60. Zhongshan County, District 12, Zhongxing township (1953), GDPA: 237-1-3.
61. Raoping County, District 1, Dong'ao Township (1953), GDPA: 237-1-3.
62. Guangzhou City (1953), GDPA: 237-1-3.
63. This includes data from Guangzhou City, Bao'an County (Songlian and Aohu Townships), Zhongshan County (Zhongxing Township), Zhongshan County (Datong Township), Kaiping County, Chaoyang County (District 14), Chenghai County, Dinghai County (Longdu District, Liangou Township), and Raoping County (District 1, Dongao Township). GDPA: 237-1-3.
64. Dinghai County, Longdu District, Lian'gou Township (1953), GDPA: 237-1-3.
65. Zhongshan Xian, District 12, Zhongxing Township, 3 villages (1953), GDPA: 237-1-3.
66. Zhongshan Xian, District 12, Zhongxing Township, 3 villages (1953), GDPA: 237-1-3.
67. Zhongshan Xian, District 12, Zhongxing Township, 3 villages (1953), GDPA: 237-1-3.

68. Raoping County, District 1, Dong'ao Township (1953), GDPA: 237-1-3.

69. Hainan District, Qiongdong County, Futian Township (1953), GDPA: 237-1-3.

70. Guangzhou City and Zhongshan County, District 12, Zhongxing Township (1953), GDPA: 237-1-3.

71. Raoping County, District 1, Dong'ao Township (1953), GDPA: 237-1-3; Chenghai County, Huibei District (1953), GDPA: 237-1-3; Dinghai County, Longdu District, Qianmei Township (1953), GDPA: 237-1-3.

72. Dinghai County, Longdu District, Qianmei Township (1953), GDPA: 237-1-3.

73. Report from Wenchang Law Court (1956), GDPA: 250-1-8, 43.

74. Dinghai County, Longdu District, Qianmei Township (1953), GDPA: 237-1-3.

75. Fengshun County, He'an Village (1953), GDPA: 237-1-3.

76. Fengshun County, He'an Village (1953), GDPA: 237-1-3.

77. Fengshun County, He'an Village (1953), GDPA: 237-1-3.

78. "Guangdongsheng huaqiao hunyin anjian shenpan gongzuo chubu zongjie chugao" [A draft preliminary report on the adjudication of huaqiao marriage cases in Guangdong province], April 12, 1957, GDPA: 250-1-8.

79. "Guangdongsheng huaqiao hunyin anjian shenpan gongzuo chubu zongjie chugao."

80. Beijing guiguo huaqiao lianyihui, ed., *Guanyu qiaowu zhengce ji qita ruogan wenti de dafu* [Concerning answers to several questions about the policies on overseas Chinese affairs] (Beijing: Beijing guiguo huaqiao lianyihui, May 1956).

81. *Guanyu qiaowu zhengce ji qita ruogan wenti de dafu.*

82. "Guangdongsheng huaqiao hunyin anjian shenpan gongzuo chubu zongjie chugao."

83. "Guangdongsheng huaqiao hunyin anjian shenpan gongzuo chubu zongjie chugao."

84. "Guangdongsheng huaqiao hunyin anjian shenpan gongzuo chubu zongjie chugao."

85. "Guangdongsheng huaqiao hunyin anjian shenpan gongzuo chubu zongjie chugao."

86. "Guangdongsheng huaqiao hunyin anjian shenpan gongzuo chubu zongjie chugao."

87. "Guangdongsheng huaqiao hunyin anjian shenpan gongzuo chubu zongjie chugao."

88. Report from Wenchang Law Court (1956), GDPA: 250-1-8.

89. Report from Wenchang Law Court (1956), GDPA: 250-1-8.

90. Report from Shunde County People's Court (1956), GDPA: 250-1-8.

91. Report from Shunde County People's Court (1956), GDPA: 250-1-8.

92. "Guangdongsheng huaqiao hunyin anjian shenpan gongzuo chubu zongjie chugao."

93. Report from Wenchang Law Court (1956), GDPA: 250-1-8.

94. Report from Wenchang Law Court (1956), GDPA: 250-1-8.

95. Report from Wenchang Law Court (1956), GDPA: 250-1-8.
96. "Taishan xian meizhou qiaohui qingkuang diaocha baogao."
97. "Taishan xian meizhou qiaohui qingkuang diaocha baogao."
98. "Taishan xian meizhou qiaohui qingkuang diaocha baogao."
99. "Taishan xian meizhou qiaohui qingkuang diaocha baogao."
100. "Taishan xian meizhou qiaohui qingkuang diaocha baogao."
101. "Muqian Taishan cunzai de yixie youguyan huaqiao zhengce wenti baogao."
102. "Muqian Taishan cunzai de yixie youguyan huaqiao zhengce wenti baogao."

Chapter 5: Homecomings

1. "Zhou Enlai zongli dui Miandian huaqiao de jianghua" ["Premier Zhou Enlai speaking to the overseas Chinese in Burma"] (December 18, 1956), *Qiaowu zhengce wenji* [Overseas Chinese Policy Document Collection] (Beijing: Beijing renmin chubanshe, 1957), 1–10.
2. Aung Myoe Maung, *In the Name of Pauk-Phaw: Myanmar's China Policy since 1948* (Singapore: Institute of Southeast Asian Studies, 2011), 13. See also David Mozingo, *China's Policy towards Indonesia* (Ithaca, NY: Cornell University Press, 1976).
3. Guangdong sheng difang shizhi bianzuan weiyuanhui, ed., *Guangdong sheng zhi: Huaqiao zhi* [Guangdong Provincial Gazetteer: Overseas Chinese Gazetteer] (Guangzhou: Guangdong renmin chubanshe, 1996), 223.
4. *Guangdong sheng zhi*, 223.
5. For returnees from Indonesia, see Michael R. Godley, "'The Sojourner:' Returned Overseas Chinese in the People's Republic of China," *Pacific Affairs* 62, no. 3 (fall 1989): 330–53; Michael R. Godley and Charles A. Coppel, "The Pied Piper and the Prodigal Children: A Report on the Indonesian Chinese Students Who Went to Mao's China," *Archipel* 39 (1990): 179–98; and Wang Cangbai, *Huozai biechu: Xianggang yinni huaren koushu lishi* [Life is elsewhere: Stories of the Indonesian Chinese in Hong Kong] (Hong Kong: Centre for Asian Studies, University of Hong Kong, 2006).
6. For an insightful analysis of the term *guiqiao*, see Wang Cangbai, "Guiqiao Returnees as Policy Subject in China," *The Newsletter* (International Institute for Asian Studies) 50 (spring 2009): 7.
7. Peterson, *Overseas Chinese*, 55–74.
8. Peterson, *Overseas Chinese*, 55–74.
9. Guangzhou City Archives (GZCA): 194-2 (1954). Ezra F. Vogel, *Canton under Communism: Programs and Politics in a Provincial Capital, 1949–1968* (Cambridge, MA: Harvard University Press, 1969), 369.
10. Zhuang Guotu, "Zhongguo zhengfu dui *guiqiao*, qiaojuan zhengce de yanbian, 1949–1966," *Nanyang wenti yanjiu* 3 (July 1992): 49–56.

11. GZCA: 194-18 (1955).
12. GZCA: 194-35 (May 28, 1956), 95.
13. GZCA: 194-18 (1955).
14. GZCA: 194-18 (1955).
15. GZCA: 194-35 (1955).
16. GZCA: 194-18 (1955).
17. GZCA: 194-18 (1955).
18. GZCA: 194-18 (1955).
19. GZCA: 194-22 (1956).
20. GZCA: 194-22 (1956).
21. GZCA: 194-22 (1956).
22. GZCA: 194-28 (1956).
23. GZCA: 194-35 (December 13, 1956).
24. GZCA: 194-35 (December 13, 1956).
25. Vogel, *Canton under Communism*, 66.
26. GZCA: 194-23 (1956).
27. Peterson, *Overseas Chinese*, 114–18; Han Xiaorong, "The Demise of China's Overseas Chinese State Farms," *Journal of Chinese Overseas* 9 (2013): 33–58.
28. Han, "The Demise of China's Overseas Chinese State Farms," 39.
29. *Guangdong sheng zhi*, 213–14.
30. "Guanyu Huangbeixiang huaqiao nongmuchang qingkuang baogao" [Report concerning the condition of the Huangbeixiang overseas Chinese farm and ranch], Guangdong Provincial Archives (GDPA): 35-143-53.
31. "Guanyu Huangbeixiang huaqiao nongmuchang qingkuang baogao," GDPA: 35-143-53.
32. "Guanyu Huangbeixiang huaqiao nongmuchang qingkuang baogao," GDPA: 35-143-53.
33. See also Peterson, *Overseas Chinese*, 122.
34. Guangzhou huaqiao xincun bianjizu, *Guangzhou huaqiao xincun* [Guangzhou overseas Chinese new village] (Beijing: Jianzhu gongcheng chubanshe, 1959), preface by Zhu Guang (Major of Guangzhou).
35. *Guangzhou huaqiao xincun*, preface.
36. GZCA: 194-79 (year unspecified).
37. GZCA: 194-86 (1960).
38. Lin Jinzhi, "Qiaohui dui Zhonguo jingji fazhan yu qiaoxiang jieshe de zuoyong," *Nanyang wenti yanjiu* 2 (April 1992): 21–34.
39. GZCA: 194-48 (1958).
40. GZCA: 194-48 (1958).
41. GZCA: 194-90 (1960).
42. Stephen Fitzgerald, *China and the Overseas Chinese: A Study of Peking's Changing Policy, 1949–1970* (Cambridge: Cambridge University Press, 1972), 145. For the 1960 conflict between Indonesia and China, see Mozingo, *China's Policy towards Indonesia*, 157–91; J. A. C. Mackie, "Anti-Chinese Outbreaks in Indonesia,

1959–1968," in *The Chinese in Indonesia: Five Essays* (Melbourne: Nelson, 1976), 82–96; and Charles A. Coppel, *Indonesian Chinese in Crisis* (Kuala Lumpur: Oxford University Press, 1983).

43. GZCA: 194-90 (1960).
44. GZCA: 194-90 (1960).
45. GZCA: 194-90 (1960).
46. GZCA: 194-98 (1961).
47. GZCA: 194-91 (1960).
48. GZCA: 194-91 (December 1960).
49. GZCA: 194-91 (December 1960).
50. GZCA: 194-91 (December 1960).
51. Han Xiaorong, "The Demise of China's Overseas Chinese State Farms," 35.
52. Guangdong Provincial Archives (GDPA): 232-1-51 (May 1, 1961).
53. GDPA: 232-1-51 (May 1, 1961).
54. GZCA: 194-86 (1960).
55. GZCA: 194-86 (1960).
56. GZCA: 194-86 (1960).
57. GZCA: 194-86 (1960).
58. GZCA: 194-86 (1960).
59. GZCA: 194-86 (1960).
60. GZCA: 194-86 (1960).
61. Roderick MacFarquhar, *The Origins of the Cultural Revolution*, vol. 3 (New York: New York University Press, 1974–97), 334.
62. GDPA: 216-1-368 (1963).
63. GZCA: 192-34 (1966).
64. GZCA: 192-34 (1966).
65. GZCA: 192-34 (1966).
66. GZCA: 192-66 (1966).
67. GZCA: 194-68 (1966).
68. GZCA: 194-68 (1966).
69. For the returnees who remigrated to Hong Kong, see Michael R. Godley and Charles A. Coppel, "The Indonesian Chinese in Hong Kong: A Preliminary Report on a Minority Community in Transition," *Issues and Studies* 26, no. 7 (July 1990): 94–108, and Wang Cangbai and Siu-lun Wong, "Home as a Circular Process: A Study of the Indonesian Chinese in Hong Kong," in *Beyond Chinatown: New Chinese Migrants and China's Global Expansion*, ed. Mette Thunø (Copenhagen: Nordic Institute of Asian Study Press, 2007), 183–209.

Conclusion and Epilogue

1. See, for example, Donna R. Gabaccia, *Italy's Many Diasporas* (Seattle: University of Washington Press, 2000); Sunil S. Amrith, *Migration and Diaspora in Modern Asia* (New York: Cambridge University Press, 2011), and *Crossing the*

Bay of Bengal: The Furies of Nature and the Fortunes of Migrants (Cambridge, MA: Harvard University Press, 2013); Tara Zahra, *The Great Departure: Mass Migration from Eastern Europe and the Making of the Free World* (New York: W. W. Norton, 2016); and Linda Reeder, *Widows in White: Migration and the Transformation of Rural Italian Women, Sicily, 1880–1920* (Toronto: University of Toronto Press, 2003).

2. For a comparative historical account, see David Scott FitzGerald and David Cook-Martín, *Culling the Masses: The Democratic Origins of Racist Immigration Policy in the Americas* (Cambridge, MA: Harvard University Press, 2014).

3. See Leo Douw, Cen Huang, and Michael R. Godley, *Qiaoxiang Ties: Interdisciplinary Approaches to "Cultural Capitalism" in South China* (London: Kegan Paul International, 1999), and Carolyn L. Cartier, *Globalizing South China* (Malden, MA: Blackwell, 2001). For an excellent critique of contemporary fascination with diaspora history, see Ana Maria Candela, "Qiaoxiang on the Silk Road: Cultural Imaginaries as Structures of Feeling in the Making of a Global China," *Critical Asian Studies* 45, no. 3 (2013): 431–58.

4. See Liu Hong, "Haiwai huaren yu jueqi de Zhongguo: Lishi xing, guojia yu guoji guanxi" [Chinese overseas and rising China: History, nation, and international relations], *Open Times* 8 (2010): 79–93; Li Minghuan, "Ershi yi shiji chu Ou'zhou huaren shetuan fazhan xin qushi" [New trends in the community development of Chinese in early twenty-first-century Europe], *Overseas Chinese History Studies* 4 (December 2015): 1–8; and Zhuang Guotu, "Jingmao yu yimin hudong: Dongnanya yu Zhongguo guanxi de xin fazhan" [The interaction between trade and migration: New developments in the relationship between Southeast Asia and China], *Journal of Contemporary Asia-Pacific Studies* 2 (2008): 83–104. See also several edited volumes, including Gregor Benton and Frank N. Pieke, eds., *The Chinese in Europe* (Houndmills, UK: Macmillan, 1998); Pál Nyíri and I. R. Savel'ev, eds., *Globalizing Chinese Migration: Trends in Europe and Asia* (Aldershot, UK: Ashgate, 2002); Leo Suryadinata, ed., *Migration, Indigenization, and Interaction: Chinese Overseas and Globalization* (Hackensack, NJ: World Scientific, 2011); Gregor Benton and Edmund Terence Gomez, eds., *The Chinese in Britain, 1800–Present: Economy, Transnationalism, Identity* (Basingstoke, UK: Palgrave Macmillan, 2008); and Felix B. Chang and Sunnie T. Rucker-Chang, eds., *Chinese Migrants in Russia, Central Asia and Eastern Europe* (London: Routledge, 2012).

5. Cheng Xi, "Liuxuesheng di dailiu yu Zhongguo zhengfu di duice" [The Chinese students who remain abroad and the response of the Chinese government], *Overseas Chinese History Studies* 2 (1999): 63–76.

6. For the emigration and return of students and professionals, see David Zweig, Chen Changgui, and Stanley Rosen, "Globalization and Transnational Human Capital: Overseas and Returnee Scholars to China," *China Quarterly* 179 (September 2004): 735–57; Xiang Biao, "A Ritual Economy of 'Talent': China and Overseas Chinese Professionals," *Journal of Ethnic and Migration Studies* 37, no. 5

(2011): 821–38; and Liu Lisong, *Chinese Student Migration and Selective Citizenship: Mobility, Community and Identity between China and the United States* (London: Routledge 2016). For labor and entrepreneurial emigration, see Pál Nyíri, *Chinese in Eastern Europe and Russia: A Middleman Minority in a Transnational Era* (London: Routledge, 2007), and Frank N. Pieke, *Transnational Chinese: Fujianese Migrants in Europe* (Stanford, CA: Stanford University Press, 2004).

7. For studies on this subject, see Li Zhang, *Strangers in the City: Reconfigurations of Space, Power, and Social Networks within China's Floating Population* (Stanford, CA: Stanford University Press, 2001); Yan Hairong, *New Masters, New Servants: Migration, Development, and Women Workers in China* (Durham, NC: Duke University Press, 2008); and Pun Ngai, *Made in China: Women Factory Workers in a Global Workplace* (Durham, NC: Duke University Press, 2005).

8. Lisa Rofel, *Desiring China: Experiments in Neoliberalism, Sexuality, and Public Culture* (Durham, NC: Duke University Press, 2007).

9. For a rare volume that juxtaposes Chinese internal and international migration, see Hein Mallee and Frank N. Pieke, eds., *Internal and International Migration: Chinese Perspectives* (Richmond, UK: Curzon, 1999). For a discussion of "sea turtle" (*haigui*) and "seagull" (*hai'ou*), see Liu Hong, "Haiwai huaren yu jueqi de Zhongguo," 86, and Wang Cangbai, Wong Siu-lun, and Sun Wenbin, "Haigui: A New Area in China's Policy towards Chinese Diaspora?" *Journal of Chinese Overseas* 2, no. 2 (2006): 294–309.

10. Pál Nyíri, *Mobility and Cultural Authority in Contemporary China* (Seattle: University of Washington Press, 2010), 5.

11. See, for example, Pál Nyíri and Juan Zhang, with Merriden Varrall, "China's Cosmopolitan Nationalists: 'Heroes' and 'Traitors' of the 2008 Olympics," *China Journal* 63 (January 2010): 25–55; Pál Nyíri, "Chinese Entrepreneurs in Poor Countries: A Transnational 'Middleman Minority' and Its Futures," *Inter-Asia Cultural Studies* 12 (2011): 145–53, and *Mobility and Cultural Authority*, 35–44.

12. Liu Hong, "Haiwai huaren yu jueqi de Zhongguo," 85.

13. For a discussion of the variety of interests and motives among the new migrants beyond a state-centered approach, see Hong Liu and Els van Dongen, "China's Diaspora Policies as a New Mode of Transnational Governance," *Journal of Contemporary China* 25, no. 102 (2016): 805–21.

14. Aihwa Ong, *Flexible Citizenship: The Cultural Logics of Transnationality* (Durham, NC: Duke University Press, 1999).

15. For the history of the Cold War in East Asia, see Zheng Yangwen, Hong Liu, and Michael Szonyi, eds., *The Cold War in Asia: The Battle for Hearts and Minds* (Leiden: Brill, 2010); Priscilla Roberts and John M. Carroll, *Hong Kong in the Cold War* (Hong Kong: Hong Kong University Press, 2016); Lin Zhiling and Thomas W. Robinson, *The Chinese and Their Future: Beijing, Taipei, and Hong Kong* (Washington, DC: AEI Press, 1994); Michael Share, *Where Empires Collided: Russian and Soviet Relations with Hong Kong, Taiwan, and Macao* (Hong Kong: Chinese University Press, 2007); Nancy Bernkopf Tucker, *Taiwan, Hong Kong, and the United*

States, 1945–1992: Uncertain Friendships (New York: Twayne, 1994); and Chi-Kwan Mark, *Hong Kong and the Cold War: Anglo-American Relations, 1949–1957* (Oxford: Clarendon, 2004).

16. For Hong Kong, see Tai-lok Lui, "A Missing Page in the Grand Plan of 'One Country, Two Systems': Regional Integration and Its Challenges to Post-1997 Hong Kong," *Inter-Asia Cultural Studies* 16, no. 3 (2015): 396–409, and Christopher Hutton, "The Tangle of Colonial Modernity: Hong Kong as a Distinct Linguistic and Conceptual Space within the Global Common Law," *Law Text Culture* 18 (2014): 221–48. For Taiwan, see Stephen Allen, "Recreating 'One China': International Self-Determination, Autonomy and the Future of Taiwan," *Asia-Pacific Journal on Human Rights and the Law* 1 (2003): 21–51, and Jean-Pierre Cabestan, "Review of Su Chi, *Taiwan's Relations with Mainland China: A Tail Wagging Two Dogs*," *China Perspectives* 4 (2009): 2–5.

17. Evan N. Dawley, "The Question of Identity in Recent Scholarship on the History of Taiwan," *China Quarterly* 198 (2009): 442–52.

18. For examples of the vast literature on contemporary Hong Kong and Taiwan, see Angelina Chin, "Diasporic Memories and Conceptual Geography in Post-Colonial Hong Kong," *Modern Asian Studies* 48, no. 6 (2014): 1566–93; Thomas Kwan-choi Tse, "Constructing Chinese Identity in Post-Colonial Hong Kong: A Discursive Analysis of the Official Nation-Building Project," *Studies in Ethnicity and Nationalism* 14, no. 1 (2014): 188–206; Hui-Ching Chang and Rich Holt, "Taiwan and ROC: A Critical Analysis of President Chen Shui-bien's Construction of Taiwan Identity in National Speeches," *National Identities* 11, no. 3 (September 2009): 301–30; and Stéphane Corcuff, "The Liminality of Taiwan: A Case-Study in Geopolitics," *Taiwan in Comparative Perspective* 4 (December 2012): 34–64.

19. Matthew Pratt Guterl, "Comment: The Futures of Transnational History," *American Historical Review* 181, no. 1 (February 2013): 131.

20. Guterl, "Comment," 139.

21. For "worlding," see Rob Wilson and Christopher Leigh Connery, eds., *The Worlding Project: Doing Cultural Studies in the Era of Globalization* (Berkeley, CA: North Atlantic, 2007). For Asian America in Asia, see Andrea Louie, *Chineseness across Borders: Renegotiating Chinese Identities in China and the United States* (Durham, NC: Duke University Press, 2004); Eleana Kim, *Adopted Territory: Transnational Korean Adoptees and the Politics of Belonging* (Durham, NC: Duke University Press, 2010); Chih-ming Wang, *Transpacific Articulations: Student Migration and the Remaking of Asian America* (Honolulu: University of Hawai'i Press, 2013); Eiichiro Azuma, "'Pioneers of Overseas Japanese Development': Japanese American History and the Making of Expansionist Orthodoxy in Imperial Japan," *Journal of Asian Studies* 67, no. 4 (November 2008): 1187–226; and Michael Jin, "Americans in the Pacific: Rethinking Race, Gender, Citizenship, and Diaspora at the Crossroads of Asian and Asian American Studies," *Critical Ethnic Studies* 2, no. 1 (2016): 128–47. For a broader consideration of the United States

and the Americas, see Evelyn Hu-Dehart, ed., *Across the Pacific: Asian Americans and Globalization* (Philadelphia: Temple University Press, 1999); Rhacel Salazar Parreñas and Lok C. D. Siu, eds., *Asian Diasporas: New Formations, New Conceptions* (Stanford, CA: Stanford University Press, 2007); Cindy I-Fen Cheng, *Citizens of Asian America: Democracy and Race during the Cold War* (New York: New York University Press, 2013); Madeline Hsu, *The Good Immigrants: How the Yellow Peril Became the Model Minority* (Princeton, NJ: Princeton University Press, 2015); Laura Madokoro, *Elusive Refuge: Chinese Migrants in the Cold War* (Cambridge, MA: Harvard University Press, 2016); Katherine López, *Chinese Cubans: A Transnational History* (Chapel Hill: University of North Carolina Press, 2013); and Ana Maria Candela, "Nation, Migration and Governance: Cantonese Migrants to Peru and the Making of Overseas Chinese Nationalism, 1849–2013" (Ph.D. diss., University of California, Santa Cruz, 2013). For critical refugee studies, see Yến Lê Espiritu, *Body Counts: The Vietnam War and Militarized Refuge(es)* (Berkeley: University of California Press, 2014), and Viet Thanh Nguyen, *Nothing Ever Dies: Vietnam and the Memory of War* (Cambridge, MA: Harvard University Press, 2016).

22. Lisa Lowe, *The Intimacies of Four Continents* (Durham, NC: Duke University Press, 2015).

BIBLIOGRAPHY

Archival, Museum, and Library Collections

Academia Sinica Libraries, Taiwan
Amoy (Xiamen University) Library and Center for Southeast Asian Studies Library, China
Chinese University of Hong Kong Library, Hong Kong
Guangdong Provincial Archives, China
Guangzhou City Archives, China
House of Common Papers (digital), United Kingdom
National Archives of Singapore
National Library of Singapore
National University of Singapore Libraries
Overseas Chinese Museum, Taishan, China
Overseas Chinese Museum, Xiamen, China
Simon Fraser University Libraries, Burnaby, Surrey, and Vancouver, British Columbia
Sun Yat-sen University Library, Guangzhou, China
Taishan County Archives, Taishan, China
University of Hong Kong Library, Hong Kong
University of Victoria Libraries, British Columbia
University of Wisconsin Libraries

Newspapers and Periodicals

Nanyang Qingbao
Nanyang Yanjiu
Straits Chinese Magazine

Books, Articles, and Dissertations

Akashi, Yoji. *The Nanyang Chinese National Salvation Movement, 1937–1941*. Lawrence: Center for East Asian Studies, University of Kansas, 1970.
Alatas, Syed Hussein. *The Myth of the Lazy Native: A Study of the Image of the Malays, Filipinos, and Javanese from the 16th to the 20th Century and Its Function in the Ideology of Colonial Capitalism*. London: Frank Cass, 1977.

Alexander, Garth. *The Invisible China: The Overseas Chinese and the Politics of Southeast Asia*. New York: Macmillan, 1973.

Alilunas-Rodgers, Kristine, and Anthony Reid, eds. *Sojourners and Settlers: Histories of Southeast Asia and the Chinese*. Honolulu: University of Hawai'i Press, 2001.

Allen, Stephen. "Recreating 'One China': International Self-Determination, Autonomy and the Future of Taiwan," *Asia-Pacific Journal on Human Rights and the Law* 1 (2003): 21–51.

Amrith, Sunil S. *Crossing the Bay of Bengal: The Furies of Nature and the Fortunes of Migrants*. Cambridge, MA: Harvard University Press, 2013.

———. *Migration and Diaspora in Modern Asia*. New York: Cambridge University Press, 2011.

Anderson, Benedict. *Imagined Communities: Reflections on the Origin and Spread of Nationalism*. London: Verso, 2006.

———. "Nationalism, Identity, and the World-in-Motion: On the Logics of Seriality." In *Cosmopolitics: Thinking and Feeling beyond the Nation*, ed. Pheng Cheah and Bruce Robbins, 117–33. Minneapolis: University of Minnesota Press, 1998.

Ang, Ien. *On Not Speaking Chinese: Living between Asia and the West*. London: Routledge, 2001.

Arrighi, Giovanni, Takeshi Hamashita, and Mark Selden, eds. *The Resurgence of East Asia: 500, 150 and 50 Year Perspectives*. London: Routledge, 2003.

Aung Myoe, Maung. *In the Name of Pauk-Phaw: Myanmar's China Policy since 1948*. Singapore: Institute of Southeast Asian Studies, 2011.

Axel, Brian Keith. "The Context of Diaspora." *Cultural Anthropology* 19, no. 1 (2004): 26–60.

———. "The Diasporic Imaginary." *Public Culture* 14, no. 2 (2002): 411–28.

Azuma, Eiichiro. *Between Two Empires: Race, History, and Transnationalism in Japanese America*. New York: Oxford University Press, 2005.

———. "'Pioneers of Overseas Japanese Development': Japanese American History and the Making of Expansionist Orthodoxy in Imperial Japan." *Journal of Asian Studies* 67, no. 4 (November 2008): 1187–226.

Barabantseva, Elena. *Overseas Chinese, Ethnic Minorities, and Nationalism: De-Centering China*. Milton Park, UK: Routledge, 2011.

Barlow, Tani E., ed. *Formation of Colonial Modernity in East Asia*. Durham, NC: Duke University Press, 1997.

———. *The Question of Women in Chinese Feminism*. Durham, NC: Duke University Press, 2004.

Barrett, Tracy C. *The Chinese Diaspora in South-East Asia: The Overseas Chinese in Indo-China, 1870–1945*. London: I. B. Tauris, 2012.

Beijing guiguo huaqiao lianyihui, ed. *Guanyu qiaowu zhengce ji qita ruogan wenti de dafu*. Beijing: Beijing guiguo huaqiao lianyihui, May 1956.

Benton, Gregor, and Edmund Terence Gomez. *The Chinese in Britain, 1800–Present: Economy, Transnationalism, Identity*. Basingstoke, UK: Palgrave Macmillan, 2008.

Benton, Gregor, and Frank N. Pieke. *The Chinese in Europe*. Houndmills, UK: Macmillan, 1998.

Bergère, Marie-Claire. *Sun Yat-sen*. Translated by Janet Lloyd. Stanford, CA: Stanford University Press, 1998.

Bernards, Brian. *Writing the South Seas: Imagining the Nanyang in Chinese and Southeast Asian Postcolonial Literature*. Seattle: University of Washington Press, 2015.

Billioud, Sébastien, and Joël Thoraval. *The Sage and the People: The Confucian Revival in China*. Oxford: Oxford University Press, 2015.

Blaustein, Albert P., ed. *Fundamental Legal Documents of Communist China*. South Hackensack, NJ: Rothman, 1962.

Botsman, Daniel V. "Freedom without Slavery? 'Coolies,' Prostitutes, and Outcastes in Meiji Japan's 'Emancipation Moment,'" *American Historical Review* 116, no. 5 (2011): 1323–47.

Brah, Avtar. *Cartographies of Diaspora: Contesting Identities*. London: Routledge, 1996.

Brettell, Caroline, and James Frank Hollifield, eds. *Migration Theory: Talking across Disciplines*. New York: Routledge, 2015.

Brown, Jeremy, and Matthew D. Johnson, eds. *Maoism at the Grassroots: Everyday Life in China's Era of High Socialism*. Cambridge, MA: Harvard University Press, 2015.

Brown, Jeremy, and Paul Pickowicz, eds. *City versus Countryside in Mao's China: Negotiating the Divide*. New York: Cambridge University Press, 2012.

———. *Dilemmas of Victory: The Early Years of the People's Republic of China*. Cambridge, MA: Harvard University Press, 2007.

Brubaker, Rogers. "The 'Diaspora' Diaspora." *Ethnic and Racial Studies* 28, no. 1 (January 2005): 1–19.

Buckley, Charles Burton. *An Anecdotal History of Old Times in Singapore: From the Foundation of the Settlement under the Honourable the East India Company on February 6th, 1819 to the Transfer to the Colonial Office as Part of the Colonial Possessions of the Crown on April 1st, 1867*. Singapore: Fraser and Neave, 1902.

Butler, Kim D. "Defining Diaspora, Refining a Discourse." *Diaspora* 10, no. 2 (fall 2001): 189–219.

Cabestan, Jean-Pierre. Review of Su Chi, *Taiwan's Relations with Mainland China: A Tail Wagging Two Dogs*. *China Perspectives* 4 (2009): 2–5.

Cai, Shijun, and Xu Yunqiao, eds. *Xinma huaren kangri shiliao, 1937–1945*. Singapore: Wenshi chuban siren gongsi, 1984.

Callahan, William A. *China Dreams: 20 Visions of the Future*. Oxford: Oxford University Press, 2013.

———. *Contingent States: Greater China and Transnational Relations*. Minneapolis: University of Minnesota Press, 2004.

Campbell, Persia Crawford. *Chinese Coolie Emigration to Countries within the British Empire*. London: P. S. King and Son, 1923.

Candela, Ana Maria. "Nation, Migration and Governance: Cantonese Migrants to Peru and the Making of Overseas Chinese Nationalism, 1849–2013." Ph.D. diss., University of California, Santa Cruz, 2013.

———. "*Qiaoxiang* on the Silk Road: Cultural Imaginaries as Structures of Feeling in the Making of a Global China." *Critical Asian Studies* 45, no. 3 (2013): 431–58.

Cartier, Carolyn L. *Globalizing South China*. Malden, MA: Blackwell, 2001.

Cassel, Pär Kristoffer. *Grounds of Judgment: Extraterritoriality and Imperial Power in Nineteenth-Century China and Japan*. Oxford: Oxford University Press, 2012.

Chakrabarty, Dipesh. *Provincializing Europe: Postcolonial Thought and Historical Difference*. Princeton, NJ: Princeton University Press, 2000.

Chan, Anthony. "'Orientalism' and Image Making: The Sojourner in Canadian History." *Journal of Ethnic Studies* 9 (1981): 37–46.

Chan, Shelly. "The Case for Diaspora: A Temporal Approach to the Chinese Experience." *Journal of Asian Studies* 74, no. 1 (February 2015): 107–28.

———. "The Disobedient Diaspora: Overseas Chinese Students in Mao's China, 1958–66." *Journal of Chinese Overseas* 10, no. 2 (2014): 220–38.

———. "A Maidservant of the Revolution: He Xiangning and Chinese Feminist Nationalism in the 1920s–1930s." Occasional Paper No. 185, Hong Kong Institute of Asia Pacific Studies, Chinese University of Hong Kong, May 2007.

———. "The Overseas Chinese Project: Nation, Culture, and Race in Modern China." Ph.D. diss., University of California, Santa Cruz, 2009.

———. "Rethinking the 'Left-Behind' in Chinese Migrations: A Case of Liberating Wives in Emigrant South China in the 1950s." In *Proletarian and Gendered Mass Migrations: A Global Perspective on Continuities and Discontinuities from the Nineteenth to the Twenty-First Centuries*, ed. Dirk Hoerder and Amarjit Kaur. Boston: Brill, 2013.

Chan, Sucheng. *Asian Americans: An Interpretive History*. New York: Twayne, 1991.

Chang, Felix B., and Sunnie T. Rucker-Chang, eds. *Chinese Migrants in Russia, Central Asia and Eastern Europe*. London: Routledge, 2012.

Chang, Hui-Ching, and Rich Holt. "Taiwan and ROC: A Critical Analysis of President Chen Shui-bien's Construction of Taiwan Identity in National Speeches." *National Identities* 11, no. 3 (September 2009): 301–30.

Chang, Kornel S. *Pacific Connections: The Making of the Western U.S.-Canadian Borderlands*. Berkeley: University of California Press, 2012.

Charney, Michael W., Brenda S. A. Yeoh, and Chee Kiong Tong, eds. *Chinese Migrants Abroad: Cultural, Educational, and Social Dimensions of the Chinese Diaspora*. Singapore: Singapore University Press, 2003.

Chen, Da, and Bruno Lasker. *Emigrant Communities in South China: A Study of Overseas Migration and Its Influence on Standards of Living and Social Change*. New York: Institute of Pacific Relations, 1940.

———. *Nanyang Hua qiao yu Min Yue she hui.* Changsha: Shang wu yin shu guan, 1938.

Chen, Hansheng, ed. *Huagong chuguo shiliao huibian*, vol. 1, pt. 1–4. Beijing: Zhonghua shuju, 1984.

Chen, Kuan-Hsing. *Asia as Method: Toward Deimperialization.* Durham, NC: Duke University Press, 2010.

Chen, Mong Hock. *The Early Chinese Newspapers of Singapore, 1881–1912.* Singapore: University of Malaya Press, 1967.

Chen, Yong. *Chinese San Francisco, 1850–1943: A Trans-Pacific Community.* Stanford, CA: Stanford University Press, 2000.

Chen, Yusong (Tan Yeok Seong). *Yeyinguan wencun* [Collected writings from the Ya-Yin studio], vol. 3. Singapore: South Seas Society, ca. 1983.

Cheng, Cindy I-Fen. *Citizens of Asian America: Democracy and Race during the Cold War.* New York: New York University Press, 2013.

Cheng, Xi. "Liuxuesheng di dailiu yu Zhongguo zhengfu di duice" [The remaining abroad of Chinese students and the response of the Chinese government]. *Overseas Chinese History Studies* 2 (1999): 63–76.

Chin, Angelina. "Diasporic Memories and Conceptual Geography in Post-Colonial Hong Kong." *Modern Asian Studies* 48, no. 6 (2014): 1566–93.

"China—A New Field for Straits Enterprise. An Interview with Mr. Lew Yuk Lin, Acting Consul for China at Singapore." *Straits Chinese Magazine* 2, no. 7 (1898): 102–4.

Chirot, Daniel, and Anthony Reid, eds. *Essential Outsiders: Chinese and Jews in the Modern Transformation of Southeast Asia and Central Europe.* Seattle: University of Washington Press, 1997.

Cho, Lily. "The Turn to Diaspora." TOPIA: *Canadian Journal of Cultural Studies* 17 (spring 2007): 11–30.

Chou, Grace Ai-Ling. *Confucianism, Colonialism, and the Cold War: Chinese Cultural Education at Hong Kong's New Asia College, 1949–76.* Leiden: Brill, 2012.

Chu, Julie Y. *Cosmologies of Credit: Transnational Mobility and the Politics of Destination in China.* Durham, NC: Duke University Press, 2010.

Chu, Richard T. *Chinese and Chinese Mestizos of Manila: Family, Identity, and Culture, 1860s–1930s.* Leiden: Brill, 2010.

Chua, Beng Huat. "Arrested Development: Democratization in Singapore." *Third World Quarterly* 15, no. 4 (1994): 655–68.

———. *Communitarian Ideology and Democracy in Singapore.* London: Routledge, 1995.

Clifford, James. *Routes: Travel and Translation in the Late Twentieth Century.* Cambridge, MA: Harvard University Press, 1997.

Cochran, Sherman. *Chinese Medicine Men: Consumer Culture in China and Southeast Asia.* Cambridge, MA: Harvard University Press, 2006.

Cochran, Sherman, and Paul Pickowicz, eds. *China on the Margins*. Ithaca, NY: Cornell East Asia Program, 2010.

Cochran, Sherman, and David Strand, eds. *Cities in Motion: Interior, Coast, and Diaspora in Transnational China*. Berkeley: Institute of East Asian Studies, University of California, Berkeley, and Center for Chinese Studies, University of California, Berkeley, 2007.

Cohen, Paul. *Discovering History in China: American Historical Writing on the Recent Chinese Past*. New York: Columbia University Press, 1984.

Cohen, Robin. *Global Diasporas: An Introduction*. Seattle: University of Washington Press, 1997.

Cook, James A. "Rethinking 'China': Overseas Chinese and China's Modernity." In *Visualizing Modern China: Image, History, and Memory, 1750–Present*, ed. James A. Cook, Joshua L. Goldstein, Matthew D. Johnson, and Sigrid Schmalzer, 127–43. Lanham, MD: Lexington, 2014.

Cook, James A., Joshua L. Goldstein, Matthew D. Johnson, and Sigrid Schmalzer. *Visualizing Modern China: Image, History, and Memory, 1750–Present*. Lanham, MD: Lexington, 2014.

Coppel, Charles. *Indonesian Chinese in Crisis*. Kuala Lumpur: Oxford University Press, 1983.

Corcuff, Stéphane. "The Liminality of Taiwan: A Case-Study in Geopolitics." *Taiwan in Comparative Perspective* 4 (December 2012): 34–64.

The Cuba Commission Report: A Hidden History of the Chinese in Cuba: The Original English-Language Text of 1876. Baltimore: Johns Hopkins University Press, 1993.

Curtin, Philip D. *Cross-Cultural Trade in World History*. Cambridge: Cambridge University Press, 1984.

Cushman, Jennifer Wayne. *Chinese American Transnationalism: The Flow of People, Resources, and Ideas between China and America during the Exclusion Era*. Philadelphia: Temple University Press, 2006.

———. *Family and State: The Formation of a Sino-Thai Tin-Mining Dynasty, 1797–1932*. Singapore: Oxford University Press, 1991.

Dawley, Evan N. "The Question of Identity in Recent Scholarship on the History of Taiwan." *China Quarterly* 198 (2009): 442–52.

DeBernardi, Jean Elizabeth, Gregory L. Forth, and Sandra A. Niessen, eds. *Managing Change in Southeast Asia: Local Identities, Global Connections*. Montreal: CASA Secretariat, 1995.

Delgado, Grace. *Making the Chinese Mexican: Global Migration, Localism, and Exclusion in the U.S.-Mexico Borderlands*. Stanford, CA: Stanford University Press, 2012.

Diamant, Neil. *Revolutionizing the Chinese Family: Politics, Love, and Divorce in Urban and Rural China, 1949–1968*. Berkeley: University of California Press, 2000.

Dirlik, Arif. "Bringing History Back In: Of Diasporas, Hybridities, Places, and Histories." In *Postmodernity's Histories: The Past as Legacy and Project*. Lanham, MD: Rowman and Littlefield, 2000.

———. "Confucius in the Borderlands: Global Capitalism and the Reinvention of Confucianism." *boundary 2* 22, no. 3 (autumn 1995): 229–73.

———. "Critical Reflections on 'Chinese Capitalism' as Paradigm." *Identities* 3, no. 3 (1997): 303–30.

———. "Guoxue/National Learning in the Age of Global Modernity." *China Perspectives* 1 (2011): 4–13.

Douw, Leo, Cen Huang, and Michael R. Godley, eds. *Qiaoxiang Ties: Interdisciplinary Approaches to Cultural Capitalism*. London: Kegan Paul International, 1999.

Douw, Leo, and Peter Post, eds. *South China: State, Culture and Social Change during the Twentieth Century*. Amsterdam: Royal Netherlands Academy of Arts and Sciences, 1996.

Drake, Fred W. *China Charts the World: Hsu Chi-yü and His Geography of 1848*. Cambridge, MA: East Asian Research Center, Harvard University, 1975.

Dressler, Markus, and Arvind-pal Singh Mandair. *Secularism and Religion-Making*. New York: Oxford University Press, 2011.

Duara, Prasenjit. *The Global and Regional in China's Nation-Formation*. Abingdon, UK: Routledge, 2009.

———. "Nationalists among Transnationals: Overseas Chinese and the Idea of China, 1900–1911." In *Ungrounded Empires: The Cultural Politics of Modern Chinese Transnationalism*, ed. Aihwa Ong and Donald Nonini, 39–60. New York: Routledge, 1997.

———. "Religion and Citizenship in China and the Diaspora." In *Chinese Religiosities: Afflictions of Modernity and State Formation*, ed. Mayfair Mei-Hui Yang, 43–64. Berkeley: University of California Press, 2008.

———. *Rescuing History and the Nation: Questioning Narratives of Modern China*. Chicago: University of Chicago Press, 1997.

———. *Sovereignty and Authenticity: Manchukuo and the East Asian Modern*. Lanham, MD: Rowman and Littlefield, 2003.

Dufoix, Stéphane. *Diasporas*. Berkeley: University of California Press, 2008.

Elegant, Robert S. *The Dragon's Seed: Peking and the Overseas Chinese*. New York: St. Martin's, 1959.

Espiritu, Yến Lê. *Body Counts: The Vietnam War and Militarized Refuge(es)*. Berkeley: University of California Press, 2014.

Eyferth, Jan Jacob Karl. *Eating Rice from Bamboo Roots: The Social History of a Community of Handicraft Papermakers in Rural Sichuan, 1920–2000*. Cambridge, MA: Harvard University Asia Center, 2009.

Fairbank, John King. *Trade and Diplomacy on the China Coast: The Opening of the Treaty Ports, 1842–1854*. Cambridge, MA: Harvard University Press, 1953.

Finanne, Antonia. *Speaking of Yangzhou: A Chinese City, 1550–1850*. Cambridge, MA: Harvard University Press, 2004.
Fitzgerald, C. P. *The Third China: The Chinese Communities of South-East Asia*. Vancouver: University of British Columbia Publications Centre, 1965.
FitzGerald, David, and David Cook-Martín. *Culling the Masses: The Democratic Origins of Racist Immigration Policy in the Americas*. Cambridge, MA: Harvard University Press, 2014.
Fitzgerald, Stephen. *China and the Overseas Chinese: A Study of Peking's Changing Policy, 1949–1970*. Cambridge: Cambridge University Press, 1972.
Freedman, Maurice. *Chinese Lineage and Society: Fukien and Kwangtung*. London: Athlone, 1966.
———. *Lineage Organization in Southeastern China*. London: Athlone, 1965.
Fried, Morton H., ed. *Colloquium on Overseas Chinese*. New York: Institute of Pacific Relations, 1958.
Frost, Mark Ravinder. "Asia's Maritime Networks and the Colonial Public Sphere, 1840–1920," *New Zealand Journal of Asian Studies* 6, no. 2 (December 2004): 63–94.
Fujian Shifan Daxue, ed. *Wanqing haiwai biji xuan*. Beijing: Haiyang chubanshe: Xinhua shudian Beijing faxingsuo faxing, 1983.
Gabaccia, Donna R. *Italy's Many Diasporas*. Seattle: University of Washington Press, 2000.
Gabaccia, Donna R., and Dirk Hoerder, eds. *Connecting Seas and Connected Ocean Rims: Indian, Atlantic, and Pacific Oceans and China Seas Migrations from the 1830s to the 1930s*. Leiden: Brill, 2011.
Ghosh, Amitav. "The Diaspora in Indian Culture." *Public Culture* 2, no. 1 (1989): 73–78.
Gilroy, Paul. *The Black Atlantic: Modernity and Double Consciousness*. Cambridge, MA: Harvard University Press, 1993.
"Go beyond Mandarin to Connect with China." *Straits Times*, June 24, 2004.
Godley, Michael R. "The Late Ch'ing Courtship of the Chinese in Southeast Asia." *Journal of Asian Studies* 34, no. 2 (1975): 361–85.
———. *The Mandarin-Capitalists from Nan-Yang: Overseas Chinese Enterprise in the Modernization of China, 1893–1911*. New York: Cambridge University Press, 1981.
———. "The Sojourner: Returned Overseas Chinese in the People's Republic of China." *Pacific Affairs* 62, no. 3 (fall 1989): 330–53.
Godley, Michael R., and Charles A. Coppel. "The Indonesian Chinese in Hong Kong: A Preliminary Report on a Minority Community in Transition." *Issues and Studies* 26, no. 7 (July 1990): 94–108.
Godley, Michael R., and Charles A. Coppel. "The Pied Piper and the Prodigal Children: A Report on the Indonesian-Chinese Students Who Went to Mao's China." *Archipel: Études interdisciplinaires sur le monde insulindien* 39 (1990):179–98.

González, Fredy. "We Won't Be Bullied Anymore: Chinese-Mexican Relations and the Chinese Community in Mexico, 1931–1971." Ph.D. diss., Yale University, 2013.

Goodman, Bryna. *Native Place, City, Nation: Regional Networks and Identities in Shanghai, 1853–1937*. Berkeley: University of California Press, 1995.

"Good Model for Bilingual Elite." *Straits Times*, December 19, 1998.

Gotō, Ken'ichi. *Tensions of Empire: Japan and Southeast Asia in the Colonial and Postcolonial World*. Athens: Ohio University Press, 2003.

Gottschang, Thomas R., and Diana Lary. *Swallows and Settlers: The Great Migration from North China to Manchuria*. Ann Arbor: Center for Chinese Studies, University of Michigan, 2000.

Grossberg, Lawrence. "On Postmodernism and Articulation: An Interview with Stuart Hall." In *Stuart Hall: Critical Dialogues in Cultural Studies*, ed. Kuan-Hsing Chen David Moreley. London: Routledge, 1995.

Guangdong sheng difang shizhi biancuan weiyuanhui, ed. *Guangdong sheng zhi—huaqiao zhi*. Guangzhou: Guangdong renmin chubanshe, 1996.

Guangzhou huaqiao xincun bianjizu. *Guangzhou huaqiao xincun*. Beijing: Jianzhu gongcheng chubanshe, 1959.

Guo, Songtao, Liu Xihong, and Zhang Deyi. *The First Chinese Embassy to the West: The Journals of Kuo-Sung-T'ao, Liu Hsi-Hung and Chang Te-yi*. Translated and annotated by J. D. Frodsham. Oxford: Clarendon Press, 1974.

Guo li ji nan da xue nan yang wen hua shi ye bu. *Nan yang hua qiao jiao yu hui yi bao gao*. Shanghai: Guo li ji nan ta xue nan yang wen hua shi ye bu, 1930.

Guterl, Matthew Pratt. "Comment: The Futures of Transnational History." *American Historical Review* 181, no. 1 (February 2013): 130–39.

Hall, Catherine. *Civilising Subjects: Metropole and Colony in the English Imagination*. Chicago: University of Chicago Press, 2002.

Hall, Stuart. "Cultural Identity and Diaspora." In *Identity: Community, Culture, Difference*, ed. Jonathan Rutherford, 222–37. London: Lawrence and Wishart, 1990.

Hamashita, Takeshita. "The Intra-Regional System in East Asia in Modern Times." In *Network Power: Japan and Asia*, ed. Peter J. Katzenstein and Takashi Shiraishi, 113–35. Ithaca, NY: Cornell University Press, 1996.

Hamilton, Gary G., ed. *Cosmopolitan Capitalists: Hong Kong and the Chinese Diaspora at the End of the Twentieth Century*. Seattle: University of Washington Press, 1999.

Hanyü da cidian. Shanghai: Shanghai cishu chubanshe, 1986.

Hare, G. T. "The Straits-Born Chinese." *Straits Chinese Magazine* 1, no. 1 (1897): 3–8.

Harper, T. N., and Sunil S. Amrith. *Sites of Asian Interaction: Ideas, Networks and Mobility*. Cambridge: Cambridge University Press, 2014.

Harris, Lane J. "Overseas Chinese Remittance Firms, the Limits of State Sovereignty, and Transnational Capitalism in East and Southeast Asia, 1850s–1930s." *Journal of Asian Studies* 74, no. 1 (February 2016): 129–51.

Harrotunian, Harry. "Some Thoughts on Comparability and the Space-Time Problem." *boundary 2* 32, no. 2 (summer 2005): 23–52.

Hau, Caroline S. *The Chinese Question: Ethnicity, Nation, and Region in and beyond the Philippines*. Singapore: National University of Singapore Press, 2014.

He, Xiangning. *Shuang qing wenji*, vol. 2. Beijing: Renmin chubanshe, Xinhua shudian faxing, 1985.

Hei, Yan [Ren, Jinghe]. *Taishan qiaoxiang xuelei shi: Zhonggong baoxing lu*, part 1–3. Hong Kong: Shenzhou tushu gongsi, 1953.

Heng, Derek Thiam Soon, and Syed Muhd Khairudin Aljunied. *Singapore in Global History*. Amsterdam: Amsterdam University Press, 2011.

Hershatter, Gail. *The Gender of Memory: Rural Women and China's Collective Past*. Berkeley: University of California Press, 2011.

———. *Women in China's Long Twentieth Century*. Berkeley: University of California Press, 2007.

Hevia, James. *English Lessons: The Pedagogy of Imperialism in Nineteenth-Century China*. Durham, NC: Duke University Press, 2003.

Hicks, George L. *A Bibliography of Japanese Works on the Overseas Chinese in Southeast Asia, 1914–1945*. Hong Kong: Asian Research Service, 1992.

Hinton, Harold C. *Communist China in World Politics*. Boston: Houghton Mifflin, 1966.

Hinton, William. *Fanshen: A Documentary of Revolution in a Chinese Village*. Berkeley: University of California Press, 1966.

Ho, Elaine Yee Lin, and Julia Kuehn, eds. *China Abroad: Travels, Subjects, Spaces*. Hong Kong: Hong Kong University Press, 2009.

Hong, Lysa, and Huang Jianli. *The Scripting of a National History: Singapore and Its Pasts*. Hong Kong: Hong Kong University Press, 2008.

Honig, Emily. *Creating Chinese Ethnicity: Subei People in Shanghai, 1850–1980*. New Haven, CT: Yale University Press, 1992.

Howland, Douglas. "The *Maria Luz* Incident: Personal Rights and International Justice for Chinese Coolies and Japanese Prostitutes." In *Gender and Law in the Japanese Imperium*, ed. Susan L. Burns and Barbara J. Brooks, 21–47. Honolulu: University of Hawai'i Press, 2014.

Hsü, Immanuel C. Y. *China's Entrance into the Family of Nations: The Diplomatic Phase, 1858–1880*. Cambridge, MA: Harvard University Press, 1960.

Hsu, Madeline. *Dreaming of Gold, Dreaming of Home: Transnationalism and Migration between the United States and South China, 1882–1943*. Stanford, CA: Stanford University Press, 2000.

———. *The Good Immigrants: How the Yellow Peril Became the Model Minority*. Princeton, NJ: Princeton University Press, 2015.

Hu-Dehart, Evelyn, ed. *Across the Pacific: Asian Americans and Globalization*. Philadelphia: Temple University Press, 1999.

———. "Chinatowns and Borderlands: Inter-Asian Encounters in the Diaspora." *Modern Asian Studies* 46, no. 2 (2012): 425–51.

———. "Chinese Coolie Labour in Cuba in the Nineteenth Century: Free Labour or Neo-Slavery?" *Slavery and Abolition* 14, no. 1 (1993): 67–86.

———. "La Trata Amarilla: The 'Yellow Trade' and the Middle Passage, 1847–1884." In *Many Middle Passages: Forced Migration and the Making of the Modern World*, ed. Emma Christopher, Cassandra Pybus, and Marcus Rediker, 166–83. Berkeley: University of California Press, 2007.

Huang, Jianli. "Conceptualizing Chinese Migration and Chinese Overseas: The Contributions of Wang Gungwu." *Journal of Chinese Overseas* 6 (2010): 1–21.

———. "Umbilical Ties: The Framing of the Overseas Chinese as the Mother of the Revolution." *Frontiers of History in China* 6, no. 2 (June 2011): 183–228.

Huang, Jingwan. *Hua qiao dui zuguo de gongxian*. Shanghai: Tangdi she, 1940.

Huters, Theodore. *Bringing the World Home: Appropriating the West in Late Qing and Early Republican China*. Honolulu: University of Hawaiʻi Press, 2005.

Hutton, Christopher. "The Tangle of Colonial Modernity: Hong Kong as a Distinct Linguistic and Conceptual Space within the Global Common Law." *Law Text Culture* 18 (2014): 221–48.

Irick, Robert L. *Ch'ing Policy toward the Coolie Trade, 1847–1878*. Taipei: Chinese Materials Center, 1982.

Jin, Michael. "Americans in the Pacific: Rethinking Race, Gender, Citizenship, and Diaspora at the Crossroads of Asian and Asian American Studies." *Critical Ethnic Studies* 2, no. 1 (2016): 128–47.

Jinan Daxue xiaoshi bianxie zu [Jinan University History Editorial Group]. *Jinan Xiaoshi, 1906–1986* [The history of Jinan University, 1906–1986]. Guangzhou: Jinan Daxue, 1986.

Johnson, Kay Ann. *Women, the Family, and Peasant Revolution in China*. Chicago: University of Chicago Press, 1983.

Jung, Moon-Ho. *Coolies and Cane: Race, Labor, and Sugar in the Age of Emancipation*. Baltimore: Johns Hopkins University Press, 2006.

Karl, Rebecca E. *Staging the World: Chinese Nationalism at the Turn of the Twentieth Century*. Durham, NC: Duke University Press, 2002.

Katzenstein, Peter J., ed. *Sinicization and the Rise of China: Civilizational Processes beyond East and West*. Milton Park, UK: Routledge, 2012.

Keating, Pauline B. *Two Revolutions: Village Reconstruction and the Cooperative Movement in Northern Shaanxi, 1934–1945*. Stanford, CA: Stanford University Press, 1997.

Keeman, Faye Yuan. *Under an Imperial Sun: Japanese Colonial Literature of Taiwan and the South*. Honolulu: University of Hawaiʻi Press, 2003.

Kenley, David L. *New Culture in a New World: The May Fourth Movement and the Chinese Diaspora in Singapore, 1919–1932*. New York: Routledge, 2003.

Kern, Stephen. *The Culture of Time and Space 1880–1918*. Cambridge, MA: Harvard University Press, 1983.

Khor, Eng Hee. "A Biography of Lim Boon Keng." Translated by Li Yelin. BA honors thesis, University of Malaya, 1985–1986.

Kim, Eleana. *Adopted Territory: Transnational Korean Adoptees and the Politics of Belonging.* Durham, NC: Duke University Press, 2010.

Koselleck, Reinhart. *Futures Past: On the Semantics of Historical Time.* New York: Columbia University Press, 2004.

Kuhn, Philip. *Chinese among Others: Emigration in Modern Times.* Lanham, MD: Rowman and Littlefield, 2008.

Kuo, Eddie C. Y. "Confucianism as Political Discourse in Singapore: The Case of an Incomplete Revitalization Movement." In *Confucian Traditions in East Asian Modernity: Moral Education and Economic Culture in Japan and the Four Mini-Dragons,* ed. Tu Wei-ming, 294–393. Cambridge, MA: Harvard University Press, 1996.

Kuo, Huei-Ying. *Networks beyond Empires: Chinese Business and Nationalism in the Hong Kong-Singapore Corridor, 1914–1941.* Leiden: Brill, 2014.

———. "Social Discourse and Economic Functions: The Singapore Chinese in Japan's Southward Expansion between 1914 and 1941." In *Singapore in Global History,* ed. Derek Heng and Syed Muhd Khairudin Aljunied. Amsterdam: Amsterdam University Press, 2011.

Kwee, Hui Kian. "Cultural Strategies, Economic Dominance: The Lineage of Tan Bing in Nineteenth-Century Semarang, Java." In *Linking Destinies: Trade, Towns and Kin in Asian History,* ed. Peter Boomgaard, Dick Kooiman, and Henk Schulte Nordholt, 197–217. Leiden: KITLV Press, 2008.

Lai, Him Mark. *Becoming Chinese American: A History of Communities and Institutions.* Walnut Creek, CA: AltaMira, 2004.

Lang, Graeme, and Josephine Smart. "Migration and the Second Wife in South China: Toward Cross-border Polygyny." *International Migration Review* 36, no. 2 (summer 2002): 546–69.

Lary, Diana. *Chinese Migrations: The Movement of People, Goods, and Ideas over Four Millennia.* Lanham, MD: Rowman and Littlefield, 2012.

———. *Region and Nation: The Kwangsi Clique in Chinese Politics, 1925–1937.* London: Cambridge University Press, 1974.

Lee, Erika. "Orientalisms in the Americas: A Hemispheric Approach to Asian American History." *Journal of Asian American Studies* 8, no. 3 (2005): 235–56.

Lee, Guan Kin (Li, Yuanjin). *Dongxi wenhua de zhuangji yu xinhua zhishi fenzi de san zhong huiying: Khoo Seok Wan, Lim Boon Keng, Song Ong Siang de bijiao yanjiu.* Singapore: Xinjiapo guoli daxue zhongwen xi, bafang wenhua qiye gongsi, 2001.

———. *Lin Wenqing de sixiang: Zhongxi wenhua de huiliu yu maodun.* Singapore: Xinjiapo yazhou yanjiu hui, 1991.

———. "Lin Wenqing zou xiang Xiamen daxue—yi ge Xinjiapo haixia huaren de xungen lichen." In *Shiji zhi jiao de haiwai huaren,* ed. Zhuang Guotu et al., 514. Fuzhou: Fujian renmin chubanshe, 1998.

---. "The 1911 Revolution in the Global Context: The Significance of Singapore." In *Tongmenghui, Sun Yat Sen and the Chinese in Southeast Asia: A Revisit*, ed. Leo Suryadinata, 147–69. Singapore: Chinese Heritage Centre, 2006.

---. "Xinma rujiao yundong (1894–1911) de xiandai yiyi: Yi 1980 niandai Xinjiapo ruxue yundong yanzheng zhi (1894–1911)." In *Nanda xueren*. Singapore: Nanyang ligong daxue, Zhonghua yiyan wenhua zhongxin, 2001.

Lefebvre, Henri. *The Production of Space*. Oxford: Blackwell, 1991.

---. "The Theory of Moments." In *Critiques of Everyday Life*, vol. 2, 340–58. London: Verso, 2002.

Leonard, Jane Kate. *Wei Yuan and China's Rediscovery of the Maritime World*. Cambridge, MA: Harvard University, 1984.

Levenson, Joseph. *Confucian China and Its Modern Fate*. Berkeley: University of California Press, 1965.

Lewis, Martin W., and Kären Wigen. *The Myth of Continents: A Critique of Metageography*. Berkeley: University of California Press, 1997.

Lewis, Su Lin. *Cities in Motion: Urban Life and Cosmopolitanism in Southeast Asia, 1920–1940*. Cambridge: Cambridge University Press, 2016.

---. "Print Culture and the New Maritime Frontier in Rangoon and Penang." *Moussons* 17 (2011): 127–44.

Lew-Williams, Beth. "The Chinese Must Go: Immigration, Deportation and Violence in the 19th Century Pacific Northwest." Ph.D. diss., Stanford University, 2011.

Li, Anshan. "Zhonghua minguo shiqi Nanyang yanjiu shuping." *Jindaishi Yanjiu* 4 (2002): 290–314.

Li, Changfu. *Li Changfu wen ji*. Kaifeng Shi: Henan da xue chu ban she, 2007.

---. *Nanyang Hua qiao*. Shanghai: Shang wu yin shu guan, 1933.

---. *Nanyang Hua qiao gai kuang*. Shanghai: Guo li ji nan da xue Nanyang Meizhou wen hua shi ye bu, 1930.

---. *Nanyang Hua qiao shi*. Shanghai: Guo li ji nan da xue Nanyang wen hua shi ye bu, 1929.

---. *Nanyang shi di yu Hua qiao Hua ren yan jiu: Li Changfu xian sheng lun wen xuan ji*. Guangzhou: Jinan da xue chu ban she, 2001.

---. *Zhongguo zhimin shi* [History of China's colonization]. Shanghai: Shangwu yinshu guan, 1937.

Li, Changfu, and Ch'ang-fu Li. *Zhong guo zhi min shi*. Taipei: Tai wan shang wu, 1983.

Li, Jierong. "Jinan daxue Nanyang wenhua jiaoyu shiye bu de lishi chengjiu yu gongxian" [The historical achievements and contributions of the Department of Nanyang Cultural and Educational Affairs at Jinan University]. *Jinan Xuebao* 23, no. 5 (September 2001): 110–16.

Li, Jinsheng. "Yige Nanyang, gezi jieshuo: 'Nanyang' gainian de lishi yanbian" [One Nanyang, different interpretations: The historical evolution of the "Nanyang" concept]. *Yazhou wenhua* [Asian culture] 30 (June 2006): 113–23.

Li, Minghuan. "Ershi yi shiji chu Ou'zhou huaren shetuan fazhan xin qushi" [New trends in the community development of Chinese in early twenty-first-century Europe]. *Overseas Chinese History Studies* 4 (December 2015): 1–8.

Li, Yinghui. *Huaqiao zhengce yu haiwai minzu zhuyi (1912–1949)*. Taipei: Guoshiguan, 1997.

Liang Qichao. *Xindalu youji jielu* [Selected notes on travels to the New World]. Changsha: Hunan renmin chubanshe, 1981.

Liao, Chengzhi. *Liao cheng zhi wen ji*. Beijing: Renmin chubanshe, 1990.

Lim, Boon Keng. *The Chinese Crisis from Within*. Singapore: Select Publishing, 2007.

———. "The Chinese in Malaya." In *Present Day Impressions of the Far East and Prominent and Progressive Chinese at Home and Abroad*, ed. W. Feldwick, 875–82. London: Globe Encyclopedia, 1917.

———. *The City of Amoy, Now Named Sze-Min, or, the Island That Remembers the Ming*. Amoy [Xiamen, China]: Amoy University Press, 1936.

———. "The Confucian Ideal." *Straits Chinese Magazine* 9, no. 3 (1905): 115–19.

———, trans. *The Li Sao: An Elegy on Encountering Sorrows*. Reprint. Taipei: Ch'eng Wen, 1974.

———. "Our Enemies," Presidential Address to the Chinese Philomathic Society, March 1897. *Straits Chinese Magazine* 1, no. 2 (1897): 52–58.

———. "The Reform Movement among the Straits Chinese." *Straits Chinese Magazine* 2, no. 8 (1898): 172–75.

———. "The Renovation of China." *Straits Chinese Magazine* 2, no. 7 (1898): 88–99.

———. "The Role of the Babas in the Development of China." *Straits Chinese Magazine* 7, no. 3 (1903): 94–100.

———. "Straits Chinese Hedonism." *Straits Chinese Magazine* 4, no. 15 (1900): 108–11.

———. "Straits Chinese Reform: I. The Queue Question." *Straits Chinese Magazine* 3, no. 9 (1899): 22–25.

———. "Straits Chinese Reform: III. The Education of Children." *Straits Chinese Magazine* 3, no. 11 (1899): 102–5.

———. "Straits Chinese Reform: V. Filial Piety." *Straits Chinese Magazine* 4, no. 13 (1900): 24–25.

———. "Straits Chinese Reform: VI. Funeral Rites." *Straits Chinese Magazine* 4, no. 14 (1900): 49–47.

———. "Suggested Reforms of the Chinese Marriage Customs." *Straits Chinese Magazine* 5, no. 18 (1901): 58–60.

Lin, Jian. *Furonghupan yi sanlin: Linwenqing Linyutang Linhuixiang de Xiadasuiyue*. Xiamen Shi: Xiamen daxue chubanshe, 2011.

Lin, Jinzhi. *Jindai Huaqiao touzi guonei qiyeshi yanjiu*. Fuzhou: Fujian renmin chubanshe, 1983.

Lin, Zhiling, and Thomas W. Robinson. *The Chinese and Their Future: Beijing, Taipei, and Hong Kong*. Washington, DC: AEI Press, 1994.

Liu, Hong. "Haiwai huaren yu jueqi de Zhongguo: Lishi xing, guojia yu guoji guanxi" [Chinese overseas and rising China: History, nation, and international relations]. *Open Times* 8 (2010): 79–93.

Liu, Hong, and Els van Dongen. "China's Diaspora Policies as a New Mode of Transnational Governance." *Journal of Contemporary China* 25, no. 102 (2016): 805–21.

Liu, Lisong. *Chinese Student Migration and Selective Citizenship: Mobility, Community and Identity between China and the United States*. London: Routledge, 2016.

Liu, Lydia H. *The Clash of Empires: The Invention of China in Modern World Making*. Cambridge, MA: Harvard University Press, 2004.

———. *Translingual Practice: Literature, National Culture, and Translated Modernity—China, 1900–1937*. Stanford, CA: Stanford University Press, 1995.

Liu, Jixuan, Chi-hsuan Liu, Shih-cheng Shu, and Shicheng Shu. *Zhonghua Minzu Touzhi Nanyang Shi*. Shanghai: Shanghai yinshu guan, 1934.

Liu, Shimu, and Zhigui Xu. *Huaqiao Canzhengquan Quan'an*. Shanghai: Shanghai Huaqiao lianhehui, 1913.

———. *Huaqiao Gaiguan*. Shanghai: Zhonghua shuju, 1935.

Look Lai, Walton. *Indentured Labor, Caribbean Sugar: Chinese and Indian Migrants to the British West Indies, 1838–1918*. Baltimore: Johns Hopkins University Press, 1993.

López, Kathleen. *Chinese Cubans: A Transnational History*. Chapel Hill: University of North Carolina Press, 2013.

Louie, Andrea. *Chineseness across Borders: Renegotiating Chinese Identities in China and the United States*. Durham, NC: Duke University Press, 2004.

Louie, Kam, David M. Pomfret, and Julia Kuehn. *Diasporic Chineseness after the Rise of China: Communities and Cultural Production*. Vancouver: University of British Columbia Press, 2013.

Lowe, Lisa. *Immigrant Acts: On Asian American Cultural Politics*. Durham, NC: Duke University Press, 1996.

———. *The Intimacies of Four Continents*. Durham, NC: Duke University Press, 2015.

Lu Xun. *Lu Xun quanji*, vols. 3, 11. Beijing: Renmin wenxue chuban she, 1981.

Lui, Tai-lok. "A Missing Page in the Grand Plan of 'One Country, Two Systems': Regional Integration and Its Challenges to Post-1997 Hong Kong." *Inter-Asia Cultural Studies* 16, no. 3 (2015): 396–409.

Luo Huangchao. "Liu Shimu yu Huaqiao shiye he Nanyang yanjiu" [Liu Shimu and overseas Chinese affairs as well as South Seas studies]. *Jinan Xuebao* 3 (1983): 13–16.

Ma, Laurence J. C. "Space, Place and Transnationalism in the Chinese Diaspora." In *The Chinese Diaspora: Space, Place, Mobility, and Identity*, ed. Carolyn L. Cartier and Laurence J. C. Ma. Lanham, MD: Rowman and Littlefield, 2003.

Ma, Laurence J. C., and Carolyn L. Cartier. *The Chinese Diaspora: Space, Place, Mobility, and Identity*. Lanham, MD: Rowman and Littlefield, 2003.

MacFarquhar, Roderick. *The Origins of the Cultural Revolution*, vol. 3. New York: Columbia University Press, 1974–97.

Mackie, J. A. C. "Anti-Chinese Outbreaks in Indonesia, 1959–1968." In *The Chinese in Indonesia: Five Essays*. Melbourne: Nelson, 1976.

Madokoro, Laura. *Elusive Refuge: Chinese Migrants in the Cold War*. Cambridge, MA: Harvard University Press, 2016.

Mallee, Hein, and Frank N. Pieke, eds. *Internal and International Migration: Chinese Perspectives*. Richmond, UK: Curzon, 1999.

Madsen, Deborah L. "Diaspora, Sojourn, Migration: The Transnational Dynamics of 'Chineseness.'" In *Diasporic Histories: Cultural Archives of Chinese Transnationalism*, ed. Deborah L. Madsen and Andrea Riemenschnitter. Hong Kong: Hong Kong University Press, 2009.

Malvezin, Laurent. "The Problems with (Chinese) Diaspora: An Interview with Wang Gungwu." In *Diasporic Chinese Ventures: The Life and Work of Wang Gungwu*, ed. Hong Liu and Gregor Benton, 49–60. London: RoutledgeCurzon, 2004.

Mandair, Arvind-Pal S., and Markus Dressler. *Secularism and Religion-Making*. New York: Oxford University Press, 2011.

Manning, Patrick, and Tiffany Trimmer. *Migration in World History*. London: Routledge, 2013.

"Many Cultures, One Common Aim." *Straits Times*, June 24, 2004.

Mao, Qixiong, and Lin Xiangdong, eds. *Zhongguo qiaowu zhengce gaishu*. Beijing: Zhongguo qiaowu chubanshe, 1994.

Mar, Lisa Rose. *Brokering Belonging: Chinese in Canada's Exclusion Era, 1885–1945*. New York: Oxford University Press, 2010.

Mark, Chi-Kwan. *Hong Kong and the Cold War: Anglo-American Relations 1949–1957*. Oxford: Clarendon, 2004.

Marks, Robert. *Tigers, Rice, Silk, and Silt: Environment and Economy in Late Imperial South China*. Cambridge: Cambridge University Press, 1998.

Martin, W. A. P. *A Cycle of Cathay or China, South and North with Personal Reminiscences*, 3rd ed. Taipei: Ch'eng wen, [1900] 1966.

Masuzawa, Tomoko. *The Invention of World Religions, or, How European Universalism Was Preserved in the Language of Pluralism*. Chicago: University of Chicago Press, 2005.

McClintock, Ann. *Imperial Leather: Race, Gender, and Sexuality in the Colonial Contest*. New York: Routledge, 1995.

McHale, Shawn Frederick. *Print and Power: Confucianism, Communism, and Buddhism in the Making of Modern Vietnam*. Honolulu: University of Hawai'i Press, 2004.

McKeown, Adam. "Chinese Emigration in Global Context, 1850–1940." *Journal of Global History* 5, no. 1 (2010): 95–124.

———. *Chinese Migrant Networks and Cultural Change: Peru, Chicago, Hawaii, 1900–1936*. Chicago: University of Chicago Press, 2001.

———. "Conceptualizing Chinese Diasporas, 1842 to 1949." *Journal of Asian Studies* 58, no. 2 (1999): 306–37.

———. *Melancholy Order: Asian Migration and the Globalization of Borders*. New York: Columbia University Press, 2008.

Meagher, Arnold J. *The Coolie Trade: The Traffic in Chinese Laborers to Latin America 1847–1874*. Philadelphia: Xlibris, 2008.

Meares, Carina, Trudie Cain, and Paul Spoonley. "Bamboo Networks: Chinese Business Owners and Co-Ethnic Networks in Auckland, New Zealand." *Journal of Chinese Overseas* 7 (2011): 258–69.

Meijer, M. J. *Marriage Law and Policy in the Chinese People's Republic*. Hong Kong: Hong Kong University Press, 1971.

Meisner, Maurice J. *Mao's China and After: A History of the People's Republic*. New York: Free Press, 1999.

Mihalopoulos, Bill. *Sex in Japan's Globalization, 1870–1930: Prostitutes, Emigration and Nation Building*. London: Pickering and Chatto, 2011.

Mo, Yajun. "Itineraries for a Republic: Tourism and Travel Culture in Modern China, 1866–1954." Ph.D. diss., University of California, Santa Cruz, 2011.

Morse, Hosea Ballou. "Emigration." In *The International Relations of the Chinese Empire*, vol. 2, 163–64. New York: Longmans, Green, 1900.

Moya, Jose C., and Adam McKeown. *World Migration in the Long Twentieth Century*. Washington, DC: American Historical Association, 2011.

Mozingo, David. *China's Policy towards Indonesia*. Ithaca, NY: Cornell University Press, 1976.

Mullaney, Thomas S. *Critical Han Studies: The History, Representation, and Identity of China's Majority*. Berkeley: University of California Press, 2012.

Myers, Ramon Hawley, Mark R. Peattie, and Jingzhi Zhen. *The Japanese Colonial Empire, 1895–1945*. Princeton, NJ: Princeton University Press, 1984.

Nagano, Akira, and Chaoqin Huang. *Zhonghua min zu zhi guo wai fa zhan*. Shanghai: Guo li ji nan da xue nan yang wen hua shi ye bu, 1929.

Nanyang Huaqiao Jiaoyu Huiyi baogao. Shanghai: Guoli Jinan Daxue Nanyang Wenhua Shiyebu, 1930.

Nanyang shidi yu huaqiao huaren yanjiu: Li Changfu xianshen lunwen xuanji [The History and geography of Nanyang and the study of the overseas Chinese: A collection of Mr. Li Changfu's essays]. Guangzhou: Jinan daxue chubanshe, 2001.

"Nanyang zhi bazhe" [Hegemons of the South Seas], Speech by Umetani Mitsusada. Translated by Liu Shimu. Shanghai: Zhonghua Nanyang xiehui choubei chu: 1923.

Ng, Chin-Keong. *Trade and Society: The Amoy Network on the China Coast, 1683–1735*. Singapore: Singapore University Press, 1983.

Ng, Maria, and Philip Holden. *Reading Chinese Transnationalisms: Society, Literature, Film*. Hong Kong: Hong Kong University Press, 2006.

Ng, Wing Chung. *The Chinese in Vancouver, 1945–80: The Pursuit of Identity and Power*. Vancouver: University of British Columbia Press, 1999.

Nguyen, Viet Thanh. *Nothing Ever Dies: Vietnam and the Memory of War*. Cambridge, MA: Harvard University Press, 2016.

Northrup, David. *Indentured Labor in the Age of Imperialism, 1834–1922*. Cambridge: Cambridge University Press, 1995.

Nowotny, Helga. *The Cunning of Uncertainty*. Cambridge: Polity, 2016.

Nyíri, Pál. "Chinese Entrepreneurs in Poor Countries: A Transnational 'Middleman Minority' and Its Futures." *Inter-Asia Cultural Studies* 12 (2011): 145–53.

———. *Chinese in Eastern Europe and Russia: A Middleman Minority in a Transnational Era*. London: Routledge, 2007.

———. *Mobility and Cultural Authority in Contemporary China*. Seattle: University of Washington Press, 2010.

Nyíri, Pál, and I. R. Savel'ev. *Globalizing Chinese Migration: Trends in Europe and Asia*. Aldershot, UK: Ashgate, 2002.

Nyíri, Pál, and Juan Zhang, with Merriden Varrall. "China's Cosmopolitan Nationalists: 'Heroes' and 'Traitors' of the 2008 Olympics." *China Journal* 63 (January 2010): 25–55.

Ong, Aihwa. *Flexible Citizenship: The Cultural Logics of Transnationality*. Durham, NC: Duke University Press, 1999.

Ong, Aihwa, and Donald Nonini, eds. *Ungrounded Empires: The Cultural Politics of Modern Chinese Transnationalism*. New York: Routledge, 1997.

Oxfeld, Ellen. *Blood, Sweat, and Mahjong: Family and Enterprise in an Overseas Chinese Community*. Ithaca, NY: Cornell University Press, 1993.

Oyen, Meredith. *The Diplomacy of Migration: Transnational Lives and the Making of U.S.-Chinese Relations in the Cold War*. Ithaca, NY: Cornell University Press, 2015.

Pan, Lynn, ed. *The Encyclopedia of the Chinese Overseas*. Cambridge, MA: Harvard University Press, 1999.

———. *Sons of the Yellow Emperor: A History of the Chinese Diaspora*. Boston: Little, Brown, 1990.

Parreñas, Rhacel S., and Lok C. D. Siu, eds. *Asian Diasporas: New Formations, New Conceptions*. Stanford, CA: Stanford University Press, 2007.

Peattie, Mark R. "The Nan'yō: Japan in the South Pacific, 1885–1945." In *The Japanese Colonial Empire, 1895–1945*, ed. Ramon Hawley Myers, Mark R. Peattie, and Jingzhi Zhen. Princeton, NJ: Princeton University Press, 1984.

———. *Nan'yo: The Rise and Fall of the Japanese in Micronesia, 1885–1945*. Honolulu: University of Hawai'i Press, 1988.

Peterson, Glen D. "Migration and China's Urban Reading Public: Shifting Representations of 'Overseas Chinese' in Shanghai's *Dongfang Zazhi* (Eastern Miscellany), 1904–1948." In *Migration, Indigenization and Interaction: Chinese Overseas and Globalization*, ed. Leo Suryadinata, 277–96. Singapore: World Scientific, 2011.

———. *Overseas Chinese in the People's Republic of China*. Abingdon, UK: Routledge, 2012.

———. "Socialist China and the Huaqiao: The Transition to Socialism in the Overseas Chinese Areas of Rural Guangdong, 1949–1956," *Modern China* 14, no. 3 (July 1988): 311.

Pieke, Frank N. *Transnational Chinese: Fujianese Migrants in Europe*. Stanford, CA: Stanford University Press, 2004.

Pomeranz, Kenneth. *The Great Divergence: China, Europe, and the Making of the Modern World Economy*. Princeton, NJ: Princeton University Press, 2000.

Price, John. *Orienting Canada: Race, Empire, and the Transpacific*. Vancouver: University of British Columbia Press, 2011.

"The Pull of Two Worlds." *The Straits Times*, April 8, 2001.

Pun, Ngai. *Made in China: Women Factory Workers in a Global Workplace*. Durham, NC: Duke University Press, 2005.

Purcell, Victor. *The Chinese in Malaya*. Oxford: Oxford University Press, 1948.

———. *The Chinese in Southeast Asia*. Oxford: Oxford University Press, 1965.

Qiaowu zhengce wenji. Beijing: Renmin chubanshe, 1957.

Qin, Yucheng. *The Diplomacy of Nationalism: The Six Companies and China's Policy toward Exclusion*. Honolulu: University of Hawai'i Press, 2009.

Qiu, Hanping. *Huaqiao wenti*. Shanghai: Shangwu yinshu guan, 1936.

Ransmeier, Johanna S. *Sold People: Traffickers and Family Life in North China*. Cambridge, MA: Harvard University Press, 2017.

Rea, Christopher G., and Nicolai Volland. *The Business of Culture: Cultural Entrepreneurs in China and Southeast Asia, 1900–65*. Vancouver: University of British Columbia Press, 2015.

Reeder, Linda. *Widows in White: Migration and the Transformation of Rural Italian Women, Sicily, 1880–1920*. Toronto: University of Toronto Press, 2003.

Reid, Anthony. *Southeast Asia in the Age of Commerce, 1450–1680*. New Haven, CT: Yale University Press, 1988.

Remer, C. F. *Foreign Investments in China*. New York: H. Fertig, 1968.

Rhoads, Edward. *Stepping Forth into the World: The Chinese Educational Mission to the United States, 1872–81*. Hong Kong: Hong Kong University Press, 2011.

Riemenschnitter, Andrea, and Deborah L. Madsen, eds. *Diasporic Histories: Cultural Archives of Chinese Transnationalism*. Hong Kong: Hong Kong University Press, 2009.

Roberts, Priscilla, and John M. Carroll. *Hong Kong in the Cold War*. Hong Kong: Hong Kong University Press, 2016.

Rofel, Lisa. *Desiring China: Experiments in Neoliberalism, Sexuality, and Public Culture*. Durham, NC: Duke University Press, 2007.

Safran, William. "Diasporas in Modern Societies: Myths of Homeland and Return." *Diaspora* 1, no. 1 (1991): 83–99.

Schiavone Camacho, Julia María. *Chinese Mexicans: Transpacific Migration and the Search for a Homeland, 1910–1960*. Chapel Hill: University of North Carolina Press, 2012.

Schiffrin, Harold Z. *Sun Yat-sen and the Origins of the Chinese Revolution.* Berkeley: University of California Press, 1970.

———. *Visuality and Identity: Sinophone Articulations across the Pacific.* Berkeley: University of California Press, 2007.

Seah, Leander. "Conceptualizing the Chinese World, Jinan University, Nanyang Migrants, and Trans-Regionalism, 1900–1941." Ph.D. diss., University of Pennsylvania, 2011.

Sewell, William H. *Logics of History: Social Theory and Social Transformation.* Chicago: University of Chicago Press, 2005.

Share, Michael. *The Soviet Union, Hong Kong, and the Cold War, 1945–1970.* Washington, DC: Woodrow Wilson International Center for Scholars, 2003.

———. *Where Empires Collided: Russian and Soviet Relations with Hong Kong, Taiwan, and Macao.* Hong Kong: Chinese University Press, 2007.

Shen, Huifen. *China's Left-Behind Wives: Families of Migrants from Fujian to Southeast Asia, 1930s–1950s.* Honolulu: University of Hawai'i Press, 2012.

Shih, Shu-mei. "Against Diaspora: The Sinophone as Places of Cultural Production." In *Global Chinese Literature: Critical Essays,* ed. David Dewei Wang and Jing Tsu, 29–48. Leiden: Brill, 2010.

Shimizu, Hajime. *Southeast Asia in Modern Japanese Thought: Essays on Japanese–Southeast Asian Relationship, 1880–1940.* Nagasaki: Nagasaki Prefectural University, 1997.

Shimizu, Hiroshi, and Hirakawa Hitoshi. *Japan and Singapore in the World Economy: Japan's Economic Advance into Singapore, 1870–1965.* London: Routledge, 1999.

Shiraishi, Saya, and Shiraishi Takashi, eds. *The Japanese in Colonial Southeast Asia.* Ithaca, NY: Southeast Asia Program, Cornell University, 1993.

Sinn, Elizabeth. *Pacific Crossing: California Gold, Chinese Migration, and the Making of Hong Kong.* Hong Kong: Hong Kong University Press, 2013.

Skinner, G. W. *Chinese Society in Thailand: An Analytical History.* Ithaca, NY: Cornell University Press, 1957.

———, ed. *The City in Late Imperial China.* Stanford, CA: Stanford University Press, 1977.

Skinner, G. William, and Hugh D. R. Baker, eds. *The City in Late Imperial China.* Stanford, CA: Stanford University Press, 1977.

Smith, Arthur. *Chinese Characteristics.* New York: Fleming H. Revell, 1894.

So, Billy K. L. *Prosperity, Region, and Institutions in Maritime China: The South Fukien Pattern, 946–1368.* Cambridge, MA: Harvard University Asia Center, 2000.

Soja, Edward W. *Postmodern Geographies: The Reassertion of Space in Critical Social Theory.* London: Verso, 1989.

Song Ong Siang (Song, Wangxiang). *One Hundred Years' History of the Chinese in Singapore.* Singapore: Oxford University Press, [1923] 1984.

———. "The Position of Chinese Women," *Straits Chinese Magazine* 1, no. 1 (1897): 16–23.

Stacey, Judith. *Patriarchy and Socialist Revolution in China*. Berkeley: University of California Press, 1983.
Stern, Steve J. "The Tricks of Time: Colonial Legacies and Historical Sensibilities in Latin America." In *Colonial Legacies: The Problem of Persistence in Latin American History*, ed. Jeremy Adelman, 135–50. New York: Routledge, 1999.
Stewart, Watt. *Chinese Bondage in Peru*. Durham, NC: Duke University Press, 1951.
Sugihara, Kaoru. *Japan, China, and the Growth of the Asian International Economy, 1850–1949*. Oxford: Oxford University Press, 2005.
Suryadinata, Leo, ed. *Chinese Diaspora Since Admiral Zheng He with Special Reference to Maritime Asia*. Singapore: Chinese Heritage Centre and HuayiNet, 2007.
———, ed. *Migration, Indigenization, and Interaction: Chinese Overseas and Globalization*. Hackensack, NJ: World Scientific, 2011.
———. *Peranankan Chinese Politics in Java, 1917–1942*. Singapore: Singapore University Press, 1981.
———. *Southeast Asia's Chinese Businesses in an Era of Globalization: Coping with the Rise of China*. Singapore: Institute of Southeast Asian Studies, 2006.
Suyama, Taku. "Pang Societies and the Economy of Chinese Immigrants in Southeast Asia." In *Papers on Malayan History*, ed. K. G. Tregonning, 193–213. Singapore: Department of History, University of Singapore, 1962.
Szonyi, Michael. *Cold War Island: Quemoy on the Front Line*. Cambridge: Cambridge University Press, 2008.
———. "Mothers, Sons and Lovers: Fidelity and Frugality in the Overseas Chinese Divided Family before 1949." *Journal of Chinese Overseas* 1, no. 1 (May 2005): 43–64.
Tagliacozzo, Eric. *Secret Trades, Porous Borders: Smuggling and States along a Southeast Asian Frontier, 1865–1915*. New Haven, CT: Yale University Press, 2005.
Tagliacozzo, Eric, and Wen-Chin Chang. *Chinese Circulations: Capital, Commodities, and Networks in Southeast Asia*. Durham, NC: Duke University Press, 2011.
Taishan qiaowu bangongshi, ed. *Taishan xian huaqiao zhi*. Taishan: Taishan qiaowu chubanshe, 1992.
Takaki, Ronald T. *Strangers from a Different Shore: A History of Asian Americans*. Boston: Little, Brown, 1989.
Tan, Chee Beng. *The Baba of Melaka: Culture and Identity of a Chinese Peranakan Community in Malaysia*. Petaling Jaya: Selangor, 1988.
———. *Chinese Transnational Networks*. London: Routledge, 2007.
———. *Southern Fujian: Reproduction of Traditions in Post-Mao China*. Hong Kong: Chinese University Press, 2006.
Tan, Kah Kee. *Nanqiao huiyi lu* [Memoirs of a Nanyang overseas Chinese]. Singapore: Yihe xuan, 1946.
Tanaka, Stefan. *New Times in Modern Japan*. Princeton, NJ: Princeton University Press, 2004.

Tang, Xiaobing. *Global Space and the Nationalist Discourse of Modernity: The Historical Thinking of Liang Qichao*. Stanford, CA: Stanford University Press, 1996.

———. "'Poetic Revolution,' Colonization and Form at the Beginning of Chinese Literature." In *Rethinking the 1898 Reform Period: Political and Cultural Change in Late Qing China*, ed. Rebecca Karl and Peter Zarrow, 245–65. Cambridge, MA: Harvard University Press, 2002.

Taylor, Jeremy E. *Rethinking Transnational Chinese Cinemas: The Amoy-Dialect Film Industry in Cold War Asia*. London: Routledge, 2011.

Teng, Emma. *Taiwan's Imagined Geography: Chinese Colonial Travel Writing and Pictures, 1683–1895*. Cambridge, MA: Harvard University Asia Center, 2004.

Teng, Ssu-yü, and John King Fairbank. *China's Response to the West: A Documentary Survey, 1839–1923*. Cambridge, MA: Harvard University Press, 1961.

"Three Men, Three Models: The Chinese Divide." *Straits Times*, April 8, 2001.

Tölölyan, Khachig. "Rethinking Diaspora(s): Stateless Power in the Transnational Moment." *Diaspora* 5 (1996): 3–36.

Topley, Marjorie. "Marriage Resistance in Rural Kwangtung." In *Women in Chinese Society*, ed. Margery Wolf and Roxane Witke. Stanford, CA: Stanford University Press, 1975.

Trocki, Carl A. *Opium and Empire: Chinese Society in Colonial Singapore, 1800–1910*. Ithaca, NY: Cornell University Press, 1990.

Tse, Thomas Kwan-choi. "Constructing Chinese Identity in Post-Colonial Hong Kong: A Discursive Analysis of the Official Nation-Building Project." *Studies in Ethnicity and Nationalism* 14, no. 1 (2014): 188–206.

Tsin, Michael Tsang-Woon. *Nation, Governance, and Modernity in China: Canton, 1900–1927*. Stanford, CA: Stanford University Press, 1999.

Tsing, Anna Lowenhaupt. *Friction: An Ethnography of Global Connection*. Princeton, NJ: Princeton University Press, 2005.

Tu, Wei-ming. *Confucian Traditions in East Asian Modernity: Moral Education and Economic Culture in Japan and the Four Mini-Dragons*. Cambridge, MA: Harvard University Press, 1996.

———. "Cultural China: The Periphery as the Center." In *The Living Tree: The Changing Meaning of Being Chinese Today*, 1–34. Stanford, CA: Stanford University Press, 1994.

———. *The Living Tree: The Changing Meaning of Being Chinese Today*. Stanford, CA: Stanford University Press, 1994.

Tucker, Nancy Bernkopf. *Taiwan, Hong Kong, and the United States, 1945–1992: Uncertain Friendships*. New York: Twayne, 1994.

Van Slyke, Lyman P. *Yangtze: Nature, History, and the River*. Reading, MA: Addison-Wesley, 1988.

Vaughan, J. D. *The Manners and Customs of the Chinese of the Straits Settlements*. Singapore: Mission, 1879.

Vogel, Ezra F. *Canton under Communism: Programs and Politics in a Provincial Capital, 1949–1968*. Cambridge, MA: Harvard University Press, 1969.

Wakeman, Frederick E. *Strangers at the Gate: Social Disorder in South China, 1839–1861*. Berkeley: University of California Press, 1966.

Wang, Cangbai. "Guiqiao Returnees as Policy Subject in China." *Newsletter* (International Institute for Asian Studies) 50 (spring 2009): 7.

———. *Huozai biechu: xianggang yinni huaren koushu lishi* [Life Is Elsewhere: Stories of the Indonesian Chinese in Hong Kong]. Hong Kong: Centre for Asian Studies, University of Hong Kong, 2006.

Wang, Cangbai, and Wong Siu-lun. "Home as a Circular Process: A Study of the Indonesian Chinese in Hong Kong." In *Beyond Chinatown: New Chinese Migrants and China's Global Expansion*, ed. Mette Thunø, 183–209. Copenhagen: Nordic Institute of Asian Study Press, 2007.

Wang, Cangbai, Wong Siu-Lun, and Wenbin Sun. "Haigui: A New Area in China's Policy toward the Chinese Diaspora?" *Journal of Chinese Overseas* 2 (2006): 294–309.

Wang, Chih-ming. *Transpacific Articulations: Student Migration and the Remaking of Asian America*. Honolulu: University of Hawai'i Press, 2013.

Wang, Gungwu. *China and the Chinese Overseas*. Singapore: Times Academic Press, 1991.

———. *The Chinese Overseas: From Earthbound China to the Quest for Autonomy*. Cambridge, MA: Harvard University Press, 2000.

———. *Community and Nation: China, Southeast Asia and Australia*. North Sydney: Allen and Unwin, 1992.

———. *Don't Leave Home: Migration and the Chinese*. Singapore: Times Academic Press, 2001.

———. "Merchants without Empire: The Hokkien Sojourning Communities." In *The Rise of Merchant Empires: Long-Distance Trade in the Early Modern World, 1350–1750*, ed. James D. Tracy. Cambridge: Cambridge University Press, 1993.

———. *The Nanhai Trade: The Early History of Chinese Trade in the South China Sea*. Singapore: Times Academic Press, 1998.

———. "A Note on the Origins of Hua-Ch'iao." In *Community and Nation: Essays on Southeast Asia and the Chinese*, ed. Anthony Reid, 118–27. Singapore: Heinemann Educational, 1981.

———. "A Single Chinese Diaspora? Some Historical Reflections." In *Imagining the Chinese Diaspora: Two Australian Perspectives*, ed. Annette Shun Wah and Wang Gungwu. Canberra: Centre for the Study of the Chinese Diaspora, Australian National University, 1999.

———. "South China Perspectives on Overseas Chinese." *Australia Journal of Chinese Affairs* 13 (January 1985): 69–84.

Wang, Gungwu, and Jennifer Wayne Cushman, eds. *Changing Identities of the Southeast Asian Chinese since World War II*. Hong Kong: Hong Kong University Press, 1988.

Wang, Gungwu, and Chin-Keong Ng. *Maritime China in Transition 1750–1850*. Wiesbaden: Harrassowitz Verlag, 2004.

Wang, Gungwu, and L. Ling-chi Wang, eds. *The Chinese Diaspora: Selected Essays.* Singapore: Times Academic Press, 1998.

Ward, A. H. C., Raymond W. Chu, and Janet Salaff, eds. and trans. *The Memoirs of Tan Kah Kee.* Singapore: Singapore University Press, 1994.

Wasserstrom, Jeffrey N. *Global Shanghai, 1850–2010: A History in Fragments.* London: Routledge, 2009.

Watson, James L. *Emigration and the Chinese Lineage: The Mans in Hong Kong and London.* Berkeley: University of California Press, 1975.

Wen Xiongfei. *Nanyang huaqiao tongshi* [A general history of the overseas Chinese in Nanyang]. Shanghai: Dongfang yinshu guan, 1929.

Wickberg, Edgar. *The Chinese in Philippine Life, 1850–1898.* New Haven, CT: Yale University Press, 1965.

Wilbur, C. Martin. *Sun Yat-sen: Frustrated Patriot.* New York: Columbia University Press, 1976.

Williams, Lea E. *The Future of the Overseas Chinese in Southeast Asia.* New York: McGraw-Hill, 1966.

Willmott, Donald E. *The Chinese of Semarang: A Changing Minority Community in Indonesia.* Ithaca, NY: Cornell University Press, 1960.

Wilson, Rob, and Arif Dirlik, eds. *Asia/Pacific as Space of Cultural Production.* Durham, NC: Duke University Press, 1995.

Wilson, Rob, and Christopher Leigh Connery, eds. *The Worlding Project: Doing Cultural Studies in the Era of Globalization.* Berkeley, CA: North Atlantic, 2007.

Wong, Roy Bin. *China Transformed: Historical Change and the Limits of European Experience.* Ithaca, NY: Cornell University Press, 1997.

Wong, Sin Keong. *China's Anti-American Boycott Movement in 1905: A Study in Urban Protest.* New York: Peter Lang, 2002.

Woon, Yuen-fong. *The Excluded Wife.* Montreal: McGill-Queen's University Press, 1998.

———. *Social Organization in South China, 1911–49: The Case of the Kuan Lineage of K'ai-p'ing County.* Ann Arbor: Center for Chinese Studies, University of Michigan, 1984.

Wright, Mary Clabaugh. *The Last Stand of Chinese Conservatism: The T'ung-Chih Restoration, 1862–1874.* Stanford, CA: Stanford University Press, 1957.

Wu, Chun-hsi. *Dollars, Dependents, and Dogma: Overseas Chinese Remittances to Communist China.* Stanford, CA: Hoover Institution on War, Revolution, and Peace, 1967.

Wu, Lien-te. *Plague Fighter: The Autobiography of a Modern Chinese Physician.* Cambridge: Heffer, 1959.

Xiang, Biao. "A Ritual Economy of 'Talent': China and Overseas Chinese Professionals." *Journal of Ethnic and Migration Studies* 37, no. 5 (2011): 821–38.

Xue, Fucheng. *The European Diary of Hsieh Fucheng: Envoy Extraordinary of Imperial China.* Translated by Helen Hsieh Chien; introduced and annotated by Douglas Howland. New York: St. Martin's Press, 1993.

Yan, Chunbao. *Yi sheng zhen wei you shui zhi: Da xue xiao zhang Lin Wenqing.* Fuzhou: Fujian jiao yu chu ban she, 2010.

———, ed. *Essays of Lim Boon Keng on Confucianism: with Chinese Translations.* Singapore: World Scientific, 2014.

Yan, Hairong. *New Masters, New Servants: Migration, Development, and Women Workers in China.* Durham, NC: Duke University Press, 2008.

Yang, Bin. "Under and Beyond the Pen of Eileen Chang: Shanghai, Nanyang, Huaqiao, and Greater China." *Frontiers of History in China* 11, no. 3 (2016): 458–84.

Yang, C. K. *A Chinese Village in Early Communist Transition.* Cambridge: Technology Press, Massachusetts Institute of Technology, 1959.

Yang, Jiancheng. "Dongnanya huaqiao yanjiu riwen mingzhu yicong jianjie" [An introduction to the translated works of important Japanese studies on Chinese in the South Seas]. In *Sanshi niandai Nanyang huaqiao qiaohui touzi diaocha baogao shu* [An investigative report on the remittance investment of Chinese in the South Seas in the 1930s]. Taipei: Zhonghua xueshu yuan Nanyang yanjiusuo [Chinese Academy, Institute for South Seas Studies], 1983.

———, ed. *Nanyang Yanjiu Shiliao Chongkan* [Nanyang studies series]. Taipei: Zhonghua xueshuyuan Nanyang yanjiusuo, 1984.

———. *Sanshi niandai Nanyang Huaqiao qiaohui touzi diaocha baogaoshu.* Zhonghua Minguo Taibei Shi Yangmingshan Huagang: Zhonghua xue shu yuan Nanyang yan jiu suo, 1983.

Yang, Jiancheng, and Guanqin Huang. *Zhongguo guo min dang yu Hua qiao wen xian chu bian: 1908 nian—1945 nian.* Zhonghua min guo Taibei Shi Yangmingshan Huagang: Zhonghua xue shu yuan Nanyang yan jiu suo, 1984.

Yang, Mayfair Mei-hui, ed. *Chinese Religiosities: Afflictions of Modernity and State Formation.* Berkeley: University of California Press, 2008.

Yao, Nan. *Xingyun yeyu ji.* Singapore: Singapore News and Publications, 1984.

Yen, Ching-hwang. *Community and Politics: The Chinese in Colonial Singapore and Malaysia.* Singapore: Times Academic Press, 1995.

———. "The Confucian Revival Movement in Singapore and Malaya, 1899–1911." *Journal of Southeast Asian Studies* 7, no. 1 (March 1976): 33–57.

———. *Coolies and Mandarins: China's Protection of Overseas Chinese during the Late Ch'ing Period, 1851–1911.* Singapore: Singapore University Press, 1985.

———. *The Overseas Chinese and the 1911 Revolution, with Special Reference to Singapore and Malaya.* Kuala Lumpur: Oxford University Press, 1976.

———. *A Social History of the Chinese in Singapore and Malaya, 1800–1911.* Singapore: Oxford University Press, 1986.

Yi, Meihou. "Guangdongsheng gedi qiaolian gongzuo gaikuang." In *Zhonghua quanguo guiguo huaqiao lianhe hui chengli dahui tekan.* Beijing: Zhonghua quanguo guiguo huaqiao lianhe hui, 1957.

Yong, C. F. *Chinese Leadership and Power in Colonial Singapore.* Singapore: Times Academic Press, 1992.

———. *Tan Kah-Kee: The Making of an Overseas Chinese Legend.* Singapore: Oxford University Press, 1987.

Yong, C. F., and R. B. McKenna. *The Kuomintang Movement in British Malaya, 1912–1949.* Singapore: Singapore University Press, National University of Singapore, 1990.

Young, Elliott. *Alien Nation: Chinese Migration in the Americas from the Coolie Era through World War II.* Chapel Hill: University of North Carolina Press, 2014.

Young, Louise. *Beyond the Metropolis: Second Cities and Modern Life in Interwar Japan.* Berkeley: University of California Press, 2013.

———. *Japan's Total Empire: Manchuria and the Culture of Wartime Imperialism.* Berkeley: University of California Press, 1998.

Yu, Henry. "The Intermittent Rhythms of the Cantonese Pacific." In *Connecting Seas and Connected Ocean Rims: Indian, Atlantic, and Pacific Oceans and China Seas Migrations from the 1830s to the 1930s,* ed. Donna R. Gabaccia and Dirk Hoerder. Leiden: Brill, 2011.

———. *Thinking Orientals: Migration, Contact, and Exoticism in Modern America.* New York: Oxford University Press, 2001.

Yun, Lisa. *The Coolie Speaks: Chinese Indentured Laborers and African Slaves in Cuba.* Philadelphia: Temple University Press, 2008.

Yung, Judy. *Unbound Feet: A Social History of Chinese Women in San Francisco.* Berkeley: University of California Press, 1995.

Yung, Judy, Gordon H. Chang, and H. Mark Lai. *Chinese American Voices: From the Gold Rush to the Present.* Berkeley: University of California Press, 2006.

Yung, Wing. *My Life in China and America.* New York: Henry Holt, 1909.

Zahra, Tara. *The Great Departure: Mass Migration from Eastern Europe and the Making of the Free World.* New York: W. W. Norton, 2016.

Zhang, Li. *Strangers in the City: Reconfigurations of Space, Power, and Social Networks within China's Floating Population.* Stanford, CA: Stanford University Press, 2001.

Zhang, Wenhai. *Huang He zisha yu Hong Xiannü.* Hong Kong: Wenhai shu wu, 1957.

Zhang, Xiangshi. *Huaqiao Zhongxin zhi Nanyang.* Haikou: Hainan shuju, 1927.

Zhang, Yaqun. *Zi qiang bu xi, zhi yu zhi shan: Xiamen da xue xiao zhang Lin Wenqing.* Jinan Shi: Shandong jiao yu chu ban she, 2012.

Zhao Canpeng. "Jinan daxue Nanyang wenhua shiye bu de lishi yange" [The historical development of the Nanyang Cultural Affairs Department at Jinan University]. *Dongnanya yanjiu* 6 (2007): 5–12.

Zhen, Dong. *Zhonggong zenyang duidai huaqiao?* Hong Kong: Youlian chubanshe, 1953.

———. *Zhonggong zenyang jieduo huaqiao.* Taipei: Haiwai chubanshe, 1955.

Zheng, Fuhong. "Wenge shiqi de guonei qiaowu yu guiqiao qiaojuan shenghuo." *Nanyang wenti yanjiu* 81 (April 1995): 40–47.

Zheng, Yangwen, Hong Liu, and Michael Szonyi, eds. *The Cold War in Asia: The Battle for Hearts and Minds.* Leiden: Brill, 2010.

Zhuang, Guotu. "Jingmao yu yimin hudong: Dongnanya yu Zhongguo guanxi de xin fazhan" [The interaction between trade and migration: New developments in the relationship between Southeast Asia and China]. *Journal of Contemporary Asia-Pacific Studies* 2 (2008): 83–104.

———. *Zhongguo fengjian zhengfu de huaqiao zhengce*. Xiamen: Xiamen Daxue, 1989.

———. "Zhongguo zhengfu dui guiqiao, qiaojuan zhengce de yanbian, 1949–1966." *Nanyang wenti yanjiu* 3 (July 1992): 49–56.

Zou, Rong. *The Revolutionary Army*. Translated by John Lust. The Hague: Mouton, 1968.

Zweig, David, Chen Changgui, and Stanley Rosen. "Globalization and Transnational Human Capital: Overseas and Returnee Scholars to China." *China Quarterly* 179 (September 2004): 735–57.

INDEX

Amoy University (Xiamen University), 75; Lim Boon Keng and, 75–76, 98–101; Lu Xun and, 75–76, 101; Tan Kah Kee and, 98–99, 103

babas, 61, 79, 81, 87, 102
Barkly, Henry, 21, 26
Bowring, John, 21, 27, 28
Britain, 18, 21–31, 35

capitalism, 68–69; imperialism and, 18, 23–24; neoliberal, 192. *See also* indentured laborers, Chinese
Chen Lanbin, 42, 46
Christian missionary discourses, 90–94
class struggle: against transnational families, 111–15; renewal of, 176–77
colonialism: racial ideologies and, 56, 88. *See also* Confucian revivalism; religion-making
Communist period: idea of modern marriage, 130; land reform, 107, 108, 111–25; local and central responses to excesses of land reform, 115–25; marriage reform, 107, 108, 125–41; policies on transnational families, 108–10
Confucian revivalism, 75–76, 79; colonialism in Asia and, 76–77, 104–5; global capitalism and, 105–6
coolies. *See* indentured laborers, Chinese
Cuba Commission, The, 41–42

Deng Xiaoping, 187–88, 192
diaspora: global history and, 195–96; as historical method, 193–95; meanings and criticisms of, 8–9; as means of reintegration, 191–93; as temporal, 11–13, 189
diaspora moments: as challenges caused by returns, 147–49, 183; in Confucian revivalism, 78, 90, 104–6; in creation of sovereignty, 20, 45; definition of, 14, 16; in formation of national narratives, 73; in global identity formation, 90, 104–6; as means to reinterpret national history, 185–89; as signs of discrepant modes of development, 109, 144
diaspora studies: focus on spatiality and, 11
diaspora time: definition of, 12–13, 16; as intersecting, 185–87; as ruptured, 30–31, 45
Dirlik, Arif, 100
Duara, Prasenjit, 50, 78

emigrants, Chinese: as free in British colonial discourses, 21–31; impact on China, 185. *See also* emigration, Chinese
emigration, Chinese: after 1978, 188–91; as civilizing mission, 56–57; as colonization, 56, 62, 63–66; end of Qing ban on, 17–18; impact on South China, 107, 108–9; in impact-response model, 19–20; in push-pull model, 22; Qing indifference to, 31–32; in scholarship, 3–9; scope and impact of, 1–3
Emigration Convention, The, 35
Encyclopedia of Chinese Overseas, The, 6–7

Fairbank, John King, 19
family. *See* transnational families
fanshen (to turn over the body), 112, 124

"father tongue," 83
France, 18, 35
Fujian province, 109

gender of emigration, 108–9, 117–18
global history, 193–95; Chinese, 6–9. *See also* transnational turn
Great Leap Forward, 160, 166–67
Greater China. *See* Hong Kong; Taiwan
Gu Hongming, 78, 89
Guangdong province, 107–8; Higher People's Court, 136–39. *See also* Kaiping; Taishan
Guangzhou Huaqiao New Village, 161–67
Guangzhou Overseas Affairs Bureau, 150–57
guiqiao (returned huaqiao), 147; as "difficult," 149–60; "capitalist tendencies" of, 147–48, 167–70, 175–76, 180, 183; from British Malaya, 153–54, 153–56, 178; from Indonesia, 154, 157, 170–73, 182; lack of class analysis of, 148–49, 152, 155, 160; origins and numbers of, 147; resettlement in Guangzhou Huaqiao New Village, 160–70; resettlement in state farms, 148, 156–60, 171–73; in Socialist Education Movement, 177–78; as term, 147
guoxue (national studies), 99–100

Hershatter, Gail, 12, 108
homeland-nation: China as, 10–11, 63, 71, 185
Hong Kong, 191–94
Hsu, Madeline, 109
huaqiao (Chinese diaspora): as "black elements," 182; as a special but temporary category, 109–10, 119, 145, 149–50; letters complaining about land reform, 111–15; as mode of family production, 109; as mutually constitutive with zuguo, 2, 9–11; temporality and, 10–12. *See also* diaspora

indentured laborers, Chinese: African slavery and, 18, 21, 36; destinations and numbers of, 24; as different from traditional migrants, 21–23; efforts to protect, 34–35; free trade and, 23–24; images of, 25–27; impact on sovereignty and diplomacy, 20–21, 31–45; kidnapping of, 28–29, 34, 41; riots and mutinies related to, 28–29, 36–37, 38–39; treatment of, 36–37, 39–44; tribute system and, 30; world press and, 37–38; Zongli Yamen and, 33–35
Indian Ocean, 74
Indonesia: repatriations from, 170–73. *See also* Southeast Asia
intellectuals, Chinese: migration to Southeast Asia, 49–50
Irick, Robert, 20

Japan: interest in Nanyang Chinese, 48, 55–56; occupation of Singapore, 104; "southward advance," 49, 55, 57
Jinan University (Shanghai), 71; research and publications on Nanyang, 48–49. *See also* Nanyang

Kaiping, 109, 137
Karl, Rebecca, 47

Lee Guan Kin, 76, 79, 90, 104
Lee Kuan Yew, 76
Li Changfu, 49, 58–61, 62, 65–67
Li Hongzhang, 41–42
Liang Qichao, 63–65
Liao Chengzhi, 119, 121
Lim Boon Keng, 61; on ancestor worship, 86; biography of, 80–81; China's modernization and, 88–90; Christianity and, 92–94; claims of cultural authenticity by, 77; European culture and, 85, 87; Lu Xun and, 75–76, 91, 99–101; Malay culture and, 87; on marriage practices, 86; May Fourth culture and, 98–99, 101–3; portrayals of, 76–78; secularization of Confucianism and, 94–95, 97–98; study of *Li Sao* by, 101–3; Victorian gender norms and, 81–82, 96–97; on women, 86–87, 95–97

Lin Zexu, 54
Liu, Hong, 190
Liu Shimu, 48, 61, 71
Lowe, Lisa, 22, 195
Lu Xun, 75–76, 91, 101

Macao, 38–39, 44
McKeown, Adam, 22
Meagher, Arnold J., 36
migration, contemporary Chinese: global, 188–91; rural-to-urban, 189–90
migration, global mass: first wave, 1, 185

Nanyang (The South Seas): Chinese interest in maritime Asia and, 53–56; as cultural frontier, 49–50; as different from the Japanese term *Nan'yō*, 55; as field of study, 48–49; as region, 49–52, 73–74; as term, 52–53
Nanyang Chinese: as incomplete colonists, 65–66; as synchronized with China's evolution, 62–63, 66–67
Nanyang studies: Chinese national identity and, 59–62; colonial thought and, 50, 51, 56–59; Guomindang and, 48, 71–73; "rise of the West" and, 68–70
national character, 94
Nationalist period, 48, 70–72
Nyiri, Pal, 190
nyonyas, 79, 82

Opium Wars, 32, 53; impact on indentured labor migration, 18–19, 23–24, 32–33
Overseas Chinese. See *huaqiao*
"Overseas Chinese landlords," 107, 111–21
"Overseas Chinese marriages," 107, 127–30

peranakan, 70, 78
Peru, 41; petitions from Chinese in, 39–41
Peru Commission, 41–43
Peterson, Glen, 110, 149, 157
Prince Gong, 33–34

qiao (temporarily located), 10
qiaofu (wives of huaqiao), 111; attempts to limit divorces of, 134–42; images of, 125–30; length of separation from husbands, 128; resistance to marriage reform, 130–33
qiaogong (huaqiao laborer), 120
qiaojuan (family dependents of huaqiao): official accounts of, 121–25; Socialist Education Movement and, 177–79; as targets of mobilization, 142–44; as term, 111
qiaoshang (huaqiao merchant), 120
Qing dynasty: edict to invite returns, 17–18; tribute system, 30, 53
queue-cutting, 83

refugees. See guiqiao
religion-making, 77, 91–92, 97–98
remittances: accommodation of transnational families and, 119; image of female dependency and, 129; land reform and, 118; land reform review and, 121–22; significance of, 110
returnees. See guiqiao

settler colonialism, Chinese discussions of, 62–63
Shih, Shu-mei, 9
Singapore, 76, 78–79
Socialist Education Movement, 177–79
Song Ong Siang, 61, 80, 82
South China, 107–8
Southeast Asia: returnees from, 146–47. See also Nanyang
Spain, 35
Stern, Steve J., 11
Straits Chinese, 78–79, 88–89; colonialism and, 84–86; reformism and, 81–84
Straits Chinese Magazine, 80–81. See also Lim Boon Keng

Taishan, 109, 112–18, 142–44
Taiwan, 191–94
Tan Kah Kee, 71, 76, 98–99, 103–4

Tan Tingxiang, 31–32
Tanaka, Stefan, 11
Tang, Xiaobing, 63–64
temporalities, multiple, 11–12. *See also* diaspora moments; diaspora time
temporalities of development: campaign time, 109; huaqiao versus socialist, 109; national time, 187, 194
time, concepts of, 11–12. *See also* diaspora moments; diaspora time
totok, 70
transnational families: as "overseas Chinese landlords," 111–15; and women as intermediaries, 142–44
transnational turn: focus on spatiality, 11–12; impact on scholarship, 4–6; through diaspora, 193–95. *See also* diaspora; diaspora moments; diaspora time; global history
tusheng, 61. *See also* babas; peranakan

Wang Gungwu: on Chinese identity, 11; on end of emigration ban, 17; on huaqiao as term, 10; on Nanhai and Nanyang, 52–53

Wei Yuan, 54
Wen Xiongfei, 56, 67–68
White, James T., 24–25, 27
women in transnational families: as intermediaries, 142–44
Woon, Yuen-fong, 109
Wu Liande, 61, 78, 84

Xi Jinping, 189
xin yimin (new migrants), 188–91
Xu Qianshen, 43–44
Xue Fucheng, 17–18

Yang, Mayfair, 92
Yen Ching-hwang, 79
Young, Louise, 11–12
Yung Wing, 42–43, 46

Zhang Xiangshi, 58, 65, 68–69
Zhou Enlai: in Burma, 146
Zongli Yamen, 32–35, 38
zuguo (ancestral homeland): as mutually constitutive with huaqiao, 2; to mean "permanent," 9–10. *See also* huaqiao

www.ingramcontent.com/pod-product-compliance
Lightning Source LLC
Chambersburg PA
CBHW070756230426
43665CB00017B/2388